## A GUIDE TO THE **HOY DÍA** ICONS

### ACTIVITY TYPES

| | | |
|---|---|---|
| | **Pair Activity** | Indicates that the activity is designed to be done by students working in pairs. |
| | **Group Activity** | Indicates that the activity is designed to be done by students working in small groups. |
| | **Audio** | Indicates that related audio material is available in MySpanishLab as well as on CDs and on the Companion Website. |
| | **World Wide Web** | Includes helpful links and activities found on the *Hoy día* Companion Website and in MySpanishLab. |
| | **Video** | Indicates that the video resources are available on a DVD or in MySpanishLab. |
| | **Student Activities Manual** | Indicates that additional practice activities are available in the Student Activities Manual. The manual is available in MySpanishLab as well as in printed form. |
| ¡Hola! | **MySpanishLab** | Indicates that additional resources are available in MySpanishLab. For example, in MySpanishLab you will find a pronunciation guide, a mnemonic dictionary with tips to help you learn each chapter's vocabulary, and specialized information related to professions and careers. |

# Hoy día

## Spanish for **Real Life**

### John T. McMinn
Austin Community College

### Nuria Alonso García
Providence College

**Prentice Hall**

Boston   Columbus   Indianapolis   New York   San Francisco
Upper Saddle River   Amsterdam   Cape Town   Dubai   London
Madrid   Milan   Munich   Paris   Montreal   Toronto   Delhi   Mexico City
Sao Paulo   Sydney   Hong Kong   Seoul   Singapore   Taipei   Tokyo

**Executive Editor, Elementary Spanish:** Julia Caballero
**Editorial Assistant:** Andrea Arias
**Executive Marketing Manager:** Kris Ellis-Levy
**Senior Marketing Manager:** Denise Miller
**Marketing Coordinator:** Bill Bliss
**Development Editor:** Celia Meana
**Development Editor for Assessment:** Melissa Marolla Brown
**Senior Managing Editor for Product Development:** Mary Rottino
**Associate Managing Editor (Production):** Janice Stangel
**Senior Production Project Manager:** Nancy Stevenson
**Media/Supplements Editor:** Meriel Martínez
**Senior Media Editor:** Samantha Alducin
**Senior Art Director:** Pat Smythe
**Art Director:** Miguel Ortiz
**Art Manager:** Gail Cocker
**Line Art:** Daisy DePuthod
**Senior Manufacturing & Operations Manager, Arts & Sciences:** Nick Sklitsis
**Operations Specialist:** Cathleen Petersen
**Text & Cover Designer:** Lisa Delgado, Delgado and Company, Inc.
**Manager, Rights & Permissions:** Zina Arabia
**Manager, Visual Research:** Beth Brenzel
**Manager, Cover Visual Research & Permissions:** Karen Sanatar
**Image Permission Coordinator:** Richard Rodrigues
**Full-Service Project Management:** Melissa Sacco, Pre-Press PMG
**Composition:** Pre-Press PMG
**Printer/Binder:** LSC Communications
**Cover Printer:** LSC Communications
**Publisher:** Phil Miller

This book was set in Palatino 10/12.

KV 07.31.2018 0803

**Library of Congress Cataloging-in-Publication Data**
McMinn, John T.
  Hoy dia : Spanish for real life / John T. McMinn.
    p. cm.
  Includes bibliographical references and index.
  ISBN-13: 978-0-205-75602-5 (alk. paper : student ed.)
  ISBN-10: 0-205-75602-6 (alk. paper : student ed.)
  ISBN-13: 978-0-205-76152-4 (alk. paper : student ed.)
  ISBN-10: 0-205-76152-6 (alk. paper : student ed.)
  1. Spanish language--Textbooks for foreign speakers--English. 2. Spanish language--Grammar--Problems, exercises, etc.  I. García, Nuria Alonso.
II. Title.
  PC4129.E5M434 2010
  468.2'421—dc22                    2009046118

Student Edition, Volume 1 ISBN-10: 0-205-75602-6
Student Edition, Volume 1 ISBN-13: 978-0-205-75602-5
Student Edition, Volume 2 ISBN-10: 0-205-76152-6
Student Edition, Volume 2 ISBN-13: 978-0-205-76152-4
Annotated Instructor's Edition, Volume 1 ISBN-10: 0-205-76982-9
Annotated Instructor's Edition, Volume 1 ISBN-13: 978-0-205-76982-7
Annotated Instructor's Edition, Volume 2 ISBN-10: 0-205-76983-7
Annotated Instructor's Edition, Volume 2 ISBN-13: 978-0-205-76983-4

**Prentice Hall**
is an imprint of

www.pearsonhighered.com

# Brief Contents

# Scope & Sequence

Today's text for today's instructors, students, and classrooms...

### *Hoy día:*
Spanish for **Real Life**

Instructors are busy, students are busy. Classes are bigger, courses meet less frequently, and students want to be able to apply what they learn in class immediately. Today's instructors and students need a solution that fits with real life. *Hoy día:* **Spanish for Real Life** focuses on the Spanish students' need for everyday communication. It teaches them to function in a variety of real-world settings—at work and in their neighborhoods, traveling abroad, or doing service in their local communities. *Hoy día* helps students focus on what they need to know now to use Spanish effectively in real life.

As Spanish becomes more and more indispensable in daily life, students will find *Hoy día:* **Spanish for Real Life** an excellent tool that facilitates both their immersion in the Spanish language and their connection to the people who speak it.

## REAL LIFE CONNECTIONS...

### help students use Spanish effectively in their daily lives.

■ **Vocabulary** is presented via illustrations or photos and focuses on contexts in which a broad range of students—traditional college-aged students, working adults, or retirees returning to school—find themselves in real life.

■ *¿Y tú?* activities prompt students to personalize and share information with a partner. By making the activities personal, students see the connection between what they are practicing and its relationship to their own real lives.

■ *Otra conversación* activities have students adapt the communicative situation modeled in *Una conversación* to talk about their own real lives.

■ *En la vida real* sections integrate thematic review activities into real-life scenarios that help students understand the value of what they are learning and how it can be used in their daily lives.

■ *Entre profesionales,* the last activity in the *En la vida real* section, focuses on expanding students' knowledge of Spanish for a particular career. Students are encouraged to go to MySpanishLab to learn more about this career path and practice with similar real scenarios and activities.

■ Authentic video segments in the *Voces de la calle* section feature real people using Spanish in their local communities in North America. By showing how important it is to be bilingual in our multicultural society, they help students tie what they are learning in class to their real lives.

# ACCESSIBLE AND PRACTICAL ORGANIZATION...

## makes it easy for students to organize their learning and for instructors to plan their classes.

▶ **Chapters 1–5 and 7–11** are divided into four interrelated sections or *Temas*. All material is presented in easy-to-follow two-page modules, with presentation of new material at the top of the left page of the spread, followed by practice on the facing page. The first three *Temas* of each chapter begin with a vocabulary presentation, followed by two grammar sections. The fourth *Tema* begins with a vocabulary presentation, but instead of new grammar presentations, it includes a review of material presented earlier in the chapter with activities integrated into a real-life situation. The final *Hoy día* section of each chapter offers readings, video activities, and structured composition topics through which students can apply their language skills to real life.

| ORGANIZATION OF CHAPTERS 1–5 AND 7–11 | |
|---|---|
| **Chapter opener** with communicative objectives and cultural advance organizer | |
| **Tema 1** | Title |
| | Vocabulary<br>Grammar<br>Grammar |
| **Tema 2** | Title |
| | Vocabulary<br>Grammar<br>Grammar |
| **Tema 3** | Title |
| | Vocabulary<br>Grammar<br>Grammar |
| **Tema 4** | Title |
| | Vocabulary<br>*Resumen de gramática*<br>*En la vida real* |
| **Hoy día** | |
| | *Lectores de hoy*<br>*Voces de la calle*<br>*Escritores en acción* |
| **Vocabulary summary** | |

▶ **Review chapters 6 and 12** feature real-life scenarios spread over four *Temas*.
Each review-chapter *Tema* recycles previously introduced vocabulary to
encourage conversation while adding some new words to provide appropriate
context and have students apply the comprehension strategies they have
learned in previous chapters. Each of these chapters also reviews all of the
grammar taught in the preceding five chapters.

| ORGANIZATION OF REVIEW CHAPTERS 6 AND 12 | |
|---|---|
| **Chapter opener** with communicative objectives and cultural advance organizer | |
| **Tema 1** | Title |
| | Thematic vocabulary |
| | *Repaso 1* |
| | *Repaso 2* |
| | *Repaso 3* |
| | *Repaso 4* |
| **Tema 2** | Title |
| | Thematic vocabulary |
| | *Repaso 1* |
| | *Repaso 2* |
| | *Repaso 3* |
| | *Repaso 4* |
| **Tema 3** | Title |
| | Thematic vocabulary |
| | *Repaso 1* |
| | *Repaso 2* |
| | *Repaso 3* |
| | *Repaso 4* |
| **Tema 4** | Title |
| | Thematic vocabulary |
| | *Repaso 1* |
| | *Repaso 2* |
| | *Repaso 3* |
| | *Repaso 4* |

# ADAPTABLE AND FLEXIBLE DESIGN...

### supports instructors teaching face-to-face, hybrid, and fully online courses.

▶ **For classes with reduced contact hours,** the modular, two-page spreads in each *Tema* allow for maximum flexibility. The real-life communicative activities ensure that the content is immediately applicable. The wealth of additional content in MySpanishLab, including oral practice, tutorials, and more, allows you to assign meaningful practice outside of class, perfect for hybrid and fully online courses.

▶ **For classes with more contact hours,** the extensive instructor's annotations include numerous additional activities, allowing instructors to provide more practice in class with the meaningful linguistic input that students need. MySpanishLab also offers you premium content to enhance your class experience. Some of the content you can find includes the following:

  ▶ Mnemonic dictionary (memory aids designed to help students with chapter vocabulary)

  ▶ *Entre profesionales* (activities related to a variety of professions and careers)

  ▶ Podcasts

  ▶ *Escapadas* (a travelogue that takes students on a virtual voyage to different sites all over the Hispanic world)

  ▶ Games

  ▶ Pronunciation guide and practice

And much more...

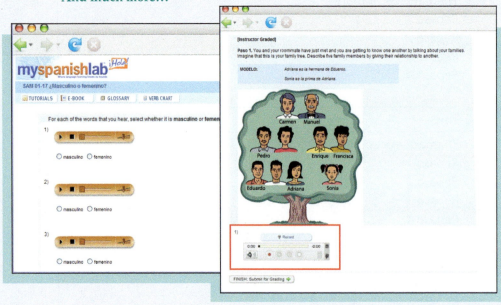

# MORE TOOLS FOR STUDENT SUCCESS...

## support students as they learn Spanish through clearly organized review tools and meaningfully sequenced activities.

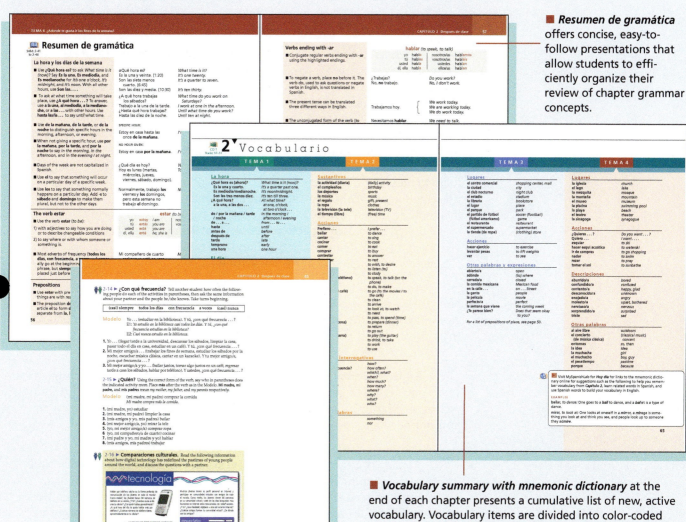

■ *Resumen de gramática* offers concise, easy-to-follow presentations that allow students to efficiently organize their review of chapter grammar concepts.

■ *Vocabulary summary with mnemonic dictionary* at the end of each chapter presents a cumulative list of new, active vocabulary. Vocabulary items are divided into color-coded sections that correspond to the *Temas* in which they appear, making it easy for students to study for quizzes and exams. Each vocabulary list also refers students to an online mnemonic dictionary that helps them remember new words more easily. For example, for the verb **mirar**, it points out that you *look at* yourself in a *mirror*. It also lists other Spanish words with the same root, helping students to make connections and expand their vocabulary. For **mirar**, it points out that **una mirada** is *a glance* or *a look*.

■ *Meaningful activities.* To support students as they use their new language skills, all vocabulary and grammar activities are designed to promote meaningful communication on topics about which students really have something to say. These activities are structured so that students must understand what they are saying in order to answer correctly. The numerous activities are carefully sequenced in order to build students' confidence as they use new structures, going from simple recognition, where students answer with a word or a brief phrase, to more global, personalized activities that allow students to speak about their own real experiences in Spanish.

**Integrated program components** give students and instructors what they need to make teaching and learning Spanish a meaningful, successful, and gratifying experience. *Hoy día* is available in two paperback volumes: Volume 1: Chapters 1–6, and Volume 2: Chapters 7–12.

## Student Resources

▶ 📖 Student Activities Manual. The organization of the **Student Activities Manual** (SAM) parallels that of the student text. Activities corresponding to each *Tema* in the textbook recycle and reinforce the vocabulary and grammar presented in the textbook. The *Diario* at the end of the activities for *Temas* 2 and 4 guides students in writing paragraphs on the topics of the chapter. As in the textbook, the communicative nature of activities has been maintained so that students are required to think about the meaning of what they are writing, and grammatical forms are not practiced without relating them to meaning. The order of the activities follows directly the order of presentation of vocabulary and grammar in the corresponding *Tema* of the textbook, so that instructors who cover only part of a *Tema* during a class can easily assign the matching activities from that *Tema* of the SAM. As in the textbook, the final *Tema* of the SAM reviews material from throughout the chapter contextualized in a real-life setting.

▶ Answer Key for the Student Activities Manual. A separate, optional **Answer Key for the Student Activities Manual** allows students to check their own work if the instructor wishes.

▶ 🔊 Audio CDs for the Student Activities Manual. CD recordings provide easy access to each listening comprehension activity in the Student Activities Manual. The recordings are also accessible in MySpanishLab and on the Companion Website.

▶ 🔊 Audio CDs for the Student Textbook. CD recordings corresponding to each listening activity in the textbook, as well as the dialogues, vocabulary presentations, and the end-of-chapter vocabulary lists, allow students flexibility in practicing listening comprehension and pronunciation at home. The recordings are also accessible in MySpanishLab and on the Companion Website.

▶ 🎬 Student Video DVD. Filmed especially for *Hoy día*, the *Voces de la calle* video features approximately 25 speakers from various Spanish-speaking countries and from diverse backgrounds and professions who use Spanish in their communities. Students can listen firsthand to the personal and professional experiences of journalists, students, artists, business owners, and others. Pre-, during-, and post-viewing activities are featured in the *Voces de la calle* section at the end of each chapter. The video script is also available for self-checking of the activities or to facilitate comprehension of the video content.

## Instructor Resources

▶ **Annotated Instructor's Edition**

Available in two paperback volumes (Volume 1: Chapters 1–6, Volume 2: Chapters 7–12) the **Annotated Instructor's Edition** contains numerous marginal annotations with warm-up and expansion activities, as well as additional cultural information. Also included are an array of tips and ideas designed specifically for graduate teaching assistants or adjunct faculty who may have limited preparation time or who may be teaching Spanish for the first time.

▶ **Instructor's Resource Manual**

The Instructor's Resource Manual (IRM) includes sample syllabi and lesson plans, the scripts for the SAM audio program and the video, and a guide to rubrics.

▶ **The Testing Program**

The Testing Program is closely correlated with the content of the textbook and includes a bank of activities that assess the vocabulary, grammar, and listening, reading, and writing skills for each chapter of the text. This flexible, modular approach allows instructors to customize tests to fit their classes. Complete, ready-to-use tests are also provided, and can either be administered by the instructor or used as models.

▶  **Audio CD for the Testing Program**

This CD contains the audio that accompanies the listening comprehension section for each test.

▶ **Instructor Resource Center**

Several of the instructor supplements listed above—the Instructor's Resource Manual and the Testing Program, as well as the SAM audio script and the video script—are available for download at the access-protected *Hoy día* Instructor Resource Center (www.pearsonhighered.com). An access code will be provided at no charge to instructors once their faculty status has been verified.

## Online Resources

▶ *¡Hola!* MySpanishLab

**MySpanishLab** is Pearson's nationally hosted online learning system created specifically for students in college-level language courses. It brings together—in one convenient, easily navigable site—a wide array of language-learning tools and resources, an electronic version of the *Hoy día* student text, an interactive version of the *Hoy día* Student Activities Manual, and all materials from the *Hoy día* audio and video programs. Readiness checks, chapter tests, and tutorials for both Spanish and English grammar personalize instruction to meet the unique needs of individual students. Instructors can use the system to make assignments, set grading parameters, listen to student-created voice recordings, and provide feedback on student work. Instructor access is provided at no charge. Students can purchase access codes online or at their local bookstore.

▶ 🖱️ **Companion Website**

The open-access Companion Website™ has been specifically created to accompany *Hoy día*. The Website features access to the *Hoy día* audio program (Textbook and SAM) as well as links for completing the *¡Navega!* activities within the textbook.

# ACKNOWLEDGMENTS

*Hoy día* is the result of a collaborative effort among the authors, our publisher, and our colleagues and students. We are especially thankful to many members of the Spanish teaching community for their time and insightful suggestions as they reviewed the drafts of *Hoy día*. Their critiques and recommendations helped us to sharpen our pedagogical focus and improve the overall quality of the program. We gratefully acknowledge the contributions of our faculty reviewers.

### Core panel of faculty reviewers

Darren Broome, *Gordon College, Georgia*
Lori Fry, *Indian River State College*
Khedija Gadhoum, *Clayton State University*
Frozina Goussak, *Collin County Community College*
David Migaj, *Wright City College of Chicago*
Dennis Miller, *Clayton State University*
Charles Molano, *Lehigh Carbon Community College*
Milagros Juan-Ojermark, *Diablo Valley College*
Sadie Nickelson-Requejo, *The University of Puget Sound*
Michele Shaul, *Queens University of Charlotte*
Sabrina Spannagel, *South Seattle Community College*

We also wish to acknowledge our student reviewers who gave us comprehensive feedback on the mnemonic dictionary. A total of 30 students from the following 15 colleges and universities participated.

**Colleges and Universities**
Arizona State University
Austin Community College
Miami Dade Community College
Oklahoma University
Providence College
The University of California, Los Angeles
University of Colorado, Boulder
University of Florida
University of Maryland, College Park
University of Nebraska, Lincoln
University of North Carolina, Greensboro
University of Pennsylvania
University of Pittsburgh
University of Texas, San Antonio
University of Washington

### Students

Susan E Bendernagel, Rachel Brickner, Clint Cornett, Drue Dorsey, Alexis Fabrizio, Amanda Fakhir, Jessica Garza, Christopher Gast, Allissa Goldberg, Dianna He, Adam Hughes, Jason Hustedt, Amanda Kudron, Bridget D. Landry, Alex R. Langlois, Michael Long, Jr, Colleen R. McGreal, Samantha L. Mills, Laura Morel, Rachel Nekolaichuk, Timothy B. O'Mara, Meghana Reddy, Sasha Rodriquez, Drew Rudebusch, Evan Skinner, Nicolas Trilla, Caroleena Vargas, Cheryl Walker, Whitney E. Washousky, Alyssa Whitwell.

We are also grateful for the guidance of Celia Meana, development editor, for all of her work, suggestions, attention to detail, and dedication to the text. Her support and spirit helped us to achieve the final product. We would also like to thank the contributor who assisted us in the preparation the Student Activities Manual: Stéphanie Panichelli-Batalla. We are very grateful to other colleagues and friends at Prentice Hall: Meriel Martínez, Media Editor, for helping us produce such a great video, audio program, and Companion Website; and Melissa Marolla Brown, Development Editor for Assessment, for the diligent coordination among the text, Student Activities Manual, and Testing Program. We are very grateful to our MySpanishLab team, Bob Hemmer, Samantha Alducin, and Mary Reynolds, for the creation of *Hoy día* materials for MySpanishLab. Thanks to Andrea Arias, Editorial Assistant, for her hard work and efficiency in obtaining reviews and attending to many administrative details.

We are very appreciative of our marketing team, Kris Ellis-Levy, Denise Miller, and Bill Bliss, for their creativity and efforts in coordinating all marketing and promotion of the *Hoy día* program. Thanks, too, to our production team, Mary Rottino, Senior Managing Editor for Product Development, Janice Stangel, Associate Managing Editor, and Nancy Stevenson, Senior Production Project Manager, who guided *Hoy día* through the many stages of production; to our partners at Pre-Press PMG, especially Melissa Sacco, Senior Project Manager, for her careful and professional editing and production services. We also thank our art team, Pat Smythe, Miguel Ortiz, Gail Cocker, and Maria Piper. Special thanks to Lisa Delgado for the beautiful interior and cover designs. Finally, we would like to express our sincere thanks to Phil Miller, Publisher, and Julia Caballero, Executive Editor, for their guidance and support through every aspect of *Hoy día*.

*John T. McMinn*
*Nuria Alonso García*

# 1 En la universidad

In this chapter, you will learn about the growing importance of Hispanic cultures in the United States. It is important to understand some common cultural customs in order to avoid misunderstandings when meeting or working with Hispanics.

Hispanics generally expect people arriving at gatherings to shake hands or give kisses on the cheek to everyone in the group. When leaving, it is expected to say good-bye to everyone in the same manner.

- ▶ Do you feel comfortable giving or receiving kisses on the cheek?
- ▶ How often do you shake hands?
- ▶ How might a Hispanic feel if not acknowledged in this way?

Some Hispanics may move their hands more and stand closer when talking.

- ▶ What do you usually think when someone stands closer to you than most people?
- ▶ How might someone feel if you backed away?

In most Hispanic countries, people have a different sense of fashion and are less likely to wear shorts, T-shirts, and tennis shoes.

- ▶ Do people's clothes sometimes affect your impression of them? In what ways?

**Vocabulario** Saludos y despedidas

SAM: 1-1
to 1-6

 CD 1
Track 1

**Una conversación informal**

ANTONIO: **Buenos días. Soy**
Antonio. **¿Y tú? ¿Cómo**
**te llamas?**

DAVID: **Hola.** Me llamo David.

ANTONIO: **Mucho gusto,** David.

DAVID: **Igualmente. ¿De dónde**
**eres,** Antonio?

ANTONIO: Soy **de aquí.** ¿Y tú?

DAVID: Soy de Miami.

ANTONIO: ¿Eres estudiante?

DAVID: Sí, soy estudiante de la universidad Panamericana.

Use the expressions in the preceding conversation to introduce yourself to a classmate or to other people with whom you have an informal relationship. Use **tú** to say *you* to a classmate or friend.

**Una conversación formal**

SR GONZÁLEZ: **Buenas noches.** Soy Carlos
González. ¿Y usted? ¿Cómo
se llama?

SRA DELGADO: Me llamo María Delgado.

SR GONZÁLEZ: Mucho gusto.

SRA DELGADO: Igualmente. ¿De dónde es
usted, señor González?

SR GONZÁLEZ: Soy de México. ¿Y usted,
señora Delgado?

SRA DELGADO: Soy de Puerto Rico.

SR GONZÁLEZ: ¿Es usted profesora o estudiante?

SRA DELGADO: Soy profesora de español de la universidad Panamericana.

Use **usted** for *you* when talking to someone to whom you want to show respect, such as a professor or an adult you do not know well. A different form of the verb is also used with **usted.**

**Más saludos y despedidas**

JOSÉ: ¡Hola, Celia! **¿Cómo estás?**

CELIA: **¡Buenas tardes,** José! **Estoy muy bien,**
**gracias.** ¿Y tú?

JOSÉ: **Regular. No estoy mal.**

CELIA: **Pues, adiós. Hasta mañana.**

JOSÉ: Sí, **hasta luego.**

Use **¿Cómo estás?** when asking how a friend, classmate, or someone with whom you have an informal relationship is doing, and **¿Cómo está (usted)?** when talking to a professor or an adult you do not know well.

**¡Ojo!**

■ You should learn all vocabulary appearing in the **Vocabulario** sections. Words needing additional explanations are boldfaced and glossed at the bottom of the page. You can also find a list with translations of all the new vocabulary from each **Tema** at the end of the chapter.

■ Note that the letter **h** is silent in Spanish and is not pronounced in **hola** or **hasta**, and the **ll** in words like **llamo** is pronounced similarly to an English **y** sound.

 **¿Cómo se pronuncia?** ¡Hola!

***The vowels a, e, i, o, u***

The Pronunciation Guide for Spanish can be found in your MySpanishLab™ course. This guide will help you communicate more clearly in Spanish. Occasionally, marginal notes will suggest appropriate times to study pronunciation explanations. Now is a good time to learn how to pronounce the vowels **a, e, i, o, u** by accessing the Pronunciation Guide in **Capítulo 1**. The proper pronunciation of the vowels is the most basic key to good pronunciation in Spanish.

---

**Buenos días.** *Good morning.* **Soy** *I am* **¿Y tú?** *And you?* **¿Cómo te llamas?** *What's your name?* **Hola.** *Hi.* **Mucho gusto.** *Pleased to meet you.* **Igualmente.** *Likewise.* **¿De dónde eres?** *Where are you from?* **de** *from, of* **aquí** *here* **Buenas noches.** *Good evening.* **saludos** *greetings* **despedidas** *saying good-bye* **¿Cómo estás?** *How are you?* **Buenas tardes.** *Good afternoon* **Estoy muy bien, gracias** *I'm doing very well, thank you* **Regular.** *As usual.* **No estoy mal.** *I'm not bad.* **Pues, adiós.** *Well, good-bye.* **Hasta mañana.** *See you tomorrow.* **hasta luego** *see you later, good-bye*

**El alfabeto**

Here is how you can ask people to spell their names or other words.

**¿Cómo se escribe** González? ¿Se escribe **con** o **sin** acento?

| | | | | | |
|---|---|---|---|---|---|
| **a** | a | **k** | ka | **s** | ese |
| **b** | be (grande) | **l** | ele | **t** | te |
| **c** | ce | **m** | eme | **u** | u |
| **d** | de | **n** | ene | **v** | uve, ve (chica), |
| **e** | e | **ñ** | eñe | | ve (corta) |
| **f** | efe | **o** | o | **w** | uve doble, |
| **g** | ge | **p** | pe | | doble ve, doble u |
| **h** | hache | **q** | cu | **x** | equis |
| **i** | i | **r** | ere | **y** | i griega |
| **j** | jota | **rr** | erre | **z** | zeta |

CD 1
Track 2

Una conversación. Two students are meeting for the first time.

JUAN: Buenos días. ¿Cómo estás?

ISABEL: Hola, estoy bien gracias. ¿Y tú?

JUAN: Bien, gracias. ¿Cómo te llamas?

ISABEL: Me llamo Isabel Ramos. ¿Y tú?

JUAN: Soy Juan Mosquera.

ISABEL: ¿Cómo se escribe Mosquera?

JUAN: Se escribe M-O-S-Q-U-E-R-A. ¿De dónde eres, Isabel?

ISABEL: Soy de Denver. ¿Y tú, Juan?

JUAN: Soy de aquí.

ISABEL: Mucho gusto.

JUAN: Igualmente.

CD 1, Track 3

**¡A escuchar!**

Listen to another conversation in which two students meet. What are their names and where are they from?

**1-1 ▶ Respuestas.** Which responses from the box are logical if someone says the following to you?

| | | |
|---|---|---|
| Adiós. | Estoy regular. | Mucho gusto. |
| Buenas tardes. | Hola. | Soy Daniel Reyna. |
| Buenos días. | Igualmente. | Soy de aquí. |
| Estoy muy bien, gracias. | Me llamo Anita López. | |

**1.** ¡Hola!    **4.** ¿De dónde eres?    **7.** Mucho gusto.

**2.** ¿Cómo te llamas?    **5.** Soy Carlos González.    **8.** ¿Cómo estás?

**3.** ¿Cómo se llama usted?    **6.** Buenas tardes.    **9.** Hasta mañana.

**1-2 ▶ ¿Cómo se escribe?** Spell the names of your favorite people and things in Spanish. Your classmates will try to name them.

Modelo    tu restaurante favorito

P-a-n-c-h-o-s (pe-a-ene-ce-hache-o-ese)

**1.** tu restaurante favorito    **2.** tu actor favorito    **3.** tu auto favorito

**1-3 ▶ Otra conversación.** With a partner, reread *Una conversación* between Juan and Isabel at the top of the page. Then change the conversation to talk about yourselves.

**¿Cómo se escribe . . . ?** *How do you write . . . ? How is . . . spelled?* **con** *with* **sin** *without*

# 📖 Gramática 1

SAM: 1-7
to 1-8

## Deciding how to address people: Using **tú** or **usted**

### Para averiguar

There are **Para averiguar** self-check questions with each grammar explanation. After reading the explanation, you should be able to answer these questions.

1. What does **tú** mean? What does **usted** mean? With whom do you use each one?
2. Do you usually use subject pronouns like **yo** (*I*) and **tú** (*you*) in Spanish?
3. Is there always a one-to-one correspondence between words in Spanish and English sentences?

■ There are two ways to say *you* to someone in Spanish. Use the familiar form **tú** when talking to a friend, a classmate, a family member, or a child. Use the formal form **usted** to address an adult you do not know or someone to whom you wish to show respect. **Usted** is often abbreviated **Ud.**

■ Verb forms are different for each of the subject pronouns.

| **tú** (*you, familiar*) | **usted** (*you, formal*) | |
|---|---|---|
| ¿Cómo te llamas (tú)? | ¿Cómo se llama (usted)? | *What is your name?* |
| ¿Cómo estás (tú)? | ¿Cómo está (usted)? | *How are you?* |
| ¿De dónde eres (tú)? | ¿De dónde es (usted)? | *Where are you from?* |

■ In Spanish, subject pronouns like **yo** (*I*) and **tú** (*you,* familiar) are normally omitted because the verb ending indicates who the subject is. The pronoun **usted** (*you,* formal) is used more often than **yo** and **tú,** but it is often omitted as well. For example, both **soy** and **yo soy** are translated as *I am.* The word **yo** is included only when you want to put emphasis on the word *I.*

■ You should not expect to be able to translate word for word from English to Spanish. The lack of one-to-one correspondence can also be seen in the expressions used to give names.

| SPANISH | LITERAL TRANSLATION | ENGLISH EQUIVALENT |
|---|---|---|
| (Yo) me llamo . . . | (*I*) *myself call. . . .* | *My name is. . . .* |

**1-4 ▶ ¿Tú o usted?**   In which situation would you more likely use the following phrases, A or B?

A    B

1. ____ ¿Cómo te llamas?
2. ____ ¿Cómo se llama usted?
3. ____ ¿Cómo está usted?
4. ____ ¿Cómo estás?
5. ____ Me llamo Pablo Zamora, ¿y usted?
6. ____ Me llamo Alicia, ¿y tú?
7. ____ ¿De dónde es usted?
8. ____ ¿Eres de México?
9. ____ ¿De dónde eres?
10. ____ ¿Es usted de Miami?

**1-5 ▶ ¿Cómo se llama usted? ¿Cómo te llamas?** How would you ask these people their names?

Modelo     an elderly neighbor
            *¿Cómo se llama usted?*

**1.** a professor
**2.** a classmate
**3.** your classmate's little brother
**4.** a salesclerk

**5.** your roommate's grandmother
**6.** your roommate's girlfriend/boyfriend
**7.** your father's boss
**8.** your mother's secretary

**1-6 ▶ ¿Cómo está usted? ¿Cómo estás?** How would you ask the people in the preceding activity how they are?

Modelo     an elderly neighbor
            *¿Cómo está usted?*

**1-7 ▶ ¿Cómo estás?** With a partner, prepare brief exchanges where these people greet each other and ask how they are doing. Do they use **¿Cómo estás?** or **¿Cómo está usted?**

Modelo     E1: *Buenas tardes. ¿Cómo está usted?*
            E2: *Estoy muy bien, gracias. ¿Y usted?*
            E1: *Estoy bien, gracias.*

**Gramática 2**   Describing yourself and others:
SAM: 1-9
to 1-12            Introduction to **ser** and **estar**

SAM: 1-9
to 1-12

## Para averiguar

1. What are the two verbs meaning *to be* in Spanish? How do you say *I am, you are* (familiar), and *you are* (formal) with each?

2. Do you use the forms of **ser** or **estar** to say who people are? Where they are from? What they are like? How they are doing?

3. What are three adjectives you can use with **estar** to say how you are doing? Do you use the ending **-o** or **-a** for males? For females?

■ There are two verbs meaning *to be* in Spanish.

| **ser** *(to be)* | | | **estar** *(to be)* | | |
|---|---|---|---|---|---|
| yo | soy | *I am* | yo | estoy | *I am* |
| tú | eres | *you are* | tú | estás | *you are* |
| usted | es | *you are* | usted | está | *you are* |

■ The verbs **ser** and **estar** cannot be used interchangeably. Use the forms of **ser** to say who people are, where they are from originally, or what they are like. Use the forms of **estar** to say how people are feeling or doing. Remember that subject pronouns (**yo, tú, usted**) are often dropped in Spanish and you rely on the form of the verb to determine who the subject is.

**Soy** estudiante / profesor (profesora).   *I am a student / professor.*
**Soy** de Estados Unidos.                   *I am from the United States.*
**Estoy** muy bien hoy.                       *I am very well today.*

■ Whereas the verb *to be* is negated in English by placing *not* after it, verbs in Spanish are negated by placing **no** before them.

Anita **no es** estudiante. Es profesora.   *Anita **is not** a student. She's a professor.*
**No soy** de aquí.                          *I am **not** from here.*

■ Some nouns and adjectives change forms depending on whether they describe males or females, such as **profesor** (*male*) and **profesora** (*female*). Here are some adjectives you might use with **estar** to say how you are doing. Use the ending **-o** for males and **-a** for females.

**¿Cómo estás?**

¿Cansado/a?          ¿Enfermo/a?          ¿Ocupado/a?

**1-8 ▶ Presentaciones.** Complete the following sentences by selecting the words in parentheses that describe you best, or by using others like them.

1. Soy ____. (estudiante, profesor, profesora)
2. Soy ____. (de aquí, de Chicago, de Dallas, de Atlanta, de Baltimore, . . .)
3. Hoy estoy ____. (bien, mal, regular, cansado/a, enfermo/a, ocupado/a)

 **¿Y tú?** Now, ask another student the same information by completing the following questions with the appropriate verbs in the form of **tú**.

¿____ estudiante o profesor/a?
¿De dónde ____?
¿Cómo ____ hoy?

**1-9 ► ¿Cómo estás?** Your friends are doing the following things when you call. How might they answer when you ask how they are? Using **cansado/a, enfermo/a, ocupado/a,** or **muy bien,** prepare short exchanges with a classmate, who will play the role of the person in the picture.

Modelo   Eduardo
E1: *Hola, Eduardo. ¿Cómo estás?*
E2: *Estoy enfermo.*

**1.** Ramón        **2.** Pedro        **3.** Alicia

**1-10 ► Mucho gusto.** Get acquainted with a classmate using the following conversation as a model. Change the formal **usted** forms to familiar **tú** forms and make additional changes as needed.

— Buenas tardes. Soy Ximena Duarte. ¿Y usted? ¿Cómo se llama?
— Me llamo Enrique Contreras.
— Mucho gusto, señor Contreras.
— Igualmente. ¿Cómo está usted?
— Estoy muy bien. ¿Y usted?
— Bien, gracias. ¿De dónde es usted, señora Duarte?
— Soy de Miami. ¿Y usted?
— Soy de aquí.

**1-11 ► Comparaciones culturales** Imagine that you are at an event at the Hispanic Chamber of Commerce in your area and you are meeting people from the following places. Ask each of them if they are from the capital city. Refer to the maps in the back of the book, if necessary.

Modelo   México
          *¿Es usted de la ciudad de México?*

**1.** Puerto Rico
**2.** Cuba
**3.** El Salvador
**4.** la República Dominicana
**5.** Guatemala
**6.** Colombia
**7.** Honduras
**8.** Ecuador
**9.** Perú

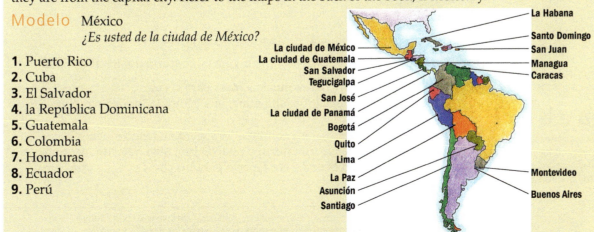

# 📖 Vocabulario  En la clase

SAM: 1-13 to 1-16

## ¿Sabías que...?

In order to get maximum use out of classroom space, public school children in Mexico attend class in shifts. Morning school is approximately from 7:30 AM until 1:00–1:30 PM, and afternoon school from 1:00–1:30 PM until 7:30 PM. Do you think this system would work where you live? Why or why not?

## ¡Ojo!

Different words are sometimes used for certain things in different regions of the Spanish-speaking world. For example, in Mexico, people say **una pluma** instead of **un bolígrafo**. In Spain, people say **un ordenador** for **una computadora**, and **un computador** is used in parts of Latin America.

🔊 CD 1 Track 4

¿**Qué hay** en el salón de clase? ¿Hay muchos estudiantes en la clase de español?

En **mi cuarto,** en el escritorio, **tengo . . .**

🔊 CD 1, Track 6

## ¡A escuchar!

Now, listen to two students talk about what they have and need for class. What does Julio have in his backpack? What does Ernesto have instead?

🔊 CD 1 Track 5

**Una conversación.** Two roommates are talking about what they have.

MARCO:  Hola, Luis. **¿Tienes** muchas **cosas** para el cuarto?

LUIS:  Tengo un escritorio, **una cama,** una computadora y un estante con **varios** libros. ¿Y tú?

MARCO:  **Como** tú, tengo una computadora, **pero** no tengo muchos libros. **También** tengo un estéreo y un televisor. **Sólo necesito** una cama.

LUIS:  No hay problema. Hay espacio **para tus** cosas y tengo **otra** cama.

---

**qué** *what*  **hay** *there is, there are, is there, are there*  **mi(s)** *my*  **un cuarto** *a room*  **tengo** *I have*
**Tienes** *(do) you have*  **una cosa** *a thing*  **una cama** *a bed*  **varios/as** *several*  **Como** *like, as*  **pero** *but*
**También** *also, too*  **Sólo** *only*  **necesito** *I need*  **para** *for*  **tu(s)** *your*  **otro/a** *another, other*

**1-12 ▶ ¿Qué es?** Which word from the list can be used to describe each item?

| | |
|---|---|
| una computadora | una estudiante de mi clase |
| un cuarto | un estudiante de mi clase |
| un libro | una mesa con una silla para estudiantes |
| un señor | un profesor o una profesora con un grupo |
| *una señora* | de estudiantes |

Modelo    Una profesora es *una señora*.

1. Un profesor es . . .
2. Un compañero de clase es . . .
3. Una compañera de clase es . . .
4. Un diccionario es . . .
5. Un salón de clase es . . .
6. Una calculadora es . . .
7. Una clase es . . .
8. Un pupitre es . . .

**1-13 ▶ Productos.** An international student is asking about product names. Which product from the list do you associate with each of these brand names?

| | |
|---|---|
| un bolígrafo | un diccionario |
| *una calculadora* | un estéreo |
| una cama | un reloj |
| una computadora | |

Modelo    Texas Instruments, Casio, Sharp
          *una calculadora*

1. Dell, Hewlett Packard, Gateway, Apple
2. Bic, Parker, Cross
3. Timex, Elgin, Rolex, Fossil, Pulsar
4. Merriam-Webster, American Heritage
5. Bose, Sony, Sharp, Panasonic
6. Serta, Sealy Posturepedic, Simmons

**1-14 ▶ ¿Qué hay?** A student is talking about what she has. Put each noun in parentheses in the logical blank. Then, indicate whether the sentence is true **(cierto)** or false **(falso)** for you. Note that **en** can mean both *in* or *on*.

Modelo    Tengo *un bolígrafo en mi mochila.* (mochila, bolígrafo)
          *Cierto.*

1. Tengo mucho _____ en mi _____. (papel, cuaderno)
2. Hay muchas _____ en mi _____. (mochila, cosas)
3. Tengo una _____ en mi _____. (computadora, escritorio)
4. Hay muchos _____ en mi _____. (estante, libros)
5. Tengo un _____ en mi _____. (cuarto, televisor)
6. No hay muchas _____ en mi _____. (ventanas, cuarto)

**1-15 ▶ Mis cosas.** Say what items presented on the preceding page can be found in the following places.

Modelo    En mi pupitre, *hay un cuaderno y un bolígrafo.*

1. En mi pupitre . . .
2. En mi cuarto . . .
3. En mi mochila . . .

**1-16 ▶ Otra conversación.** With a partner, reread *Una conversación* between Marco and Luis. Then, imagine that one of you is moving in with the other and talk about what you have.

## ¡Ojo!

- Note that there are two different forms of the word for *a* (**un** and **una**). You will learn how to determine when to use **un** vs. **una** in the next grammar section. For now, use the form you see with each word in these vocabulary activities.
- The word **de** can mean either *from* or *of*, and it is also used before a noun that modifies another noun. In the second case, the modifying noun follows the noun it describes: **un salón de clase** *a classroom*, **un/a compañero/a de clase** *a classmate*, **una clase de español** *a Spanish class*.
- Use **mi** or **tu** before singular nouns to say *my* or *your* (familiar) and **mis** or **tus** before plural nouns.

## ¿Cómo se pronuncia? ¡Hola!

*Syllabification and Stress*

It is easy to determine which syllable to stress in Spanish words with just a few simple rules. These rules are explained in the Pronunciation Guide found in MySpanishLab for your course.

# Gramática 1

SAM: 1-17
to 1-20

## Saying what there is: Gender and number of nouns, the indefinite article, and **hay**

Para **averiguar**

1. For nouns that do not refer to humans or animals, can you tell their gender from what they mean?
2. What endings generally indicate that a noun is masculine? That a noun is feminine? Are the following cognates masculine or feminine: **familia, actividad, video, definición**?
3. What is the plural ending for nouns ending with a vowel? For those ending with a consonant? What happens to a final **z** before the **-es** ending?
4. What are the two forms of the word for *a/an* in Spanish? For *some*? When do you use each?
5. How do you say *there is, there are, is there,* and *are there* in Spanish?
6. How do you say *not any* before a masculine noun? Before a feminine noun?

■ All nouns in Spanish have gender and are classified as masculine or feminine. Nouns naming humans or animals are generally masculine or feminine according to their sex, but you cannot guess the gender of nouns naming things from their meaning. For example, the word for *dress* **(vestido)** is masculine.

■ The words for *a/an* and *some*, known as indefinite articles, have different forms, depending on whether they are used with masculine or feminine nouns.

### Indefinite Articles

|  | Masculine | | | Feminine | | |
|---|---|---|---|---|---|---|
| SINGULAR | un | libro | *a book* | una | mesa | *a table* |
| PLURAL | unos | libros | *some books* | unas | mesas | *some tables* |

■ Make nouns plural by adding **-s** if they end with a vowel and **-es** if they end with a consonant. A final **-z** changes to **-c-** before the **-es** plural ending.

| una mesa | ⟶ | unas mesa**s** |
|---|---|---|
| un profesor | ⟶ | unos profesor**es** |
| un lápiz | ⟶ | unos lápi**ces** |

■ Generally, nouns ending with **-o** or **-l** are masculine and those ending with **-a, -dad, -tad, -sión,** or **-ción** are feminine. There are exceptions, such as **un día** (*a day*) and many nouns ending with **-ma** like **un problema** (*a problem*), which are masculine. The gender of nouns ending with other vowels or consonants is usually not predictable, so you should learn them with the article.

■ Nouns referring to people generally have distinct forms for masculine or feminine. Masculine nouns ending in **-o** change the final **-o** to **-a** for the feminine form. An **-a** is added to a noun ending in a consonant for its feminine form.

| un compañero de clase | *a classmate (male)* |
|---|---|
| una compañe**ra** de clase | *a classmate (female)* |
| un profesor | *a professor (male)* |
| una profesor**a** | *a professor (female)* |

■ Nouns ending with other vowels or the ending **-ista** generally have the same form for both males and females. Refer to **un** or **una** to determine gender.

| **un** estudiante | *a student (male)* |
|---|---|
| **una** estudiante | *a student (female)* |
| **un** artista | *an artist (male)* |
| **una** artista | *an artist (female)* |

■ Use **hay** to say what there is. **Hay** is used with both singular and plural nouns and can have four different translations: *there is, there are, is there,* or *are there.*

| **Hay** un diccionario en mi mochila. | *There is a dictionary in my backpack.* |
|---|---|
| ¿**Hay** muchos estudiantes? | *Are there a lot of students?* |

■ To say that there is not something, place **no** before **hay.** To say *not any,* use **ningún** before a masculine noun or **ninguna** before a feminine noun instead of **un** or **una.**

| **No** hay **ningún** libro aquí. | *There is not (isn't) any book here.* |
|---|---|
| **No** hay **ninguna** computadora. | *There is not (isn't) any computer.* |

■ Like the word *some* in English, **unos** and **unas** are usually omitted in Spanish.

| Hay (unos) libros en el estante. | *There are (some) books on the shelf.* |
|---|---|

**1-17 ▶ En la universidad.** Here are some Spanish nouns that are cognates. You can determine whether the following nouns are masculine or feminine by their endings. Indicate whether you use **un** or **una** to translate *a* or *an* before each one.

Modelo    *una* residencia para estudiantes

1. ____ cafetería
2. ____ museo
3. ____ teatro
4. ____ administración
5. ____ facultad de medicina
6. ____ gimnasio
7. ____ supermercado
8. ____ discoteca
9. ____ laboratorio de biología
10. ____ orquesta sinfónica
11. ____ competición de golf
12. ____ estatua de un presidente

¡Ojo!

Cognates are words that look similar and have the same meaning in two languages. You will learn more about cognates in the *Reading strategy* in this chapter.

**¿Y tú?** Using **hay**, take turns with a partner to say whether the preceding items in this activity can be found at your university.

Modelo    *Hay una residencia para estudiantes. / Hay residencias para estudiantes. / No hay ninguna residencia para estudiantes.*

**1-18 ▶ En la biblioteca.** Say what there is in this library.

Modelo    *Hay una puerta.*

**1-19 ▶ En el salón de clase.** A student will name one of the objects found in your classroom. The following students will repeat everything that has already been named and add one more item to the list until everything in your classroom has been named.

Modelo    E1: *En el salón de clase hay un escritorio.*
E2: *En el salón de clase hay un escritorio y pupitres.*
E3: *En el salón de clase hay un escritorio, pupitres y libros . . .*

# Gramática 2

SAM: 1-21
to 1-25

## Saying how many: Numbers from 0 to 100

## Para averiguar

1. Which numbers agree for masculine or feminine?
2. What are the forms of **uno** before masculine and feminine nouns?
3. Is there any difference in how you say *one class* and *a class*?
4. Which numbers between 16 and 99 are written as single words? Which must be written as three separate words?
5. When do you use **cien** to say *one hundred*? When do you use **ciento**?
6. Do you use **un/a** before **otro/a** to say *another*?

■ Here are the numbers 0–100 in Spanish. Use **cuántos** before a masculine noun and **cuántas** before a feminine noun to ask *how many*.

| | | | |
|---|---|---|---|
| 0 cero | | | |
| 1 uno | 11 once | 21 veintiuno | 31 treinta y uno |
| 2 dos | 12 doce | 22 veintidós | 32 treinta y dos . . . |
| 3 tres | 13 trece | 23 veintitrés | |
| 4 cuatro | 14 catorce | 24 veinticuatro | 40 cuarenta (cuarenta y uno . . .) |
| 5 cinco | 15 quince | 25 veinticinco | 50 cincuenta (cincuenta y uno . . .) |
| 6 seis | 16 dieciséis | 26 veintiséis | 60 sesenta (sesenta y uno . . .) |
| 7 siete | 17 diecisiete | 27 veintisiete | 70 setenta (setenta y uno . . .) |
| 8 ocho | 18 dieciocho | 28 veintiocho | 80 ochenta (ochenta y uno . . .) |
| 9 nueve | 19 diecinueve | 29 veintinueve | 90 noventa (noventa y uno . . .) |
| 10 diez | 20 veinte | 30 treinta | 100 cien (ciento uno, ciento dos . . .) |

■ The number **uno** changes to **un** before a masculine noun and **una** before a feminine noun. Note that **un** and **una** can be translated as *one* or *a/an* before a noun.

| | |
|---|---|
| Tengo **un** diccionario. | *I have one dictionary. / I have a dictionary.* |
| Hay **una** computadora. | *There is one computer. / There is a computer.* |

■ Similarly, **veintiuno** changes to **veintiún** and **veintiuna**, and numbers like **treinta y uno** change to **treinta y un** and **treinta y una** before masculine and feminine nouns. The numbers 16–29 are written as single words, but similar numbers above 30 are written as three separate words.

| | |
|---|---|
| Hay **veintiún** estudiantes en mi clase. | *There are twenty-one students in my class.* |
| Hay **treinta y una** sillas. | *There are thirty-one chairs.* |
| Hay **cuarenta y cinco** días de clase. | *There are forty-five days of class.* |

■ Use **cien** to say *one hundred* exactly, but **ciento** for the numbers 101–199. Do not use **y** directly after **ciento**

100 = cien
101 = ciento uno/a
145 = ciento cuarenta y cinco

■ If you do not know the exact number of something, you may also use the following words to express how many. These adjectives all agree with the nouns they describe for masculine or feminine.

| | |
|---|---|
| **mucho(s) / mucha(s)** | *much, many* |
| **poco(s) / poca(s)** | *little, few* |
| **varios / varias** | *several* |
| **otro(s) / otra(s)** | *another, other* |

| | |
|---|---|
| No tengo **mucho** papel. | *I don't have much paper.* |
| Hay **muchos** estudiantes internacionales. | *There are many international students.* |

■ Note that **otro** and **otra** mean *another* and you do not use **un** or **una** before them.

| | |
|---|---|
| ¿Hay **otro** examen? | *Is there another exam?* |

**1-20 ▶ En la clase de matemáticas.** Use **más** (+) and **son** (=) to read the following math problems. Be sure to include the answers.

Modelo   10 + 12 = ____
         *Diez más doce son veintidós.*

**1.** 8 + 7 = ____          **5.** 15 + 12 = ____          **9.** 61 + 15 = ____
**2.** 6 + 10 = ____         **6.** 34 + 22 = ____          **10.** 84 + 15 = ____
**3.** 4 + 14 = ____         **7.** 49 + 13 = ____          **11.** 91 + 7 = ____
**4.** 13 + 11 = ____        **8.** 58 + 24 = ____          **12.** 63 + 37 = ____

**1-21 ▶ ¿Cuál es tu número de teléfono?** Say the following telephone numbers aloud. Read the first digit alone, then read the last six as pairs.

Modelo   223-7607
         *dos, veintitrés, setenta y seis, cero, siete*

**1.** 907-1531          **4.** 305-6484          **7.** 257-1707
**2.** 759-4152          **5.** 414-9099          **8.** 654-1511
**3.** 878-9505          **6.** 302-1213          **9.** 512-6743

 **¿Y tú?** Now, ask three classmates their telephone numbers in case you need to call them to ask something about class.

Modelo   — ¿Cuál es tu número de teléfono?
         — Es el 835-1324. *(ocho, treinta y cinco, trece, veinticuatro)*

**1-22 ▶ Comparaciones culturales.** Hispanics represent 15% of the population of the United States. Read the top ten states' rankings for the percentage of the population that is Hispanic. The first one has been done as an example. Note that commas are used instead of decimal points in Spanish.

Modelo   *Nuevo México es el número uno con el cuarenta y cuatro coma dos por ciento.*

**1.** Nuevo México: 44,2%          **6.** Florida: 20,1%
**2.** California: 35,9%            **7.** Colorado: 19,7%
**3.** Texas: 35,7%                 **8.** Nueva York: 16,3%
**4.** Arizona: 29,7%               **9.** Nueva Jersey: 15,6%
**5.** Nevada: 24,4%                **10.** Illinois: 14,7%

**Zonas con alta concentración de hispanos**

Más de 50.000
De 10.000 a 49.999
De 1.000 a 9.999
Menos de 999

#  Vocabulario En el campus universitario

SAM: 1-26
to 1-28

CD 1
Track 7

¿**Cómo es** la universidad? ¿el laboratorio de **lenguas**? ¿el gimnasio? ¿Cómo es **la comida** de la cafetería?

Los edificios son . . .

**nuevos y modernos**

**viejos**

La biblioteca es . . .

**grande**

**pequeña**

## ¡Ojo!

In Spanish, the word *the* (**el, la, los, las**) and adjectives have various forms, depending on the nouns they modify. On what do you think their forms depend? You will learn more about how to use them in the next grammar section.

Las residencias son . . .

**bonitas**

**feas**

Los profesores y los estudiantes son . . .

## ¡Ojo!

Normally **y** is used to translate *and*, but before words beginning with **i** or **hi** it changes to **e**. Similarly, **o** is used to say *or*, except before words beginning with **o** or **ho**, where it changes to **u**.

buenos e interesantes
optimistas
**simpáticos** y pacientes
responsables y **trabajadores**
serios, inteligentes e intelectuales
**divertidos** y extrovertidos

malos y **aburridos**
pesimistas
**antipáticos** e impacientes
irresponsables y **perezosos**
**tontos**
tímidos

---

¿**Cómo es/son** . . . ? *How is/are . . . ? What is/are . . . like?* **una lengua** *a language* **la comida** *food* **pequeño/a** *little, small* **bonito/a** *pretty* **feo/a** *ugly* **aburrido/a** *boring* **simpático/a** *nice* **antipático/a** *unpleasant* **trabajador/a** *hardworking* **perezoso/a** *lazy* **tonto/a** *stupid, silly* **divertido/a** *fun*

Una conversación. Two friends are talking about their classes.

MARIELA: ¿Cómo son tus clases este semestre?
ADELMA: Tengo tres clases difíciles y dos **fáciles**.
MARIELA: ¿Y tus profesores? ¿Son interesantes?
ADELMA: **Todos** son interesantes menos uno **que** es aburrido.
MARIELA: ¿Y los estudiantes? ¿Son simpáticos?
ADELMA: Sí, tengo dos clases con mi **novio**, una con mi **mejor amiga**, otra con mi **compañera de cuarto** y hay otros amigos en todas mis clases.

CD 1, Track 9

## ¡A escuchar!

Now, listen to a conversation in which two students are talking about their campus. What do they say about the buildings? What are three things they say about the library? What are Paloma's friend's dorm room and roommate like? What is the cafeteria like?

**1-23 ► Mi universidad.** Describe your university, your classes, and yourself by completing the following sentences with the appropriate words in italics.

1. La universidad es *grande / pequeña*. También es *moderna / vieja*.
2. Los edificios son *nuevos / viejos*. Muchos son *bonitos / feos*.
3. Hay *muchos / pocos* libros en la biblioteca. Es *grande / pequeña*.
4. Mis clases son *interesantes / aburridas*. Tengo clases *difíciles / fáciles*.
5. Mi clase de español es *grande / pequeña*. Hay *muchos / pocos* estudiantes.
6. Mis compañeros de clase son *inteligentes / tontos*. También son *divertidos / aburridos*.

**1-24 ► ¿Cómo son?** Claudia, a student, is describing her university. Complete each sentence with the most logical adjective in parentheses.

Modelo    La biblioteca es nueva y *moderna*. (vieja, moderna)

1. La biblioteca es grande y _____. (pequeña, buena)
2. Los edificios son bonitos y _____. (modernos, feos)
3. Los estudiantes son extrovertidos y _____. (tímidos, divertidos)
4. Los estudiantes son responsables y _____. (perezosos, trabajadores)
5. Los profesores son pacientes y _____. (simpáticos, antipáticos)
6. Las clases son difíciles, pero _____. (buenas, fáciles)
7. Las clases son interesantes y _____. (aburridas, divertidas)
8. Mi compañera de cuarto es simpática y _____. (mala, buena)

**1-25 ► ¿Cómo eres?** Complete the following sentences with the adjectives from the list that describe you best. Where two endings are given, use **-a** if you are female. Then, describe your best friend (*mejor amigo/a*).

| | | | |
|---|---|---|---|
| aburrido/a | impaciente | paciente | simpático/a |
| antipático/a | inteligente | perezoso/a | tímido/a |
| divertido/a | interesante | responsable | tonto/a |
| extrovertido/a | irresponsable | serio/a | trabajador/a |

Soy _____ y (e) _____. No soy _____ ni *(nor)* _____.

Mi mejor amigo/a es _____ y (e) _____. No es _____ ni _____.

**1-26 ► Otra conversación.** With a classmate, reread *Una conversación* between Mariela and Adelma. Then, change the conversation so that it describes your classes.

---

**fácil** *easy*   **todo/a/os/as** *all*   **que** *that*   **un novio/una novia** *a boyfriend/a girlfriend*   **un/a mejor amigo/a** *a best friend*   **un/a compañero/a de cuarto** *a roommate*

**Gramática 1**

SAM: 1-29
to 1-34

# Specifying people and things and describing them: The definite article and adjectives

## Para averiguar

1. What are the four forms of the word for *the* in Spanish? When do you use each?
2. When is the definite article used in Spanish, but not in English?
3. Which nouns and adjectives generally have different forms for masculine and feminine? Which do not?
4. When do you add **-s** to an adjective to make it plural? When do you add **-es**?
5. Where do you place adjectives with respect to the nouns they describe?
6. What are four adjectives that are placed before the noun? What happens to **bueno** and **malo** before masculine singular nouns? What does **grande** mean when it is after the noun? What does it mean before the noun? How does its form change before singular nouns?

■ There are four ways to say *the* (the definite article) in Spanish. The form you use depends on whether a noun is masculine or feminine and singular or plural.

**Definite Articles**

|  | **Masculine** | **Feminine** |
|---|---|---|
| SINGULAR | el  edificio *the building* | la  residencia *the residence hall* |
| PLURAL | los  edificios *the buildings* | las  residencias *the residence halls* |

■ The definite article is not only used to translate the word *the*, it is also used when making a generalized description of a category of people or things. In such cases, there is no article in English.

**Los** cursos técnicos son difíciles.      *Technical courses are difficult.*
**Los** amigos son importantes.      *Friends are important.*

■ Adjectives also have different forms, depending on whether they describe a masculine or feminine noun, and whether the noun is singular or plural. Adjectives ending with **-o** or **-or** in the masculine form end with **-a** or **-ora** in the feminine form. Adjectives ending with other letters or **-ista** have just one form for both masculine and feminine.

|  | **Masculine** | **Feminine** | **Masculine** | **Feminine** |
|---|---|---|---|---|
| SINGULAR | tímido | tímida | inteligente | inteligente |
| PLURAL | tímidos | tímidas | inteligentes | inteligentes |

Mi novio es tímido, inteligente,      *My boyfriend is shy, intelligent,*
  trabajador y optimista.       *hardworking, and optimistic.*
Mi novia es tímida, inteligente,      *My girlfriend is shy, intelligent,*
  trabajadora y optimista.       *hardworking, and optimistic.*

■ As with nouns, make adjectives plural by adding **-s** if they end with a vowel and **-es** if they end with a consonant. Use the masculine plural form of adjectives to describe a group with both males and females.

Juan es intelectual y serio.   ⟶   Juan y María son intelectual**es** y serio**s**.
*Juan is intellectual and serious.*   ⟶   *Juan and Maria are intellectual and serious.*

■ Unlike adjectives in English, most Spanish adjectives are placed after the nouns they modify.

una clase **difícil**       *a difficult class*
un edificio **feo**       *an ugly building*

■ The adjectives **bueno** (*good*), **malo** (*bad*), and **mejor** (*best*) may be placed before nouns. Like the number **uno**, the final **-o** of the masculine form of **bueno** and **malo** is dropped before singular nouns.

un **buen** amigo   una buena amiga   los buenos amigos   las buenas amigas
un **mal** día      una mala idea      los malos hábitos   las malas condiciones

■ The adjective **grande** means *big* or *large* when it is placed after the noun, but it means *great* when it is placed before it. Before masculine or feminine singular nouns it shortens to **gran**.

una universidad **grande**       *a big university*
una **gran** universidad       *a great university*

**1-27 ▶ La universidad.** Complete the following statements with the correct forms of the definite article.

Modelo    *Las* residencias son modernas.

**1.** _____ universidad es grande.
**2.** _____ edificios son nuevos.
**3.** _____ clase de español es divertida.
**4.** _____ estudiantes son trabajadores.
**5.** _____ biblioteca es nueva y moderna.
**6.** _____ laboratorio de lenguas es viejo.

**¿Y tú?** Take turns with a partner saying whether the preceding statements in this activity are true (**cierto**) or false (**falso**) for your university. Correct the false statements. Use **No hay . . .** to say there is not something at your university.

Modelo    *Cierto. Las residencias son modernas. | Falso. Las residencias son viejas. |*
          *Falso. No hay residencias.*

**1-28 ▶ ¿Es igual?** Compare studying at the university with studying at your high school using **más** *(more)* or **menos** *(less)* with the appropriate form of the adjective in parentheses. You may also respond with: **No hay mucha diferencia.**

Modelo    clases (fácil)
          *Las clases son más fáciles en la universidad. | Las clases son menos fáciles*
          *en la universidad. | No hay mucha diferencia.*

**1.** clases (difícil)
**2.** edificios (moderno)
**3.** biblioteca (pequeño)
**4.** estudiantes (trabajador)
**5.** clases (aburrido)
**6.** gimnasio (grande)

**1-29 ▶ Dos universidades.** In groups, prepare at least six sentences comparing these two universities. Which group can make the most comparisons?

Modelo    *Los edificios son más modernos en la Universidad Del Monte*
          *y son más viejos en la Universidad Del Valle.*

La Universidad del Monte                    La Universidad del Valle

# Gramática 2

SAM: 1-35 to 1-40

## Saying who it is: Subject pronouns and the verb **ser**

■ You have already seen most of the forms of the verb **ser** *(to be)*. Use **ser** to identify people, to say where they are from, or to describe what they are like. Here are all of its forms with the corresponding subject pronouns. The feminine pronouns **nosotras, vosotras,** and **ellas** are used for all-female groups. For groups containing males, use **nosotros, vosotros,** and **ellos.**

| | | | **ser** *(to be)* | | | |
|---|---|---|---|---|---|---|
| yo | soy | *I am* | nosotros/as | somos | *we are* |
| tú | eres | *you are (familiar)* | vosotros/as | sois | *you are (plural, familiar)* |
| usted | es | *you are (formal)* | ustedes | son | *you are (plural)* |
| él | es | *he is* | ellos | son | *they are (males or mixed groups)* |
| ella | es | *she is* | ellas | son | *they are (females only)* |

■ Subject pronouns are generally not used in Spanish, unless they are needed for clarity or to emphasize who you are talking about.

Somos amigos.                    *We are friends.*
¿Eres de aquí?                   *Are you from here?*

■ The form of the verb used with **usted, él,** and **ella** is the same for all verbs in all tenses. Similarly, the form for **ustedes, ellos,** and **ellas** is the same. Do not drop these pronouns if they are needed to clarify who the subject is.

Usted es muy bueno/a.            *You are very good.*
Él/Ella es muy bueno/a.          *He/She is very good.*

■ The pronoun **vosotros/as** is not generally used in Latin American Spanish. In Spain, it is used as the plural of familiar **tú** to talk to a group of friends or classmates, and **ustedes** is the plural of formal **usted.** In Latin American Spanish, use **ustedes** to say *you* (plural) to all groups, formal or familiar. Note that **ustedes** is often abbreviated **Uds.**

Vosotros/as sois mis amigos/as.  *You are my friends. (familiar, plural in Spain)*
Ustedes son mis amigos/as.       *You are my friends. (familiar, plural in America)*
Ustedes son mis mejores profesores.  *You are my best professors. (formal, plural, in all regions)*

■ When the names of people or things are the subjects of sentences, use the **él/ella** form of the verb if the subject is singular and the **ellos/ellas** form if it is plural. Use the **nosotros/as** form when including yourself in a group. Remember to place **no** before verbs to negate them.

Carlos es mi mejor amigo.        *Carlos is my best friend.*
Mis amigos son muy trabajadores. *My friends are very hardworking.*
Mis amigos y yo no somos perezosos. *My friends and I are not lazy.*

■ **Es** is also used to say *it is.* The subject pronoun *it* is not translated in Spanish.

Es una clase divertida.          *It's a fun class.*

**1-30 ▶ ¿Cierto o falso?** Complete the following sentences with the correct forms of **ser.** Then, indicate whether each one is true (**cierto**) or false (**falso**) for you.

Modelo    Mi mejor amigo/a *es* paciente.
*Cierto. Mi mejor amigo/a es paciente.* /
*Falso. Mi mejor amigo/a no es paciente.*

**1.** Yo _____ tímido/a.
**2.** Mi mejor amigo/a _____ de México.
**3.** Muchos de mis amigos _____ estudiantes.
**4.** Mis amigos y yo _____ muy trabajadores.
**5.** Mi profesor/a de español _____ de Costa Rica.
**6.** Mis compañeros de clase _____ simpáticos.

**1-31 ▶ Entrevista.** Complete the following questions with the correct forms of the verb **ser.**

**1.** ¿De dónde _____ (tú)? ¿De dónde _____ tu mejor amigo/a? ¿_____ (él/ella) estudiante también? ¿_____ Uds. muy parecidos/as (*similar*)? ¿Quién (*Who*) _____ más paciente, él/ella o tú? ¿Quién _____ más extrovertido/a?

**2.** ¿Cómo _____ tus clases este semestre/trimestre? ¿_____ (tú) un/a buen/a estudiante? ¿_____ (tú) muy trabajador/a o un poco perezoso/a? ¿_____ muy intelectuales tus amigos y tú? ¿_____ (Uds.) muy serios? ¿_____ tus clases más importantes o menos importantes que (*than*) tus amigos?

**¿Y tú?** Now, use the preceding questions to interview a classmate. Remember to use **mi** before a singular noun and **mis** before a plural noun to say *my*. Afterwards, report what you found out about your partner to the class. Use **su** before a singular noun and **sus** before a plural noun to say both *his* and *her*.

**1-32 ▶ Comparaciones culturales.** A Latino is talking about Hispanics in the United States at a meeting of the Hispanic Chamber of Commerce. Complete each sentence with the appropriate form of the verb **ser.**

Modelo    Nosotros *somos* la minoría más grande de Estados Unidos. El 15% (por ciento) de la población *es* hispano y el 13% de la población es afro-americano.

**1.** El oeste (*west*) y el sur (*south*) _____ las dos regiones con más hispanos. La región con menos hispanos _____ el medio oeste (*midwest*).

**2.** Uno de cada (*each*) cuatro hispanos _____ monolingüe en español, uno _____ monolingüe en inglés y dos _____ bilingües.

**3.** Para la oficina del censo de Estados Unidos (*U.S. Census Bureau*), los términos **hispano** y **latino** _____ sinónimos, pero para muchas personas, los latinos _____ sólo de origen latinoamericano y los hispanos _____ de Latinoamérica, España y otras regiones también.

**4.** **Hispano** _____ el término preferido por el 22% de nosotros y **latino** _____ el término preferido por el 11%. Los dos términos _____ iguales (*equal*) para el 67% de nuestra (*our*) comunidad.

**5.** Cuatro de cada diez de nosotros _____ inmigrantes y seis de nosotros _____ originarios de Estados Unidos.

**6.** La edad promedio (*average age*) de la población de Estados Unidos _____ de 36 años (*years old*), pero la edad promedio de los hispanos _____ de sólo 27 años.

**Vocabulario** Los cursos universitarios y frases útiles

SAM: 1-41
to 1-49

 CD 1
Track 10

— **¿Qué estudias** en la universidad? ¿Qué clases tienes este semestre/trimestre?
— **Estudio** . . . Este semestre / trimestre tengo . . .

### ¿Sabías que...?

In many Hispanic countries, university studies are very specialized. Students complete three years of **Preparatoria** from the ages of 15 to 18, and then may enter directly into specialized degree programs like medicine or law, which have an average duration of five years. These degree plans are not postgraduate, as in the United States. Would you like your university studies to be more specialized?

### ¡Ojo!

- Do not use an article with course names after verbs like **estudio** (*I'm studying*) or **tengo** (*I have*). However, unlike in English, the definite article is used in Spanish when describing courses with an adjective as in the following sentences: **El español es interesante. / La física es difícil.**
- The word for *psychology* is spelled with a **p** in some regions and without a **p** in others.

CIENCIAS SOCIALES:
historia
ciencias políticas
sociología
(p)sicología

LENGUAS:
español (*m*)
francés (*m*)
**alemán** (*m*)
japonés (*m*)
inglés (*m*)

CIENCIAS:
biología
**química**
física

BELLAS ARTES (*F PL*):
música
arte (*m*)
teatro

CURSOS TÉCNICOS:
matemáticas
**informática**

ADMINISTRACIÓN (*F*)
DE EMPRESAS:
**contabilidad** (*f*)
economía

HUMANIDADES (*F PL*):
literatura
filosofía

*Here are some instructions your Spanish instructor might give you in class:*

| | |
|---|---|
| ¡Abran el libro en la página 37, por favor! | *Open the book to page 37, please!* |
| ¡Lean cada pregunta | *Read each question!* |
| ¡Repitan las siguientes palabras, por favor! | *Repeat the following words, please!* |
| ¡Hagan el mismo ejercicio en parejas! | *Do the same exercise in pairs!* |
| ¡Contesten en oraciones completas, por favor! | *Answer in complete sentences, please!* |
| ¡Escriban las respuestas en la pizarra! | *Write the answers on the board!* |
| ¡Aprendan estas palabras para mañana! | *Learn these words for tomorrow!* |

*Here are some things you might need to say to your instructor:*

| | |
|---|---|
| ¿Hay tarea para la próxima clase? | *Is there homework for the next class?* |
| No comprendo. Repita, por favor. | *I don't understand. Please repeat.* |
| No sé la respuesta. | *I don't know the answer.* |
| ¿Qué significa . . . en inglés? | *What does . . . mean in English?* |
| ¿Cómo se dice . . . en español? | *How do you say . . . in Spanish?* |

---

**¿Qué estudias?** *What do you study?, What are you studying?*  **Estudio** *I study, I am studying*
**alemán** *German*  **química** *chemistry*  **informática** *computer science*  **contabilidad** *accounting*

Track 11

**Una conversación.** Two students are talking about their classes.

ENRIQUE: **¿Te gustan** tus clases?

VERÓNICA: **Me gustan** todas mis clases menos la clase de historia.

ENRIQUE: ¿Por qué no te gusta?

VERÓNICA: El profesor no es muy interesante y hay mucha tarea que no es muy **útil.**

ENRIQUE: ¿Cuántos exámenes hay?

VERÓNICA: Sólo hay dos, **un examen parcial** y un examen final.

CD 1, Track 12

## ¡A escuchar!

Listen to another conversation in which a student is talking to a friend about her classes. What classes does she have? Which ones does she like? Which one does she not like? Why? Which is her favorite (*favorita*)? Why?

**1-33 ▶ Las clases.** With which class(es) do you associate the following things?

Modelo   el cubismo → *arte*

1. un concierto de piano
2. una computadora
3. una calculadora
4. los débitos y los créditos
5. una novela realista
6. la lógica
7. la palabra *monsieur*
8. la inflación
9. las plantas y los animales
10. el oxígeno y el hidrógeno
11. la teoría de la relatividad
12. los procesos mentales

**1-34 ▶ ¿Te gusta(n)?** Ask a classmate if he/she likes the following things. Use **te gusta** to ask about a singular noun and **te gustan** if it is plural.

Modelos   ¿la clase de español?
   E1: *¿Te gusta la clase de español?*
   E2: *Sí, me gusta.*

¿los cursos técnicos?
   E1: *¿Te gustan los cursos técnicos?*
   E2: *No, no me gustan.*

1. ¿la universidad?
2. ¿el campus?
3. ¿los edificios?
4. ¿las clases muy fáciles?
5. ¿las lenguas?
6. ¿más las ciencias o las artes?
7. ¿más la biología o la química?
8. ¿más la música o la literatura?

## ¡Ojo!

Use **me gusta(n)** to say what you like and **te gusta(n)** to ask what a friend or classmate likes. Literally, **me gusta(n)** means that something *is* or some things *are pleasing to me*. Use **me/te gusta** (*is pleasing*) without **-n** if what you like is singular, and use **me/te gustan** (*are pleasing*) with **-n** if it is plural. In these structures, the definite article is used with the noun that follows (**Me gustan *los* exámenes fáciles.**), unless it is replaced by another word such as **tu(s)** or **mi(s)** (**Me gustan *mis* clases.**).

**¿Y tú?** Now in pairs, share with the class each other's preferences using **le gusta(n).** Note in the Modelo that if you include the name of the person you are talking about, **a** is inserted before it.

Modelo   *A Carlos le gusta mucho la clase de español.*

**1-35 ▶ Instrucciones.** Working with a partner, how many logical classroom commands can you form using words from each column? Include the article **el, la, los,** or **las** before each noun.

Modelo   *Hagan los ejercicios en el cuaderno.*

| | | | |
|---|---|---|---|
| Abran | oraciones | | página 54 |
| Hagan | respuestas | | pizarra |
| Escriban | tarea | | cuaderno |
| Repitan | libro | en | escritorio |
| Lean | ejercicios | | libro |
| Contesten | palabras | | computadora |
| Aprendan | preguntas | | |

**1-36 ▶ Otra conversación.** With a partner, reread *Una conversación* between Enrique and Verónica. Then, change the conversation to talk about your own classes.

**Te gusta(n)** *do you like*   **Me gusta(n)** *I like*   **útil** *useful*   **un examen parcial** *a mid-term exam*

#  Resumen de gramática

SAM: 1-50
to 1-53

## Nouns and articles

- All nouns in Spanish have gender and are classified as masculine or feminine.

- The indefinite article (*a, some*), and the definite article (*the*) have different forms and must agree with the nouns that follow them.

- Generally, nouns ending with **-o** or **-l** are masculine and those ending with **-a, -dad, -tad, -sión,** or **-ción** are feminine. There are exceptions, such as **un día** (*a day*) and many nouns ending with **-ma** like **un problema** (*a problem*), which are masculine.

- Make nouns plural by adding **-s** if they end with a vowel and **-es** if they end with a consonant.

- A final **-z** changes to **-c-** before the **-es** plural ending.

### Indefinite Articles

| | Masculine | | Feminine | |
|---|---|---|---|---|
| SINGULAR | un | ejercicio | una | pregunta |
| PLURAL | unos | ejercicios | unas | preguntas |

### Definite Articles

| | Masculine | | Feminine | |
|---|---|---|---|---|
| SINGULAR | el | ejercicio | la | pregunta |
| PLURAL | los | ejercicios | las | preguntas |

¿Hay **un** diccionario?　　　*Is there a dictionary?*
¿Dónde está **el** diccionario?　　*Where is the dictionary?*

| Masculine | Feminine |
|---|---|
| -o:  el libro | -a: la tarea |
| -l:  el papel | -dad/-tad: la universidad |
| | -ción/-sión: la oración |

### Plurals of Nouns

ENDING WITH A VOWEL:  la silla  → las sillas
ENDING WITH A CONSONANT:  el papel → los papeles
ENDING WITH -Z:  el lápiz  → los lápices

## Numbers

- The number one (**uno**) changes to **un** before a masculine noun or **una** before a feminine noun, and looks like the indefinite article.

uno, dos, tres . . .
un libro, dos libros, tres libros . . .
una silla, dos sillas, tres sillas . . .

## Adjective agreement

- Adjectives agree in number and gender with the nouns they modify.

- Adjectives ending with **-o** or **-or** change to **-a** or **-ora** for the feminine form.

- Adjectives ending with other letters or **-ista** generally have the same form for both genders.

| | Masculine | Feminine |
|---|---|---|
| SINGULAR | nuevo | nueva |
| PLURAL | nuevos | nuevas |

| | Masculine | Feminine |
|---|---|---|
| SINGULAR | fácil | fácil |
| PLURAL | fáciles | fáciles |

Mi profesor es simpático, intelectual y optimista.

*My (male) professor is nice, intellectual, and optimistic.*

Mi profesora es simpática, intelectual y optimista.

*My (female) professor is nice, intellectual, and optimistic.*

- Make adjectives plural by adding -s if they end with a vowel and -es if they end with a consonant.

Mis amigos son intelectuales y extrovertidos.

*My friends are intellectual and extroverted.*

## Adjective placement

- Adjectives are placed after the nouns they modify.

| un profesor simpático | *a nice profesor* |
| una clase aburrida | *a boring class* |

- The adjectives **bueno** (*good*), **malo** (*bad*), and **mejor** (*best*) may be placed before nouns. The final **-o** of the masculine form of **bueno** and **malo** is dropped before singular nouns.

| un buen examen | *a good exam* |
| un mal examen | *a bad exam* |
| una buena idea | *a good idea* |
| una mala idea | *a bad idea* |

- After a noun, **grande** means *big* or *large*.

| una universidad grande | *a big university* |

- Before a noun, **grande** is shortened to **gran** and means *great*.

| una gran universidad | *a great university* |

## Subject pronouns and the verb *ser*

- The verb **ser** means *to be* and is used to identify and describe people or things.

- Subject pronouns (**yo, tú . . .**) are generally omitted in Spanish. Insert them only to emphasize or clarify who the subject is.

- Use **nosotras, vosotras,** and **ellas** for all-female groups. For groups containing males, use **nosotros, vosotros,** and **ellos.**

- Use **tú** with a friend, a classmate, a family member, or a child. Use **usted** with an adult you do not know well or to show respect.

- **Vosotros/as** is used in Spain as the plural of **tú**. In Latin American Spanish, **ustedes** is used to say *you* (plural) to all groups.

- **Usted** and **ustedes** are abbreviated **Ud.** and **Uds.**

### Subject Pronouns and *ser*

| Singular | | | Plural | | |
|---|---|---|---|---|---|
| yo | soy | *I am* | nosotros/as | somos | *we are* |
| tú | eres | *you are* | vosotros/as | sois | *you are* |
| usted | es | *you are* | ustedes | son | *you are* |
| él | es | *he is* | ellos | son | *they are* |
| ella | es | *she is* | ellas | son | *they are* |

| ¿De dónde eres? | Where are you from? |
| Soy de Miami. | I'm from Miami. |

| ¿Eres mi compañero de clase? | Are you my classmate? |
| ¿Es Ud. mi profesor? | Are you my professor? |

| IN SPAIN: | Vosotros sois amigos. | You are friends. |
| IN LATIN AMERICA: | Ustedes son amigos. | You are friends. |

## Expressing *to be*

- Use **ser** (**yo soy, tú eres, Ud. es . . .**) to say who or what people or things are, where they are from, or what they are like.

| Soy Mariela Martínez. | *I am Mariela Martínez.* |
| Soy de México. | *I'm from Mexico.* |
| Soy tímida. | *I'm shy.* |

- Use **estar** (**yo estoy, tú estás, Ud. está . . .**) to say how people are feeling or doing, or where someone or something is.

| Estoy un poco enferma hoy. | *I am a little sick today.* |

- Use **hay** instead of **ser** or **estar** to say *there is, there are, is there,* or *are there.*

| Hay veintiún estudiantes en mi clase. | *There are twenty-one students in my class.* |

SAM: 1-54 to 1-58

## EN EL CENTRO DE ESTUDIANTES INTERNACIONALES

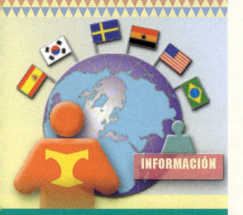

INFORMACIÓN

In this chapter, you learned how to greet people and get to know them, as well as describe yourself and your friends, your university, and your classes. Now, you will practice what you have learned in a real-life simulation of working at the international students' center at your university or college.

**1-37 ▸ ¿Qué hay?** Some new students are asking you about your school. Complete the following questions logically with either the correct form of the definite article (**el, la, los, las**) or the indefinite article (**un, una**).

Modelo    ¿Hay libros en español en *la* biblioteca?

**1.** ¿Hay _____ biblioteca grande en _____ universidad?
**2.** ¿Son todas _____ clases en inglés o hay clases en español?
**3.** ¿Hay computadoras para los estudiantes en _____ biblioteca?
**4.** ¿Hay residencias para _____ estudiantes?
**5.** ¿Hay _____ cafetería? ¿Es buena _____ comida?
**6.** ¿Son todas _____ clases por la mañana (*in the morning*) o por la tarde o hay clases por la noche también?
**7.** ¿Hay _____ laboratorio de lenguas para _____ clases de lengua?
**8.** ¿Hay clases de inglés como segunda lengua para _____ estudiantes internacionales?

**¿Y tú?** Now, ask a classmate the preceding questions about your school.

**1-38 ▸ Descripciones.** You are talking to a new student about your university. Use the correct form of one of the adjectives below to describe the italicized noun in each sentence. You may negate any sentence if you wish

| | | | |
|---|---|---|---|
| aburrido | divertido | inteligente | pequeño |
| antipático | fácil | interesante | perezoso |
| bonito | feo | malo | simpático |
| bueno | grande | moderno | trabajador |
| difícil | intelectual | nuevo | viejo |

Modelo    Hay muchos *estudiantes.*
         *Hay muchos estudiantes trabajadores.* /
         *No hay muchos estudiantes antipáticos.*

**1.** Hay muchos *profesores.*
**2.** Hay *una biblioteca.*
**3.** Me gustan *los edificios.*
**4.** Me gustan *las clases.*
**5.** Este semestre/trimestre tengo más *clases.*
**6.** Me gustan *los exámenes.*

**1-39 ▸ Comparaciones culturales.** You are meeting some international students from the following Hispanic countries. Guess which population in millions (**millones**) goes with each country. Your instructor will answer more (**más**) or less (**menos**) until you give the correct answer.

3 — 4 — 6 — 11 — 14 — 17 — 27 — 28 — 40 — 44 — 46 — más de 100

**1.** México _____
**2.** España _____
**3.** Perú _____
**4.** Ecuador _____
**5.** Argentina _____
**6.** Venezuela _____
**7.** Costa Rica _____
**8.** Cuba _____
**9.** Colombia _____
**10.** Uruguay _____
**11.** Chile _____
**12.** Paraguay _____

**1-40 ▸ Ciudades natales.** You are filling out forms for some international students and they are spelling out the name of their hometowns. A classmate will spell the capital of a Hispanic country and the rest of the class will write it down and name the the country.

Modelo    E1:              L-I-M-A
          CLASS WRITES:    *Lima, Perú*

**1-41 ▸ Estudiantes internacionales.** Some international students from Mexico are asking you the following things. Complete their questions using either **hay** or the correct form of the verb **ser** as appropriate.

Modelo    *¿Hay* muchos estudiantes internacionales?

1. ¿Hay muchos estudiantes de México? ¿_____ (nosotros) el grupo de estudiantes internacionales más grande o _____ más estudiantes internacionales de otro país (*country*)?
2. ¿_____ todas las clases de dos o tres días a la semana (*per week*) en la universidad o _____ clases de un día a la semana o de cuatro o cinco?
3. ¿_____ muy importantes los deportes (*sports*) en la universidad?
4. ¿_____ un estadio (*stadium*) grande?
5. ¿_____ caros (*expensive*) los libros para las clases?
6. ¿_____ una librería (*bookstore*) en el campus?

**¿Y tú?** Now, play the role of an international student from Mexico and ask a classmate the preceding questions in this activity.

Modelo    *¿Hay* muchos estudiantes internacionales?
          *Ustedes son el cinco o diez por ciento de los estudiantes.*

### ¡Hola!  Entre profesionales

With the fast-growing Hispanic populations in North America, sooner or later you will have a need for Spanish in your professional interactions. Visit MySpanishLab for *Hoy día* for links to *Entre profesionales* to learn useful Spanish for a particular field of work for each chapter. In this first chapter, instead of learning about a specific career, you will be introduced to the diverse groups of Hispanics you will encounter, and you will find more activities such as the following one.

**La diversidad hispana.** You are at a gathering with students from different countries and you hear students use the following expressions to ask *What's up*? With a partner, prepare a conversation in which a student from one of these places greets you and asks "what's up" using one of the expressions below. You respond, and ask if he/she is from the appropriate place.

| Una chilena: | *¿Qué hay (de nuevo)?* | Un cubano: | *¿Qué bolá?* |
|---|---|---|---|
| Un salvadoreño: | *¿Qué onda?* | Una puertorriqueña: | *¿Qué es la que hay?* |
| Una colombiana: | *¿Quiubo?* | Un dominicano: | *¿Qué lo que?* |
| Un mexicano: | *¿Qué pasó?* | Una española: | *¿Qué tal?* |

27

### 📖 Estudiar en el extranjero

SAM: 1-59
to 1-60

### Antes de leer

Do you like to travel, see interesting places, and meet fascinating people? Studying abroad offers an unparalleled opportunity to do all of these things. Before reading the brochure for a study abroad program, read the following strategy to help you improve your comprehension.

> ▶ **Reading Strategy** *Recognizing cognates* There are many words in Spanish whose meaning can be guessed, because they are similar to an English word. Such words are called cognates. You have already seen some cognates in this chapter (**profesor, responsable, . . .**) Cognates can help you understand new texts in Spanish.

### Ahora tú

1-42 ▶ **Cognados.** Note that the endings **-mente** and **-ado/a** correspond to *-ly* and *-ed* in English (**generalmente** = *generally,* **interesado/a** = *interested*). Skim the reading and identify as many cognates as possible as **verbos, sustantivos** (*nouns*), **adjetivos,** and **adverbios.**

---

## SIN FRONTERAS: ¿Necesitas perfeccionar tu español? ¿Estás interesado/a en aprender más de la cultura hispánica? SIN FRONTERAS tiene un programa para ti.

**¿Quién habla español en el mundo?** El español es la tercera[1] lengua del mundo[2] en número de hablantes[3] después del[4] chino mandarín y el inglés. Actualmente hay más de 400 millones de hablantes de español en el mundo. En Estados Unidos hablan español aproximadamente 34 millones de personas y el español es la lengua más estudiada en las universidades.

**¿Por qué estudiar en el extranjero?** Estudiar en el extranjero, conectar con la lengua en su elemento y aprender[5] la cultura de sus hablantes ofrecen la oportunidad de vivir[6] la lengua en todas sus dimensiones. SIN FRONTERAS prepara a los estudiantes para mirar[7] al mundo con una mente abierta[8].

**¿Qué ofrece SIN FRONTERAS?** SIN FRONTERAS ofrece programas en varios países[9] de Latinoamérica adaptados a los intereses del estudiante. ¿Interesado en estudiar la cultura maya? El programa de Mérida, en Yucatán, México es tu mejor opción. ¿Es tu interés aprender sobre las tradiciones incas? Lima, Perú, te espera[10].

La duración de los programas es flexible. Hay programas de semestre, año[11] académico o verano[12].

Todos los programas ofrecen:

- Clases diarias[13] con atención personalizada
- Profesorado especializado y dinámico
- Seminarios de cultura y civilización
- Excursiones a sitios de interés turístico

Las instalaciones incluyen:

- Residencias modernas y seguras[14]
- Cafetería
- Salas para actividades sociales
- Zonas Wi-Fi para acceso a Internet

*Chichén Itzá, Yucatán, México*

*Universidad de Guanajuato*

### ¡SIN FRONTERAS te conecta con el espíritu de la cultura hispana!

---

[1]*third* [2]*world* [3]*speakers* [4]*after* [5]*to learn* [6]*to live* [7]*to look at* [8]*an open mind* [9]*countries* [10]*awaits you* [11]*year* [12]*summer* [13]*daily* [14]*safe, secure*

## Después de leer

**1-43 ► ¿Cierto o falso?** Complete the following sentences logically with either **hay** or a form of **ser**. Then, indicate whether the following statements are true (**cierto**) or false (**false**) and correct the false statements.

|  | Cierto (*True*) | Falso (*False*) |
|---|:---:|:---:|
| **1.** El español _____ la tercera lengua del mundo. El inglés y el francés _____ las dos lenguas con más hablantes. | ☐ | ☐ |
| **2.** Estudiar en el extranjero _____ una buena manera de conectar con una lengua y la cultura de sus (*its*) hablantes. | ☐ | ☐ |
| **3.** _____ un programa de *Sin fronteras* en Lima, Perú para estudiar las tradiciones mayas. | ☐ | ☐ |
| **4.** Todos los programas de *Sin fronteras* _____ de un año académico. No _____ ningún programa durante el verano. | ☐ | ☐ |
| **5.** Las clases _____ todos los días. | ☐ | ☐ |
| **6.** _____ seminarios de cultura y civilización. | ☐ | ☐ |
| **7.** Los estudiantes viven (*live*) en casas particulares con familias. No _____ ninguna residencia para los estudiantes. | ☐ | ☐ |
| **8.** Las instalaciones de *Sin fronteras* _____ modernas y seguras. | ☐ | ☐ |

**1-44 ► ¿Qué hay?** Work in groups to see how many sentences you can create using **hay** to describe the **Sin fronteras** study abroad programs.

Modelo    *Hay programas en varios países.*
*Hay oportunidades de conectar con la lengua en su elemento . . .*

**1-45 ► ¿No hay . . .?** In groups, write three additional questions you would like to ask a representative about **Sin fronteras**.

Modelo    *¿Cuántos estudiantes hay en las clases? ¿Son grandes?*
*¿Hay un programa en Costa Rica?*

**1-46 ► Intereses.** Interview another student to find out his/her feelings about studying abroad.

1. ¿Estás interesado/a en estudiar en otro país?
2. ¿Tienes más interés en la cultura maya de México o en la cultura inca de Perú? ¿En qué otros países hispanos tienes interés?
3. En un programa de estudios en el extranjero, ¿es mejor vivir en una casa particular (*private*) con una familia local o en una residencia con otros estudiantes extranjeros? ¿Por qué?
4. ¿Hay oportunidades en Estados Unidos de estudiar español en un contexto de inmersión total?

**1-47 ► Inmersión cultural.** Do you think that it is important to study abroad? Find words or phrases in the reading that suggest its value. Then, in groups, discuss these and other benefits of studying at a university in Latin America or Spain. Present your group's opinions to the class.

## 📖 Señas de identidad

SAM: 1-61
to 1-62

### Antes de ver

The United States is home to many people of Hispanic origin who wish to preserve their language and traditions. In this first segment of *Voces de la calle*, various people will introduce themselves and talk about their Hispanic heritage and current lives.

**1-48 ▶ Reflexiones.** What are some indicators of the Hispanic presence in today's American society? Besides Hispanics, what other cultures are represented in the United States? What percentage of the population do Hispanics represent?

▶ **Listening strategy** *Anticipating content.* Working with a partner, list the five things people from around the world would most likely say when introducing themselves and what phrases they might use to express each in Spanish.

### Ahora tú

 **1-49 ▶ Verifica.** Listen to our video participants and check if the information that you have anticipated is given in the video.

### Después de ver

**1-50 ▶ ¿Qué dicen?** Read the following statements from the video segment and identify the person who said each one: Jorge, Dennis, Edgar, or Analissa.

1. "Soy periodista (*journalist*), vivo (*I live*) en Nueva York, soy mitad (*half*) colombiano, mitad argentino, escribo para revistas como *Urban Latino* magazine."
2. "Como músico, me encanta (*I love*) estar con mi chelo, primeramente, tocar (*to play*) mi instrumento."
3. "¡Hola! [. . .]. Soy puertorriqueño. Vivo aquí en el Bronx, en Nueva York [. . .] desde 1982."
4. "Soy pintor y [. . .] estamos aquí en Queens, Nueva York, y estamos muy contentos de estar aquí."

**1-51 ▶ ¿De dónde son?** Complete the following sentences indicating the origin of the people from the video. Use the appropriate form of **ser** and the place of origin or residence.

1. Analissa Martínez _____ de _____, Texas.
2. Michelle y Alejandro _____ de _____.
3. Edgar Alcaraz _____ de _____.
4. Gloria Celaya _____ de _____ y su esposo Héctor _____ de _____.

##  Una consulta

SAM: 1-63

### Antes de escribir

In this section of each chapter, you will use what you have learned to complete a writing task. For this first assignment, you are going to write an email to your professor introducing yourself and asking for a clarification about something in class. Use the writing strategy at the right to help you write more effectively.

### Antes de escribir

**1-52 ▶ ¡Prepárate!** Before you write your email to your professor, review the topics and structures presented in this chapter and consider the following questions. Which did you find the most difficult to understand? What adjectives can you use in Spanish to describe how you feel about the class and the students in it? Which ones describe you as a foreign language learner?

### Ahora tú

**1-53 ▶ Una consulta.** Write your email to your Spanish professor asking him/her a question about a grammar or vocabulary structure that you do not understand well. Remember to use expressions such as **No comprendo** or **¿Qué significa . . .?** Then, describe your personality as a foreign language student. Also include your views of the class in general.

### Después de escribir

 **1-54 ▶ ¡Edita!** Working with a partner, edit each other's emails and discuss possible errors or areas that are unclear.

**1-55 ▶ ¡Repasa!** Review your email using the checklist below to check your grammar:

❑ Did you use the verb **ser** to say who you are, and to identify yourself as a student from the class?
❑ Did you make the adjectives agree with the nouns in your descriptions?
❑ Did you include expressions such as **No comprendo** or **¿Qué significa . . . ?** to indicate the structure or vocabulary from the chapter that you do not understand well?
❑ Did you address your professor as **profesor** or **profesora**?

**1-56 ▶ ¡Navega!** Visit your online resource for *Hoy día* for the link to the *Centro Virtual Cervantes*. It offers a discussion forum, *Foro didáctico*, for students to search postings related to Spanish grammar and vocabulary, reading and writing. Click on *Foro didáctico*, and browse through the topics posted. Select one that might interest you, and see if you can grasp its content. Then, post the question that you have asked your professor by clicking on the **Nuevo mensaje** link at the top of the page. Fill out the **Nuevo mensaje** form. Send your question by clicking on **Enviar formulario**. See how other users around the world respond!

> **▶ Writing strategy**
> *Identifying your audience.*
> When you write a letter or an email to a professor or a supervisor requesting information, it is essential to organize it logically and to use the correct tone. In this type of formal communication, you are expected to address the audience with the **usted** form rather than the **tú** form. Make your email polite and clear, and remember to address your professor as **profesor** or **profesora.** What phrases can you use to greet your professor and ask how he/she is?

# 1 Vocabulario

| TEMA 1 | TEMA 2 |
|---|---|

## Saludos (Greetings)

| | |
|---|---|
| Buenos días. | Good morning. |
| Buenas tardes. | Good afternoon. |
| Buenas noches. | Good evening. Good night. |
| Hola. | Hi. |
| ¿Cómo estás? | How are you? (familiar) |
| ¿Cómo está usted? | How are you? (formal) |
| hoy | today |
| Estoy . . . | I am . . . , I'm . . . |
| (muy) bien | (very) well |
| (un poco) cansado/a | (a little) tired |
| enfermo/a | sick, ill |
| mal | bad(ly) |
| ocupado/a | busy |
| regular | as usual |
| gracias | thank you |
| ¿Y tú/usted? | And you? (familiar/formal) |
| Pues . . . | Well, . . . , So, . . . . |

## Presentaciones (Introductions)

| | |
|---|---|
| ¿Cómo te llamas? | What is your name? (familiar) |
| ¿Cómo se llama usted? | What is your name? (formal) |
| señor (Sr.) | Mr., sir |
| señora (Sra.) | Mrs., Mme. |
| señorita (Srta.) | Miss |
| Me llamo . . . | My name is . . . |
| Soy . . . | I am, I'm . . . |
| ¿Cómo se escribe? | How is that written? |
| con / sin acento | with / without an accent |
| Mucho gusto. | Pleased to meet you. |
| Igualmente. | Likewise. |
| ¿De dónde eres? | Where are you from? (familiar) |
| ¿De dónde es usted? | Where are you from? (formal) |
| Soy de . . . | I'm from . . . |
| aquí | here |

## Despedidas (Expressions for saying good-bye)

| | |
|---|---|
| Adiós. | Good-bye. |
| Hasta luego. | See you later. |
| Hasta mañana. | See you tomorrow. |

## Otras palabras (Other words)

| | |
|---|---|
| el estudiante | student (male) |
| la estudiante | student (female) |
| el profesor | professor (male) |
| la profesora | professor (female) |
| la universidad | university |

## En el salón de clase

| | |
|---|---|
| un bolígrafo | pen |
| una calculadora | calculator |
| una cama | bed |
| una clase (de español) | (Spanish) class |
| un/una compañero/a de clase | classmate (male) |
| una computadora | computer |
| una cosa | thing |
| un cuaderno | notebook |
| un cuaderno de ejercicios | workbook |
| un cuarto | room |
| un diccionario | dictionary |
| un escritorio | desk |
| un estante | shelf |
| un estéreo | stereo |
| un lápiz | pencil |
| un libro | book |
| una mesa | table |
| una mochila | bookbag, backpack |
| un papel | (piece of) paper |
| una pizarra | blackboard |
| una planta | plant |
| una puerta | door |
| un pupitre | student desk |
| un reloj | clock, watch |
| un salón de clase | classroom |
| una silla | chair |
| un televisor | television set |
| una ventana | window |

## Otras palabras y expresiones

| | |
|---|---|
| como | like, as |
| de | of, from |
| en | in, on, at |
| hay | there is, there are, is there, are there |
| más | more, plus |
| mi/s | my |
| mucho/a/os/as | much, many, a lot of |
| Necesito . . . | I need . . . |
| ningún/ninguna | no, not . . . any |
| otro/a | other, another |
| para | for |
| pero | but |
| poco/a/os/as | little, few |
| sólo | only |
| también | also, too |
| (no) tengo . . . | I (don't) have . . . |
| ¿Tienes . . . ? | Do you have . . . ? |
| todo/a/os/as | all, every |
| tu/s | your (familiar) |
| un/a | a, an |
| unos/as | some |
| varios/as | several |

*For the numbers 0–100, see page 14.*

## En el campus universitario

| | |
|---|---|
| la biblioteca | library |
| la cafetería | cafeteria |
| la comida | food |
| el/la compañero/a de cuarto | roommate |
| el edificio | building |
| el gimnasio | gym(nasium) |
| el laboratorio de lenguas | language lab |
| el/la mejor amigo/a | best friend |
| el/la novio/a | boyfriend/girlfriend |
| la residencia | residence hall, dormitory |

## Descripciones

| | |
|---|---|
| ¿Cómo es . . . ? | How is . . . ? What's . . . like? |
| aburrido/a | boring |
| antipático/a | unpleasant |
| bonito/a | pretty |
| bueno/a | good |
| difícil | difficult |
| divertido/a | fun |
| extrovertido/a | outgoing, extroverted |
| fácil | easy |
| feo/a | ugly |
| grande | big |
| (im)paciente | (im)patient |
| intelectual | intellectual |
| inteligente | intelligent |
| interesante | interesting |
| (ir)responsable | (ir)responsible |
| malo/a | bad |
| moderno/a | modern |
| nuevo/a | new |
| optimista | optimistic |
| pequeño/a | little, small |
| perezoso/a | lazy |
| pesimista | pessimistic |
| serio/a | serious |
| simpático/a | nice |
| tímido/a | shy, timid |
| tonto/a | stupid, silly |
| trabajador/a | hardworking |
| viejo/a | old |

*¡Hola!*

## Otras palabras

| | |
|---|---|
| menos | minus, less, except |
| que | that |

*For the subject pronouns and the forms of **ser**, see page 20.*

## Los estudios (*Studies*)

| | |
|---|---|
| ¿Qué estudias? | What are you studying? |
| Estudio . . . | I'm studying . . . |
| ¿Qué clases tienes? | What classes do you have? |
| Este semestre/trimestre tengo . . . | This semester/trimester I have . . . |

*For a list of courses, see page 22.*

## En el libro de texto

| | |
|---|---|
| el ejercicio | exercise |
| la oración | sentence |
| la página | page |
| la palabra | word |
| la respuesta | answer, response |
| la tarea | homework |

## Otras palabras y expresiones

| | |
|---|---|
| cada | each |
| ¿Cómo se dice . . . en español? | How do you say . . . in Spanish? |
| mismo/a | same |
| No comprendo. | I don't understand. |
| No sé. | I don't know. |
| por favor | please |
| próximo/a | next |
| ¿Qué significa . . . en inglés? | What does . . . mean in English? |
| siguiente | following |
| ¿Te gusta . . . ? / (+ singular noun) | |
| ¿Te gustan . . . ? (+ plural noun) | Do you like . . . ? |
| (No) me gusta . . . / (+ singular noun) | |
| (No) me gustan . . . (+ plural noun) | I (don't) like . . . |
| útil | useful |

*For a list of classroom commands, see page 22*

Visit MySpanishLab for *Hoy día* for links to the mnemonic dictionary online and for suggestions to help you remember vocabulary from *Capítulo 1*, learn related words in Spanish, and use Spanish words to build your vocabulary in English.

### EXAMPLES

**día,** day: This word is related to the English adjective *diurnal*. A *diurnal* animal is one that is active in the daytime. It is also related to *diary*, which is a daily journal. Related word in Spanish: **diario/a,** *daily*

**noche,** *night:* This word is related to the English adjective *nocturnal*. A *nocturnal* animal is one that is active at night. Related word in Spanish: **nocturno/a,** *nocturnal*

# 2 Después de clase

In this chapter, you will learn to talk about schedules and leisure activities. Although there are cultural differences among Hispanics, their concept of time regarding punctuality often varies significantly from that of other cultures.

Hispanics tend to be very flexible with time. It is not considered impolite to arrive ten or fifteen minutes late to informal gatherings.

- ▶ Do you consider yourself a punctual person?
- ▶ Is it important to be punctual? Why?

It is a common custom among Hispanic families to share mealtimes. In some Hispanic countries, work schedules allow time for people to have lunch at home with their families.

- ▶ How important do you think it is to share mealtimes with the family?
- ▶ What do you think of a work schedule that allows longer lunch hours?

In most Hispanic countries, people place a great emphasis on socializing with friends and family. Work schedules tend to be less demanding than in the United States.

- ▶ Do you think that work schedules in the United States are very demanding?
- ▶ Do you feel overwhelmed by the responsibilities of your schedule?

# Vocabulario    Mi horario

SAM: 2-1
to 2-4

 CD 1 Track 25   ¿Qué hora es?

## ¿Sabías que...?

In most Hispanic countries, Sunday is a day of rest. Traditionally, some people attend church in the morning, and then take a stroll around the town, visit the Sunday market, and go for a drink (**un aperitivo**). In the early afternoon, families gather around a special lunch that takes place between two and three, and usually lasts for hours. How do you usually spend your Sundays?

## ¡Ojo!

Use **es la una** to say *it is one o'clock*, but **son las . . .** to say *it is* with the other hours. Use **a la una** to say *at one o'clock* and **a las . . .** to say *at* with other hours. Use **hasta la una** or **hasta las . . .** to say *until* a certain hour. Also note that **mañana** might be translated as either *morning* or *tomorrow*, and **tarde** can mean either *afternoon* or *late*. The context will clarify the meaning. You will learn more about telling time in the next grammar explanation.

Son las ocho.

Son las nueve y diez.

Son las diez y cuarto.

Son las once y veinte.

Es la una.

Es la una y media.

Son las dos menos veinte.

Son las cinco menos cuarto.

¿Qué día es? ¿Qué días tienes clases? ¿A qué hora? ¿Te gusta tu **horario**? ¿Tienes otra clase **antes** o **después de** la clase de español?

| Octubre | | | | | | |
|---|---|---|---|---|---|---|
| lunes | martes | miércoles | jueves | viernes | sábado | domingo |
| 8 | 9 | 10 | 11 | 12 | 13 | 14 |

¿Dónde estás generalmente los lunes a las diez **de la mañana**? ¿a la una **de la tarde**? ¿a las diez **de la noche**?

¿en casa? ¿en la cama?

¿en clase o en la biblioteca?

¿en el trabajo? ¿en la oficina?

¿con tus amigos?

---

**el horario** *the schedule*  **antes de** *before*  **después de** *after*  **de la mañana** *in the morning*  **de la tarde** *in the afternoon*  **de la noche** *at night*

Track 26

**Una conversación.** Read the following conversation in which two students talk about their schedules.

JOSÉ: Hola, Inés. ¿Qué días tienes clases?

INÉS: Tengo clases de literatura, historia y biología los lunes, miércoles y viernes. Mi clase de ciencias políticas es los martes y jueves.

JOSÉ: ¿A qué hora son tus clases?

INÉS: Los martes y jueves, mi clase de ciencias políticas es a las nueve. Los lunes, miércoles y viernes estoy en clase **todo el día de** diez **a** tres.

JOSÉ: ¡Estás muy ocupada! ¿**Trabajas** también?

INÉS: Sí, **esta semana trabajo** cuatro **horas** el lunes, miércoles y viernes y todo el día el sábado. Con frecuencia trabajo los domingos también, pero **este fin de semana** no trabajo el domingo.

JOSÉ: ¿**Te gustaría estudiar conmigo** el domingo?

INÉS: Sí, me gustaría estudiar **juntos**. No me gusta estudiar **sola**. ¿A qué hora?

JOSÉ: No **demasiado temprano**. Estoy en la cama hasta **tarde** los domingos. ¿A las dos?

INÉS: Está bien.

CD 1, Track 27

## ¡A escuchar!

Listen to another conversation in which Sara asks Elena about her schedule this semester. What classes does Elena have, what days, and at what times? When does she work?

---

**2-1 ▶ Mis clases.** Change the words in italics in the following sentences so that they describe you. If they are already true for you, read them as they are.

1. Mi clase de español es los *lunes y miércoles*.
2. Mi clase de español es a *las diez y cuarto de la mañana*.
3. Tengo *una clase* los martes y jueves.
4. No tengo ninguna clase los *viernes, sábados y domingos*.
5. Tengo *una clase* antes de la clase de español.
6. *No* tengo *ninguna clase* después de la clase de español.
7. Me gustan más las clases a *las nueve o diez de la mañana*.
8. No me gustan las clases a *las cuatro de la tarde*.

**2-2 ▶ ¿Dónde estás?** Using the forms of **estar** as in the Modelo, ask where a classmate generally is at the indicated times. Some possible locations are provided in the box.

| | | | |
|---|---|---|---|
| con mi familia | en casa | en el trabajo | en la universidad, |
| con mis amigos | en clase | en la biblioteca | pero no en clase |

Modelo    los sábados a las 10:30 de la noche
E1: *¿Dónde estás los sábados a las diez y media de la noche?*
E2: *Los sábados a las diez y media de la noche, generalmente estoy con mis amigos.*

1. los lunes a las 9:00 de la mañana
2. los martes a la 1:15 de la tarde
3. los miércoles a las 7:30 de la mañana
4. los jueves a las 11:30 de la noche
5. los viernes a las 5:45 de la tarde
6. los domingos a las 3:20 de la tarde

**2-3 ▶ Otra conversación.** With a partner, reread *Una conversación* between José and Inés at the top of the page. Then, change it to talk about your schedule.

---

**todo el día** *all day*   **de . . . a . . .** *from . . . to . . .*   **trabajas** *(do) you work*   **esta semana** *this week*   **trabajo** *I work*   **horas** *hours*   **este fin de semana** *this weekend*   **¿Te gustaría . . . ?** *Would you like . . . ?*   **estudiar** *to study*   **conmigo** *with me*   **juntos/as** *together*   **solo/a** *alone*   **demasiado** *too, too much*   **temprano** *early*   **tarde** *late*

# Gramática 1

SAM: 2-5
to 2-9

## Describing your schedule: Time and the days of the week

### Para averiguar

1. When do you use **es** instead of **son** to say what time it is?
2. When do you say **son las dos**? When do you say **a las dos**?
3. When do you say **de la mañana** for *in the morning*? When do you say **por la mañana**?
4. When do you use **el** with a day of the week? When do you use **los**?
5. What do **hasta, de . . . a, antes de,** and **después de** mean? After which of these do you drop **la, las, el, los** with hours and days?

■ Use **¿Qué hora es?** to ask *What time is it (now)?* Say **Es la una** for *It's one o'clock,* **Es mediodía** for *It's noon,* and **Es medianoche** for *It's midnight.* With all other hours, use **Son las . . .** To express an amount of time until an hour, say that it's the hour minus (**menos**) the number of minutes.

— ¿Qué hora es?
— Es la una y cuarto. (1:15) / Son las tres menos diez. (2:50)

■ To ask at what time something takes place, use **¿A qué hora . . . ?** To answer, use **a la una, al mediodía, a la medianoche,** or **a las . . .** with other hours. Unlike *at* in English, **a** cannot be dropped in questions.

— **¿A** qué hora es tu clase de historia?     — *(At) what time is your history class?*
— Es **a** las diez.                           — *It's at ten.*

■ You may use the following expressions to distinguish times in the morning, afternoon, or evening.

| | | |
|---|---|---|
| **de la mañana** | A las ocho de la mañana. | *At eight in the morning.* |
| **de la tarde** | A la una de la tarde. | *At one in the afternoon.* |
| **de la noche** | A las once de la noche. | *At eleven in the evening.* |

■ If you are not giving a specific hour, use **por la mañana, por la tarde,** and **por la noche** to say *in the morning, in the afternoon,* and *in the evening / at night.*

SPECIFIC HOUR:     Trabajo a las ocho y media **de la mañana.**
                   *I work at eight thirty (half past eight) in the morning.*

NO HOUR GIVEN:     Trabajo **por la mañana.**
                   *I work in the morning.*

■ Use the following expressions to ask and tell what day it is. Days of the week are not capitalized in Spanish and Monday (**lunes**) is the first day of the week on calendars, not Sunday (**domingo**).

— ¿Qué día es hoy?
— Hoy es lunes (martes, miércoles, jueves, viernes, sábado, domingo).

■ Use **el** to say that something will occur *on* a particular day. Although *on* may be dropped in English, **el** may not be dropped in this context in Spanish.

Esta semana, no tengo clase **el** miércoles.     *This week, I don't have class (on) Wednesday.*

■ To say that something normally happens every week *on* a day, use **los.** Add **-s** to **sábado** and **domingo** to make them plural, but not to days that already end with **-s.**

Trabajo **los** viernes y domingo**s.**     *I work (on) Fridays and Sundays.*

■ You may also use **hasta** (*until*), **antes de** (*before*), **después de** (*after*) or **de . . . a** (*from . . . to*) with days of the week or times. After **de . . . a,** the article is dropped before days or hours.

Estoy en clase **de** lunes **a** viernes **de** nueve **a** dos.     *I am in class Monday through Friday from nine to two.*

Estoy en casa **hasta** las ocho y **después de** las tres.     *I'm at home until eight and after three.*

**2-4 ▶ ¿Qué hora es?** Look at the clocks below and say what time it is.

Modelo   *Son las once y media de la mañana.*

1.    2.    3.    4.    5.

**2-5 ▶ ¿Qué palabra es?** Complete the following conversation by choosing the correct word in parentheses.

RAÚL: ¿Tienes más clases (1) _____ (de, por) la mañana o (2) _____ (de, por) la tarde este semestre/trimestre?

SERGIO: Tengo química (3) _____ (el, los) martes y jueves (4) _____ (son, a) las diez de la mañana. Mis clases de matemáticas e inglés son (5) _____ (de, por) la tarde (6) _____ (el, los) lunes, miércoles y viernes.

RAÚL: ¿Te gustaría estudiar química juntos en la biblioteca este fin de semana?

SERGIO: ¡Claro! ¿(7) _____ (El, Los) sábado o (8) _____ (el, los) domingo?

RAÚL: ¿(9) _____ (El, Los) domingo (10) _____ (a, son) las tres (11) _____ (de, por) la tarde está bien?

SERGIO: Me gusta más estudiar (12) _____ (son, a) las siete (13) _____ (el, los) domingos.

RAÚL: Está bien (14) _____ (son, a) las siete. ¿Qué hora es ahora?

SERGIO: (15) _____ (Son, A) las dos y veinte.

RAÚL: Tengo clase (16) _____ (son, a) las dos y media. Hasta (17) _____ (el, los) domingo.

SERGIO: Hasta luego.

**2-6 ▶ Entrevista.** Ask another student the following questions. Afterwards, be prepared to tell the class about your partner. You will need these verb forms to talk about him/her: **le gusta(n), él/ella está, él/ella tiene, él/ella trabaja.**

**1.** ¿Te gusta tu horario este semestre? ¿Qué días estás en clase? ¿Qué días no tienes clase?

**2.** ¿Tienes más clases por la mañana, por la tarde o por la noche? ¿A qué hora te gustan más las clases? ¿A qué hora son tus clases este semestre?

**3.** ¿Qué días trabajas? ¿A qué hora?

**2-7 ▶ Comparaciones culturales.** In official schedules such as movie times or bus, train, and flight schedules, times in Hispanic countries are generally posted using the 24-hour clock. Do you think it would be good to use the 24-hour clock in official schedules here? Why or why not? Convert the following movie times from the 24-hour clock to conversational time.

Modelo   13:50
*Las trece horas y cincuenta minutos son las dos menos diez de la tarde.*

| | | | |
|---|---|---|---|
| **1.** 19:00 | **3.** 16:45 | **5.** 21:35 | **7.** 22:25 |
| **2.** 20:30 | **4.** 15:10 | **6.** 14:40 | **8.** 17:55 |

**¡Ojo!**

To convert from a 24-hour clock to a 12-hour clock, simply subtract 12 from the time given. For example, 15:00 is 3:00 PM (15 − 12 = 3). With the 24-hour clock, state the number of minutes (31–59 minutes) after the hour instead of using **menos** to say the number of minutes until the next hour.

#  Gramática 2 Saying where you are: The verb **estar**

SAM: 2-10 to 2-14

## Para averiguar

1. What are two uses of the verb **estar**? What are its forms?
2. Which two adverbs indicating frequency are placed directly before the verb? Where may the other adverbs of frequency be placed?

## ¿Cómo se pronuncia? ¡Hola!

**Written accent marks.**

Written accents are used on some of the forms of **estar** to indicate which syllable is stressed. Refer to the Pronunciation Guide in your MySpanishLab course under Word Stress to learn the rules for using accent marks.

■ You have already used the verb **estar** (*to be*) with adjectives to say how you are doing.

— ¿Cómo **estás**?
— **Estoy** un poco enferma y muy cansada.

■ Here is the full conjugation of **estar**.

### estar *(to be)*

| | | | | | |
|---|---|---|---|---|---|
| yo | estoy | *I am* | nosotros/as | estamos | *we are* |
| tú | estás | *you are (familiar)* | vosotros/as | estáis | *you are (familiar plural)* |
| usted | está | *you are (formal)* | ustedes | están | *you are (plural)* |
| él, ella | está | *he, she is* | ellos/as | están | *they are* |

■ Also use **estar** to say where or with whom someone or something is.

— ¿**Estás** en clase los jueves?
— Sí, **estoy** en clase hasta las dos y después **estoy** con mis amigos.

— *Are you in class on Thursdays?*
— *Yes, I'm in class until two and afterwards I'm with my friends.*

■ Use the following adverbs with verbs to say how often. **(Casi) siempre** and **(casi) nunca** are most commonly placed just before the verb. The other adverbs may go at the beginning or end of a clause.

| | | | |
|---|---|---|---|
| **(casi) siempre** | *(almost) always* | **una vez a la semana** | *once a week* |
| **(casi) nunca** | *(almost) never* | **dos veces al mes** | *twice a month* |
| **todo el día** | *all day long* | **tres veces al año** | *three times a year* |
| **todos los días** | *every day* | **los lunes** | *on Mondays* |
| **generalmente** | *generally* | **los fines** | |
| **con frecuencia** | *frequently* | **de semana** | *on weekends* |
| **a veces** | *sometimes, at times* | **de lunes a viernes** | *Monday through Friday* |

— ¿**Siempre** estás en casa por la mañana?
— No, **a veces** estoy en la biblioteca.

— *Are you always at home in the morning?*
— *No, sometimes I'm at the library.*

**2-8 ▶ ¿Con qué frecuencia?** Complete each sentence with the correct form of **estar** and an appropriate adverb of frequency to describe yourself and your acquaintances.

Modelo (Yo) _____ muy cansado/a por la mañana.
*Casi siempre estoy muy cansado/a por la mañana.*

**1.** (Yo) _____ muy ocupado/a los fines de semana.
**2.** Los domingos, mis padres _____ en casa todo el día.
**3.** Mi mejor amigo/a y yo _____ juntos/as los fines de semana.
**4.** Mi mejor amigo/a _____ en clase conmigo.
**5.** (Yo) _____ en la biblioteca antes de la clase de español.
**6.** El/La profesor/a de español _____ en el salón de clase cuando yo llego (*when I arrive*).
**7.** Mis compañeros de clase y yo _____ confundidos (*confused*) en clase.

**2-9 ▶ ¿Dónde están?** José is talking about himself and others. Refer to the illustrations and use the correct form of (**no**) **estar** with each item in parentheses to describe where or with whom these people are, or how they are doing.

Modelo   Mi compañero de cuarto . . . (conmigo, en la cama, cansado)
*Mi compañero de cuarto no está conmigo. Está en la cama. Está cansado.*

**1.** Mi padre . . . (en casa, en la oficina, ocupado, solo, con clientes)

**2.** Los clientes . . . (en un sofá, juntos en la misma mesa, interesados en la presentación)

**3.** Yo . . . (en un restaurante, en el trabajo, solo, con mi novia)

**4.** Mi novia y yo . . . (con otros amigos, solos en la mesa, solos en el restaurante)

**2-10 ▶ Entrevista.** Complete each question with the indicated form of the verb **estar**. After **me/te gusta**, leave **estar** unconjugated: **Me gusta estar . . .** (*I like to be . . .* ).

**1.** ¿Dónde _____ (tú) generalmente antes de la clase de español? ¿Dónde _____ (tú) generalmente después de la clase? ¿Dónde _____ tus padres normalmente a la hora de la clase de español? ¿en casa? ¿en el trabajo? ¿en un café o un restaurante?

**2.** ¿_____ tu casa/apartamento/residencia cerca de (*near*) la universidad, lejos de (*far from*) la universidad o en el campus? ¿Hasta qué hora _____ (tú) en tu casa/apartamento/residencia por la mañana? ¿Cuántas horas _____ (tú) en la universidad generalmente los días que (nosotros) _____ en esta clase?

**3.** ¿Te gusta más _____ con tus amigos o solo/a los fines de semana? Los fines de semana, ¿ _____ (tú) más con tu familia o con tus amigos? ¿Qué días _____ ustedes juntos generalmente? A veces, ¿te gusta _____ solo/a?

**¿Y tú?** Use the preceding questions to interview another student.

Hola, ¿cómo estás?

#  Vocabulario  Las actividades diarias

SAM: 2-15 to 2-18

 CD 1 Track 28 ¿Qué te gusta **hacer** después de clase? ¿Con **quién** te gusta pasar **el tiempo libre**? ¿Cuáles son tus actividades **diarias**?

Generalmente después de clase, me gusta . . .

tomar **algo** con otros estudiantes en un café

hablar por teléfono con mi mejor amigo/a

mirar la tele solo/a en casa

Hoy después de clase, necesito . . .

trabajar

regresar temprano a casa

estudiar

Este fin de semana, **deseo** . . .

escuchar música y bailar con mi novio/a

tocar la guitarra y cantar con mis amigos

pasar tiempo solo/a en casa y **descansar**

**hacer** *to do, to make*  **quién** *who, whom*  **el tiempo** *time*  **libre** *free*  **diario/a** *daily*  **algo** *something*  **desear** *to wish, to desire*  **descansar** *to rest*

Este fin de semana, necesito . . .

limpiar la casa

cocinar / preparar **una cena** especial para **el cumpleaños** de un/a amigo/a

comprar **ropa** / **un regalo** para un/a amigo/a

---

CD 1
Track 29

Una conversación. In the following conversation, two friends are talking about weekend activities.

JOSÉ: ¿Qué te gusta hacer los fines de semana?

DIEGO: Los viernes casi siempre estoy cansado. Trabajo hasta las siete y después del trabajo, **prefiero** pasar la noche en casa.

JOSÉ: ¿No trabajas los sábados **ni** los domingos?

DIEGO: No, los sábados me gusta **salir**. Me gusta **ir al cine** o a un café con mis amigos. A veces me gusta **comer** en un restaurante.

JOSÉ ¿Te gusta descansar los domingos?

DIEGO: Sí, me gusta mirar **deportes** en la televisión, pero casi siempre necesito hacer mucha tarea.

JOSÉ: Yo también tengo mucha tarea los domingos.

CD 1, Track 30

¡A **e s c u c h a r !**

Now, listen to another conversation in which two students, Amanda and Gloria, are talking about their activities after class. What do they like to do? When do they work?

**2-11 ► ¿Qué haces?** Change the italicized words so that the following sentences describe you. If the sentence is already true, answer **es cierto** and read the sentence as it is.

**1.** Hoy, después de clase, necesito *trabajar*.

**2.** Generalmente, después de clase, me gusta *descansar*.

**3.** No me gusta *bailar* con mis amigos.

**4.** Los fines de semana, me gusta *mirar la televisión*.

**5.** Tengo mucho tiempo para descansar *los jueves*.

**6.** Generalmente, necesito estudiar mucho *los lunes, miércoles y sábados*.

**7.** Me gusta pasar mucho tiempo con mis amigos *los viernes por la noche*.

**8.** Deseo pasar este fin de semana *solo/a en casa*.

 **2-12 ► Entrevista.** Interview another student with the following questions.

**1.** ¿Te gusta más tomar algo con tus amigos en un café o bailar con tus amigos en un club?

**2.** ¿Te gusta escuchar música clásica? ¿jazz? ¿rock? ¿música popular? ¿Te gusta más escuchar música de la radio o de tu iPod o MP3?

**3.** ¿Qué te gustaría hacer esta noche? ¿Y este fin de semana? ¿Qué necesitas hacer esta noche? ¿Y este fin de semana?

 **2-13 ► Otra conversación.** With a partner, reread *Una conversación* between José y Diego. Then, change it to talk about your weekend activities.

---

**una cena** *a dinner*   **el cumpleaños** *the birthday*   **la ropa** *clothes*   **un regalo** *a gift, a present*   **prefiero** *I prefer*   **ni** *nor*   **salir** *to go out*   **ir al cine** *to go to the movies*   **comer** *to eat*   **los deportes** *sports*

# 📖 Gramática 1

SAM: 2-19
to 2-21

## Talking about your activities: Regular -ar verbs

Para **averiguar**

1. What is an infinitive?
2. What are the three infinitive endings in Spanish?
3. What are the endings of regular -**ar** verbs that go with each of the subject pronouns? How do you determine the stem to which you attach these endings?

### ¡Ojo!

You will learn later how to conjugate non -**ar** verbs like **ir** (*to go*), **comer** (*to eat*), and **hacer** (*to do, to make*). Until then, just use them in the infinitive after another verb to say what you need, would like, or like to do. (**Necesito comer. Me gustaría ir a la cafetería. Me gusta hacer mi tarea en un café.**)

■ **Infinitives:** The form of the verb that you find in Spanish dictionaries or vocabulary lists is called the infinitive. Some examples of infinitives in English are *to work, to do,* and *to write.* Spanish infinitives consist of single words that end in -**ar**, -**er**, or -**ir: trabajar, hacer, escribir**. Here you will learn the different forms of -**ar** verbs in the present tense.

■ To indicate the subject of -**ar** verbs you must conjugate them by dropping the -**ar** ending of the infinitive and adding the highlighted endings shown below. As with all verbs, the subject pronouns are not used, unless they are needed for clarity or emphasis.

### trabajar *(to work)*

| | | | | | | |
|---|---|---|---|---|---|---|
| yo | trabajo | *I work* | nosotros/as | trabajamos | *we work* |
| tú | trabajas | *you work* | vosotros/as | trabajáis | *you work* |
| usted | trabaja | *you work* | ustedes | trabajan | *you work* |
| él, ella | trabaja | *he, she works* | ellos/as | trabajan | *they work* |

■ These -**ar** verbs follow the same pattern as **trabajar.**

| | | | | |
|---|---|---|---|---|
| **bailar** | *to dance* | **limpiar** | *to clean* |
| **cantar** | *to sing* | **llegar** | *to arrive* |
| **cocinar** | *to cook* | **mirar** | *to look at, to watch* |
| **comprar** | *to buy* | **necesitar** | *to need* |
| **contestar** | *to answer* | **pasar** | *to pass, to spend (time)* |
| **descansar** | *to rest* | **preparar** | *to prepare* |
| **desear** | *to wish, to desire* | **regresar** | *to return* |
| **escuchar** | *to listen (to)* | **tocar** | *to play (music, an instrument)* |
| **estudiar** | *to study* | **tomar** | *to drink, to take* |
| **hablar** | *to speak* | **usar** | *to use* |

■ Note that the simple present tense in English can be translated three different ways in Spanish.

Trabajamos hoy. { *We work today.*
*We are working today.*
*We do work today.*

■ To negate a verb, remember that you place **no** before it. Do not translate the verb *do* that is used to ask questions or negate verbs in English.

—¿**Pasas** mucho tiempo con tus padres?
—No, **no paso** mucho tiempo con ellos.

— *Do you spend much time with your parents?*
— *No, I don't spend much time with them.*

■ When there are two verbs together and the second one is the infinitive (*to . . .* ) in English, it will be translated by an infinitive in Spanish.

Necesito **estudiar** muchos verbos.

*I need to study a lot of verbs.*

■ This does not mean, however, than you cannot have several conjugated verbs in a row.

Todos los días **estoy** en clase, **trabajo, regreso** a casa y **estudio.**

*Every day, I'm in class, I work, (I) return home, and (I) study.*

**2-14 ► ¿Con qué frecuencia?** Tell another student how often the following people do each of the activities in parentheses, then ask the same information about your partner and the people he/she knows. Take turns beginning.

| (casi) siempre | todos los días | con frecuencia | a veces | (casi) nunca |
|---|---|---|---|---|

Modelo    Yo . . . (estudiar en la biblioteca). Y tú, ¿con qué frecuencia . . . ?
E1: *Yo estudio en la biblioteca casi todos los días. Y tú, ¿con qué frecuencia estudias en la biblioteca?*
E2: *Casi nunca estudio en la biblioteca.*

**1.** Yo . . . (llegar tarde a la universidad, descansar los sábados, limpiar la casa, pasar todo el día en casa, estudiar en un café). Y tú, ¿con qué frecuencia . . . ?
**2.** Mi mejor amigo/a . . . (trabajar los fines de semana, estudiar los sábados por la noche, escuchar música clásica, cantar en un karaoke). Y tu mejor amigo/a, ¿con qué frecuencia . . . ?
**3.** Mi mejor amigo/a y yo . . . (bailar juntos, tomar algo juntos en un café, regresar tarde a casa los sábados, hablar por teléfono). Y ustedes, ¿con qué frecuencia . . . ?

**2-15 ► ¿Quién?** Using the correct form of the verb, say who in parentheses does the indicated activity more. Place **más** after the verb as in the Modelo. **Mi madre, mi padre,** and **mis padres** mean *my mother, my father,* and *my parents* respectively.

Modelo    (mi madre, mi padre) comprar la comida
*Mi madre compra más la comida.*

**1.** (mi madre, yo) estudiar
**2.** (mi madre, mi padre) limpiar la casa
**3.** (mis amigos y yo, mis padres) bailar
**4.** (mi mejor amigo/a, yo) mirar la tele
**5.** (yo, mi mejor amigo/a) comprar ropa
**6.** (yo, mi compañero/a de cuarto) cocinar
**7.** (mi padre y yo, mi madre y yo) hablar
**8.** (mis amigos, mis padres) trabajar

**2-16 ► Comparaciones culturales.** Read the following information about how digital technology has redefined the pastimes of young people around the world, and discuss the questions with a partner.

tecnología

Hablar por teléfono celular es la forma preferida de comunicación de los jóvenes en todo el mundo[1]. Como media[2], los jóvenes tienen 94 números de teléfono en su celular. ¿Y tú? ¿Cuántas veces al día usas tu celular? ¿Con quién hablas generalmente? ¿A qué hora del día te gusta hablar más por teléfono? ¿Cuántos números de teléfono tienes aproximadamente en tu celular?

Muchos jóvenes tienen su perfil personal en Internet y participan en comunidades virtuales con amigos de todo el mundo. Como media, los jóvenes tienen 86 personas en su comunidad virtual y siete de las diez búsquedas más frecuentes en Internet están relacionadas con redes[6] sociales. ¿Y tú? ¿Usas *Facebook, MySpace* u otra red social en Internet? ¿Cuántos amigos forman tu comunidad virtual? ¿De dónde son tus amigos?

La comunicación digital por Internet complementa, no reemplaza[3] a la televisión. Las personalidades de la televisión y los programas populares son temas[4] frecuentes en las salas de chat y las búsquedas[5] en línea. ¿Y tú? ¿Hablas con tus amigos de los programas de televisión? ¿Qué programas te gustan más? ¿Te gusta más mirar la televisión o pasar tiempo en la computadora? A veces, ¿miras episodios pasados de programas de televisión por Internet?

myspace.latino    Buscar
Inicio   Amigos   Foros   Música
¡Chisme!   ¡Buscar a tus amigos!   INICIAR SESIÓN   REGÍSTRATE
Correo electrónico
¡Cargar fotos!   Especiales   Contraseña

[1]*worldwide*  [2]*on average*  [3]*replace*  [4]*topics*  [5]*searches*  [6]*networks*

#  Gramática 2   Asking questions: Question formation

SAM: 2-22
to 2-27

## Para averiguar

1. Where do you generally place the subject with respect to the verb in a question? In what sort of questions is the subject sometimes placed at the end?
2. What two expressions can you add to the end of a statement to check that you are right? How are they translated in English?
3. How do you say *who, what, which, where, when, why, how, how much, how many,* and *how often* in Spanish?
4. Do you use **qué** or **cuál** to translate *What is . . . ?* or *What are . . . ?* when asking for a definition? When asking for a selection out of a group of possibilities?

## ¡Ojo!

Note that all question words have written accent marks to distinguish them from other words in Spanish. For example, **cómo** means *how*, but **como** means *like*, and **qué** means *what* but **que** means *that* or *than*.

## ¿Cómo se pronuncia? ¡Hola!

### The letters cu and qu

Most question words begin with **cu** and **qu**. Words spelled with **cu** have a [w] sound when they are pronounced but those with **qu** do not. There is more practice of **cu** and **qu** in the Pronunciation Guide in your MySpanishLab course under Consonants.

■ To ask a question that may be answered *yes* or *no*, use rising intonation just as in English. Rising intonation means that the pitch of your voice goes up at the end of the question. The word *do*, used to ask questions in English, is not translated in Spanish.

¿Trabajas todos los días? ———↗        *Do you work every day?* ———↗

■ Unlike in English, where questions and statements are worded differently, questions in Spanish are often worded the same as statements. For this reason, questions in Spanish begin with an inverted question mark to cue readers from the start to read them with the correct intonation.

STATEMENT:  Trabajo mañana. ———↘        QUESTION:  ¿Trabajo mañana? ———↗
　　　　　　*I work tomorrow.*　　　　　　　　　　　　　　*Do I work tomorrow?*

■ When the subject of a verb is stated, it is generally placed after the verb in a question. It may be placed at the end of a very short question.

STATEMENTS:  Daniel estudia más que tú.        QUESTIONS:  ¿Estudia Daniel más que tú?

Daniel estudia mucho.        ¿Estudia mucho Daniel?

■ If you think you already know the answer to a question and you are just asking to be sure, attach **¿verdad?** or **¿no?** to the end of a statement.

Daniel es tu novio, **¿verdad?**        *Daniel is your boyfriend, isn't he?*
Es de Guatemala, **¿no?**        *He's from Guatemala, right?*

■ Use the following interrogative words to ask questions that will be answered with new information, such as *where, when,* or *with whom.* **Cuál(es)** and **quién(es)** have plural forms when referring to plural nouns, and **cuánto/a** and **cuántos/as** agree for number and gender.

| | | | |
|---|---|---|---|
| **¿cuál(es)?** | *which?, what?* | **¿dónde?** | *where?* |
| **¿cuándo?** | *when?* | **¿de dónde?** | *from where?* |
| **¿con qué frecuencia?** | *how often?* | **¿por qué?** | *why?* |
| **¿cuánto/a?** | *how much?* | **¿quién(es)?** | *who?* |
| **¿cuántos/as?** | *how many?* | **¿con quién(es)?** | *with whom?* |
| **¿cómo?** | *how?* | **¿qué?** | *what?* |

■ Generally **qué** translates the English word *what;* however, **cuál(es)** translates as *what* when it is followed by the verb *to be* (**ser**) and one is making a selection from a group. Use **qué** to say *what* with other verbs and with **ser** when asking for a definition.

SELECTION:   ¿Cuál es tu clase favorita?   *What is your favorite class?*
DEFINITION:   ¿Qué es un infinitivo?   *What is an infinitive?*

■ Use **qué** rather than **cuál(es)** directly before a noun.

¿Qué días trabajas?        *What days do you work?*

**2-17 ▶ La tarde de Ramón.** Use the following illustrations to complete each question with the correct question word. Then, answer each question with a complete sentence in Spanish.

**1.** ¿A _____ hora regresa Ramón del trabajo?
**2.** ¿ _____ regresa? ¿en su coche (*his car*) o en el autobús?
**3.** ¿ _____ compra antes de regresar a su casa? ¿un libro o comida?
**4.** ¿ _____ paga (*does he pay*)? ¿más de veinticinco dólares o menos?
**5.** ¿ _____ prepara la comida, Ramón o su esposa (*his wife*)?
**6.** ¿ _____ prepara la comida? ¿en la casa o en el patio?

**2-18 ▶ ¿Qué o cuál(es)?** Complete the following questions students might have for the professor with **qué** or **cuál(es)** to say *what*. Use **qué** to say *what* with verbs other than **ser.** Before a form of **ser,** use **cuál(es)** to ask for a selection and **qué** for a definition.

**1.** ¿ _____ es la tarea para la próxima clase?
**2.** ¿ _____ necesitamos estudiar para mañana?
**3.** ¿ _____ es un infinitivo?
**4.** ¿ _____ son los verbos que necesitamos estudiar para el examen?
**5.** ¿ _____ más necesitamos estudiar para el examen?
**6.** ¿ _____ significa el verbo *llegar*?
**7.** ¿ _____ son sus (*your*) horas de oficina?
**8.** ¿ _____ le gusta hacer después del trabajo?

**2-19 ▶ Preguntas.** Write the questions you would ask another student to obtain the underlined information.

Modelo    Soy de Baltimore.
          *¿De dónde eres?*

**1.** Soy tímido/a, paciente y optimista.
**2.** Este semestre, tomo tres clases.
**3.** Tengo clases de francés, matemáticas e historia.
**4.** Estoy en clase los lunes, miércoles y viernes por la mañana.
**5.** Llego a la universidad a las ocho y media.
**6.** Trabajo en un restaurante.
**7.** Estudio con mi mejor amigo.
**8.** Hoy regreso a casa después de clase.

**¿Y tú?** Now, use the questions you prepared to interview a classmate.

# 📖 Vocabulario   Lugares cerca de la universidad

SAM: 2-28
to 2-30

🔊 ¿Qué hay en **la ciudad**? ¿Qué **lugares** hay **cerca de** la universidad? ¿Qué te gusta
CD 1
Track 31   hacer después de clase?

comprar libros en una librería

**ver una película** en el cine

bailar en un club nocturno

ir al parque

levantar pesas y hacer ejercicio en el gimnasio

ver **un partido** de **fútbol** o de **fútbol americano** en el estadio

comprar ropa en **un centro comercial** con muchas tiendas

comer en un restaurante de comida mexicana

comprar comida en el supermercado y cocinar en casa

---

**la ciudad** *the city*   **un lugar** *a place*   **cerca de** *near*   **ver una película** *to see a movie*   **un partido** *a game, a match*   **el fútbol** *soccer*   **el fútbol americano** *football*   **un centro comercial** *a shopping center, a mall*

**Una conversación.** José and Inés are making plans to study together.

JOSÉ: ¿Te gustaría estudiar juntos en mi apartamento antes del examen?

INÉS: ¿Tu apartamento está cerca de aquí?

JOSÉ: Está un poco **lejos de** la universidad. Está **en la calle** Buena Vista.

INÉS: Prefiero estudiar en el café Java. Está **abierto** hasta tarde todos los días, menos los lunes que está **cerrado**.

JOSÉ: ¿Dónde está?

INÉS: Está **al lado de** un edificio de oficinas en la calle Río Grande.

JOSÉ: Está bien. ¿A qué hora?

INÉS: Me gusta estudiar después de la cena. Hay menos **gente**. ¿**Te parece bien** a las ocho?

JOSÉ: Perfecto.

CD 1, Track 33

**¡A escuchar!**

Now, listen to another conversation in which two students, Pablo and Rafael, make plans to study together. Where and when do they decide to study?

**2-20 ▶ ¿Qué día?** Complete each statement with a logical day of the week.

Modelo     Generalmente los partidos profesionales de fútbol americano son *los domingos.*

**1.** Generalmente los partidos universitarios de fútbol americano son _____.

**2.** Hay más gente en los clubes nocturnos _____.

**3.** Yo prefiero ir al cine _____.

**4.** _____ muchas tiendas están abiertas menos horas.

**5.** Me gusta comer en un restaurante _____.

**2-21 ▶ Preferencias.** Complete the following questions with a logical place.

Modelo     ¿Prefieres bailar con tus amigos en una fiesta en tu casa o en *un club nocturno?*

**1.** ¿Prefieres ver un partido de fútbol americano en la tele o en _____ ?

**2.** ¿Prefieres ver un DVD en casa o ver una película en _____ ?

**3.** ¿Prefieres comprar ropa por Internet o en _____ ?

**4.** ¿Prefieres comprar libros nuevos en _____ o ir a la biblioteca?

**5.** ¿Prefieres comer en un restaurante o comprar comida en _____ y cocinar en casa?

**6.** ¿Prefieres bailar con tus amigos en _____ o en casa?

 **¿Y tú?** Now, use the questions you prepared to interview another student.

 **2-22 ▶ Mis lugares favoritos.** Ask another student about his/her favorite places in town. Your partner will answer and say whether the place mentioned is near or far from the university and what street it is on, if he/she knows.

Modelo     un club nocturno

         E1: *¿Cuál es tu club nocturno favorito?*
         E2: *Mi club nocturno favorito es La Bamba. Está lejos de la universidad. Está en la calle Seis. / No sé cómo se llama la calle.*

**1.** un supermercado      **3.** una tienda de ropa      **5.** un parque

**2.** un cine      **4.** una librería      **6.** un restaurante

 **2-23 ▶ Otra conversación.** With a partner, reread *Una conversación* between José and Inés. Then, invite your partner to do something together. Be sure to explain where the place you are going to meet is located.

---

**lejos de** *far from*   **en la calle . . .** *on . . . Street*   **abierto/a** *open*   **cerrado/a** *closed*   **al lado de** *next to* **la gente** *people*   **¿Te parece bien . . . ?** *Does . . . seem okay to you?*

# 📖 Gramática 1

SAM: 2-31 to 2-33

## Indicating location: Prepositions of place and the contraction with **de**

### Para **averiguar**

1. Do you use **ser** or **estar** with prepositions to say where something is?
2. What happens to the word **de** when it is followed by **el** (*the*)? Does **de** contract with **la, los,** or **las?**

### ¿Cómo se **pronuncia?**

**The consonant d**

Many prepositions contain the letter **d.** You can find an explanation of how to pronounce it in the Pronunciation Guide in your MySpanishLab course under Consonants.

■ Use **estar** with these prepositions to say where something is.

| | | | |
|---|---|---|---|
| **a la derecha de** | *to the right of* | **a la izquierda de** | *to the left of* |
| **al lado de** | *next to* | **enfrente de** | *across from, facing* |
| **al este de** | *east of* | **al oeste de** | *west of* |
| **al norte de** | *north of* | **al sur de** | *south of* |
| **cerca de** | *near* | **lejos de** | *far from* |
| **con** | *with* | **sin** | *without* |
| **delante de** | *ahead of, in front of* | **detrás de** | *behind* |
| **encima de** | *on top of* | **debajo de** | *below, under* |
| **en** | *at, in, on* | **entre** | *between* |

■ **De** contracts with the singular article **el** (*the*) to form **del. De** does not contract with **la, los,** or **las.**

Tu lápiz está debajo **del** libro.     *Your pencil is under the book.*
Mi mochila está encima **de la** mesa.     *My backpack is on top of the table.*

**2-24 ▶ Lugares.** Name the building that is located in the following places in the illustration.

el estadio

la residencia

la biblioteca

la cafetería

el parque

el gimnasio

Modelo     Está detrás del gimnasio.
*El estadio está detrás del gimnasio.*

1. Está delante del estadio.
2. Están al lado de la residencia.
3. Está enfrente de la residencia.
4. Está a la izquierda de la residencia.
5. Está entre la cafetería y la biblioteca.
6. Está a la derecha de la residencia.
7. Está más lejos del gimnasio.
8. Está más cerca del gimnasio.

**2-25 ▶ ¿Quién es?** Write the name of a classmate on a sheet of paper. The rest of the class will ask questions about the location of the person whose name is on your paper until they can identify who it is. Use **ti** and **mí** as in the Modelo to say *you* and *me* after prepositions.

Modelo   E1: *¿Está detrás o delante de ti?*
         E2: *Está detrás de mí.*
         E3: *¿Está a la derecha de Raquel? . . .*

**2-26 ▶ En la calle Molino.** Sketch the street below on a sheet of paper. In random order, label each of the buildings using the names from the list. Make another sketch of the street, this time leaving out the names of the buildings. Then, working in pairs, ask each other questions using prepositions to discover where your partner's buildings are located. Continue until you have filled in the names of all the buildings on your blank sketch. When you have finished, compare papers.

| la biblioteca | el cine | el gimnasio | el restaurante | la tienda |
|---|---|---|---|---|
| el café | el club nocturno | la librería | el supermercado | de ropa |

Modelo   E1: *¿Qué está enfrente del hotel?*
         E2: *El restaurante está enfrente del hotel.*

**2-27 ▶ Comparaciones culturales.** Read the description of the geographic locations of different Hispanic countries or territories, and identify which one is being described. Refer to the maps in the back of the book, if necessary.

Modelo   Está al norte de Costa Rica.
         *Es Nicaragua.*

**1.** Está entre Costa Rica y Colombia.
**2.** Está al lado de Haití.
**3.** Está al norte de Ecuador y Perú.
**4.** Está al oeste de Argentina.
**5.** Está entre Honduras y Costa Rica.
**6.** Está al sur de Nicaragua.
**7.** Está al este de la República Dominicana.
**8.** Está al norte de Guatemala y al sur de Estados Unidos.

**Gramática 2**   Saying what you are going to do:
**Ir,** the contraction with **a, ir a** + infinitive

SAM: 2-34
to 2-36

### Para **averiguar**

1. What are the forms of the verb **ir?**
2. How do you say *I go*? How do you say *I am going*?
3. What word is placed between the conjugated form of **ir** and the infinitive that follows it when saying what someone is going to do?
4. How do you say *where* when asking where someone is going?
5. With which form of the word for *the* does **a** (*to*) contract?

■ Use the verb **ir** to say where people go.

### ir *(to go)*

| | | | |
|---|---|---|---|
| yo | voy | nosotros/as | vamos |
| tú | vas | vosotros/as | vais |
| usted | va | ustedes | van |
| él, ella | va | ellos, ellas | van |

■ Use **adónde** with **ir** to ask where someone is going. To answer, use the preposition **a** (*to*). Like **de** which contracts with **el** to form **del**, **a** contracts with **el** to form **al**. It does not contract with **la, los,** or **las.**

— ¿**Adónde** van ustedes?            — *Where are you going?*
— Vamos **al** parque y luego vamos   — *We're going to the park and then we're*
 **a la** biblioteca.                   *going to the library.*

■ Note that the forms of **ir** are used to say where someone *is going* at the moment, as well as where someone *goes* in general. To say what someone *is going to do*, conjugate **ir** followed by the preposition **a** and an infinitive.

— ¿**Vas a comer** en casa?           — *Are you going to eat at home?*
— No, **voy a comer** con mi novia.   — *No, I'm going to eat with my girlfriend.*
— ¿Qué **van a hacer** después?       — *What are you going to do afterwards?*
— **Vamos a** ir al centro comercial. — *We're going to go to the mall.*

■ Use the infinitive of **hay, haber,** to say *there is/are going to be.*

**Va a haber** una fiesta el sábado.   *There's going to be a party on Saturday.*

■ The following adverbs express when something is going to happen.

| | |
|---|---|
| **esta mañana** | *this morning* |
| **esta tarde** | *this afternoon* |
| **esta noche** | *tonight, this evening* |
| **este fin de semana** | *this weekend* |
| **mañana (por la mañana, por la tarde,** | *tomorrow (morning, afternoon,* |
|  **por la noche)** | *night)* |
| **la semana (el mes, el año) que viene** | *next week (month, year)* |

**2-28** ▶ **Lugares favoritos.** Complete the following statements with the correct form of the verb **ir** and the name of a specific place to say where these people go in order (**para**) to do each activity.

Modelos   Para bailar, muchos estudiantes *van al club Carnaval.*
            Para comer comida italiana, yo *voy al restaurante Casa Toscana.*

**1.** Para ver una película, mis amigos y yo . . .
**2.** Para pasar una tarde tranquila, yo . . .
**3.** Para comprar ropa, mi mejor amigo/a . . .
**4.** Para tomar algo, mis amigos y yo . . .
**5.** Para comprar libros, muchos estudiantes . . .
**6.** Para comer comida mexicana, yo . . .

**2-29 ▶ ¿Con qué frecuencia?** Say how often these people go to the indicated places. Use an expression from the list and the correct form of **ir**.

| (casi) siempre | con frecuencia | (casi) nunca |
|---|---|---|
| todos los días | a veces | |

Modelo   después de clase, mis amigos y yo / la biblioteca
*Después de clase, mis amigos y yo vamos a la biblioteca a veces.*

**1.** mi padre / el trabajo
**2.** mi mejor amigo y yo / el gimnasio
**3.** yo / un restaurante de comida mexicana
**4.** mis padres / el parque
**5.** los sábados por la tarde, yo / el estadio
**6.** los sábados, mis amigos y yo / un club
**7.** mis amigos y yo / el cine
**8.** mi mejor amigo/a / el centro comercial

**2-30 ▶ Predicciones.** Say whether the following people are going to do each activity in parentheses tomorrow.

Modelo   Yo . . . (ir al trabajo, estar en clase)
*No voy a ir al trabajo mañana. Voy a estar en clase mañana.*

**1.** Yo . . . (estar ocupado/a, estar en casa por la mañana, ir al parque, salir con mis amigos, comer en un restaurante)
**2.** Mi mejor amigo/a . . . (trabajar, ir a la universidad, estar en la cama hasta el mediodía, pasar el día conmigo, comer conmigo, salir a bailar, estudiar mucho)
**3.** Mi mejor amigo/a y yo . . . (hablar por teléfono, tomar algo en un café, ir al centro comercial, estar juntos/as todo el día)
**4.** Mis padres (*my parents*) . . . (trabajar, estar en casa por la mañana, comer conmigo, descansar, estar en casa por la noche)

**2-31 ▶ ¿Qué vas a hacer?** In pairs, ask what your partner is going to do at the following times.

Modelo   esta noche
E1: *¿Qué vas a hacer esta noche?*
E2: *Voy a pasar esta noche en casa. No voy a hacer nada en especial.*

**1.** hoy después de clase      **4.** este sábado por la tarde
**2.** esta noche                     **5.** este sábado por la noche
**3.** mañana por la mañana    **6.** la semana que viene

**2-32 ▶ Entrevista.** Complete the following questions with the correct forms of **ir**.

**1.** ¿Adónde _____ (tú) generalmente después de la clase de español? ¿a casa? ¿a otra clase? ¿al trabajo? ¿a la biblioteca? ¿Prefieres estudiar con tus amigos en la biblioteca o prefieres _____ a un café?
**2.** ¿ _____ (tú) a salir con tus amigos este fin de semana? ¿Adónde _____ ustedes generalmente los fines de semana? ¿ _____ (ustedes) en tu coche (*car*), en el coche de un amigo o en el autobús?
**3.** ¿ _____ (tú) al cine con frecuencia? ¿ _____ (tú) más al cine por la tarde o por la noche? ¿Quién _____ más contigo (*with you*) al cine? ¿ _____ (tú) solo/a al cine a veces? ¿ _____ (tú) a ver una película hoy?

 **¿Y tú?** Now, ask a classmate the preceding questions in this activity.

# 📖 Vocabulario  Los pasatiempos

SAM: 2-37 to 2-40

CD 1
Track 44

¿Te gustan las actividades **al aire libre**? ¿Te gusta . . . ?

## ¿Sabías que...?

Although Hispanics embrace other faiths, Catholicism is prevalent in Hispanic countries. In Mexico, 89% of the population is Catholic and 47% attend church each week. In Argentina, where 78% of the population is Catholic, 28% of them go to church weekly, but 25% do not attend regularly. In Spain, where 76% of the people are Catholic, only one out of five Spanish Catholics attends church weekly, and 54% hardly ever go to church. Nineteen percent of Spaniards say they are non-religious. In the United States, 68% of Hispanics are Catholic, 20% are Protestant, and 8% are non-religious.

ir a **la piscina** (al **lago**, a **la playa**) y **nadar, tomar el sol** o hacer esquí acuático

ir a la montaña y esquiar

¿Te gustan más las actividades culturales o espirituales? ¿Te gusta . . . ?

ir al museo, al teatro o a un concierto de música clásica

ir a la iglesia (a la sinagoga, a la mezquita), cantar y **rezar**

Si estás solo/a en casa los sábados por la noche . . .

Si **un/a muchacho/a desconocido/a** habla contigo . . .

¿estás **aburrido/a** y **triste porque** estás solo/a en casa?
¿estás **enojado/a** o **molesto/a** porque prefieres salir?

¿estás nervioso/a porque eres tímido/a?
¿estás **contento/a** porque eres muy sociable?
¿estás **sorprendido/a** o **confundido/a**?

---

**los pasatiempos** *pastimes*  **al aire libre** *outdoors*  **la piscina** *the swimming pool*  **el lago** *the lake*  **la playa** *the beach*  **nadar** *to swim*  **tomar el sol** *to sunbathe*  **rezar** *to pray*  **aburrido/a** *bored*  **triste** *sad*  **porque** *because*  **enojado/a** *angry, mad*  **molesto/a** *bothered, upset*  **un muchacho** *a boy, a guy* **una muchacha** *a girl*  **desconocido/a** *unknown*  **contento/a** *happy, glad*  **sorprendido/a** *surprised* **confundido/a** *confused*

**Una conversación.** José and Inés are making plans for this evening.

JOSÉ: Bueno Inés, ¿qué **quieres** hacer esta noche?

INÉS: No sé. ¿Por qué no vamos al centro comercial?

JOSÉ: No, no **quiero ir de compras**. ¡Vamos al cine! Quiero ver la nueva película de Benicio del Toro.

INÉS: Está bien. ¿Quieres ir a comer algo antes?

JOSÉ: ¡Buena idea! ¿A qué hora paso por tu casa?

INÉS: ¿A las seis y media?

JOSÉ: Muy bien. **Entonces**, hasta las seis y media.

INÉS: Sí. Hasta luego.

CD 1, Track 36

## ¡A escuchar!

Now, listen to another conversation in which two friends are making plans for the weekend. What do they decide to do and when?

**2-33 ► ¿Dónde?** Ask a classmate where he/she prefers to do these things.

Modelo   nadar (en la piscina, en el lago o en la playa)
E1: *¿Prefieres nadar en la piscina, en el lago o en la playa?*
E2: *Generalmente, prefiero nadar en la piscina. / No me gusta nadar.*

1. tomar el sol (en la piscina, en el lago, en la playa o en el patio)
2. hacer ejercicio (en casa, en un gimnasio, en una piscina o en un parque)
3. tomar algo con los amigos (en casa, en un club o en un café)
4. cantar (en la iglesia / la sinagoga / la mezquita, en un bar o en casa)
5. ver una exposición (en un museo de arte o en un museo de ciencias naturales)
6. hablar con los amigos (por teléfono, en casa, en un café o en un bar)
7. ver una película (en el cine o en la televisión)
8. comer con los amigos (en casa, en un restaurante o en un parque)
9. bailar (en casa o en un club nocturno)

**2-34 ► Reacciones.** Describe how you feel in the following situations. Use **estoy** with an adjective from this list: **aburrido/a, nervioso/a, contento/a, triste, enojado/a, molesto/a, sorprendido/a,** or **confundido/a.**

Modelo   Un/a estudiante desconocido/a quiere tu número de teléfono.
*Estoy nervioso/a.*

1. Una persona desconocida llama por teléfono a las dos de la mañana.
2. Estás solo/a en casa el sábado por la noche, pero te gustaría salir con tus amigos.
3. Vas a una fiesta y todos miran un partido de fútbol americano en la tele.
4. Vas a la casa de un amigo para estudiar y hay una fiesta para tu cumpleaños.
5. Tu novio/a está con otro/a muchacho/a.

**2-35 ► Otra conversación.** With a partner, reread *Una conversación* between José and Inés. Then, change the conversation to make plans to do something together.

**2-36 ► Comparaciones culturales.** You are planning a trip to Mexico City. Compare the schedules of the following places of interest and services there with those of similar ones in your own city.

1. El Museo Nacional de Antropología es el museo más importante de la ciudad. Está abierto todos los días de nueve de la mañana a siete de la tarde, menos los lunes que está cerrado.
2. Muchos centros comerciales en la ciudad de México están abiertos de once de la mañana a nueve de la noche. Los domingos están cerrrados.
3. El metrobús (*city bus*) funciona desde (*starting from*) las cuatro y media de la mañana hasta la medianoche.

**quieres** *(do) you want* · **quiero** *I want* · **ir de compras** *to go shopping* · **Entonces** *so, then*

# Resumen de gramática

SAM: 2-41 to 2-46

## La hora y los días de la semana

- Use **¿Qué hora es?** to ask *What time is it (now)?* Say **Es la una, Es mediodía,** and **Es medianoche** for *It's one o'clock, It's midnight,* and *It's noon.* With all other hours, use **Son las. . . .**

- To ask *at* what time something will take place, use **¿A qué hora . . . ?** To answer, use **a la una, al mediodía, a la medianoche,** or **a las . . .** with other hours. Use **hasta las/la . . .** to say *until* what time.

| | |
|---|---|
| ¿Qué hora es? | *What time is it?* |
| Es la una y veinte. (1:20) | *It's one twenty.* |
| Son las siete menos cuarto. (6:45) | *It's a quarter to seven.* |
| Son las diez y media. (10:30) | *It's ten thirty.* |
| ¿A qué hora trabajas los sábados? | *What time do you work on Saturdays?* |
| Trabajo a la una de la tarde. | *I work at one in the afternoon.* |
| ¿Hasta qué hora trabajas? | *Until what time do you work?* |
| Hasta las diez de la noche. | *Until ten at night.* |

- Use **de la mañana, de la tarde,** or **de la noche** to distinguish specific hours in the morning, afternoon, or evening.

SPECIFIC HOUR:

| | |
|---|---|
| Estoy en casa hasta las once **de la mañana**. | *I'm at home until eleven in the morning.* |

- When not giving a specific hour, use **por la mañana, por la tarde,** and **por la noche** to say *in the morning, in the afternoon,* and *in the evening / at night.*

NO HOUR GIVEN:

| | |
|---|---|
| Estoy en casa **por la mañana**. | *I'm at home in the morning.* |

- Days of the week are not capitalized in Spanish.

- Use **el** to say that something will occur *on* a particular day of a specific week.

| | |
|---|---|
| ¿Qué día es hoy? | *What day is today?* |
| Hoy es lunes (martes, miércoles, jueves, viernes, sábado, domingo). | *Today is Monday (Tuesday, Wednesday, Thursday, Friday, Saturday, Sunday).* |

- Use **los** to say that something normally happens *on* a particular day. Add **-s** to **sábado** and **domingo** to make them plural, but not to the other days.

| | |
|---|---|
| Normalmente, trabajo **los** viernes y **los** domingos, pero esta semana no trabajo **el** domingo. | *Normally, I work (on) Fridays and Sundays, but this week I don't work (on) Sunday.* |

## The verb *estar*

- Use the verb **estar** (*to be*):

1) with adjectives to say how you are doing or to describe changeable conditions

2) to say where or with whom someone or something is.

**estar** *(to be)*

| yo | estoy | *I am* | nosotros/as | estamos | *we are* |
|---|---|---|---|---|---|
| tú | estás | *you are* | vosotros/as | estáis | *you are* |
| usted | está | *you are* | ustedes | están | *you are* |
| él, ella | está | *he, she is* | ellos/as | están | *they are* |

- Most adverbs of frequency (**todos los días, con frecuencia, a veces . . .** ) generally go at the beginning or end of a phrase, but **siempre** and **nunca** are placed just before the verb.

| | |
|---|---|
| Mi compañero de cuarto **casi nunca** está en casa los sábados. | *My roommate is almost never at home on Saturdays.* |
| **Con frecuencia** trabaja todo el día. | *He frequently works all day.* |

## Prepositions

- Use **estar** with prepositions to say where things are with respect to one another.

- The preposition **de** contracts with the article **el** to form **del,** but it remains separate from **la, los,** or **las.**

| | |
|---|---|
| ¿Tu residencia está al lado del gimnasio o de la biblioteca? | *Is your dorm next to the gym or the library?* |
| Está a la derecha **del** gimnasio. | *It's to the right of the gym.* |

## Verbs ending with -ar

- Conjugate regular verbs ending with -ar using the highlighted endings.

**hablar** *(to speak, to talk)*

| | | | | |
|---|---|---|---|---|
| yo | hablo | | nosotros/as | hablamos |
| tú | hablas | | vosotros/as | habláis |
| usted | habla | | ustedes | hablan |
| él, ella | habla | | ellos/as | hablan |

- To negate a verb, place **no** before it. The verb *do*, used to ask questions or negate verbs in English, is not translated in Spanish.

¿Trabajas?　　　　　　*Do you work?*
No, **no** trabajo.　　　*No, I don't work.*

- The present tense can be translated three different ways in English.

Trabajamos hoy.　　　{ *We work today.*
　　　　　　　　　　　*We are working today.*
　　　　　　　　　　　*We do work today.*

- The unconjugated form of the verb (*to work, to do . . .*) is the infinitive. When there are two verbs together and the second one is in the form *to . . .* in English, it will generally be translated by an infinitive in Spanish. However, you can have several conjugated verbs in a row.

Necesitamos **hablar**.　　*We need to talk.*
Quiero **bailar**.　　　　　*I want to dance.*

Hablamos, bailamos y cantamos.　　*We talk, (we) dance, and (we) sing.*

## The verb *ir*

- Use **adónde** with **ir** (*to go*) to ask where someone goes.

**ir** *(to go)*

| | | | | |
|---|---|---|---|---|
| yo | voy | | nosotros/as | vamos |
| tú | vas | | vosotros/as | vais |
| usted | va | | ustedes | van |
| él, ella | va | | ellos, ellas | van |

- The preposition **a** (*to*) contracts with **el** to form **al**, but it does not contract with **la, los,** or **las.**

¿**Adónde** vas?　　　　*Where are you going?*
Voy **al** gimnasio.　　　*I'm going to the gym.*

- To say what someone is going to do, conjugate **ir** followed by the preposition **a** and an infinitive. The infinitive of **hay** is **haber**.

**Va a haber** un concierto en el parque. ¿**Vas a ir?**　　*There's going to be a concert at the park. Are you going to go?*

## Asking questions

- Questions are preceded by an inverted question mark (¿) in Spanish. The words *do* and *does*, used to ask questions in English, are not translated in Spanish. The subject is generally placed after the verb in a question. It may be placed at the end of very short questions.

¿Trabaja Joel en una tienda o en un café?　　*Does Joel work at a store or at a café?*

¿Por qué nunca baila contigo tu novio?　　*Why doesn't your boyfriend ever dance with you?*

- Attach **¿verdad?** or **¿no?** to the end of a statement to confirm information.

Vas a trabajar mañana, **¿verdad?**　　*You're going to work tomorrow, aren't you?*

- **Cuál(es)** translates *what* when it is followed by the verb *to be* (**ser**) and one is asking for a selection from a group.

SELECTION:

¿**Cuál** es tu restaurante favorito?　　*What is your favorite restaurant?*

- Use **qué** to say *what* with other verbs and with **ser** to ask for a definition.

DEFINITION:

¿**Qué** es la paella?　　*What is paella?*

SAM: 2-47
to 2-52

**EN LA CÁMARA DE COMERCIO**

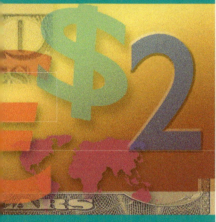

In this chapter, you learned how to talk about your schedule and activities outside of class. Now, you will practice what you have learned in a real-life simulation of working at the Hispanic Chamber of Commerce for your city.

**2-37 ▸ Horarios.** You are planning a convention with visitors from Latin America. Prepare a list of specific places of interest near your university and the times they are open. If you are not sure, choose a time that seems logical.

Modelo  un museo
*El museo de arte Laguna Gloria está abierto entre las diez de la mañana y las seis de la tarde de martes a domingo. No está abierto los lunes. | No hay ningún museo en la ciudad.*

1. una tienda de ropa     3. un gimnasio     5. un centro comercial
2. un club nocturno     4. un restaurante     6. un café

**2-38 ▸ ¿Con qué frecuencia?** Say how often you go to each place named in the preceding activity.

Modelo  *Casi nunca voy al museo de arte Laguna Gloria.*

**2-39 ▸ Preguntas.** Some visitors at a convention you have planned are asking questions about you and the city where your university is located. Complete each question with the italicized question words in Spanish.

1. ¿_____ (*Who*) es usted?
2. ¿_____ (*What, Which*) es el mejor restaurante cerca de la universidad?
3. ¿_____ (*Where*) está ese restaurante?
4. ¿_____ (*Why*) le gusta ese restaurante?
5. ¿_____ (*How many*) restaurantes de comida mexicana hay en la ciudad?
6. ¿_____ (*How*) se llama el centro comercial más cerca de la universidad?
7. ¿En _____ (*what*) calle está ese centro comercial?

 **¿Y tú?** Now, ask another student the preceding questions.

**2-40 ▸ ¿En qué orden?** You are discussing the itinerary for the day with a group of visitors. Which of the activities listed are these people going to do first, and what are they going to do later (**luego**)? Make logical sentences using **ir** as in the Modelo. Be sure to put the activities in the logical order.

Modelo  yo: contestar sus preguntas, hablar de los planes para el día
*Voy a hablar de los planes para el día y luego voy a contestar sus preguntas.*

1. nosotros: llegar al museo a las nueve, tomar el autobús para el museo a las ocho y media
2. el museo: abrir (*to open*) las puertas a las nueve de la mañana, estar abierto hasta las seis de la tarde
3. nosotros: ir de compras por la tarde, pasar la mañana en el museo
4. yo: regresar en una hora, ir a mi oficina ahora
5. varias personas: salir a un restaurante esta noche, ir a bailar después de la cena

**2-41** ▸ **Nuestra ciudad.** A group of visitors is asking for information about you and your city. Tell them what you know by completing each statement with the correct form of the verb in parentheses and an appropriate expression. You may choose from the expressions in italics or provide your own. Note that the subject **la gente** takes a singular verb form like **él** or **ella**.

Modelo    Los autobuses _____ (pasar) cada *diez minutos / quince minutos / . . .*
          *Los autobuses pasan cada quince minutos.*

**1.** *Mucha / Poca* gente _____ (tomar) el autobús aquí.
**2.** Los autobuses *casi siempre / casi nunca / . . .* _____ (llegar) tarde.
**3.** Ustedes _____ (necesitar) *un día / dos días / una semana / . . .* para ver todos los sitios turísticos de la región.
**4.** *Mucha / Poca* gente _____ (hablar) español aquí.
**5.** El restaurante *Stubb's Barbecue / The Salt Lick / . . .* _____ (preparar) la mejor comida regional.
**6.** Generalmente los restaurantes _____ (estar) abiertos hasta *las nueve de la noche / las diez de la noche / . . .*
**7.** En los clubes nocturnos, la gente _____ (escuchar) más música *popular / latina / hip hop / techno / country.*
**8.** Generalmente, yo _____ (comprar) más música *popular / latina / hip hop / techno / country.*

**2-42** ▸ **Mi restaurante favorito.** Write three sentences describing the location of your favorite restaurant in the city where your university is located and read them aloud. Your classmates will guess the name of the restaurant.

Modelo    E1: *Está en la calle Riverside cerca de la calle Comal. Está al lado de una tienda de ropa. Está enfrente de Walmart.*
          E2: *¿Es Seis Salsas?*
          E1: *Sí.*

¡Hola! **Entre profesionales**

Whether you travel to Spanish speaking cities on business or you work in a service industry here that welcomes Spanish speakers to your city, you will want to communicate some basic information. Visit MySpanishLab for *Hoy día* to find more useful vocabulary, information, and activities such as the following.

**Perfil de la ciudad.** You are relocating to Mexico City for a few months on business and you found the following headings on several web pages profiling the city. Can you guess what they mean? Under which of these headings would you find each statement that follows them?

**Clima / Costo de vida / Médicos / Transporte / Vida nocturna**

**1.** El metro de la Ciudad de México tiene 17 líneas y 175 estaciones.
**2.** La temperatura media es de 16 centígrados (61 Fahrenheit).
**3.** Los clubes y lugares nocturnos ofrecen diversiones para todos los gustos.
**4.** Una visita al doctor cuesta un promedio de 250 pesos (30 dólares).
**5.** Una casa de tres recámaras cuesta un promedio de 8.000 pesos (1.000 dólares).

**Moda global**

SAM: 2-53
to 2-55

### Antes de leer

Do you think that our society is driven by consumerism? Do you think that the same trend can be observed in other countries?

> ▶ **Reading Strategy** *Guessing meaning from context.* When you approach a text in Spanish, it is important to learn to use the context to guess possible meanings of unfamiliar words. By focusing on what you understand and the accompanying visual clues, you will often be able to figure out the meanings of new words.

**2-43 ▶ ¡Practica!** Determine the meanings of the boldfaced words by looking at the context in each sentence.

1. Las familias españolas **gastan** casi 2.000 euros al año en ropa.
2. El dominicano Óscar de la Renta es uno de los iconos de **la moda** global.
3. En **una sociedad de consumo** muchas personas compran cosas que no necesitan.
4. Si vamos a ir de compras, **¿a qué esperamos?** ¿Por qué no vamos ahora?

### Ahora tú

**2-44 ▶ Una viñeta.** Now, read the following comic strip.

## Después de leer

**2-45 ▶ ¿De qué hablan?** Answer the following questions based on Leticia and Aida's conversation.

**1.** ¿De qué hablan Leticia y su amiga por teléfono?
**2.** ¿Qué es Zara? ¿Qué cosas compra la gente en Zara?
**3.** ¿Qué van a hacer las muchachas?
**4.** ¿Qué le pregunta Aida a Leticia en el autobús?
**5.** ¿Compran las muchachas algo en Zara?
**6.** ¿Cuál es el comentario de Leticia al final de la viñeta?

**2-46 ▶ ¡Cuánta tarea!** Two friends, Marisol and Julia, are studying together and one of them wants to take a break. Complete their conversation with the correct question words from the box below. Some words may be used more than once.

| cuál | cuántas | dónde | qué |
|------|---------|-------|-----|
| cuándo | cuánto | por qué | verdad |

MARISOL: (1) ¿ _____ hora es?

JULIA: Son las seis y media. Estás cansada de estudiar, (2) ¿ _____ ?

MARISOL: Sí, un poco. (3) ¿ _____ actividades más necesitamos completar para la clase de mañana?

JULIA: Sólo dos más. Y después, (4) ¿ _____ quieres hacer?

MARISOL: ¡Ir de compras! Necesito un teléfono nuevo. (5) ¿ _____ opinas (*do you think*)? ¿Vamos?

JULIA: No sé. (6) ¿ _____ vamos a terminar (*to finish*) la tarea?

MARISOL: Más tarde. (7) ¿ _____ no vamos a buscar (*to look for*) mi teléfono ahora? ¡Por favor!

JULIA: Está bien. Y (8) ¿ _____ vas a comprar?

MARISOL: No sé. Me gustaría tener un modelo compacto con todas las funciones modernas.

JULIA: (9)¿ _____ quieres gastar (*to spend*)?

MARISOL: Pues, no mucho. (10) ¿ _____ hay una tienda de teléfonos por aquí cerca?

JULIA: En el centro Las Arenas. ¿A qué esperamos? ¡Vamos! (*Let's go!*)

**2-47 ▶ La moda pasa . . .** Interview your partner using the following questions, and then share the information with the rest of the class.

**1.** ¿Qué tipo de cosas te gusta comprar? ¿Ropa, música, libros, productos electrónicos?
**2.** ¿Con que frecuencia vas de compras?
**3.** De las marcas (*brands*) de ropa, ¿cuál prefieres? ¿Por qué?
**4.** ¿Cuáles son tus tiendas favoritas?
**5.** ¿Prefieres comprar en centros comerciales o en Internet? ¿Por qué?
**6.** ¿Con quién te gusta más ir de compras: con tus amigos, con tu familia, solo/a? ¿Por qué?
**7.** ¿Qué opinas de la siguiente frase de Yves Saint Laurent: "La moda pasa, el estilo es eterno"?

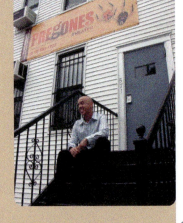

## 📖 Centros sociales comunitarios

SAM: 2-56
to 2-57

### Antes de ver

Many Hispanics devote their lives to serving the community through projects that involve the arts, health, and education. In this video segment, Jorge Merced, director of Teatro Pregones, and Jane Delgado, director of the Abrons Art Center, talk about their projects.

**2-48 ▶ Reflexiones.** What is the mission of a community center? What types of activities do they organize? Is there any community center in your area?

> ▶ **Listening strategy** *Identifying the main idea.* Pinpointing the main idea while you are listening to someone requires that you pay close attention not just to what the person is saying, but also to what words are being emphasized or repeated. First, listen for the gist and for key words that support the main ideas of the segment. Then, listen again paying special attention to the tone of the speaker to determine whether that person is offering a positive or negative view of the topic.

### Ahora tú

**2-49 ▶ Ideas principales.** As you listen to Jane and Jorge, try to identify this information:

- What are some key words that help you understand the main ideas?
- What is the tone of the speakers? Do they seem enthusiastic about their work?
- Why is this year particularly important to these community projects?

### Después de ver

**2-50 ▶ Identifica.** Indicate whether the following statements describe Teatro Pregones, Abrons Art Center, or both.

1. Apoya (*it supports*) la enseñanza (*teaching*) del baile, la música, el teatro y las artes plásticas.
2. Está en la ciudad de Nueva York.
3. Fue (*it was*) fundado en 1979 como una compañía itinerante.
4. Su misión es crear (*to create*) y presentar teatro clásico en español.
5. Su misión es educativa.
6. Tiene estudiantes de todas las áreas de Nueva York.
7. Sirve a la comunidad hispana.
8. Muchas de las obras que representa (*that it performs*) son puertorriqueñas.

**2-51 ▶ En los ratos libres.** Interview your partner using the following questions, and then share your ideas in a discussion with the entire class.

1. ¿Te gustaría ser voluntario/a en el Abrons Art Center o en el Teatro Pregones? ¿Por qué?
2. ¿Participas en algún (*some*) centro comunitario? Si no, ¿te gustaría participar?
3. En tu opinión, ¿es importante trabajar con la comunidad? ¿Por qué?
4. ¿Hay en tu universidad programas para trabajar con la comunidad?

# ESCRITORES EN ACCIÓN

## 📖 Tu perfil en Internet

SAM: 2-58

### Antes de escribir

Are you on *Facebook, MySpace,* or any other social network? How often do you use it if so? What features do social networks offer, and what makes them attractive? In this chapter, you are going to create your profile for a social network in Spanish.

**2-52 ▶ ¡Prepárate!** When you think about what information you would like to share about yourself in such a profile, what words or ideas come to your mind? Think about the following topics and jot down all of the words and ideas that occur to you in Spanish.

- tu personalidad y el tipo de estudiante que eres
- tus estudios, las clases que tomas este trimestre/semestre/año
- tu universidad y el área donde está situada
- tus actividades de tiempo libre

> ▶ **Writing strategy**
> *Brainstorming.* Brainstorming is an exercise that will help you activate existing knowledge. To brainstorm, jot down key words and ideas that come to mind relating to the topic. Generating a profusion of ideas connected to the topic will help you organize the writing activity and be better prepared to write about the topic.

### Ahora tú

**2-53 ▶ Tu perfil en Internet.** Now, complete the spaces with your personal information and write four paragraphs corresponding to the last four questions on the following screen.

### Después de escribir

**2-54 ▶ ¡Edita!** Exchange your Internet profile with a partner, and peer-edit what he/she wrote. Is there any relevant information missing? Offer suggestions to improve the grammar and organization of your partner's writing.

**2-55 ▶ ¡Revisa!** Review your profile, including the suggestions that your partner has given you, and make sure that it contains the following elements:

- ❑ vocabulary to describe yourself
- ❑ vocabulary to describe your classes and talk about your schedule
- ❑ vocabulary to describe the university
- ❑ verbs to talk about your after-class activities

**2-56 ▶ ¡Navega!** Visit your online resource for *Hoy día* for links to social networks in Spanish. Compare each site with the social network site that you currently use. Does it contain similar information? How is it different? Do you like it better?

**TEMA 1**

**TEMA 2**

### La hora

| | |
|---|---|
| ¿Qué hora es (ahora)? | *What time is it (now)?* |
| Es la una y cuarto. | *It's a quarter past one.* |
| Es mediodía/medianoche. | *It's noon/midnight.* |
| Son las tres menos diez. | *It's ten till three.* |
| ¿A qué hora? | *At what time?* |
| a la una, a las dos . . . | *at one, o'clock, at two o'clock . . .* |
| de / por la mañana / tarde / noche | *in the morning / afternoon / evening* |
| de . . . a . . . | *from . . . to . . .* |
| hasta | *until* |
| antes de | *before* |
| después de | *after* |
| tarde | *late* |
| temprano | *early* |
| una hora | *one hour* |

### El día

| | |
|---|---|
| ¿Qué día es hoy? | *What day is today?* |
| lunes | *Monday* |
| martes | *Tuesday* |
| miércoles | *Wednesday* |
| jueves | *Thursday* |
| viernes | *Friday* |
| sábado | *Saturday* |
| domingo | *Sunday* |
| ¿Qué días trabajas? | *What days do you work?* |
| Trabajo el lunes. | *I work on Monday. (a particular week)* |
| Trabajo los lunes. | *I work on Mondays.* |

### Adverbios de frecuencia

| | |
|---|---|
| (casi) siempre | *(almost) always* |
| (casi) nunca | *(almost) never* |
| todo el día | *all day* |
| todos los días | *every day* |
| generalmente | *generally* |
| con frecuencia | *frequently* |
| a veces | *sometimes, at times* |
| los fines de semana | *on weekends* |
| una vez a la semana / al mes / al año | *once a week / a month / a year* |

### Otras palabras y expresiones

| | |
|---|---|
| conmigo | *with me* |
| demasiado | *too, too much* |
| en el trabajo / la oficina | *at work / the office* |
| esta semana | *this week* |
| el horario | *schedule* |
| juntos/as | *together* |
| Me / Te gustaría . . . | *I / You would like . . .* |
| solo/a | *alone* |

### Sustantivos

| | |
|---|---|
| la actividad (diaria) | *(daily) activity* |
| el cumpleaños | *birthday* |
| los deportes | *sports* |
| la música | *music* |
| el regalo | *gift, present* |
| la ropa | *clothes* |
| la televisión (la tele) | *television (TV)* |
| el tiempo (libre) | *(free) time* |

### Acciones

| | |
|---|---|
| Prefiero . . . | *I prefer . . .* |
| bailar | *to dance* |
| cantar | *to sing* |
| cocinar | *to cook* |
| comer | *to eat* |
| comprar | *to buy* |
| contestar | *to answer* |
| descansar | *to rest* |
| desear | *to wish, to desire* |
| escuchar | *to listen (to)* |
| estudiar | *to study* |
| hablar (por teléfono) | *to speak, to talk (on the phone)* |
| hacer | *to do, to make* |
| ir (al cine / al café) | *to go (to the movies / to the café)* |
| limpiar | *to clean* |
| llegar | *to arrive* |
| mirar | *to look at, to watch* |
| necesitar | *to need* |
| pasar | *to pass, to spend (time)* |
| preparar (la cena) | *to prepare (dinner)* |
| regresar | *to return* |
| salir | *to go out* |
| tocar (la guitarra) | *to play (the guitar)* |
| tomar | *to drink, to take* |
| trabajar | *to work* |
| usar | *to use* |

### Palabras interrogativas

| | |
|---|---|
| ¿cómo? | *how?* |
| ¿con qué frecuencia? | *how often?* |
| ¿cuál(es)? | *which?, what?* |
| ¿cuándo? | *when?* |
| ¿cuánto/a? | *how much?* |
| ¿cuántos/as? | *how many?* |
| ¿dónde? | *where?* |
| ¿por qué? | *why?* |
| ¿qué? | *what?* |
| ¿quién(es)? | *who?* |

### Otras palabras

| | |
|---|---|
| algo | *something* |
| ni | *nor* |

## Lugares

| el centro comercial | shopping center, mall |
| la ciudad | city |
| el club nocturno | night club |
| el estadio | stadium |
| la librería | bookstore |
| el lugar | place |
| el parque | park |
| el partido de fútbol (fútbol americano) | soccer (football) game |
| el restaurante | restaurant |
| el supermercado | supermarket |
| la tienda (de ropa) | (clothing) store |

## Acciones

| hacer ejercicio | to exercise |
| levantar pesas | to lift weights |
| ver | to see |

## Otras palabras y expresiones

| abierto/a | open |
| adónde | (to) where |
| cerrado/a | closed |
| la comida mexicana | Mexican food |
| en la calle . . . | on . . . Street |
| la gente | people |
| la película | movie |
| perfecto/a | perfect |
| la semana que viene | the coming week |
| ¿Te parece bien? | Does that seem okay to you? |

*For a list of prepositions of place, see page 50.*

## Lugares

| la iglesia | church |
| el lago | lake |
| la mezquita | mosque |
| la montaña | mountain |
| el museo | museum |
| la piscina | swimming pool |
| la playa | beach |
| el teatro | theater |
| la sinagoga | synagogue |

## Acciones

| ¿Quieres . . . ? | Do you want . . . ? |
| Quiero . . . | I want . . . . |
| esquiar | to ski |
| hacer esquí acuático | to waterski |
| ir de compras | to go shopping |
| nadar | to swim |
| rezar | to pray |
| tomar el sol | to sunbathe |

## Descripciones

| aburrido/a | bored |
| confundido/a | confused |
| contento/a | happy, glad |
| desconocido/a | unknown |
| enojado/a | angry |
| molesto/a | upset, bothered |
| nervioso/a | nervous |
| sorprendido/a | surprised |
| triste | sad |

## Otras palabras

| al aire libre | outdoors |
| el concierto (de música clásica) | (classical music) concert |
| entonces | so, then |
| la idea | idea |
| la muchacha | girl |
| el muchacho | boy, guy |
| el pasatiempo | pastime |
| porque | because |

 Visit MySpanishLab for *Hoy día* for links to the mnemonic dictionary online for suggestions such as the following to help you remember vocabulary from *Capítulo 2*, learn related words in Spanish, and use Spanish words to build your vocabulary in English.

**EXAMPLES**

**bail**ar, *to dance:* One goes to a *ball* to dance, and a *ball*et is a type of dance.

**mir**ar, *to look at:* One looks at oneself in a *mir*ror, a *mir*age is something you look at and think you see, and people look up to someone they ad*mire*.

# 3 En familia

In this chapter, you will learn about Hispanic families.

Con frecuencia, afirmaciones como las siguientes (*the following*) se usan para describir las relaciones entre las familias hispanas. ¿Crees que (*Do you think that*) son ciertas? ¿Son ciertas estas afirmaciones sobre (*about*) tu familia?

- ► En las familias hispanas, las necesidades de la familia tienen prioridad sobre las necesidades de los individuos.

- ► Los abrazos (*hugs*) y las interacciones son más importantes que el espacio personal.

- ► Para los hispanos la palabra *familia* incluye a todos los miembros de la familia y no solamente a la familia nuclear.

- ► Para los jóvenes hispanos es menos importante independizarse (*to become independent*) de sus padres que para los jóvenes norteamericanos.

# 📖 **Vocabulario**  Los familiares

SAM: 3-1
to 3-4

🔊 ¿Cuántos son ustedes en tu familia? ¿Cuántos hermanos tienes? ¿Tienes muchos
**familiares?** ¿Tienes más primos **por parte de tu madre** o por parte de tu padre?

CD 1
Track 52

**CUATRO GENERACIONES**

¿Eres más como tu padre o como tu madre? ¿Cómo son tus hermanos? **¿Cuántos
años tienen?**

---

**los familiares** *family members*   **por parte de tu madre** *on your mother's side*   **¿Cuántos años tienen?**
*How old are they?*

Track 53

**Una conversación.** Dos amigos, Daniel y Carmen, hablan de la familia de Carmen.

DANIEL: ¿Cuántos son ustedes en tu familia?
CARMEN: Somos cinco. **Vivo** con mis padres y tengo una hermana **mayor** y un hermano **menor**.
DANIEL: ¿Cómo se llaman tus hermanos?
CARMEN: Mi hermana mayor se llama Anita y mi hermano menor se llama Alberto.
DANIEL: ¿Cuántos años tienen?
CARMEN: Anita tiene veintitrés años y Alberto **sólo** tiene diez.
DANIEL: ¿Tienen **mascotas**?
CARMEN: Sí, tenemos dos **perros** y un **gato**.

CD 1, Track 54

## ¡A escuchar!

Ahora escuchen otra conversación en la cual (*in which*) dos amigos hablan de la familia. ¿Cómo es la familia de Roberto? ¿Y la de Andrea? ¿Cuál de los dos quiere tener más hijos?

**3-1 ▶ Aclaración.** Complete the following questions with the correct words to clarify the relationships between these people.

Modelo   ¿Tu sobrina es *la hija* de tu hermano o de tu hermana?

**1.** ¿Tu abuela es _____ de tu padre o de tu madre?
**2.** ¿Tu tío es _____ de tu padre o de tu madre?
**3.** ¿Tu primo es _____ de tu padre o de tu madre?
**4.** ¿Tu nieta es _____ de tu hijo o de tu hija?
**5.** ¿Tu sobrino es _____ de tu hermano o de tu hermana?
**6.** ¿Tu medio (*half*) hermano es _____ de tu madre o de tu padre?

**3-2 ▶ Otra conversación.** In pairs, reread *Una conversación* between Daniel and Carmen. Then, change the conversation to describe your own families.

**3-3 ▶ Comparaciones culturales.** What is the average household (**hogar medio**) like in Mexico, Spain, and the United States? In groups, read the following statistics for Spain and Mexico, then guess the same statistics for the United States. Afterwards, your instructor will give the correct response. Explain which of them you find the most surprising and why.

**1.** En España una persona vive sola en el 12 por ciento de los hogares y en México en el 6 por ciento. ¿Y en Estados Unidos?
**2.** En España, el 19 por ciento de los hogares son de parejas (*couples*) sin hijos y en México, el 13 por ciento. ¿Y en Estados Unidos?
**3.** El promedio de edad (*average age*) del primer matrimonio en España es 32 años para los hombres y 29 años para las mujeres. En México, el promedio de edad es 23 años para los hombres y 20 para las mujeres. ¿Y en Estados Unidos?
**4.** En España hay 24 divorcios por 100 matrimonios y en México hay 12. ¿Y en Estados Unidos?
**5.** Como promedio, en España, las mujeres tienen su primer hijo a los 31 años y en México a los 24 años. ¿Y en Estados Unidos?

---

**Vivo** *I live*   **mayor** *older*   **menor** *younger*   **sólo** *only*   **una mascota** *a pet*   **un perro** *a dog*   **un gato** *a cat*

**Gramática 1**

SAM: 3-5
to 3-6

## Saying whose it is:
## The possessive adjectives

**Para averiguar**

1. How do you say *my, your, his, her, its, our,* and *their* in Spanish?
2. Does the ending of a possessive adjective agree for number and gender with the owner or the object possessed? Would you use **su** or **sus** to translate *their house*?
3. What do you use in Spanish instead of *'s* to show possession?
4. What can **su(s)** mean? How can you clarify its meaning?

■ The following possessive adjectives are useful when talking about belongings or relationships. You have already seen **mi(s)**, **tu(s)**, and **su(s)**. Only **nuestro/a(s)** (*our*) and **vuestro/a** (*your* pl. fam.) have different forms for masculine and feminine nouns.

### Possessive Adjectives

| Before singular nouns | Before plural nouns | |
|---|---|---|
| mi | mis | *my* |
| tu | tus | *your (sing., fam.)* |
| su | sus | *your (sing., form.),his, her, its* |
| nuestro/a | nuestros/as | *our* |
| vuestro/a | vuestros/as | *your (pl., fam.)* |
| su | sus | *your (pl.), their* |

■ The endings of possessive adjectives agree for number and gender with the object possessed, not the owner. Note that you use **su casa** to say *their house* as well as *his house* or *her house*.

**Sus** padres tienen cinco gatos.                *His / Her / Their / Your parents have five cats.*

**Nuestra** casa no está lejos de aquí.           *Our house isn't far from here.*

■ In Spanish, use **el / la / los / las** + *noun* + **de** instead of *'s* to show possession. Remember that **de** contracts with **el** (*the*) to form **del**.

Es **la** casa **de** Ramón.                        *It's Ramón's house.*

Son **los** padres **del** esposo **de** mi hermana.   *They are my sister's husband's parents.*

■ Since **su(s)** can mean *your, his, her, its,* or *their,* it is often rephrased as shown below. **De** contracts with **el** (*the*) but not with **él** (*he, him*).

sus cosas ⎧ las cosas de usted(es)   *your things*
          ⎪ las cosas de él          *his things*
          ⎨ las cosas de ella        *her things*
          ⎩ las cosas de ellos/ellas *their things*

¿Es **la** casa **de él** o es **la** casa **de ella**?   *Is it his house or is it her house?*

**3-4 ▶ Cumplidos.** Give a compliment to a friend with **tu(s)** and the correct form of the logical adjective.

Modelo    padres (interesante, aburrido)
          *Tus padres son interesantes.*

1. familia (antipático, simpático)
2. hermanas (aburrido, divertido)
3. madre (trabajador, perezoso)
4. hijos (bueno, malo)
5. perro (tonto, inteligente)
6. computadora (viejo, excelente)
7. casa (feo, bonito)
8. cuarto (grande, pequeño)

**¿Y tú?** Now, describe to a partner what you know about your best friend's family and belongings using the adjectives in the preceding activity.

Modelo    *Sus padres son aburridos. / No sé si sus padres son interesantes o aburridos. / Mi mejor amigo/a no tiene padres.*

**3-5 ▶ ¿La familia de quién?** Do these sentences describe Felicia's family or Marco's family? Rephrase each sentence to clarify whose family is being described.

Modelo    Su padre es alto.
          *El padre de Felicia es alto.*

1. Su familia es más grande.
2. Son cinco en su familia.
3. Sus hermanos son mayores.
4. Sus hermanos son menores.
5. Su madre es más alta que su padre.
6. Su hermana está con su esposo
   y el bebé de ellos.
7. Sus abuelos están con su familia.
8. Su familia está en el patio.
9. Su familia está en el sofá.
10. Hay muchas plantas en su casa.

La familia de Marco          La familia de Felicia

**3-6 ▶ Nuestra clase.** Complete the following sentences with **nuestro**, **nuestra**, **nuestros**, or **nuestras** and the appropriate ending from the choices in parentheses, or use one of your own.

Modelo    _____ clase es (por la mañana / por la tarde / por la noche).
          *Nuestra clase es por la mañana.*

1. _____ tarea (es muy larga todos los días / no es muy larga generalmente / es muy larga a veces / . . . ).
2. Las horas de oficina de _____ profesor/a son (antes de clase / después de clase / antes y después de clase / . . . ).
3. _____ profesor/a contesta _____ preguntas (en inglés generalmente / en español generalmente / en inglés a veces y en español a veces).
4. _____ exámenes (son fáciles / son difíciles / no son fáciles ni difíciles).
5. _____ próximo examen es (esta semana / la próxima semana / en dos o tres semanas / . . . ).

**3-7 ▶ ¿Cierto o falso?** Complete the following sentences with the logical possessive adjective.

Modelo    Tengo cinco tíos por parte de mi padre. Todos *sus* hermanos son
          mayores que él.

1. Tengo una tía por parte de mi madre. _____ tía es menor que ella.
2. Somos cinco en mi familia, mis dos hermanos y yo y _____ padres.
3. Mis hermanos invitan a _____ amigos a la casa con frecuencia.
4. Mis hermanos y yo pasamos mucho tiempo con _____ primos.
5. Mis abuelos vienen a mi casa con frecuencia porque _____ casa está cerca de donde vivo.
6. Tengo tres sobrinos. Son los hijos de _____ hermana mayor.

**¿Y tú?** With a partner, take turns telling each other whether the sentences in the preceding activity are true (**cierto**) or false (**falso**) for you. If a sentence is false, change it so that it describes your family.

Modelo    Tengo cinco tíos por parte de mi padre. Todos *sus* hermanos son
          mayores que él.

          *Falso. Tengo dos tíos por parte de mi padre. Uno de sus hermanos es
          mayor que él. / No tengo tíos por parte de mi padre. / No tengo padre.*

# Gramática 2 Describing relationships: The verbs **tener** and **venir**

SAM: 3-7
to 3-11

SAM: 3-7
to 3-11

## Para averiguar

1. How do you say *to have* and *to come* in Spanish? What are their forms? In which two forms do they have different endings?
2. What word precedes an infinitive after **tener** when saying what someone *has to do*?

■ The verb **tener** (*to have*) is useful when describing family or possessions. You have already seen some of its forms. Below is its full conjugation. The verb **venir** (*to come*) is similar to **tener**.

### tener (to have)

| | | | | |
|---|---|---|---|---|
| yo | tengo | | nosotros/as | tenemos |
| tú | tienes | | vosotros/as | tenéis |
| Ud., él, ella | tiene | | Uds., ellos/as | tienen |

### venir (to come)

| | | | | |
|---|---|---|---|---|
| yo | vengo | | nosotros/as | venimos |
| tú | vienes | | vosotros/as | venís |
| Ud., él, ella | viene | | Uds., ellos/as | vienen |

**Tengo** muchos primos que **vienen** a nuestra casa con frecuencia.  *I have a lot of cousins that come to our house frequently.*

■ It is common to leave out the indefinite article (**un/una**) when saying what someone does or does not have with an unmodified noun. In the singular, the indefinite article (**un, una**) is generally used if the noun is modified.

WITHOUT THE ARTICLE: No tengo gato. Tengo perro.
*I don't have a cat. I have a dog.*

WITH THE ARTICLE: Tengo un perro viejo y gordo.
*I have an old, fat dog.*

■ Use **tener que** followed by an infinitive to say that someone *has to do* something.

**Tenemos que** limpiar la casa.  *We have to clean the house.*

**3-8 ▶ ¿Qué tienen?** Say whether the following people have each relative or item indicated in parentheses.

Modelo    mis abuelos (muchos nietos, una casa grande)
*Mis abuelos tienen muchos nietos. No tienen una casa grande.*

1. yo (muchos primos, hijos, sobrinos, padres estrictos, perro, gato)
2. mis padres (nietos, mucho trabajo, una casa grande, muchas plantas)
3. mi madre y yo (mucho en común, una buena relación, muchas diferencias de opinión)
4. mi mejor amigo/a (hijos, mucho dinero, muchos problemas, mucha paciencia)

**3-9 ▶ La clase de español.** Complete each sentence with the correct form of **venir.**

1. (Nosotros/as) _____ a la clase de español todos los días.
2. A veces (yo) _____ a clase enfermo/a porque no me gusta faltar a (*to miss*) clase.
3. Nadie _____ a clase conmigo. (Yo) _____ solo/a.
4. A veces mis compañeros de clase _____ a mi casa / apartamento / residencia para estudiar conmigo los fines de semana.
5. Muchos estudiantes están contentos si sus profesores no _____ a clase porque no tienen que trabajar. El/La profesor/a de español siempre _____ a clase.

**¿Y tú?** With a partner, take turns changing the preceding sentences so that they describe your class. If a sentence is already true, read it as it is and say **Es cierto.**

**3-10 ▶ ¿Qué tienes? ¿Cómo es?** Ask another student whether the following people have the things or pets shown. Your partner should describe what they have using an adjective.

Modelo   E1: *¿Tienen computadora tus abuelos?*
E2: *Sí, tienen una computadora vieja. / No, mis abuelos no tienen computadora.*

MODELO:
tus abuelos

2. tú

1. tus padres

4. tú

3. tu mejor amigo

**3-11 ▶ Una fiesta de cumpleaños.** What do these people have to do? Complete each sentence with **tener que** and the logical activity from the list.

| | | |
|---|---|---|
| *comprar un regalo para ella* | **limpiar** | **preparar las enchiladas** |
| **decorar la casa para la fiesta** | **llegar temprano** | **trabajar** |
| **hablar español** | | |

Modelo   El cumpleaños de mi madre es mañana. Mis hermanos y yo *tenemos que comprar un regalo para ella.*

1. La fiesta para mi mamá es una sorpresa (*surprise*). Si vienes, (tú) . . .
2. Mis abuelos no hablan inglés. Con ellos, (yo) . . .
3. Mi hermano mayor no viene a la fiesta porque (él) . . .
4. Vamos a servir comida mexicana en la fiesta. Mis hermanos . . .
5. La fiesta va a ser en mi casa y ahora es un desastre. Esta noche, (yo) . . .
6. Casi todos mis hermanos van a venir temprano mañana. (Nosotros) . . .

**3-12 ▶ Entrevista.** Complete each pair of questions logically using the correct form of **tener** in one blank and the correct form of **venir** in the other. Be sure to use the appropriate verb in each blank.

1. ¿Cuántos tíos y primos _____ (tú)? ¿_____ (ellos) a visitar a tu familia con frecuencia?
2. ¿_____ (tú) casa, apartamento o cuarto en una residencia? ¿Quiénes _____ a pasar más tiempo contigo, tus primos o tus amigos?
3. ¿Qué días _____ (tú) a la universidad? ¿Qué día(s) _____ (tú) más clases?
4. ¿_____ (tú) compañero/a de cuarto? ¿_____ (Uds.) juntos/as a la universidad?
5. ¿Qué días _____ el/la profesor/a a su oficina? ¿A qué hora _____ (él/ella) horas de oficina?
6. ¿_____ (tú) que trabajar los días que hay clase de español? ¿_____ (tú) a la clase de español antes de ir al trabajo o después?

 **¿Y tú?** Now, use the questions to interview another student.

# 📖 **Vocabulario**   Un día típico

SAM: 3-12
to 3-13

 CD 1
Track 55

## ¿Sabías que...?

Una situación bastante (*fairly*) común para los hijos en España y en muchos países (*countries*) de Latinoamérica es vivir con sus padres hasta los 25 o los 30 años. Independizarse no es la tendencia general entre los jóvenes hispanos, como ocurre en Estados Unidos, y los hijos viven en la casa de sus padres sin presión (*pressure*) hasta encontrar (*until finding*) un buen trabajo.

## ¡Ojo!

Both **tomar** and **beber** mean *to drink,* but **tomar** is commonly used in expressions such as **tomar un café, un té** or in the expression **tomar algo** *to have a drink.* In Latin America, **tomar** is used in most contexts to refer to drinking.

Por la mañana . . .

Leo el periódico o **una revista** y tomo café. Tomo mucho café porque **tengo sueño**.

Por la tarde . . .

Como con mis amigos. Nunca **bebo vino** al mediodía.

Por la noche . . .

Escribo y leo correos electrónicos. Recibo muchos correos electrónicos.

Corro temprano por el parque.

**Asisto a** mis clases. Vivo cerca de la universidad.

Leo mis libros de texto, escribo **ensayos** para mis clases y aprendo vocabulario para mi clase de español.

---

 CD 1
Track 57

**Una conversación.** Ernesto habla con su padre de sus clases durante la primera semana del semestre.

PADRE: Ernesto, ¿tienes clases todos los días?

ERNESTO: Sí, asisto a dos clases los lunes, miércoles y viernes por la mañana y a una por la tarde. Los martes y jueves tengo una clase a las nueve de la mañana.

PADRE: Ah, y ¿tienes que comprar muchos libros para las clases?

ERNESTO: Necesito leer cinco libros para mi clase de literatura pero sólo uno en cada otra clase.

PADRE: ¿Tienes que escribir muchos ensayos para las clases?

ERNESTO: Sí, tres para mi clase de literatura, uno para mi clase de historia y otro para mi clase de ciencias políticas.

PADRE: ¿Vas a hablar con tus profesores durante sus horas de oficina si no comprendes algo?

ERNESTO: Sí, pero hasta ahora todo va bien.

PADRE: ¿Te gustan todas tus clases?

ERNESTO: Me gustan todas menos la clase de ciencias políticas. No aprendo mucho en **esa** clase.

 CD 1, Track 56

## ¡A escuchar!

Ahora escuchen otra conversación en la cual (*in which*) Beatriz habla con su novio de su día. ¿Cuántas clases tiene Beatriz hoy? ¿Qué desea hacer su novio? ¿Por qué no tienen mucho tiempo?

---

**una revista** *a magazine*   **tener sueño** *to be sleepy*   **beber vino** *to drink wine*   **asistir a** *to attend*
**un ensayo** *an essay, a paper*   **ese/esa** *that*

**3-13 ▶ ¿Por qué?** Select the most logical ending for each sentence from the choices on the right.

1. Como en un restaurante . . .
2. Corro por el parque . . .
3. Tomo café por la mañana . . .
4. Leo las explicaciones del libro . . .
5. Aprendo bien el vocabulario . . .
6. Escribo muchos correos electrónicos . . .

a. porque tengo sueño.
b. porque necesito ejercicio.
c. porque no me gusta preparar la comida.
d. porque no me gusta hablar por teléfono.
e. porque estudio todos los días.
f. si no comprendo algo.

**3-14 ▶ ¿Con qué frecuencia?** Insert one of the following adverbs or adverbial phrases in each of the following sentences to say how often you do each activity.

| (casi) siempre | todos los días | con frecuencia | a veces | (casi) nunca |
|---|---|---|---|---|

Modelo     Como mucho por la mañana.
           *Nunca como mucho por la mañana.*

1. Como solo/a al mediodía.
2. Corro por el parque o la calle.
3. Asisto a mi clase de español.
4. Aprendo mucho en mis clases.
5. Escribo ensayos para mis clases.
6. Asisto a un partido de básquetbol.
7. Como pizza.
8. Recibo correos electrónicos.
9. Leo novelas románticas.
10. Escribo poemas.
11. Asisto a un concierto.
12. Leo el periódico.

Generalmente, ¿dónde comes al mediodía?

**3-15 ▶ ¿En qué clases?** In which classes do you do these things?

Modelo     Escribo más ensayos.
           *Escribo más ensayos en mi clase de inglés. | Escribo muchos ensayos en
           todas mis clases. | No escribo ningún ensayo para ninguna clase.*

1. Aprendo mucho.
2. Leo más.
3. A veces no asisto a clase.
4. Casi siempre comprendo bien.
5. A veces no comprendo.
6. A veces tengo sueño.

**3-16 ▶ Otra conversación.** In pairs, reread *Una conversación* between Ernesto and his father. Then, imagine one of you is talking to a family member about your classes and prepare a similar conversation.

# 📖 Gramática 1

SAM: 3-14
to 3-18

## Describing your daily activities: Regular -er and -ir verbs

Para **averiguar**

1. How do -er verb endings differ from those for the -ar verbs you learned in *Capítulo 2*?
2. Verbs ending with -ir are conjugated like -er verbs except in two forms. Which ones?

■ The endings for regular **-er** verbs are similar to those for **-ar** verbs. Just replace the letter **a** in the **-ar** verb endings with an **e**. Regular **-ir** verbs are conjugated like **-er** verbs, except in the **nosotros/as** and **vosotros/as** forms.

### comer *(to eat)*

| | | | |
|---|---|---|---|
| yo | como | nosotros/as | comemos |
| tú | comes | vosotros/as | coméis |
| Ud., él, ella | come | Uds., ellos/as | comen |

### vivir *(to live)*

| | | | |
|---|---|---|---|
| yo | vivo | nosotros/as | vivimos |
| tú | vives | vosotros/as | vivís |
| Ud., él, ella | vive | Uds., ellos/as | viven |

■ The following **-er** and **-ir** verbs are conjugated like **comer** and **vivir**.

| -ER VERBS | | -IR VERBS | |
|---|---|---|---|
| **aprender (a . . .)** | *to learn (to . . .)* | **abrir** | *to open* |
| **beber** | *to drink* | **asistir (a)** | *to attend* |
| **comprender** | *to understand* | **compartir** | *to share* |
| **correr** | *to run* | **escribir** | *to write* |
| **creer** | *to believe* | **recibir** | *to receive* |
| **deber** | *must, should* | | |
| **leer** | *to read* | | |
| **vender** | *to sell* | | |

**¿Cómo se pronuncia?** ¡Hola!

*The letters b and v*

In Spanish, the letters **b** and **v** are pronounced alike. Refer to the Pronunciation Guide in your MySpanishLab course under Consonants to learn more about their pronunciation in words like **beber**, **vivir**, and **escribir**.

■ Use the preposition **a** before nouns following **asistir** and before infinitives following **aprender**.

| | |
|---|---|
| Mis padres asisten **a** clases de baile. | *My parents are attending dance classes.* |
| Aprenden **a** bailar salsa. | *They are learning to dance salsa.* |

■ Like the verb *must* in English, **deber** can be followed by an infinitive to indicate obligation or supposition (a guess). When it indicates obligation, it is similar in meaning to **tener que**. When it indicates supposition, it is generally followed by **de** before the infinitive.

OBLIGATION:

| | |
|---|---|
| Uds. **deben** pasar más tiempo juntos. | *You must spend more time together.* |
| (Tienen que pasar más tiempo juntos.) | *(You have to spend more time together.)* |

SUPPOSITION:

| | |
|---|---|
| Ellos **deben de** ser hermanos. | *They must be brothers.* |

**3-17 ▶ ¿Sí o no?** Say whether the following people do each of the activities listed in parentheses in your Spanish class.

Modelo   Yo . . . (comer antes de venir a clase)
*Sí, como antes de venir a clase. | No, no como antes de venir a clase.*

1. Yo . . . (comprender todas las preguntas en clase, vender mis libros al final del semestre, deber escuchar bien en clase para aprender, deber mirar mi celular constantemente en clase)
2. Nosotros . . . (aprender francés en esta clase, leer muchos libros, asistir a clase todos los días, escribir muchos ensayos en español)
3. El/La profesor/a . . . (escribir mucho en la pizarra, recibir a muchos estudiantes en su oficina, deber repetir si los estudiantes no comprenden)

**3-18 ▶ ¿Quién?** Ask your partner who in his/her family does the following things. To say nobody, use **nadie** with the same verb form as for **él/ella**.

Modelo    leer mucho
E1: *¿Quién de tu familia lee mucho?*
E2: *Yo leo mucho. | Todos leemos mucho. | Nadie lee mucho.*

1. comer mucha comida mexicana
2. correr con frecuencia
3. asistir a muchos conciertos
4. creer en Santa Claus
5. aprender español
6. vivir solo/a
7. leer el periódico todos los días
8. comprender otra lengua

**3-19 ▶ Entrevista.** Complete these questions logically with the correct forms of the verbs in parentheses. Note that the verbs are not in the correct order.

1. ¿_____ (tú) con tus padres? ¿_____ (tú) tu propio (*own*) cuarto o _____ (tú) el cuarto con otra persona? (compartir, vivir, tener)
2. ¿_____ muchos de tus tíos y primos cerca de aquí? ¿_____ Uds. más correos electrónicos o _____ (Uds.) más por teléfono? (escribir, vivir, hablar)
3. ¿_____ (tú) todos los correos electrónicos que _____ (tú) de tus amigos y familiares? ¿_____(tú) los correos no deseados (o el spam) generalmente? (recibir, abrir, leer)
4. ¿Siempre _____ (tú) todos tus problemas con tus padres o no _____ (tú) hablar de algunas (*some*) cosas con ellos? ¿Quién de tu familia _____ mejor tus problemas? (compartir, comprender, deber)

**¿Y tú?** Now, use the preceding questions to interview a classmate.

**3-20 ▶ Comparaciones culturales.** Read the following statistics about schedules and life in Spain and translate the verbs in parentheses in the appropriate forms.

Modelo    En España el 62,5% de las estudiantes y el 55,7% de los estudiantes varones (*male*) <u>asisten</u> (*attend*) regularmente a clase. ¿Y los estudiantes de tu universidad? ¿<u>Asisten</u> (*Do they attend*) más regularmente a clase?

1. El 49% de las mujeres y el 34% de los hombres en España _____ (*share*) mucho tiempo con sus familias. ¿Y tú? ¿Cuánto tiempo _____ (*do you share*) con tu familia? ¿Quién _____ (*shares*) más tiempo contigo, tu padre o tu madre?
2. Los días laborales, el 24% de las mujeres y el 26% de los hombres _____ (*eat*) durante una hora o más al mediodía, pero el 42% de cada grupo se toma sólo un cuarto de hora o menos para _____ (*to eat*). Y tú, ¿durante cuánto tiempo _____ (*do you eat*) al mediodía?
3. El 9% de las mujeres y el 14% de los hombres _____ (*believe*) que los españoles _____ (*live*) mejor que el resto de Europa y el 23% de las mujeres y el 24% de los hombres _____ (*believe*) que el resto de Europa _____ (*lives*) mejor. ¿_____ (*do we live*) mejor aquí que en otras regiones? ¿Qué _____ (*do you believe*)?

**¿Y tú?** With a partner, take turns answering the preceding questions to express your opinion or situation.

Modelo    *Creo que los estudiantes asisten más regularmente a clase aquí. | Creo que los estudiantes asisten menos regularmente a clase aquí.*

# 📖 Gramática 2    Describing people: Idiomatic expressions with **tener**

SAM: 3-19 to 3-23

## Para **averiguar**

1. What are some expressions with **tener** that are translated by the verb *to be* in English?
2. Why do you use **mucho/a** instead of **muy** to say one *is very hungry / thirsty / cold . . .*?
3. How do you say how old someone is? How do you say what you feel like doing and what you have to do?

■ There are a few idiomatic expressions in Spanish with **tener** (*to have*) followed by a noun that say how old people are or describe conditions they have. In English, these conditions are expressed using the verb *to be*.

| | | | |
|---|---|---|---|
| **tener . . . años** | *to be . . . years old* | **tener prisa** | *to be in a hurry* |
| **tener calor** | *to be hot* | **tener razón** | *to be right* |
| **tener frío** | *to be cold* | **tener sed** | *to be thirsty* |
| **tener hambre** | *to be hungry* | **tener sueño** | *to be sleepy* |
| **tener miedo (de)** | *to be afraid (of)* | **tener suerte** | *to be lucky* |

¿Tienes prisa?                        *Are you in a hurry?*
Sí, tengo miedo de llegar tarde.      *Yes, I'm afraid of arriving late.*

■ Since the words following **tener** in the preceding expressions are nouns, rather than adjectives, use **mucho/a** rather than **muy** to modify them.

                                      LITERALLY:
Tengo **mucha** hambre.                *I have a lot of hunger. = I'm very hungry.*

■ Use the expression **tener ganas de** (+ infinitive) to say what someone *feels like doing* or is *in the mood to do.*

**Tengo ganas de** comer.              *I feel like eating.*

■ Remember that you use **tener que** before an infinitive to say what someone has to do.

**Tengo que** aprender estas          *I have to learn these expressions.*
    expresiones.

### 3-21 ▶ ¿Deseo o necesidad?  Indicate whether you generally feel like doing the following activities or you have to do them.

Modelo    trabajar    *Tengo que trabajar.*
          descansar   *Tengo ganas de descansar.*

1. estudiar para un examen          6. asistir a clase
2. ir al cine                       7. asistir a un concierto
3. limpiar la casa                  8. leer mis libros de texto
4. preparar la comida               9. leer una revista
5. comer en un restaurante          10. escribir un ensayo para una clase

### 3-22 ▶ En otras palabras.  Give another way to express the same idea using an expression from the list.

| | | | |
|---|---|---|---|
| tener ganas de | tener miedo de | tener razón | tener sueño |
| tener hambre | tener prisa | tener sed | |

Modelo    ¿Estás nervioso cuando hablas en clase?
          *¿Tienes miedo de hablar en clase?*

1. ¿Tienes ganas de comer algo?     4. Tu respuesta es correcta.
2. ¿Necesitas una siesta?           5. ¿Deseas ir al cine esta noche?
3. ¿Tienes ganas de tomar algo?     6. ¿Por qué corres?

**3-23 ▶ El día de Ramón.** Describe Ramón's day by completing each sentence logically with the expressions in parentheses.

Modelo    Ramón siempre *tiene mucho sueño* por la mañana y *tiene miedo* de quedarse dormido (*oversleep*). (tener miedo, tener mucho sueño)

1. Ramón casi siempre _____ por la mañana porque si no llega a tiempo para el autobús _____ esperar (*to wait*) veinte minutos por el siguiente. (tener prisa, tener que)
2. Al mediodía, (él) _____ comer en la oficina porque siempre está muy ocupado y _____ por terminar su presentación para la tarde. (tener mucha prisa, tener que)
3. Come una ensalada con frecuencia porque no _____. Generalmente no bebe mucho tampoco (*either*) porque no _____. (tener mucha hambre, tener mucha sed)
4. Por la tarde, Ramón _____ hacer una presentación para sus colegas. Todos respetan las ideas y la opinión de Ramón porque casi siempre _____. (tener que, tener razón)
5. A veces sus colegas _____ tomar café durante la presentación porque Ramón tiene una voz (*voice*) monótona y porque (ellos) _____ después de comer. (tener que, tener sueño)
6. Ramón casi siempre _____ pasar por el supermercado después del trabajo porque sus hijos siempre _____ y comen mucho. (tener mucha hambre, tener que)
7. Generalmente, Ramón _____ preparar la comida porque su esposa regresa tarde del trabajo. A veces comen en un restaurante cuando (ellos) no _____ de cocinar. (tener ganas, tener que)
8. Su esposa casi siempre _____ después de comer y no _____ de hablar mucho por la noche. (tener ganas, tener sueño)

**3-24 ▶ Una pareja (*couple*) incompatible.** Complete each sentence logically with an idiomatic expression with **tener** to describe this incompatible couple. Some expressions are used more than once.

Modelo    Él siempre pone (*puts*) el aire acondicionado al máximo porque *tiene calor*.

1. Ella pone el aire acondicionado al mínimo porque _____.
2. Él siempre come solo porque ella nunca _____.
3. Ella está enojada si él no está de acuerdo (*doesn't agree*) con ella porque ella cree que siempre _____.
4. Ella siempre _____ durante las películas de terror.
5. Él siempre _____ durante las películas de amor porque está aburrido.
6. Él siempre se toma su tiempo cuando ella _____.
7. Ella siempre está en la cama antes de las diez de la noche, pero él nunca _____ hasta la una o las dos de la mañana.
8. Ella _____ de divorciarse y él también.

# 📖 Vocabulario   Más pasatiempos

SAM: 3-24
to 3-27

## ¿Cómo se pronuncia? ¡Hola!

### The letter g

Many of the verb forms shown here contain the letter **g**. Refer to the Pronunciation Guide in your MySpanishLab course under Consonants for an explanation of how to pronounce it.

🔊 ¿Qué haces los sábados?

CD 1
Track 58

A veces, **traigo** mucho trabajo a casa los fines de semana.

Hago ejercicio.

Veo la tele o una película.

Pongo mi iPod (la radio, un CD).

Salgo con mis amigos a un restaurante (al cine, a un bar, a bailar, a un evento deportivo).

A veces, hago un viaje en coche a las montañas o a la playa.

Si estoy cansado/a, no hago nada en especial. Paso mucho tiempo en casa.

---

**traigo** / *bring*

**Una conversación.**  Dos primos, Laura y Rafael, hablan de los fines de semana.

LAURA:  Rafael, ¿qué haces generalmente los fines de semana?
RAFAEL:  Pues, con frecuencia los sábados y a veces los viernes por la noche salgo con mis amigos a comer o a bailar. Si estoy cansado, a veces no hago nada en especial los viernes. Veo la tele o un DVD en casa.
LAURA:  A veces, ¿regresas muy tarde a casa?
RAFAEL:  Sí, a veces regreso a las dos o las tres de la mañana.
LAURA:  ¿Qué haces los domingos por la tarde?
RAFAEL:  Los domingos hago mi tarea y leo mucho para mis clases. Si no tengo mucha tarea, a veces veo un partido de fútbol en la tele.

CD 1, Track 60

## ¡A escuchar!

Ahora escuchen otra conversación en la cual dos amigos, Ernesto y Javier, hacen planes. ¿Adónde van esta tarde? ¿Con quién? ¿Adónde van esta noche? ¿Con quién?

**3-25 ▶ Qué haces?**  Select the words in italics that describe you best or provide your own if you prefer.

**1.** Para escuchar música en el coche, generalmente pongo *la radio / un CD / mi iPod / . . .*
**2.** Veo más *películas de terror / dramas / comedias / películas de aventuras / películas de acción.*
**3.** Veo más partidos de *fútbol americano / fútbol / básquetbol / béisbol / tenis* en la televisión.
**4.** Hago más viajes *a la playa / a las montañas / a Nueva York / a Los Ángeles / . . .*
**5.** Generalmente *los fines de semana / los sábados por la noche / los domingos por la tarde / . . . ,* no hago nada en especial.
**6.** Salgo más con mis amigos *los sábados por la noche / los domingos por la tarde / . . .*
**7.** Salgo más con mis amigos *al cine / a bailar / a un café / a un restaurante / . . .*

**3-26 ▶ En otras palabras.**  Rephrase the following sentences by replacing the words in italics with the verb phrases from the list that express the same ideas.

| | | | |
|---|---|---|---|
| hago algo | hago un viaje | no pongo | veo |
| hago ejercicio | *no hago nada* | no salgo | |

Modelo    Generalmente, *descanso* los fines de semana.
          *Generalmente, no hago nada los fines de semana.*

**1.** Generalmente, *no me gusta mirar* la tele durante la cena (*dinner*).
**2.** A veces *voy* en coche a otra ciudad si no hay nada interesante que hacer aquí.
**3.** Casi siempre *paso tiempo* con mi mejor amigo los fines de semana.
**4.** Con frecuencia *asisto a* un partido de fútbol americano en el estadio.
**5.** *Corro o voy al gimnasio* todos los días.
**6.** Generalmente, *estoy en casa* los domingos.

**¿Y tú?**  Tell your partner whether the sentences in the preceding activity are true (**cierto**) for you. Change the false statements to describe yourself correctly, and then ask about your partner.

Modelo    E1: *No es cierto. Casi siempre salgo con mis amigos los sábados. ¿Y tú?*
          E2: *Yo casi siempre trabajo los fines de semana, pero no hago nada si no trabajo.*

**3-27 ▶ Otra conversación.**  With a partner, reread *Una conversación* between Laura and Rafael. Then, change it to talk about your own weekends.

¿Sales más al cine o ves más películas en casa?

# Gramática 1

## Talking about your activities: The verbs **hacer, salir, poner, traer, ver,** and **oír;** and the personal **a**

Para **averiguar**

1. What is irregular about the verbs **hacer, poner, traer, salir,** and **ver** in the present tense?
2. What are the forms of the verb **oír**? What does **oír** mean?
3. What are three idiomatic expressions with **hacer**?
4. Which verb can be used to say that you *turn on* something?
5. What word precedes direct objects referring to people? What happens to **a** when it is followed by **el** (*the*)?

■ The following verbs are conjugated like regular **-er** and **-ir** verbs in the present indicative, except for the **yo** forms.

| | **hacer**<br>*(to do / to make)* | **poner**<br>*(to put / to set)* | **traer**<br>*(to bring)* | **salir**<br>*(to go out / to leave)* | **ver**<br>*(to see)* |
|---|---|---|---|---|---|
| yo | hago | pongo | traigo | salgo | veo |
| tú | haces | pones | traes | sales | ves |
| Ud., él, ella | hace | pone | trae | sale | ve |
| nosotros/as | hacemos | ponemos | traemos | salimos | vemos |
| vosotros/as | hacéis | ponéis | traéis | salís | veis |
| Uds., ellos/as | hacen | ponen | traen | salen | ven |

— ¿Qué **haces** los fines de semana?  — *What do you do on weekends?*
— No **hago** nada en especial. ¿Y tú?  — *I don't do anything special. And you?*
— Casi siempre **salgo** con mis amigos.  — *I almost always go out with my friends.*

■ The verb **oír** has a slightly different pattern.

**oír** *(to hear)*

| | | | | |
|---|---|---|---|---|
| yo | oigo | | nosotros/as | oímos |
| tú | oyes | | vosotros/as | oís |
| Ud., él, ella | oye | | Uds., ellos/as | oyen |

— ¿**Oyes** algo?  — *Do you hear something?*
— No, no **oigo** nada.  — *No, I don't hear anything.*

■ **Hacer** is used in the following idiomatic expressions:

| **hacer una pregunta** | *to ask a question* |
|---|---|
| **hacer un viaje** | *to take a trip* |
| **hacer una fiesta** | *to have a party* |

■ After **salir,** you must use the preposition **de** before the name of the place you are leaving.

Salimos **de** la casa a las siete.    *We leave the house at seven.*

■ The verb **poner** can be used to say that you put on music or you turn on the radio or television.

¿Por qué **pones** la tele si vamos a salir?    *Why are you turning on the TV if we're going to leave?*

■ In Spanish, when the object of a verb is a person, the preposition **a** precedes the noun. In this context, it is called the personal **a**, and has no English equivalent. Do not use the personal **a** after the verb **tener** to talk about friends or family members you have. Also, remember that when **a** is followed by **el** (*the*), the two words contract to form **al**.

¿Oyen ustedes bien **al** profesor?    *Do you hear the professor well?*
Siempre traigo **a** mis hijos.    *I always bring my children.*

**3-28 ▶ ¿Qué hacen ustedes?** Ask a classmate whether he/she and the following people do the first activity in parentheses. After responding, your partner will ask whether you and others do the second activity.

Modelo   tú (hacer la comida en casa, salir mucho a comer)
E1: *¿Haces la comida en casa?*
E2: *A veces yo hago la comida y a veces mi esposo hace la comida. (No, generalmente no hago la comida en casa.) ¿Y tú? ¿Sales mucho a comer?*
E1: *Con frecuencia salgo a comer los fines de semana.*

1. tú (poner tu iPod a veces durante las clases, traer un iPod en tu mochila)
2. tus amigos y tú (salir más los viernes o los sábados, salir a bailar con frecuencia)
3. tus padres y tú (salir mucho a comer juntos, comer en un restaurante con frecuencia)
4. tus amigos (hacer algo en especial para tu cumpleaños generalmente, hacer una fiesta para tu cumpleaños)

**3-29 ▶ ¿A quién?** Complete the following sentences with the personal **a** and the names of people.

Modelo   A veces oigo . . . tarde por la noche.
*A veces oigo a la gente que vive al lado tarde por la noche. / Generalmente no oigo a nadie tarde por la noche.*

1. Veo . . . todos los días.
2. Me gustaría ver más . . .
3. A veces, no comprendo . . .
4. Con frecuencia invito . . . a salir conmigo.
5. Traigo . . . a la universidad en mi coche.
6. Visito . . . con frecuencia.

**3-30 ▶ Comparaciones culturales.** Complete the following sentences about families in Spain by translating the verbs in parentheses in the correct form. Then, answer the questions to compare the situations in Spain with those of your own family and friends.

Modelo   Según un estudio publicado por la Fundación la Caixa, en España, los padres <u>salen</u> (*leave*) del trabajo, por término medio (*on average*), a las 6:20 de la tarde y las madres a las 5:30. ¿Y tus padres? ¿A qué hora *salen* (*do they leave*) del trabajo?

*Mi madre sale del trabajo más o menos a la misma hora que en España, pero mi padre sale más temprano.*

1. Los hijos _____ (*see*) la televisión un promedio (*an average*) de 1 hora y 54 minutos al día. ¿Y tú? ¿Cuánto tiempo _____ (*do you see*) la televisión todos los días?
2. El 35% de las hijas y el 44% de los hijos varones mayores de 15 años _____ (*go out*) con sus amigos casi todos los fines de semana por la noche. ¿Y tú? ¿_____ (*do you go out*) con tus amigos casi todos los fines de semana?
3. Los padres españoles _____ (*put*) una hora límite de llegar a casa por la noche al 80% de las hijas y al 71% de los hijos varones. ¿Y tus padres? ¿_____ (*do they put*) una hora límite de llegar a casa?
4. Sólo el 8% de las hijas y el 5% de los hijos varones _____ (*believe*) que su padre es muy estricto. El 57% de las hijas y el 61% de los hijos varones _____ (*believe*) que su padre es poco estricto o que no es nada estricto. ¿Y tú? ¿_____ (*do you believe*) que tu padre es muy estricto?
5. El 36% de los abuelos maternos y el 16% de los abuelos paternos _____ (*see*) a sus nietos casi todos los días. ¿Y tú? ¿Con qué frecuencia _____ (*do you see*) a tus abuelos?

# 📖 Gramática 2

SAM: 3-32
to 3-34

## Talking about what you do with friends and family: Pronouns used after prepositions

### Para averiguar

1. Which two pronouns used after prepositions are different from the subject pronouns?
2. How do you say *with me* and *with you* (singular, familiar)? How do you say *with him* (*her, us, them*)?
3. After which three prepositions do you use the pronouns **yo** and **tú**, rather than **mí** and **ti**?

■ The pronouns used after prepositions (*for* **me**, *behind* **them**, *in front of* **us** . . . ) in Spanish are the same as the subject pronouns, except **mí** is used instead of **yo** and **ti** instead of **tú**. There is an accent mark on **mí** (*me*) to distinguish it from the possessive adjective **mi** (*my*).

### Prepositional Pronouns

| para | mí | *for me* | para | nosotros/as | *for us* |
|------|------|----------|------|-------------|----------|
| para | ti | *for you* | para | vosotros/as | *for you* |
| para | usted | *for you* | para | ustedes | *for you* |
| para | él | *for him* | para | ellos | *for them* |
| para | ella | *for her* | para | ellas | *for them* |

■ As with **para** in the chart, the same pronouns are used after the other prepositions you learned in *Capítulo 2*.

| ¿Quién está **detrás de ti** en la foto? | *Who is behind you in the photo?* |
|---|---|
| Mi familia nunca hace viajes **sin mí**. | *My family never takes trips without me.* |

■ With the preposition **con**, use **conmigo** to say *with me* and **contigo** for *with you* (sing., fam.). The other prepositional pronouns do not change after **con**.

| ¿Vas **conmigo** o **con ellos**? | *Are you going with me or with them?* |
|---|---|
| ¿Tienes ganas de hacer algo **con nosotros**? | *Do you feel like doing something with us?* |

■ Use the pronouns **yo** and **tú** instead of **mí** and **ti** after the prepositions **entre**, **menos** (*minus, except*), or **excepto** (*except*).

| No hay secretos **entre tú y yo**. | *There are no secrets between you and me.* |
|---|---|
| En mi familia, todos son altos **menos yo**. | *In my family, they are all tall except me.* |

 **3-31 ▶ Interacciones.** Ask another student the following questions. He/She should answer using a prepositional pronoun.

Modelo   E1: *¿Haces muchos viajes con tus padres?*
E2: *No, no hago muchos viajes con ellos.*

1. ¿Vives con tus padres?
2. ¿Vives cerca de tu mejor amigo/a?
3. ¿Te gusta bailar con tus primos?
4. ¿Sales a comer con tus padres con frecuencia?
5. ¿Pasas mucho tiempo con tu madre?
6. ¿Asistes a clase con tu mejor amigo/a?
7. ¿Compartes el coche con tu hermano?
8. ¿Recibes correos electrónicos de tus profesores?
9. ¿Quién come contigo todos los días?
10. ¿Quién es más importante para ti?
11. ¿Quién habla mal de ti a veces?
12. ¿Quién comparte sus secretos contigo a veces?

¿Quién comparte sus secretos contigo?

**3-32** ▶ **¿Qué haces con ellos?** What are two things you do (or don't do) with the following people? Use a prepositional pronoun in your answer, as in the Modelo.

| | |
|---|---|
| salir a comer / a bailar | trabajar |
| asistir a un concierto / a clase | limpiar la casa |
| hacer un viaje / una fiesta | tomar algo en un café |
| estudiar para los exámenes | hablar español / inglés / por |
| ir de compras / al cine / al parque | teléfono |
| ver la tele / un DVD / un partido de | . . . |
| fútbol americano | |

Modelo    con tus abuelos
          *Hablo inglés con ellos. Salgo a comer con ellos. / Nunca estoy con ellos.*

**1.** con tu madre    **3.** con tus abuelos    **5.** con tus amigos
**2.** con tu padre    **4.** con tus compañeros de clase    **6.** con tu mejor amigo/a

**¿Y tú?** Ask a partner what the preceding people do with you.

Modelo    E1: *¿Qué hacen tus abuelos contigo?*
          E2: *A veces mis abuelos van de compras conmigo. /*
              *Mis abuelos nunca hacen nada conmigo.*

**3-33** ▶ **Una foto.** Mariela is describing her family in this photo. Read her statements to determine who each person is. The first answer has been given in the Modelo.

Modelo    *Su mamá es el número 1.*

Ésta es una foto de una fiesta para el cumpleaños de mi sobrino Eduardo.
Mi abuela está delante de mí y mi mamá está a mi lado.
Delante de ella está mi abuelo y mi tía Mónica está al lado de él.
Enfrente de mi tía Mónica está mi sobrino Eduardo.
A su derecha está su hermano Daniel y a su izquierda, enfrente de mi abuelo, está su papá, mi cuñado (*brother-in-law*) Alejandro.
Mi hermana Ximena está al lado de ellos.
Mi padre está cerca de ella, al lado de la mesa, y mi prima Aura está entre nosotros.
Mis otros primos están detrás de ella, más cerca de la casa.

# 📖 Vocabulario   El aspecto físico y el carácter

SAM: 3-35 to 3-40

🔊 CD 1 Track 61  ¿Cómo es tu padre / madre? ¿Es **guapo/a?** ¿Tiene el pelo **largo** o **corto**?

Es rubia. Tiene el pelo rubio.

Es moreno. Tiene el pelo **negro / castaño**.

Es pelirroja. Tiene el pelo rojo.

Es canosa. Tiene el pelo canoso.

Tiene los ojos . . .

Mi padre también tiene . . .

azules

marrones / color café

gafas

bigote

barba

verdes

grises

De carácter, ¿eres más como tu madre o más como tu padre? ¿Cómo es? ¿Es . . . ?

| | |
|---|---|
| chistoso/a o serio/a | *funny (likes to joke around) or serious* |
| relajado/a o estricto/a | *easy-going or strict* |
| liberal o conservador/a | *liberal or conservative* |
| cariñoso/a o frío/a | *loving (affectionate) or cold* |
| generoso/a o egoísta | *generous or selfish* |
| tranquilo/a o temperamental | *calm or moody* |
| amistoso/a o presumido/a | *friendly or stuck-up* |
| comprensivo/a o mandón / mandona | *understanding or bossy* |
| flexible o terco/a | *flexible or stubborn* |
| realista y normal o raro/a | *down-to-earth and normal or weird* |

🔊 CD 1 Track 64

**Una conversación.**  Dos amigas, Elena y Sonia, hablan de sus padres.

ELENA: ¿Cómo son tus padres? ¿Eres más como tu madre o tu padre?

SONIA: Físicamente soy más como mi papá. Es alto y tiene el pelo castaño y los ojos verdes como yo. Mi madre tiene el pelo canoso y los ojos azules. De carácter, soy más como ella. Es chistosa, cariñosa y un poco impulsiva. **No soy nada como** mi papá. Es temperamental, muy estricto y serio. ¿Y tú? ¿Eres más como tu madre o tu padre?

ELENA: Pues, físicamente, no soy como ninguno de los dos porque soy adoptada. En el carácter, soy más como mi papá. Nosotros dos somos reservados, pero mi mamá es muy extrovertida y sociable.

🔊 CD 1, Track 63

## ¡A escuchar!

Ahora escuchen otra conversación en la cual dos amigas, Marta y Ana, hablan del novio de una de ellas. ¿Cómo es su aspecto físico? ¿Y su carácter?

**el aspecto físico** *physical appearance*  **guapo/a** *good-looking, handsome*  **largo/a** *long*  **corto/a** *short* (in length)  **negro/a** *black*  **castaño/a** *brown* (for hair)  **no soy nada como** *I'm not anything like*

**3-34 ▶ ¿Cómo es?** Complete each description with the correct form of the logical adjective from the list.

| | | |
|---|---|---|
| amistoso/a | mandón / mandona | sociable |
| comprensivo/a | *presumido/a* | temperamental |
| frío/a | raro/a | terco/a |

Modelo    Todas mis tías por parte de mi madre creen que son mejores que nosotros. Son *presumidas.*

1. Mi madre siempre comprende todos mis problemas. Es muy _____.
2. A veces mi hermano está bien y luego, de pronto (*all of a sudden*) está enojado. Es _____.
3. Mi hermano es muy _____. Para él, es muy difícil admitir que no tiene razón.
4. Mi hermana habla con todo el mundo (*everyone*) y tiene muchos amigos. Es muy _____ y _____.
5. Tengo una tía muy _____. Nunca habla con nosotros y es indiferente si su familia necesita ayuda. (*help*)
6. Mi abuela por parte de mi madre insiste en controlar a todos sus hijos. Es muy _____.
7. Tengo un primo _____. Es muy excéntrico.

 **¿Y tú?** Reread each sentence that you completed above and tell a partner whether the adjective you used describes anyone in your family.

Modelo    *Tengo un primo presumido por parte de mi madre. /*
*No hay nadie presumido en mi familia.*

**3-35 ▶ Descripciones.** Describe the following people as in the Modelo.

Modelo    Mi madre *tiene el pelo castaño y los ojos verdes. De carácter es paciente y cariñosa. No es mandona. / No tengo madre.*

| | | |
|---|---|---|
| **1.** Mi padre . . . | **3.** Mi hermano/a menor . . . | **5.** Mi tío/a favorito/a . . . |
| **2.** La madre de mi padre . . . | **4.** Mi hermano/a mayor . . . | **6.** Mi mejor amigo/a . . . . |

 **3-36 ▶ Otra conversación.** With a partner, reread *Una conversación* between Elena and Sonia. Then, change it to describe your own parents.

 **3-37 ▶ Comparaciones culturales.** Working in groups guess what men and women in Spain prefer in a partner, according to a survey of more than 1,300 Spaniards conducted by an online matchmaking service. Select one of the answers in italics. Afterwards, your instructor will give the correct results from this survey.

Para las españolas, el hombre ideal . . .

- es *rubio / moreno / pelirrojo.*
- tiene el pelo *largo / corto.*
- tiene los ojos *azules / marrones / verdes.*
- es *mayor / menor* que ellas.
- es *divertido / serio.*
- está *un poco musculoso / muy musculoso / delgado.*
- *comparte / no comparte* los gastos (*expenses*) al 50%.
- *trabaja para vivir / vive para trabajar.*

Para los hombres, la mujer ideal . . .

- es *rubia / morena / pelirroja.*
- tiene el pelo *largo / corto.*
- tiene los ojos *azules / marrones / verdes.*
- es *mayor / menor* que ellos.
- es *aventurera / reservada.*
- *sale con su pareja / prefiere pasar tiempo en casa.*
- *comparte / no comparte* el trabajo doméstico.
- *es económicamente independiente / no trabaja.*

#  Resumen de gramática

SAM: 3-41
to 3-44

## Possessive Adjectives

- Possessive adjectives agree in number and gender with the object possessed, not the possessor.

- Use **el / la / los / las** + *noun* + **de** instead of *'s* to show possession in Spanish.

- Since **su(s)** can mean *your, his, her, its,* or *their,* it is often rephrased as shown here.

### Possessive Adjectives

| mi(s) | *my* | nuestro/a(s) | *our* |
| tu(s) | *your* | vuestro/a(s) | *you* |
| su(s) | *your, his, her, its* | su(s) | *your, their* |

No es **su** casa.  *It's not his house.*
Es **la casa de** su padre.  *It's his father's house.*

su hijo
{
el hijo de usted(es)  *your son*
el hijo de él  *his son*
el hijo de ella  *her son*
el hijo de ellos / ellas  *their son*

¿Es el hijo **de él** o **de ella**?  *Is he **his** or **her** son?*

## Verbs ending in *-er* and *-ir*

- Regular **-er** and **-ir** verb endings differ only in the **nosotros/as** and **vosotros/as** forms.

-ER VERBS: **aprender (a . . . )** *to learn (to . . . ),* **beber** *to drink,* **comer** *to eat,* **comprender** *to understand,* **correr** *to run,* **creer** *to believe,* **deber** *must, should,* **leer** *to read,* **vender** *to sell*

-IR VERBS: **abrir** *to open,* **asistir (a)** *to attend,* **compartir** *to share,* **escribir** *to write,* **recibir** *to receive,* **vivir** *to live*

- Use the preposition **a** before nouns following **asistir** and before infinitives following **aprender.**

- **Deber** can indicate obligation or supposition. When it indicates supposition, **deber** may be followed by **de** before the infinitive.

|  | **leer** (*to read*) | **escribir** (*to write*) |
|---|---|---|
| yo | leo | escribo |
| tú | lees | escribes |
| Ud., él, ella | lee | escribe |
| nosotros/as | leemos | escribimos |
| vosotros/as | leéis | escribís |
| Uds., ellos/as | leen | escriben |

Asisto **a** muchos conciertos.  *I attend a lot of concerts.*

Aprendo **a** tocar la guitarra.  *I'm learning to play the guitar.*

**Debemos** hacer algo.  *We must do something.*

**Debe de** estar enfermo.  *He must be sick.*

## The personal *a*

- Insert the preposition **a** before human direct objects, but not before things. Do not use it after **tener** to say you have friends or family members.

No comprendo **a** mi hermano.  *I don't understand my brother.*

## The verbs *hacer, poner, traer, salir, ver,* and *oír*

■ The verbs **hacer, poner, traer, salir,** and **ver** are like regular **-er** and **-ir** verbs in the present indicative, except for the **yo** forms. **Oír** is irregular in other forms as well.

■ Idiomatic expressions with **hacer** include: **hacer una pregunta** *to ask a question,* **hacer un viaje** *to take a trip,* and **hacer una fiesta** *to have a party.*

| | **hacer**<br>*(to do / to make)* | **poner**<br>*(to put / to set)* | **traer**<br>*(to bring)* |
|---|---|---|---|
| yo | hago | pongo | traigo |
| tú | haces | pones | traes |
| Ud., él, ella | hace | pone | trae |
| nosotros/as | hacemos | ponemos | traemos |
| vosotros/as | hacéis | ponéis | traéis |
| Uds., ellos/as | hacen | ponen | traen |

| | **salir**<br>*(to go out / to leave)* | **ver**<br>*(to see)* | **oír**<br>*(to hear)* |
|---|---|---|---|
| yo | salgo | veo | oigo |
| tú | sales | ves | oyes |
| Ud., él, ella | sale | ve | oye |
| nosotros/as | salimos | vemos | oímos |
| vosotros/as | salís | veis | oís |
| Uds., ellos/as | salen | ven | oyen |

El hombre que vive al lado está furioso si oye la música cuando hago una fiesta y pongo el estéreo a todo volumen.

*The man who lives next door is furious if he hears the music when I have a party and I put on the stereo full blast.*

## The verbs *tener* and *venir*

■ The verbs **tener** and **venir** have similar forms.

■ Use **tener que** with an infinitive to say that someone *has to do* something and **tener ganas de . . .** for *to be in the mood for / to . . . , to feel like . . . .*

■ **Tener** is also used in these expressions: **tener hambre / sed / frío / calor / miedo (de) / suerte / sueño / prisa / razón / . . . años** *to be hungry / thirsty / cold / hot / afraid (of) / lucky / sleepy / in a hurry / right / . . . years old.*

| | **tener**<br>*(to have)* | **venir**<br>*(to come)* |
|---|---|---|
| yo | tengo | vengo |
| tú | tienes | vienes |
| Ud., él, ella | tiene | viene |
| nosotros/as | tenemos | venimos |
| vosotros/as | tenéis | venís |
| Uds., ellos/as | tienen | vienen |

¿Tienes hambre?

*Are you hungry?*

¿Tienes ganas de venir conmigo a comer o tienes que trabajar?

*Do you feel like coming with me to eat or do you have to work?*

## Prepositional pronouns

■ The pronouns used after prepositions are the same as the subject pronouns, except **mí** and **ti** are used instead of **yo** and **tú**.

■ With the preposition **con**, use **conmigo** to say *with me* and **contigo** to say *with you* (sing., fam.).

■ After the prepositions **entre, menos** (*minus, except*), and **excepto** (*except*), use **yo** and **tú** instead of **mí** and **ti**.

| | |
|---|---|
| sin **mí** | *without **me*** |
| cerca de **ti** | *near **you*** |
| delante de **usted** | *in front of **you*** |
| detrás de **él** | *behind **him*** |
| al lado de **ella** | *next to **her*** |
| con **nosotros/as** | *with **us*** |
| para **vosotros/as** | *for **you*** |
| entre **ustedes** | *between **you*** |
| lejos de **ellos/as** | *far from **them*** |

**EN EL CENTRO DE SERVICIOS FAMILIARES**

SAM: 3-45 to 3-49

In this chapter, you learned how to describe your family and talk about your activities. Now, you will practice what you have learned in a real life simulation of working in a center providing family services to Spanish-speakers.

**3-38** ► **Mi familia.** With a partner, imagine that the mother in this photo is describing her family. Prepare a conversation in which she says who each family member is and gives his/her age.

Modelo   E1: *¿Cómo se llama usted?*
E2: *Me llamo Isabel García Ochoa.*
E1: *¿Cuántos son ustedes en la familia?*
E2: *Somos cinco y los padres de mi esposo también viven con nosotros . . .*

**3-39** ► **¿Cómo son?** Another woman with whom you are talking is describing her family members' personalities. Complete the following sentences with the appropriate possessive adjectives in the shaded blanks, and the logical adjectives from the parentheses in the other blanks.

Modelo   No tengo un esposo muy *sociable. Mi* esposo es muy tímido y *reservado.* (reservado, sociable)

**1.** Mi esposo tiene una madre muy simpática y _____.
_____ madre no es _____. (cariñosa, mandona)
**2.** Mi esposo tiene hermanos egoístas y _____. _____
hermanos no son _____. (flexibles, tercos)
**3.** Mi esposo y yo tenemos hijos relajados y _____. _____
hijos no son _____. (tranquilos, temperamentales)
**4.** Tengo un esposo serio y _____. _____ esposo no es
_____. (trabajador, perezoso)
**5.** Tenemos una familia simpática y _____. _____ familia
no es _____. (presumida, amistosa)

**3-40 ▶ En la foto.** Isabel Ochoa is explaining who each person is in the photo on the previous page. Prepare sentences using prepositional pronouns to explain where each person is with respect to her and other family members.

Modelo    *Mi esposo está detrás de mí y sus padres están . . .*

**3-41 ▶ Una familia perfecta.** If a mother wants to give the impression that she has a perfect family life, would she say that the following people always (**siempre**), sometimes (**a veces**), or never (**nunca**) do each of the following things?

Modelo    Nuestros hijos . . . (asistir a la escuela, tener problemas en la escuela)
          *Nuestros hijos siempre asisten a la escuela. Nunca tienen problemas en la escuela.*

1. Yo . . . (hacer algo bueno de comer, recibir regalos de mi esposo, comprender a mi familia, creer en un futuro mejor para nosotros)
2. Mi esposo . . . (salir con sus amigos sin mí, tener ganas de estar conmigo, venir a casa después del trabajo, beber demasiado, comprender mis problemas, tener paciencia con nuestros hijos, hacer una fiesta para mi cumpleaños)
3. Mi esposo y yo . . . (comer con nuestros hijos, salir a bailar, hacer un viaje juntos, tener muchos problemas, compartir nuestros sentimientos, creer en la importancia de la comunicación, tener miedo de hablar)
4. Nuestros hijos . . . (traer a sus amigos a casa, hacer su tarea, aprender mucho en la escuela, tener sueño en clase, leer mucho, ver la tele todo el día, salir con sus amigos hasta tarde, deber estar en casa antes de las diez de la noche)

---

¡Hola!    **Entre profesionales**

If you work or volunteer for community organizations that provide services to Hispanic families, it is important to know how to ask about their needs and explain the services you can provide. Visit MySpanishLab for *Hoy día* to find more useful vocabulary, information, and activities such as the following one.

**¿En qué puedo servirle?** Here are some of the Spanish names for common types of assistance social organizations provide. Can you guess what they mean? For each statement that follows, offer the appropriate type of assistance from the list.

> *asistencia de empleo* / cuidado de niños / ayuda alimentaria / protección contra la violencia doméstica / vivienda

Modelo    No sé qué voy a hacer. No tengo trabajo.
          *¿Necesita asistencia de empleo?*

1. Tengo miedo de mi esposo cuando bebe demasiado.
2. Mi esposo está sin trabajo hasta la semana que viene y no tiene dinero para comprar comida para la familia esta semana.
3. Mis hijos y yo no tenemos donde vivir. Ahora estamos en un refugio para inmigrantes.
4. Necesito trabajar, pero tengo un hijo de tres años.

## LECTORES DE HOY

 ### Publicidad en español

SAM: 3-50
to 3-52

### Antes de leer

You are going to read about advertising to Hispanics. Think about the following questions before you approach the reading: *¿Qué productos o servicios crees que son más populares y venden más entre* (among) *las familias hispanas? ¿Reflejan estas preferencias valores* (values) *y tradiciones hispanas?*

> ▶ **Reading Strategy** *Skimming.* Skimming is a reading technique used for obtaining the main ideas in a text. When you skim you do not read every word; instead, you glance over the reading to seek clues that provide background information, and help you get the "gist." Look at the title, slogan, subtitle, and paragraph headings, and try to identify the main topic.

### Ahora tú

3-42 ▶ **Una lista.** Look at the ads and identify the products and services offered in each. Then, make a list of the most important words and explain how they relate to the images.

*Aló, ¿familia?*
*Cerca de ti, cerca de los tuyos*

Ahora *Aló* trae a tu casa el servicio móvil *Cerca de ti.* ¿Lo oyes? Con *Cerca de ti* puedes tener hasta cinco líneas sin costo adicional y hablar los fines de semana gratis con tus familiares y amigos. Nadie te ofrece nada igual. *Aló,* diez años de servicio a las familias hispanas con tarifas competitivas.

*¡En telefonía, no tenemos rival!*

*Secura . . . y viaja tranquilo*
**Porque tu familia tiene que viajar *Secura.***

*Secura* te trae un nuevo concepto de vehículo familiar. Robusto, seguro y cómodo. Con capacidad para ocho personas, es la alternativa ideal para las salidas de fin de semana. En viajes largos o excursiones de día, *Secura* viene a por ti.

**¡Para salir en familia, *Secura*!**

## Casadenés, comidas con tradición
*Es lo auténtico, es Casadenés.*

Casadenés pone en tu mesa productos de calidad, seleccionados especialmente para satisfacer la dieta de toda tu familia. Alimentos[1] naturales perfectos para el desayuno[2], la comida y la cena de pequeños y mayores. Protege la salud[3] de tu familia, protege tus tradiciones.

**¡Comer en familia es compartir Casadenés!**

[1]food  [2]breakfast  [3]health

📖 Después de leer

SAM: 3-1 to 3-4

3-43 ▶ **Comprensión.** Answer the following questions related to the advertisements.

1. ¿Qué es *Cerca de Ti*? ¿Qué te permite (*does it allow you*) hacer?
2. ¿Crees que el anuncio de *Aló* conecta bien con las familias hispanas? ¿Por qué?
3. ¿Cómo son los productos *Casadenés*? ¿Por qué son los productos *Casadenés* atractivos para las familias hispanas?
4. ¿Por qué es *Secura* un buen automóvil para la familia?
5. ¿Qué miembros de la familia crees que están interesados en los productos y servicios que ofrecen (*offer*) los anuncios?
6. ¿Crees que estos anuncios funcionan (*these ads work*) para el público no-hispano?

3-44 ▶ **Palabras relacionadas.** Skim the ads for words related to those in the diagrams below and write them around the corresponding circle. Then, complete the diagrams with other related words or expressions you have learned in this chapter.

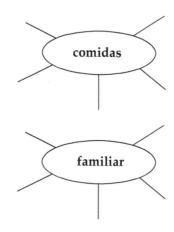

3-45 ▶ **Un buen automóvil.** Paco is talking with his brother-in-law, Daniel, about his new automobile. Complete their conversation with the appropriate words from the list and read it with a partner.

| familia | ganas | nietos | traer | suerte |
|---------|-------|--------|-------|--------|
| fin de semana | hacer | padres | salir | ver |

PACO: ¿Qué vas a (1) _____ este fin de semana?

DANIEL: Susana y yo vamos a (2) _____ una película con los niños. ¿Y ustedes?

PACO: Vamos a (3) _____ de excursión en mi nueva Secura.

DANIEL: ¿Vienen tus (4) _____ a pasar el fin de semana con ustedes?

PACO: Sí, vienen a ver a sus (5) _____ y el sábado planeamos ir a la playa.

DANIEL: Tienes (6) _____ de tener un vehículo tan (*so*) bueno.

PACO: Sí, es un vehículo práctico y cómodo para toda la (7) _____.

DANIEL: Susana y yo también tenemos (8) _____ de un auto nuevo. ¿Tienen planes para el domingo?

PACO: Sí, generalmente los domingos a los niños les gusta (9) _____ a sus amigos a casa y así pasan la tarde.

DANIEL: Eso es bueno. Buen (10) _____.

PACO: Igualmente.

## 📖 Crecer en una familia hispana

SAM: 3-53
to 3-55

### Antes de ver

Family is extremely important in Hispanic cultures. In this video segment, you are going to hear different Hispanics talking about their families and the great support (*apoyo*) they receive from their family members.

**3-46 ▶ Reflexiones.** Think about a typical Hispanic family and reflect on the following questions: *¿Cómo es? ¿Qué actividades crees que hacen sus miembros los fines de semana? ¿Qué rutina crees que tienen durante la semana? ¿Son las actividades similares a las que haces tú con tu familia?*

> **▶ Listening Strategy** *Listening for specific information.* As you listen, direct your attention to specific information you expect the speaker to mention rather than trying to understand every single word. For example, when people are talking about their family, you might listen for where they are from, how many there are in their family, or what their family is like. Try to listen for specific words that will target this information.

### 🎬 Ahora tú

**3-47 ▶ Somos una familia . . .** Listen attentively to Itandehui, Analissa and Edgar talk about their families. Answer the following questions about each one.

- ¿Cuál es su origen?
- ¿Cuántos son en su familia?
- ¿Cómo describe a su familia?

### Después de ver

**3-48 ▶ Una familia unida.** Watch the video segment once again and answer the following questions about Rafael Escansiani and his family.

1. ¿Cuántos miembros hay en la familia Escansiani?
2. ¿Quién es el padre? ¿Y la madre?
3. Describan físicamente a los miembros de la familia Escansiani.
4. ¿Cuál crees que es la rutina diaria de los padres? ¿Y la de los hijos?
5. ¿Qué crees que hace la familia los fines de semana?

**3-49 ▶ En sus ratos libres.** Describe what you think the following people do in their free time.

1. Itandehui es estudiante de literatura y medios de comunicación. En sus ratos libres . . .
2. Rosal va a empezar (*to begin*) en la universidad y quiere ser actriz. En sus ratos libres . . .
3. Alejandro trabaja en una bodega (*food store*). En sus ratos libres . . .
4. La pasión de Analissa es la música y toca el chelo. En sus ratos libres . . .

## 📖 Retrato de familia

SAM: 3-56

### Antes de escribir

Think about your family and try to visualize each one of its members as you prepare your answers to the following questions: *¿Cuáles son sus características más peculiares? Piensa en cómo pasa el día tu familia y en las actividades de fin de semana. ¿Tienes una familia grande? ¿Con qué frecuencia vienen tus familiares a tu casa? ¿Qué tradiciones comparten los miembros de tu familia?*

> ▶ **Writing strategy** *Visualizing your topic.* When writing, it often helps to visualize what you are describing. To write a description of your family, start by creating a family tree to visualize your family organization. Then, think about what your family members are like and what they like to do before beginning to write.

**3-50 ▶ ¡Prepárate!** List any words or ideas you associate with the following four categories.

- los miembros de tu familia: su aspecto físico y su carácter
- tu rutina de la semana y la rutina de tu familia
- tus fines de semana y los fines de semana de tu familia
- las tradiciones familiares

### Ahora tú

**3-51 ▶ Tu retrato de familia.** Now, write four paragraphs about your family using the information you prepared for each of the preceding categories.

### Después de escribir

**3-52 ▶ ¡Edita!** Exchange your composition with a classmate. As you read the description of his/her family, prepare three or four additional questions about information your partner did not mention that you would like to know.

**3-53 ▶ ¡Revisa!** Revise your composition to include the answers to your partner's questions. Also make sure that your composition includes:

- ❏ appropriate vocabulary to talk about family members
- ❏ structures to express possession
- ❏ verbs to talk about daily activities
- ❏ vocabulary to talk about weekend activities

**3-54 ▶ ¡Navega!** Visit your online resource for *Hoy día* and use the links provided to read about famous Hispanics and their families. Compare the descriptions you find with your composition. Does it contain useful information you could include in describing your own family?

## La familia

| | |
|---|---|
| **¿Cuántos son por parte de tu madre / padre?** | *How many are there on your mother's / father's side?* |
| **el/la abuelo/a (los abuelos)** | *grandfather / grandmother (grandparents)* |
| **el familiar** | *family member, relative* |
| **el/la hermano/a (los hermanos)** | *brother / sister (brothers and sisters)* |
| **el/la hijo/a (los hijos)** | *son / daughter (children)* |
| **la mascota / el perro / el gato** | *pet / dog / cat* |
| **el/la nieto/a (los nietos)** | *grandson / granddaughter (grandchildren)* |
| **el padre / la madre (los padres)** | *father / mother (parents)* |
| **el/la primo/a (los primos)** | *cousin (cousins)* |
| **el/la sobrino/a (los sobrinos)** | *nephew / niece (nephews and nieces)* |
| **el/la tío/a (los tíos)** | *uncle / aunt (aunts and uncles)* |

## Descripciones

| | |
|---|---|
| **alto/a** | *tall, high* |
| **bajo/a** | *short (in height), low* |
| **casado/a** | *married* |
| **de estatura mediana** | *of medium height* |
| **delgado/a** | *thin* |
| **de mediana edad** | *middle-aged* |
| **divorciado/a** | *divorced* |
| **gordo/a** | *fat* |
| **joven** | *young* |
| **mayor** | *older, oldest* |
| **mejor** | *better, best* |
| **menor** | *younger, youngest* |
| **soltero/a** | *single* |

## Otras palabras y expresiones

| | |
|---|---|
| **Se llama (Se llaman) . . .** | *His / Her name is (Their names are) . . .* |
| **tener** | *to have* |
| **tener . . . años** | *to be . . . years old* |
| **venir** | *to come* |
| **Vivo con . . .** | *I live with . . .* |

## Adjetivos posesivos

| | |
|---|---|
| **mi(s)** | *my* |
| **tu(s)** | *your (sing., fam.)* |
| **nuestro/a(s)** | *our* |
| **vuestro/a(s)** | *your (pl., fam.)* |
| **su(s)** | *your (sing., form.; pl.), his, her, its, their* |

## Medios de comunicación

| | |
|---|---|
| **un correo electrónico** | *e-mail* |
| **un ensayo** | *essay, paper* |
| **un libro de texto** | *textbook* |
| **un periódico** | *newspaper* |
| **una revista** | *magazine* |

## Acciones

| | |
|---|---|
| **abrir** | *to open* |
| **aprender (a . . .)** | *to learn (to . . .)* |
| **asistir (a)** | *to attend* |
| **beber** | *to drink* |
| **compartir** | *to share* |
| **comprender** | *to understand* |
| **correr** | *to run* |
| **creer (en / que)** | *to believe (in / that)* |
| **deber** | *must, should* |
| **escribir** | *to write* |
| **leer** | *to read* |
| **recibir** | *to receive* |
| **vender** | *to sell* |

## Otras palabras

| | |
|---|---|
| **el café** | *coffee* |
| **durante** | *during* |
| **ese / esa (esos / esas)** | *that (those)* |
| **el vino** | *wine* |

*For expressions with **tener**, see page 78.*

## Lugares y eventos

| | |
|---|---|
| el bar | bar |
| el evento deportivo | sports event |

## Expresiones verbales

| | |
|---|---|
| hacer una fiesta | to have a party |
| hacer una pregunta | to ask a question |
| hacer un viaje | to take a trip |
| oír | to hear |
| poner | to put, to place, to set |
| poner la radio (el iPod, el CD, el DVD) | to put on, to turn on the radio (the iPod, the CD, the DVD) |
| salir | to leave, to go out |
| traer | to bring |

## Otras expresiones

| | |
|---|---|
| un coche | car |
| contigo | with you |
| nada en especial | nothing in particular, nothing special |

## El aspecto físico

| | |
|---|---|
| Físicamente, es . . . | Physically, he / she is . . . |
| canoso/s | gray-haired, white-haired |
| guapo/a | good-looking, handsome |
| moreno/a | dark-complexioned |
| pelirrojo/a | red-haired |
| rubio/a | blond-haired |
| Tiene bigote / barba. | He has a mustache / beard. |
| Tiene gafas. | He / She has glasses. |
| Tiene el pelo . . . | His / Her hair is . . . |
| canoso | gray |
| castaño | brown |
| corto | short |
| largo | long |
| negro | black |
| rojo | red |
| rubio | blond |
| Tiene los ojos . . . | His / Her eyes are . . . |
| azules | blue |
| grises | gray |
| marrones (color café) | brown |
| verdes | green |

## El carácter

| | |
|---|---|
| De carácter, es . . . | Personality-wise, he / she is . . . |
| amistoso/a | friendly |
| cariñoso/a | loving, affectionate |
| chistoso/a | funny, likes to joke around |
| comprensivo/a | understanding |
| conservador/a | conservative |
| egoísta | selfish |
| estricto/a | strict |
| flexible | flexible |
| frío/a | cold |
| generoso/a | generous |
| liberal | liberal |
| mandón / mandona | bossy |
| normal | normal |
| presumido/a | stuck-up |
| raro/a | weird |
| realista | down-to-earth |
| relajado/a | easy-going |
| reservado/a | reserved |
| serio/a | serious |
| sociable | sociable |
| temperamental | moody |
| terco/a | stubborn |
| tranquilo/a | calm |

¡Hola!  Visit MySpanishLab for *Hoy día* for links to the mnemonic dictionary online for suggestions such as the following to help you remember vocabulary from *Capítulo 3,* learn related words in Spanish, and use Spanish words to build your vocabulary in English.

### EXAMPLES

**beber,** *to drink:* **Beber** is related to the English words *beverage* and *imbibe.* Related vocabulary in Spanish: **una bebida,** *a drink;* **bebible,** *drinkable;* **un/a bebedor/a,** *a (heavy) drinker;* **un bebedero,** *a drinking fountain* (in Mexico and Central America); *a drinking trough* (for animals).

**comer,** *to eat:* There is a little-used English word *comestible* (= *edible*) related to **comer.** Related vocabulary in Spanish: **una comida,** *a food, a meal;* **un comedor,** *a dining room;* **comestible,** *edible;* **un/a comilón / comilona,** *a big eater, a glutton;* **un comedero,** *a (bird / animal) feeder.*

# 4 En casa

En este capítulo vas a aprender a hablar de la casa, el barrio (*neighborhood*) y las actividades diarias en casa.

El concepto de barrio es muy importante en las culturas hispánicas. El barrio tiene ese sentimiento de comunidad tan importante para los hispanos. Es el lugar donde las personas forman su identidad.

▶ ¿Hay un sentimiento de comunidad en tu barrio?

El hispano conserva la idea de barrio cuando emigra fuera de su país (*out of his/her country*). Los Ángeles, Nueva York, Chicago, Miami, Houston y Riverside-San Bernardino, en California, son áreas de población con más de un millón de residentes latinos.

▶ ¿Hay algún barrio hispano cerca de tu casa o universidad? ¿Cómo es?

▶ ¿Es diferente de otros barrios de la ciudad? ¿En qué es diferente?

**Vocabulario**   La casa y los muebles

SAM: 4-1
to 4-4

CD 2
Track 1

¿Prefieres vivir en el centro de **una ciudad** grande, en **las afueras** de una ciudad o en **el campo?** ¿Qué hay en tu casa?

un árbol • un microondas • un comedor • un baño • una mesa • una estufa • una nevera • unas sillas • una cama • una cocina • un sofá • un dormitorio • una flor • un televisor • una sala • una piscina • una planta • un coche/un carro • un jardín

## ¿Sabías que...?

En la mayoría de las ciudades hispanas, la gente vive en grandes edificios de apartamentos. En general, los apartamentos tienen dos o tres dormitorios, cocina, salón-comedor y uno o dos baños. Las familias están acostumbradas a convivir (*to live together*) en espacios relativamente pequeños, donde el contacto personal es más frecuente. Es común que los abuelos vivan con la familia.

## ¡Ojo!

In Mexico, people say **una recámara** for a *bedroom*, and in other regions, you might hear **una alcoba.** You can also use **un cuarto** or **una habitación** to say *a room*. In some regions, people say **un refrigerador** instead of **una nevera** and **rentar / la renta** instead of **alquilar / el alquiler.**

CD 2, Track 3

 **¡A escuchar!**

Ahora, escuchen otra conversación en la cual un hombre llama por el anuncio (*ad*) de alquiler de un apartamento. ¿Dónde está el apartamento? ¿Cómo es? ¿Quiere ver el apartamento? ¿Por qué (no)?

CD 2
Track 2

**Una conversación.** Dos futuros compañeros de casa, Diego y Miguel, hablan.

DIEGO: ¿Dónde vives ahora, Miguel?

MIGUEL: Ahora vivo en una casa pequeña en las afueras. Mi **dirección** es calle Juárez, número 829. Me gustaría vivir en un apartamento más cerca del centro porque no me gusta trabajar en el jardín y quiero estar más cerca de la universidad. El problema es que los apartamentos en el centro son muy **caros**. Y tú, ¿dónde vives?

DIEGO: **Alquilo** un apartamento no muy lejos de aquí y no **pago** mucho de **alquiler**. Me gusta **el barrio**. Es muy **agradable** y tengo **vecinos** simpáticos, pero me gustaría tener un apartamento un poco más grande.

MIGUEL: ¿Tienes perro o gato?

DIEGO: No, no tengo animales. ¿Y tú?

MIGUEL: Tengo un perro, pero nunca está en la casa. Siempre está **afuera**.

DIEGO: ¿**Fumas**?

MIGUEL: No, ¿y tú?

DIEGO: **Yo tampoco.**

---

**una ciudad** *a city* **las afueras** *the outskirts* **el campo** *the country* **caro/a** *expensive* **la dirección** *the address* **alquilar** *to rent* **pagar** *to pay* **el alquiler** *the rent* **el barrio** *the neighborhood* **agradable** *pleasant, nice* **un/a vecino/a** *a neighbor* **afuera** *outside* **fumar** *to smoke* **Yo tampoco.** *Me neither.*

**4-1 ▶ ¿Qué es?** ¿Qué hay en estos lugares según (*according to*) la ilustración de la casa de la página anterior?

Modelo  entre la cocina y el baño
*Hay un comedor entre la cocina y el baño.*

1. detrás del dormitorio
2. al lado de la sala, en el jardín
3. debajo del árbol
4. entre la estufa y la nevera

5. a la izquierda del microondas
6. a la derecha del microondas
7. en el garaje, debajo del dormitorio
8. enfrente del televisor, en la sala

**¡Ojo!**

Starting in this chapter, instructions to activities in the textbook will be in Spanish. If you have questions about what you are to do, be sure to ask your instructor for clarification.

 **4-2 ▶ Entrevista.** Entrevista a otro/a estudiante con estas preguntas.

1. ¿Prefieres vivir en un apartamento, una casa o un cuarto en una residencia? ¿Tienes apartamento, casa o cuarto en una residencia? ¿Está cerca de aquí? ¿En qué calle está? ¿Prefieres vivir en el centro de una ciudad grande, en las afueras o en el campo?
2. ¿Cómo es tu casa (apartamento, residencia)? ¿Es nuevo/a o viejo/a? ¿Caro/a? ¿Cuántos dormitorios hay? ¿Cuántos baños? ¿Hay piscina? ¿Qué te gusta de tu casa (apartamento, residencia)? ¿Qué no te gusta?

 **4-3 ▶ Otra conversación.** En parejas, lean otra vez (*again*) *Una conversación* entre Diego y Miguel. Luego, usen la conversación como modelo para describir el lugar (*place*) donde viven y explicar por qué les gusta o no.

**4-4 ▶ Comparaciones culturales.** Lean con atención las descripciones sobre los distintos tipos de vivienda (*housing*) en los países hispanos y discutan las preguntas en grupo.

■ La arquitectura de las casas en los países hispanos es muy variada y refleja una mezcla (*mix*) de modernidad y tradicionalismo. En las ciudades es normal ver edificios altos y modernos, con muchos apartamentos, y también áreas residenciales nuevas, con viviendas unifamiliares (*single-family dwellings*) en las afueras de la ciudad. En el centro histórico de las ciudades todavía (*still*) hay casas antiguas (*old*) de arquitectura tradicional. En la ciudad donde vives, ¿hay una mezcla similar de modernidad y tradicionalismo en la arquitectura de las casas? ¿Te gustan más los edificios modernos o las casas antiguas? ¿Por qué?

■ Los colores de las casas reflejan el clima del lugar. En muchos países hispanos, los climas son tropicales y hay muchas casas de colores brillantes que repelen el calor (*heat*). En climas fríos, muchas casas están pintadas de colores oscuros (*dark*) para atraer (*to attract*) el calor. ¿Hay diferencias similares entre las casas en el norte y en el sur de Estados Unidos? ¿Reflejan las casas el clima del lugar donde están?

# Gramática 1

SAM: 4-5
to 4-9

## Giving your address and other information: Numbers above 100

### Para averiguar

1. In which of the following numbers do you translate the word *one: one hundred, one thousand, one million*?
2. Which of these numbers does not change in plural forms: **ciento, mil, un millón**? Which has feminine plural forms?
3. When do you use a period with numbers in Spanish? A comma?
4. How do you express years in Spanish?
5. When do you use **de** after **millón / millones**?

■ Here are the numbers from 100 to 999.

| | |
|---|---|
| 100 cien | 500 quinientos/as |
| 101 ciento uno (un/una) | 600 seiscientos/as |
| 102 ciento dos . . . | 700 setecientos/as |
| 200 doscientos/as | 800 ochocientos/as |
| 300 trescientos/as | 900 novecientos/as |
| 400 cuatrocientos/as | 999 novecientos/as noventa y nueve |

■ Use **cien** to say *one hundred* exactly, but use **ciento** in the numbers from 101 to 199. Do not use the word **un** before **cien** or **ciento**. Although **cien** and **ciento** do not have feminine forms in the numbers 100–199, **-cientos** changes to **-cientas** before feminine nouns in 200–999.

| | WITH MASCULINE NOUNS | WITH FEMININE NOUNS |
|---|---|---|
| 100: | cien libros | cien páginas |
| 101: | ciento un libros | ciento una páginas |
| 200: | doscientos libros | doscientas páginas |
| 720: | setecientos veinte libros | setecientas veinte páginas |

■ In contrast to English, in Spanish a period is used to designate numbers in the thousands, and a comma is used for decimal points.

| | | |
|---|---|---|
| (Spanish) 1.543 | mil quinientos cuarenta y tres | (English) 1,543 |
| (Spanish) 3,25 | tres coma veinticinco | (English) 3.25 |

■ The word for *thousand* is **mil**. **Mil** is not pluralized, nor is **un** used before it. Do not use the word **y** immediately after the words **mil** or **cien / ciento**.

| | |
|---|---|
| 1.000 | mil |
| 1.914 | mil novecientos catorce |
| 2.007 | dos mil siete |

■ Unlike in English, all years in Spanish are expressed using **mil,** not hundreds.

| | |
|---|---|
| 1492 | mil cuatrocientos noventa y dos |
| 2010 | dos mil diez |

■ When counting in the millions, say **un millón, dos millones, tres millones. . . .** Use **de** before nouns that directly follow the word **millón / millones**. If another number is between the word **millón / millones** and the noun, **de** is not used.

| | |
|---|---|
| un millón de dólares | *one million dollars* |
| un millón doscientos mil dólares | *one million, two hundred thousand dollars* |

**4-5 ▶ El alquiler.**  ¿Cuánto pagas de alquiler al mes? ¿Pagas más de la cantidad indicada o menos?

Modelo    $1.100
    *Pago más de mil cien dólares al mes. / Pago menos de mil cien dólares al mes.*

| | | | | | |
|---|---|---|---|---|---|
| **1.** $150 | **3.** $275 | **5.** $515 | **7.** $750 | **9.** $1.000 | **11.** $1.545 |
| **2.** $199 | **4.** $440 | **6.** $685 | **8.** $995 | **10.** $1.250 | **12.** $2.100 |

**4-6 ▶ Un poco de historia.** ¿En qué año ocurren estos eventos históricos? Si no estás seguro/a (*sure*), adivina (*guess*) y tu profesor/a te dirá si ocurrió (*will tell you if it happened*) **antes** o **después** hasta que selecciones el año correcto.

1492   1519   1821   1836   1846   1898   1917   1959

1. México declara su independencia de España.
2. El presidente cubano Fulgencio Batista es derrocado (*toppled*) por Fidel Castro.
3. Los puertorriqueños obtienen la nacionalidad estadounidense.
4. Cristóbal Colón llega a América por primera vez.
5. El emperador azteca, Moctezuma, se somete (*submits*) al conquistador español Hernán Cortés.
6. Texas se independiza de México.
7. Estados Unidos declara la guerra (*war*) a España.
8. Estados Unidos declara la guerra a México.

**4-7 ▶ Tus preferencias.** Cambia (*Change*) las siguientes oraciones para describir tu situación o tus preferencias.

1. Soy de *San Antonio*. La población es de aproximadamente *1.150.000* habitantes.
2. Prefiero vivir en una ciudad *pequeña*, de *no más de 25.000* habitantes.
3. Mi dirección es *calle Mérida, número 257*.
4. Para estudiar en esta universidad los estudiantes pagan más o menos *$3.500* al semestre.
5. Hay más de *15.000* estudiantes en esta universidad.
6. Generalmente, pago entre *$350 y $450* cada semestre por mis libros.
7. Hay muchos estudiantes en mi clase de *historia*. Hay *unos 150*.

**4-8 ▶ Anuncios clasificados.** Contesta las siguientes preguntas sobre estos apartamentos que se alquilan en Puerto Rico.

¿Cuántos dormitorios hay?     ¿Cuál es el número de teléfono?
¿Cuántos baños hay?           ¿Cuánto es el alquiler al mes?

1. Bonito apartamento en el segundo piso. Tres dormitorios, dos baños en excelentes condiciones. El complejo tiene piscina y cancha de tenis. $900 al mes. Teléfono: (787) 640-5823

2. Apartamento agradable y muy céntrico. 1 dormitorio/1 baño. A 5 minutos del centro. $575 al mes. Incluye agua y luz. Teléfono: (939) 644-3499

3. Precioso apartamento, 3 cuartos, 1 baño, cocina, sala, comedor, balcón. Situado en Carolina, cerca de Plaza Carolina. Acceso controlado. Precio mensual: $650. Para más información: (787) 531-7004

4. Apartamento amueblado, 2 dormitorios, 2 baños, terraza. Cerca de la piscina, cancha de tenis y playa. En excelentes condiciones. $1.200 al mes. Teléfono: (787) 864-7667

# 📖 Gramática 2

SAM: 4-10
to 4-13

# Negating: Indefinite and negative words

## Para averiguar

1. What are the opposites of **algo, alguien, alguno, también, y / o,** and **siempre**?
2. When a negative expression follows the verb, what must precede the verb? Is that word needed if another negative word precedes the verb?
3. What happens to **alguno** and **ninguno** before singular, masculine nouns? Do you generally use forms of **ninguno/a** in the plural?

■ Here is a list of the most common indefinite and negative words in Spanish.

| Indefinite | | Negative | |
|---|---|---|---|
| algo | something | nada | nothing, (not) anything |
| alguien, todos | someone, everyone | nadie | nobody, (not) anyone |
| alguno/a(s) | some, any | ninguno/a | none, not any |
| también | also, too | tampoco | neither, not . . . either |
| y, o | and, or | ni . . . ni . . . | neither . . . nor . . . |
| siempre, a veces | always, sometimes | nunca | never |

— ¿Hablas con **alguien**?
— **No** hablo con **nadie**. Es la tele.

— ¿Ves **algo** interesante?

— No, **no** veo **nada** en especial.

— *Are you talking to someone?*
— *I'm not talking with anyone. It's the TV.*

— *Are you watching something interesting?*

— *No, I'm not watching anything in particular.*

■ Unlike English, Spanish has double negatives. When a negative expression is placed after the verb, **no** is inserted before the verb.

**No** salgo **nunca**.        *I never go out.*
**No** hago **nada**.         *I don't do anything.*

■ If any negative expression precedes the verb, **no** is not used.

**Nunca** salgo.            *I never go out.*
**Nunca** hago **nada**.       *I never do anything.*

■ **Alguno** and **ninguno** must agree in number and gender with the nouns they describe. They become **algún** and **ningún** before masculine singular nouns. **Ninguno/a** is generally used in the singular, even as a response to the plural forms **algunos/as**.

¿Hay **algunos** apartamentos disponibles?   *Are there any apartments available?*
No, no hay **ningún** apartamento disponible.  *No, there is not any apartment available.*

■ Use **algún** or **ningún** directly before a singular masculine noun as in the preceding example, but use the form **alguno** or **ninguno** to replace the noun or when separated from it.

No hay **ninguno** disponible.        *There is not any available.*
**Ninguno** de los apartamentos está   *None of the apartments is available.*
  disponible.

**4-9 ▶ En una fiesta.**  Alguien tiene ganas de hablar contigo en una fiesta pero tú no estás interesado/a. Primero, completa sus preguntas con una palabra lógica de la lista. Luego contesta cada pregunta con la expresión negativa que corresponda.

| y | alguna | algún | alguien | o | algo | también |
|---|---|---|---|---|---|---|

Modelo     ¿Te gusta bailar *y* cantar?
           *No, no me gusta ni bailar ni cantar.*

1. ¿Estás solo/a o estás con _____?
2. ¿Tienes hambre? ¿Quieres comer _____? ¿Tienes sed _____?
3. ¿Va a tocar _____ grupo?
4. ¿Prefieres el reggaetón _____ el hip-hop?
5. ¿Quieres escuchar _____ música en especial?

**4-10 ▶ Una fiesta.** ¿Son las descripciones de esta fiesta ciertas o falsas? Corrige (*Correct*) las oraciones falsas.

Modelo    Hay alguna persona en el patio.
          *Falso. No hay ninguna persona en el patio.*

**1.** Algunos amigos salen al patio.
**2.** Alguien llama por teléfono.
**3.** Alguien contesta el teléfono.
**4.** Nadie oye el teléfono.
**5.** El hombre en el sofá habla con alguien.
**6.** Hay regalos para alguien.
**7.** No hay ni un perro ni un gato en la casa.
**8.** Hay algunos niños en la fiesta.
**9.** No hay nada de comer ni de beber en la fiesta.

**4-11 ▶ ¿Es cierto?** ¿Son ciertas o falsas estas oraciones para ti? Para las oraciones ciertas, da (*give*) información más específica. Contradice (*Contradict*) las oraciones falsas.

Modelo    Comparto cuarto con alguien.
          *Cierto. Comparto cuarto con mi esposo/a. | Falso. No comparto cuarto
            con nadie.*

**1.** Vivo con alguien.
**2.** Voy a salir con alguien esta noche.
**3.** Casi siempre hago algo con algún estudiante de la clase de español los fines de semana.
**4.** Voy a estudiar con alguien de la clase de español hoy después de clase y mañana también.
**5.** A veces hablo español con algún amigo o con algún familiar.
**6.** Generalmente, alguien hace algo especial para mi cumpleaños.

**4-12 ▶ En nuestra clase.** En grupos, usen las expresiones indefinidas y negativas para describir a su clase. ¿Qué grupo puede (*can*) formar más oraciones?

Modelo    *Algunos estudiantes no están en clase a veces, pero casi todos estamos en
            clase hoy.*
          *Casi todos los días alguien llega tarde.*
          *Todos trabajamos en grupo con frecuencia.*

# 📖 Vocabulario   Los muebles y los colores

SAM: 4-14
to 4-17

🔊 ¿Qué **muebles** hay en tu cuarto? ¿Está **limpio** o **sucio** tu cuarto? ¿Está **ordenado** o
CD 2 **desordenado?** ¿Está **lleno** de cosas?
Track 4

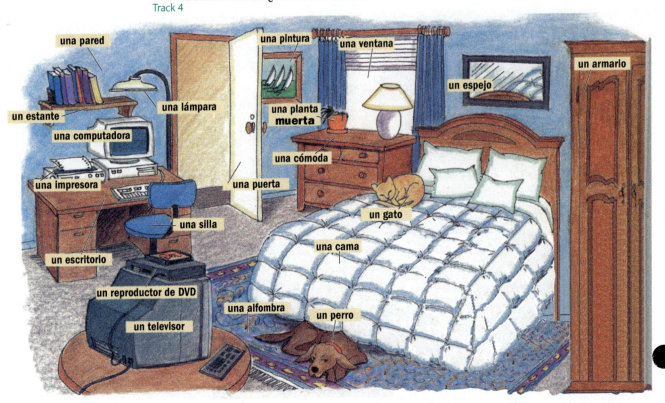

- una pared
- una pintura
- una ventana
- un armario
- un estante
- una lámpara
- un espejo
- una computadora
- una planta **muerta**
- una impresora
- una cómoda
- una puerta
- un gato
- una silla
- una cama
- un escritorio
- un reproductor de DVD
- una alfombra
- un perro
- un televisor

## ¿**Sabías** que...?

En países como México, el alquiler de
los apartamentos en las grandes
ciudades es caro en relación al nivel de
ingresos (*income level*) de las personas.
Por eso, es muy común para los
estudiantes alquilar un cuarto y no un
apartamento completo. En la mayoría
de los casos los cuartos se alquilan
amueblados (*furnished*), y las personas
que alquilan un cuarto tienen un baño
individual y una cocina común. Es una
buena solución para las personas que
buscan o necesitan independizarse sin
gastar mucho dinero.

¿De qué color es tu cuarto / tu sala?

- negro/a
- amarillo/a
- blanco/a
- verde
- marrón (café)
- azul
- beige
- rojo/a
- gris
- anaranjado/a
- rosado/a (rosa)
- morado/a

---

**los muebles** *furniture*   **limpio/a** *clean*   **sucio/a** *dirty*   **ordenado/a** *neat, tidy*   **desordenado/a** *messy*
**lleno/a** *full*   **muerto/a** *dead*

Track 5

**Una conversación.** Dos amigos, Paco y Juan, hablan del compañero de casa de uno de ellos.

PACO: ¿Vives con alguien o vives solo?

JUAN: Vivo con mi compañero de casa, Mario.

PACO: ¿Te gusta vivir con él?

JUAN: Sí y no. Es simpático, pero a veces no tiene **dinero** para pagar el alquiler y es una persona un poco desordenada. Su cuarto siempre está sucio. **Deja** su ropa en **el suelo** y hay papeles y libros **por todos lados**.

PACO: ¿Limpias la casa más que él?

JUAN: Sí, mi cuarto siempre está limpio y ordenado.

PACO: ¿Comparten ustedes baño o tienes tu **propio** baño?

JUAN: **Desafortunadamente**, tenemos que usar el mismo baño.

CD 2, Track 6

## ¡A escuchar!

Ahora, escuchen otra conversación en la cual una estudiante habla de su casa y de sus compañeras. ¿Cuánto paga al mes y cómo son sus compañeras de casa? ¿Hay problemas con ellas?

**4-13 ▶ Los colores.** ¿De qué color(es) son las siguientes cosas?

Modelo    la casa del presidente de Estados Unidos
*Es blanca.*

1. las paredes de tu cuarto
2. las paredes de tu sala
3. la alfombra de tu sala
4. tu cama
5. tu sofá
6. tu coche
7. las plantas
8. las plantas muertas
9. tu ropa hoy

**4-14 ▶ ¿De quién?** ¿Son estas pertenencias (*belongings*) de Juan, de Mario o de los dos?

el cuarto de Juan

el cuarto de Mario

Modelo    Su alfombra es azul.
*La alfombra de Juan es azul.*

1. Su cuarto está ordenado.
2. Sus paredes son blancas.
3. Su escritorio está desordenado.
4. Su ropa está en el suelo.
5. Sus gatos están en su cuarto.
6. No hay pinturas en sus paredes.
7. Todos sus libros están en el estante.
8. Hay una lámpara al lado de su cama.
9. No hay nada encima de su cama.
10. La puerta de su armario está abierta.

**4-15 ▶ Otra conversación.** En parejas, lean otra vez *Una conversación* entre Juan y Paco. Luego, cambien la conversación para hablar de la situación de uno/a de ustedes.

---

**el dinero** *money*   **dejar** *to leave*   **el suelo** *the ground, the floor*   **por todos lados** *everywhere*   **propio/a** *own*   **desafortunadamente** *unfortunately*

# 📖 Gramática 1    Describing: Using *ser* and *estar*

SAM: 4-18
to 4-21

Para **averiguar**

1. What are two uses of **estar**?
2. What are five uses of **ser**?
3. What types of adjectives do you use with **ser** to describe someone or something? What types of adjectives do you use with **estar**? What are some adjectives that can change meaning, depending on whether they are used with **ser** or **estar**?
4. In English, how would you translate **¿Cómo están tus padres?** How would you translate **¿Cómo son tus padres?**

■ Although **ser** and **estar** both mean *to be*, the two verbs are not interchangeable.

Use **estar**:

1) to describe changeable conditions, physical states, or current status with adjectives.
— **¿Está** limpio o sucio tu cuarto?
— Mi cuarto casi siempre **está** desordenado.

2) to say where or with whom someone or something is.
— ¿Dónde **está** tu compañero de casa?
— **Está** en el patio con sus amigos.

Use **ser**:

1) to describe general traits or characteristics with adjectives.
— ¿Cómo **es** la residencia donde vives?
— **Es** agradable y mi compañero de cuarto **es** simpático.

2) to say where someone is from.
— ¿De dónde **es** tu compañero de cuarto?
— **Es** de Puerto Rico.

3) to identify people and things or describe them using a noun.
— ¿Quién **es** ese muchacho?
— **Es** mi vecino. **Es** un buen amigo.

4) to talk about time.
— Mis clases **son** a las diez y a la una.

5) to say *It's (good / bad / important . . . )* when making generalizations.
— **Es** importante pagar el alquiler a tiempo.

■ Here are the adjectives you have seen that are used with **estar**.

| | | |
|---|---|---|
| **abierto/a** *open* | **enfermo/a** *sick, ill* | **nervioso/a** *nervous* |
| **aburrido/a** *bored* | **enojado/a** *angry* | **ocupado/a** *busy* |
| **cansado/a** *tired* | **juntos/as** *together* | **ordenado/a** *neat, tidy* |
| **casado/a** *married* | **limpio/a** *clean* | **solo/a** *alone* |
| **confundido/a** *confused* | **listo/a** *ready* | **sorprendido/a** *surprised* |
| **contento/a** *glad, happy* | **lleno/a** *full* | **sucio/a** *dirty* |
| **desordenado/a** *messy* | **molesto/a** *upset, bothered* | **triste** *sad* |
| **divorciado/a** *divorced* | **muerto/a** *dead* | |

■ Some adjectives can be used with either **ser** or **estar**, but have different meanings with each verb. Compare the uses of **ser** and **estar** below and in the sentences that follow.

| | | | |
|---|---|---|---|
| **estar aburrido/a** | *to be bored* | **ser aburrido/a** | *to be boring* |
| **estar listo/a** | *to be ready* | **ser listo/a** | *to be smart, clever* |

| | | |
|---|---|---|
| Tu novia **está** bonita. | *Your girlfriend is / looks pretty.* | (on a specific occasion) |
| Tu novia **es** bonita. | *Your girlfriend is pretty.* | (in general) |

■ Also compare their use in the following questions.

| | |
|---|---|
| ¿Cómo **está** tu padre? | *How is your father doing?* |
| ¿Cómo **es** tu padre? | *What is your father like?* |

**4-16 ▶ Mi casa.** Un joven habla de su casa y su familia. ¿Se usa **ser** o **estar** en las siguientes oraciones?

Mi casa (1) _____ (es / está) en las afueras y (2) _____ (es / está) muy bonita. Tengo una familia grande y cuando todos (3) _____ (somos / estamos) juntos en la casa, hay nueve personas. Comparto cuarto con mi hermano mayor y nuestro dormitorio siempre (4) _____ (es / está) desordenado. Mi hermano (5) _____ (es / está) muy perezoso y su ropa siempre (6) _____ (es / está) en el suelo y sus cosas (7) _____ (son /están) por todos lados. (8) _____ (Es / Está) difícil (9) _____ (ser / estar) en el cuarto con mi hermano todo el tiempo porque nunca (10) _____ (es / está) contento. (11) _____ (Es / Está) una persona muy temperamental y siempre (12) _____ (es / está) molesto por algo. Por eso, generalmente (13) _____ (soy / estoy) en la sala. Nuestra sala (14) _____ (es / está) muy grande y agradable y siempre (15) _____ (es / está) limpia. Mis padres (16) _____ (son / están) muy trabajadores y limpian la sala y la cocina todos los días. (17) _____ (Es / Está) bueno tener padres como ellos.

**4-17 ▶ Descripciones.** El muchacho de la actividad anterior contesta preguntas acerca de (*about*) su hermano. Completa las siguientes preguntas con la forma correcta del verbo **ser** o **estar.** Luego, contesta las preguntas según (*according to*) la ilustración.

Modelo    ¿Quién *es*? ¿Tu hermano o tu hermana?
          *Es mi hermano.*

**1.** ¿Cómo _____? ¿Moreno o rubio? ¿Guapo o feo?
**2.** ¿_____ joven or viejo?
**3.** ¿Dónde _____? ¿En casa? ¿En clase? ¿En el trabajo?
**4.** ¿Con quién _____? ¿Con sus amigos? ¿Solo?
**5.** ¿Cómo _____? ¿Contento de estar solo? ¿Molesto? ¿Aburrido?
**6.** ¿_____ ocupado?
**7.** ¿_____ en la sala o en su cuarto?
**8.** ¿De qué color _____ el sillón (*armchair*)?

**4-18 ▶ Entrevista.** Completa las siguientes preguntas con la forma correcta del verbo **ser** o **estar.**

**1.** ¿_____ (tú) muy cansado/a los fines de semana? ¿_____ (tú) muy ocupado/a los fines de semana? ¿Dónde _____ (tú) generalmente los sábados por la noche? ¿en casa? ¿con los amigos? ¿Cuál _____ tu día de la semana favorito?
**2.** ¿Quién _____ tu mejor amigo/a? ¿De dónde _____ (él/ella)? ¿_____ estudiante? ¿_____ ustedes muy parecidos/as (*alike*)?¿_____ (Uds.) juntos/as con frecuencia? ¿Dónde _____ el apartamento / la casa de tu mejor amigo/a? Generalmente, ¿_____ limpio/a o sucio/a su apartamento / casa?
**3.** ¿Cuál _____ tu restaurante favorito? ¿_____ cerca de aquí? ¿En qué calle _____? ¿_____ un restaurante mexicano? ¿Cuándo _____ abierto?

**¿Y tú?** Entrevista a un/a compañero/a de clase con las preguntas anteriores.

# 📖 Gramática 2    Making comparisons: Comparatives

SAM: 4-22
to 4-26

SAM: 4-22
to 4-26

## Para averiguar

1. How can **más . . . que** and **menos . . . que** be translated in English?
2. What does **tan . . . como** mean? And **tanto . . . como**? When does **tanto** change forms?
3. What are four adjectives and two adverbs with irregular comparatives?

■ Use the following expressions to compare people or things.

| | |
|---|---|
| **más . . . que** | *more . . . than, -er . . . than* |
| **menos . . . que** | *less . . . than, fewer . . . than* |
| **tan . . . como** | *as . . . as* |
| **tanto/a/os/as . . . como** | *as much . . . as, as many . . . as* |

| | |
|---|---|
| Tu baño es **más** grande **que** mi cocina. | *Your bathroom is bigger than my kitchen.* |
| Paso **menos** tiempo en casa **que** tú. | *I spend less time at home than you.* |
| Mi apartamento es **tan** grande **como** tu casa. | *My apartment is as big as your house.* |
| Limpio **tanto como** tú. | *I clean as much as you.* |

■ The following adjectives and adverbs have irregular comparatives and do not use **más**.

| | | | |
|---|---|---|---|
| **bueno/a** | *good* | **mejor** | *better* |
| **bien** | *well* | | |
| **malo/a** | *bad* | **peor** | *worse* |
| **mal** | *badly* | | |
| **joven** | *young* | **menor** | *younger* |
| **viejo/a** | *old* | **mayor** | *older* |

| | |
|---|---|
| Mi hermana **mayor** cocina **mejor** que yo. | *My older sister cooks better than I do.* |

■ **Tanto** (*as much, as many*) can be an adjective or an adverb. As an adjective, it must agree in number and gender with the noun that follows. As an adverb, it always ends with **-o**.

ADJECTIVE:   Tengo **tantas** ventanas en mi cuarto **como** tú.
*I have as many windows in my room as you.*

ADVERB:   Cocino **tanto como** tú.
*I cook as much as you do.*

**4-19** ▶ **Comparaciones.** ¿Estás de acuerdo (*Do you agree*) con las siguientes oraciones? Cambia cada oración si es necesario para expresar tu opinión.

Modelo    Los coches rojos son tan bonitos como los coches azules.
*Estoy de acuerdo. Los coches rojos son tan bonitos como los coches azules. / No estoy de acuerdo. Los coches rojos son más (menos) bonitos que los coches azules.*

1. Generalmente, un sofá es tan caro como un coche.
2. Para mí, las paredes amarillas son tan bonitas como las paredes rosadas.
3. Los gatos son tan inteligentes como los perros.
4. Generalmente, los apartamentos son tan caros como las casas.
5. Un televisor es tan útil (*useful*) como una computadora.
6. El precio (*price*) de una casa nueva es tan importante como el barrio.
7. Las ciudades grandes son tan interesantes como el campo.
8. Generalmente, el centro de la ciudad es tan tranquilo como las afueras.

**4-20 ▶ ¿En la ciudad o en el campo?** ¿Prefieres vivir en el centro de una ciudad, en las afueras o en el campo? En grupos, preparen comparaciones de los tres ambientes (*environments*). Pueden (*You can*) usar las ideas de la lista o sus propias ideas.

| | | |
|---|---|---|
| actividades al aire libre | jardines grandes | restaurantes |
| actividades culturales | oportunidades de | tráfico |
| árboles | empleo (*employment*) | tranquilidad |
| casas | plantas | . . . |
| gente | problemas | |

Modelo   *Hay menos tráfico en las afueras de una ciudad que en el centro, pero hay más tráfico que en el campo.*

**4-21 ▶ Comparaciones culturales.** El estilo de vida (*lifestyle*) urbano es bastante diferente entre las ciudades hispanas y las norteamericanas. Lee la siguiente información y contesta las preguntas, utilizando las estructuras para expresar comparación en español.

**1.** El metro (*subway*) de Madrid y de la ciudad de México son modelos de transporte público que millones de personas usan todos los días. En la ciudad de México no está permitido circular en coche todos los días para prevenir el aumento de la contaminación (*pollution*). ¿Crees que tanta gente tiene coche en México o España como en Estados Unidos? ¿Crees que la gente usa más el transporte público que en Estados Unidos?

**2.** La concentración mayor (*major*) de población en las ciudades hispanas está en los centros urbanos y no en las afueras. Y en Estados Unidos, ¿viven tantas personas en el centro de la ciudad como en las afueras?

**3.** La casa típica del centro de una ciudad hispana no tiene jardín ni piscina. Generalmente, ¿tienen jardín las casas en Estados Unidos? ¿Son las casas del centro tan grandes como las casas de las afueras en las ciudades norteamericanas?

**4.** En general, las ciudades tienen muchas zonas verdes, como parques y bosques (*wooded areas*). Son famosos el Parque del Retiro en Madrid y el Bosque de Chapultepec en México DF. La gente pasa mucho tiempo fuera de casa, al aire libre o de paseo (*strolling*) por las calles con la familia y los amigos. En Estados Unidos, ¿pasa la gente tanto tiempo fuera de casa como en los países hispanos?

El Parque del Retiro en Madrid, España.

# 📖 **Vocabulario**  Más actividades diarias

SAM: 4-27
to 4-28

## ¡**Ojo**!

Although the verb **almorzar** means *to eat* lunch in most Spanish-speaking areas, Mexican speakers often use it to refer to a late breakfast.

🔊 CD 2 Track 7  ¿Qué quieres hacer mañana por la mañana?

dormir hasta tarde

**desayunar** en casa / **empezar** el día con un buen desayuno

¿Qué prefieres hacer por la tarde?

**almorzar** en el parque

jugar a los videojuegos

¿Por la noche vas a . . . ?

**cenar** con unos amigos

**volver temprano** a casa después de cenar

🔊 CD 2, Track 9

## ¡A **escuchar**!

Ahora, escuchen otra conversación en la cual dos amigas hablan por teléfono de sus planes para esta tarde. ¿Qué van a hacer juntas? ¿A qué hora y dónde?

🔊 CD 2 Track 8

**Una conversación.** Dos amigos hacen planes para este fin de semana.

ESTELA: Manuel, ¿quieres jugar al tenis conmigo este viernes por la noche?

MANUEL: **Lo siento, no puedo** este viernes. Tengo que trabajar.

ESTELA: ¿Puedes jugar el sábado?

MANUEL: No sé. **Vuelvo a** trabajar el sábado por la tarde. ¿A qué hora quieres jugar?

ESTELA: ¿A qué hora vas a volver del trabajo?

MANUEL: A las seis.

ESTELA: Entonces, ¿a las siete o las siete y media en el parque?

MANUEL: Puedo jugar a las siete.

---

**desayunar** *to eat / have breakfast*   **empezar** *to begin, to start*   **almorzar** *to eat / have lunch*
**cenar** *to eat / have dinner*   **volver** *to return*   **temprano** *early*   **Lo siento.** *I'm sorry.*   **no puedo** *I can't*
**vuelvo a** (+ infinitive) *I (verb) again*

**4-22 ▶ Mañana.** Cambia las palabras en letra cursiva para describir tus planes para mañana.

1. Mañana, voy a dormir hasta *las nueve*.
2. Voy a dormir *seis o siete horas*.
3. Voy a desayunar *en The Golden Omelet*.
4. Voy a almorzar *con mi novio*.
5. Por la tarde, voy a *ir al parque y voy a jugar al tenis*.
6. Voy a volver a casa *a las cinco y media*.
7. Voy a cenar *en casa a las siete y media*.
8. Después de cenar, voy a *jugar a los videojuegos*.

**4-23 ▶ Excusas.** Utiliza el primer grupo de expresiones para invitar a un/a compañero/a de clase a hacer algo contigo esta noche, mañana y el domingo por la tarde. Tu compañero/a debe dar excusas, utilizando el segundo grupo de expresiones.

Modelo    E1: *¿Quieres volver a la biblioteca esta noche para estudiar conmigo?*
E2: *No puedo esta noche. Tengo que lavar la ropa.*
E1: *¿Puedes practicar español conmigo mañana por la mañana?*
E2: *Lo siento . . .*

**Invitaciones**

¿Quieres . . . conmigo?
¿Puedes . . . ?
¿Tienes ganas de . . . ?
¿Te gustaría . . . ?

| | | |
|---|---|---|
| cenar | desayunar | volver a la |
| jugar a los | ir al cine | biblioteca |
| videojuegos | tomar algo | para estudiar |
| almorzar | practicar español | . . . |

**Excusas**

No puedo. Tengo que . . .
Lo siento. Necesito . . .
Lo siento. No tengo
   ganas, prefiero . . .

| | |
|---|---|
| trabajar | volver a casa |
| ir a clase | ir al supermercado |
| dormir la siesta | cenar con mi hermano |
| estudiar | descansar |
| ir a la casa de . . . | lavar (*to wash*) la ropa |
| limpiar la casa | . . . |

**4-24 ▶ Entrevista.** Entrevista a un/a compañero/a de clase con estas preguntas.

1. ¿Qué días puedes dormir hasta tarde? ¿Hasta qué hora prefieres dormir los sábados? ¿Cuántas horas necesitas dormir para no estar cansado/a al día siguiente? ¿Tienes sueño a veces en tus clases?
2. ¿Desayunas todos los días? ¿Desayunas en un restaurante con frecuencia? Generalmente, ¿desayunas con alguien o desayunas solo/a? ¿Cuál es el mejor restaurante para desayunar cerca de la universidad? ¿Desayunas en la cama a veces? ¿Tienes hambre por la mañana si no desayunas o no necesitas desayunar?
3. ¿A qué hora prefieres almorzar? Generalmente, ¿traes comida para almorzar en la universidad? ¿Puedes volver a tu casa para almorzar? ¿Te gusta almorzar a veces en el parque? ¿Te gusta almorzar a veces en el patio de tu casa?
4. ¿Cenas temprano o tarde generalmente? Generalmente en casa, ¿cenas en el comedor, en la cocina o enfrente de la tele? ¿En qué restaurante cenas con más frecuencia? ¿Prefieres desayunar, almorzar o cenar en un restaurante? ¿Dónde vas a cenar esta noche?

**4-25 ▶ Otra conversación.** En parejas, lean otra vez *Una conversación* entre Estela y Manuel. Luego, preparen una conversación en la cual ustedes hacen planes para cenar, almorzar o desayunar juntos/as.

# 📖 Gramática 1

SAM: 4-29 to 4-31

## Talking about daily activities: Stem-changing verbs

### Para averiguar

1. In stem-changing verbs, **e** becomes **ie** or **i**, and **o** becomes **ue** in all forms except two. Which are they?
2. **Decir** has an irregular form for **yo**. What is it?
3. Both **decir** and **contar** can mean *to tell*. When do you use each one?
4. What do **pensar** and **volver** mean when they are followed by an infinitive?
5. What preposition do you insert before infinitives after **volver** or **empezar**?

■ Some verbs have vowel changes in the stem when they are conjugated in the present tense. The last **e** of the stem becomes **ie** or **i**, and the last **o** of the stem becomes **ue** in all of the forms except **nosotros** and **vosotros**.

**empezar (e → ie)** *(to begin)*

| | | | |
|---|---|---|---|
| yo | empi**e**zo | nosotros/as | empezamos |
| tú | empi**e**zas | vosotros/as | empezáis |
| Ud., él, ella | empi**e**za | Uds., ellos/as | empi**e**zan |

**poder (o → ue)** *(to be able, can, may)*

| | | | |
|---|---|---|---|
| yo | p**ue**do | nosotros/as | podemos |
| tú | p**ue**des | vosotros/as | podéis |
| Ud., él, ella | p**ue**de | Uds., ellos/as | p**ue**den |

**pedir (e → i)** *(to ask for, to order)*

| | | | |
|---|---|---|---|
| yo | p**i**do | nosotros/as | pedimos |
| tú | p**i**des | vosotros/as | pedís |
| Ud., él, ella | p**i**de | Uds., ellos/as | p**i**den |

Other verbs that follow these patterns are:

| e → ie | | o (u) → ue | | e → i | |
|---|---|---|---|---|---|
| cerrar | *to close* | almorzar | *to eat lunch* | decir | *to say, to tell* |
| entender | *to understand* | contar | *to count, to tell* | repetir | *to repeat* |
| pensar (en) | *to think (about)* | dormir | *to sleep* | servir | *to serve* |
| perder | *to lose, to miss* | encontrar | *to find* | | |
| preferir | *to prefer* | jugar (u → ue) | *to play* | | |
| querer | *to want* | recordar | *to remember* | | |
| | | volver | *to return* | | |

### ¡Ojo!

**Jugar** is the only verb where **u** becomes **ue**. You may hear some Spanish speakers say **Juego tenis** instead of **Juego al tenis**. Note that both forms are accepted.

■ **Decir** has an irregular form for **yo** (**yo digo** *I say*). Use **decir** for *to tell* when telling a piece of information, but **contar** when recounting a story (**una historia**) or telling a joke (**un chiste**). **Contar con** also means *to count on*.

| | |
|---|---|
| Siempre **digo** la verdad. | *I always tell the truth.* |
| Mi padre siempre **cuenta** chistes. | *My father always tells jokes.* |

■ Use **pensar** followed by an infinitive to say what you *intend* or *plan to do*. **Volver** is used with infinitives to say one redoes something or does something again. Use the preposition **a** before infinitives after **volver**, and also after **empezar** when saying what someone is beginning to do.

| | |
|---|---|
| **Pienso** estudiar francés también. | *I intend to study French too.* |
| **Vuelvo a** leer las preguntas. | *I reread the questions.* |
| **Empiezo a** entender. | *I'm beginning to understand.* |

**4-26 ▶ ¿Sí o no?** Explica si en la clase de español las siguientes personas hacen cada actividad entre paréntesis.

**Modelo**    Yo . . . (encontrar los exámenes de español difíciles)
*Yo (no) encuentro los exámenes de español difíciles.*

1. Yo . . . (dormir en clase, entender bien, recordar todo el vocabulario, querer más tarea, pensar en español)
2. El/La profesor/a . . . (decir muchas cosas en español, preferir hablar español, repetir mucho, querer buenos estudiantes, recordar mi nombre)
3. Nosotros . . . (poder hacer preguntas en inglés, volver a clase mañana, querer exámenes más difíciles, repetir muchas palabras)

**4-27 ▶ ¡Yo también!** Dos amigos describen su rutina diaria (*daily*). ¿Haces lo mismo que ellos? Cambia la forma del verbo y las palabras en letra cursiva (si es necesario) para describir lo que tú haces.

Modelo    Dormimos hasta *las nueve todos los días.*
          *Yo también duermo hasta las nueve todos los días. |*
          *Yo duermo hasta las seis y media o las siete todos los días.*

1. Por lo general, almorzamos *en McDonalds.*
2. Jugamos al tenis *todos los días.*
3. Hoy volvemos a casa a *las tres de la tarde.*
4. Generalmente, empezamos nuestra tarea a *las cuatro y media de la tarde.*
5. Preferimos cenar a *las ocho o las nueve.*
6. Pedimos una pizza *dos o tres veces a la semana.*
7. Dormimos *nueve* horas todas las noches.
8. Repetimos la misma rutina *de lunes a viernes, pero podemos hacer otras cosas los fines de semana.*

**4-28 ▶ En mi familia.** Usa uno de los verbos de la página anterior con cada expresión para describir quiénes en tu familia hacen estas cosas.

Modelo    **a.** muy tarde
          *A veces todos volvemos muy tarde a casa.*
          **b.** primero
          *Mi padre vuelve primero a casa.*
          **c.** antes de las tres
          *Nadie de mi familia vuelve a casa antes de las tres.*

1. **a.** hasta tarde
   **b.** poco
   **c.** más

2. **a.** en el trabajo
   **b.** en la universidad
   **c.** solo/a

3. **a.** bien
   **b.** todos los días
   **c.** a veces

**4-29 ▶ Entrevista.** Entrevista a un/a compañero/a de clase con estas preguntas.

1. ¿Prefieres almorzar en casa, en un restaurante o en la cafetería? ¿A qué hora almuerzas? ¿Duermes la siesta a veces después de almorzar?
2. ¿Juegas al tenis? ¿al fútbol? ¿al básquetbol? ¿a los videojuegos? ¿Con quién juegas? ¿Quién pierde generalmente? ¿Pierdes la paciencia a veces cuando juegas?
3. ¿A qué hora vuelves hoy a casa? ¿Dónde piensas cenar esta noche? ¿Qué quieres hacer después de la cena? ¿Vuelves a la universidad mañana?

## 📖 Gramática 2    Describing how you do things: Adverbs

SAM: 4-32
to 4-34

### Para averiguar

1. What ending do you use to form an adverb from an adjective in Spanish? Do you attach this ending to the masculine or feminine form of the adjective?
2. As a general rule, where do you place adverbs with respect to verbs they modify? Where do you place them if they modify a whole sentence? And if the adverbs modify an adjective?

■ Adverbs are used to say *how, where, when,* or *how much* someone does something. Just as adverbs can be formed from adjectives in English by adding the ending *-ly* (*perfect > perfectly, easy > easily*), adverbs are formed from adjectives in Spanish by adding the ending **-mente** to the end of the feminine form of the adjective. If an adjective has a written accent mark, it will be maintained on the adverb.

lógico/a → lógica**mente**
independiente → independiente**mente**
fácil → fácil**mente**

■ As a general rule, adverbs are placed just after a verb they modify.

| | |
|---|---|
| Limpio **constantemente** la casa. | *I clean the house constantly.* |
| Vuelvo **tarde** a casa los sábados. | *I return home late on Saturdays.* |

■ Adverbs may also modify adjectives or other adverbs. In that case, adverbs are placed before the adjective or other adverb that they modify.

| | |
|---|---|
| Tienes una casa **perfectamente** situada. | *You have a perfectly situated house.* |
| Juego **muy** mal al tenis. | *I play tennis very badly.* |

**4-30 ▶ En casa.** Completa cada oración con el adverbio formado del adjetivo entre paréntesis e indica si la oración te describe a ti (*describes you*).

Modelo    Duermo hasta tarde los sábados. (frecuente)
*Sí, duermo frecuentemente hasta tarde los sábados. /*
*No, no duermo frecuentemente hasta tarde los sábados.*

1. Por lo general, duermo hasta las siete. (tranquilo/a)
2. Desayuno. (regular)
3. Juego a los videojuegos. (excesivo/a)
4. Vuelvo más tarde a casa los fines de semana. (considerable)
5. Limpio la casa al menos una vez a la semana. (completo/a)
6. Pienso en mis problemas. (constante)
7. Entiendo todos los problemas de mi mejor amigo/a. (perfecto/a)
8. Pierdo la paciencia con la gente. (fácil)

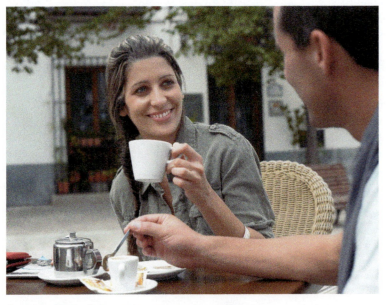

Generalmente, ¿desayunas en casa o en un café?

**4-31 ▶ Un/a buen/a compañero/a de cuarto.** Completa las siguientes oraciones lógicamente con los adverbios entre paréntesis para describir un/a buen/a compañero/a de cuarto.

Modelo    Escucha cuando hablo de problemas entre nosotros/as. No contesta sin escuchar. (rápidamente, pacientemente)
*Escucha pacientemente cuando hablo de problemas entre nosotros/as. No contesta rápidamente sin escuchar.*

1. Siempre reacciona (*reacts*) cuando hay problemas. Nunca reacciona sin pensar en lo que hace. (tranquilamente, emocionalmente)
2. Comparte el trabajo de la casa. No deja sus cosas por todos lados. (perezosamente, voluntariamente)
3. Siempre cumple (*keeps, carries out*) con su palabra. Nunca promete (*promises*) cosas que no va a cumplir. (falsamente, completamente)
4. Respeta la privacidad. No habla de mis problemas personales con todo el mundo (*everyone*). (consideradamente, públicamente)
5. No bebe en casa. Sólo bebe de vez en cuando. (socialmente, excesivamente)

**4-32 ▶ Comparaciones culturales.** Lee con atención el siguiente texto sobre la situación de muchos jóvenes en España y Latinoamérica.

En España y otros países de Latinoamérica, es realmente difícil encontrar un trabajo con un buen salario después de la universidad, y los padres hispanos entienden que deben mantener[1] a sus hijos. Por eso, los jóvenes viven en casa generalmente hasta los veinticinco o treinta años.

La dinámica familiar también es menos tradicional que en el pasado. Los padres son más permisivos, y los hijos respetan las normas familiares consideradamente. Así, padres e hijos conviven[2] armoniosamente en la casa de los padres.

A muchos jóvenes les gustaría independizarse[3] de sus padres después de terminar la universidad, pero viven en la casa de sus padres para ahorrar[4] un poco de dinero, y para poder después casarse[5] y comprar una casa.

[1]*support*  [2]*live together*  [3]*to become independent*  [4]*to save*  [5]*to get married*

Ahora, compara esta información con la situación de la gente joven donde vives. Utiliza **más . . . que, menos . . . que** o **tan . . . como** con el adverbio formado del adjetivo entre paréntesis.

Modelo    Los jóvenes viven. (independiente)
*En muchos países hispanos los jóvenes viven menos independientemente que aquí. | Aquí los jóvenes viven más independientemente que en muchos países hispanos.*

1. Los jóvenes encuentran trabajo. (fácil)
2. Los jóvenes se independizan de sus padres. (rápido)
3. Los jóvenes viven con sus padres. (tranquilo)
4. Los jóvenes ahorran dinero antes de independizarse. (paciente)
5. Los padres mantienen (*support*) a sus hijos. (voluntario)
6. Los padres aceptan la privacidad de sus hijos. (comprensivo)

# 📖 Vocabulario   El barrio y los vecinos

SAM: 4-35
to 4-38

🔊 CD 2
Track 10
¿Prefieres vivir en el centro **animado** de una ciudad donde hay más actividades culturales, pero también hay más gente, tráfico y **ruido?** ¿Te gusta . . .?

## ¿Sabías que...?

Hay una tendencia cada vez más popular en los países hispanos a vivir en las afueras. En muchas ciudades proliferan complejos residenciales muy similares a las zonas suburbanas de Estados Unidos. Muchas personas prefieren vivir allí porque es más seguro para la familia y las casas también son más grandes y más modernas que los apartamentos del centro. Muchos de estos complejos residenciales tienen seguridad (*security*) privada, y todos los servicios básicos: escuelas, supermercados, centros comerciales.

estacionar el coche en un estacionamiento

sacar la basura a la calle

lavar la ropa en una lavandería

usar el transporte público / tomar el autobús al trabajo

esperar en la parada de autobús

¿Prefieres vivir en una casa en las afueras con más espacio para las actividades al aire libre, pero también con más **quehaceres domésticos**? ¿Te gusta . . .?

arreglar cosas que no funcionan

cortar el césped

trabajar en el jardín

pagar **el recibo de la luz** (del agua, del gas)

ir a la escuela en bicicleta

🔊 CD 2, Track 12

## ¡A escuchar!

Ahora, escuchen otra conversación en la cual Daniel encuentra a un amigo, Rafael, que vive en su edificio de apartamentos. ¿Qué aspectos le gustan a Rafael? ¿Cuáles no? ¿En qué apartamento vive cada uno? ¿Cuánto cuesta el alquiler?

🔊 CD 2
Track 11

**Una conversación.** Sara habla de su nuevo barrio con Isabel.

ISABEL: ¿Te gusta tu nueva casa? ¿Cómo es el barrio?

SARA: Me gusta mucho. La calle donde vivo es muy tranquila y el barrio es **seguro** y agradable, pero está lejos de la oficina y la luz y el agua **cuestan** casi trescientos dólares al mes.

ISABEL: Y tus vecinos, ¿cómo son?

SARA: El vecino que vive al lado es muy **hablador** y **chismoso.** Siempre está afuera en el patio y es un poco **ruidoso**. En la casa de enfrente vive una familia **bastante callada**. Los dos niños siempre juegan y **andan** por la calle **en bicicleta**.

---

**animado/a** *lively*   **el ruido** *noise*   **los quehaceres domésticos** *chores*   **arreglar** *to fix, to straighten out* (a problem), *to straighten up* (a room)   **funcionar** *to work* (describing a machine, system, plan)   **el recibo de la luz** *the light bill, the electric bill*   **seguro/a** *safe*   **costar (o > ue)** *to cost*   **hablador/a** *talkative, chatty*   **chismoso/a** *gossipy*   **ruidoso/a** *noisy*   **bastante** *rather, quite*   **callado/a** *quiet*   **andar en bicicleta** *to ride a bicycle*

**4-33 ▶ Vecinos.** Indica si los siguientes adjetivos describen más a los vecinos de Carlos o a los de David.

Modelo   amistosos
*Los vecinos de Carlos son más amistosos que los vecinos de David.*

1. sociables
2. callados
3. habladores
4. tranquilos
5. ruidosos
6. animados
7. aburridos
8. divertidos

**4-34 ▶ ¿En el centro o en las afueras?** Cambia las siguientes comparaciones para expresar tu opinión de la vida (*life*) en una ciudad y en las afueras.

Modelo   Hay tanto tráfico en las afueras como en el centro.
*Hay menos tráfico en las afueras que en el centro.*

1. Cuesta tanto comprar una casa en las afueras como en el centro.
2. Hay tantos edificios de apartamentos en las afueras como en el centro.
3. Hay tanto espacio para estacionar los coches en las afueras como en el centro.
4. El alquiler es tan alto en las afueras como en el centro.
5. Es tan seguro jugar afuera o andar en bicicleta en las afueras como en el centro.
6. Los vecinos son tan chismosos en las afueras como en el centro.

**4-35 ▶ Otra conversación.** En parejas, vuelvan a leer *Una conversación* entre Isabel y Sara. Luego, cambien la conversación para hablar de su barrio.

**4-36 ▶ Comparaciones culturales.** Lee la siguiente información sobre las escuelas en los países hispanos y discute las preguntas con un/a compañero/a.

---

**La educación pública en los países hispanos**

En España y Latinoamérica la educación primaria o educación general básica (5–14 años) es obligatoria y gratuita[1] y la calidad de la educación pública es muy buena. La mayoría de los niños que asisten a escuelas públicas reciben una preparación académica excelente. Las escuelas privadas son generalmente católicas y los estudiantes toman la asignatura[2] de religión además de[3] las otras asignaturas.

Generalmente, cada barrio tiene su propia escuela o colegio público donde los niños completan su educación primaria. Sin embargo, la pobreza[4] que afecta a muchos barrios urbanos o zonas rurales de América Latina hace a muchos niños abandonar la escuela antes de completar su educación primaria. Es el caso de Bolivia, la República Dominicana, El Salvador, Guatemala, Nicaragua y Venezuela donde entre el 40 y el 80 por ciento de los estudiantes dejan de asistir[5] a la escuela antes de completar la educación primaria. Todos los miembros de la familia, incluyendo los niños, tienen que trabajar para sobrevivir[6].

---

[1]*mandatory and free*   [2]*subject*   [3]*besides*   [4]*poverty*   [5]*stop attending*   [6]*to survive*

1. En Estados Unidos, ¿creen que la calidad de la educación pública es mejor o peor que la de la educación privada? ¿Son diferentes las escuelas públicas de las afueras y las de las zonas urbanas?
2. En la educación primaria, ¿creen que el abandono escolar (*school drop-out*) es tan alto en algunos barrios de Estados Unidos como en Bolivia o Guatemala?

#  Resumen de gramática

## Numbers above 100

- Use **cien** for 100 exactly, but **ciento** in 101–199.

- Numbers 200 through 999 agree in gender with the nouns they modify, but **cien / ciento** does not in 100 through 199.

- **Mil** does not change in the plural forms.

- Use **un** in **un millón** (*one million*), but not with **cien / ciento** (*one hundred*) or **mil** (*one thousand*).

- Use **de** before nouns directly after **millón / millones**.

- Do not use **y** (*and*) immediately after the words **cien / ciento, mil,** or **millón**.

- Years are expressed using **mil**, not hundreds.

- Use a period to designate thousands, and a comma for decimals.

| MASCULINE NOUNS | FEMININE NOUNS |
|---|---|
| 100: cien libros | cien páginas |
| 101: ciento un libros | ciento un páginas |
| 200: doscientos libros | doscientas páginas |
| 710: setecientos diez libros | setecientas diez páginas |
| 3.100 tres mil cien | *three thousand one hundred* |
| 1.000 mil | *one thousand* |
| un millón de dólares | *one million dollars* |
| un millón doscientos mil dólares | *one million two hundred thousand dollars* |
| 1999 mil novecientos noventa y nueve | *nineteen ninety-nine* |
| 2011 dos mil once | *twenty eleven* |
| 1.500 mil quinientos | *one thousand five hundred* |
| 3,25 tres coma veinticinco | *three point twenty-five* |

## Indefinite and negative words

- Spanish uses multiple negatives. When the negative expressions **nada, nadie, nunca, ninguno/a, ni,** and **tampoco** are placed after the verb, **no** is inserted before it, unless another negative expression already precedes the verb.

- **Alguno/a** and **ninguno/a** become **algún** and **ningún** directly before masculine singular nouns. **Ninguno/a** is generally used in the singular.

—¿Necesitas **algo** para tu nuevo apartamento?
—No, **no** necesito **nada**.
—¿Tienes **algunos** vecinos antipáticos?
—No, **no** tengo **ningún** vecino así. / No, **no** tengo **ninguno** así. / No, **ninguno** de mis vecinos es antipático.

*Do you need anything for your new apartment?*
*No, I don't need anything.*
*Do you have any unpleasant neighbors?*
*No, I don't have any neighbors like that. / No, I don't have any like that. / No, none of my neighbors is unpleasant.*

## Using ser and estar

Use **estar** to say *to be* when talking about:

1) conditions or current status with adjectives.

2) where or with whom.

Use **ser** to say *to be* when talking about:

1) traits or characteristics with adjectives.

2) where someone / something is from.

3) who or what someone or something is.

4) when.

5) generalized judgements (*It's . . .*).

1) **Estoy** contento/a con mi casa nueva.

2) ¿En qué calle **está?**

1) Mi casa **es** muy agradable.

2) Mis vecinos **son** de Perú.

3) **Son** maestros bilingües.

4) **Es** tarde cuando vuelven.

5) **Es** malo trabajar tanto.

*I am happy with my new house.*

*On what street is it?*

*My house is very pleasant.*

*My neighbors are from Peru.*

*They are bilingual teachers.*

*It's late when they return.*

*It's bad to work so much.*

## Comparatives

- Use the following expressions to make comparisons. As an adjective, **tanto** agrees with nouns for gender and number. As an adverb, it always ends with **-o**.

| | |
|---|---|
| **más . . . que** | more / -er . . . than |
| **menos . . . que** | less / fewer . . . than |
| **tan . . . como** | as . . . as |
| **tanto/a/os/as . . . como** | as much / many . . . as |

- The following comparisons are irregular.

| | |
|---|---|
| **mejor** better | **menor** younger |
| **peor** worse | **mayor** older |

Hay **tantas** bicicletas **como** coches en la calle.
*There are as many bicycles as cars in the street.*

Mi vecina no está afuera **tanto como** yo.
*My neighbor is not outside as much as me.*

Vivo **más** cerca **que** tú.
*I live closer than you.*

Mi apartamento es **menos** caro **que** tu casa.
*My apartment is less expensive than your house.*

El baño es casi **tan** grande **como** la cocina.
*The bathroom is almost as big as the kitchen.*

No pago **tanto como** tú.
*I don't pay as much as you.*

Uno de mis vecinos es **mayor** que yo y el otro es **menor**.
*One of my neighbors is older than me and the other one is younger.*

## Stem-changing verbs

- In the following stem-changing verbs, the last vowel of the stem changes in all forms except **nosotros** and **vosotros**.

- **e > ie** verbs: **cerrar** to close; **empezar (a)** to begin (to); **entender** to understand; **pensar (en)** to think (about); **perder** to lose, to miss; **preferir** to prefer; **querer** to want

- **o > ue** verbs: **almorzar** to eat lunch; **contar (con)** to count (on), to tell (stories, jokes); **dormir** to sleep; **encontrar** to find; **jugar (u > ue)** to play; **poder** can, may, to be able; **recordar** to remember; **volver (a)** to return (to), to . . . again

- **e > i** verbs: **decir (yo digo)** to say, to tell (information); **pedir** to ask for, to order; **repetir** to repeat; **servir** to serve

### empezar (e → ie) *(to begin)*

| | | | |
|---|---|---|---|
| yo | empiezo | nosotros/as | empezamos |
| tú | empiezas | vosotros/as | empezáis |
| Ud., él, ella | empieza | Uds., ellos/as | empiezan |

### poder (o → ue) *(to be able, can, may)*

| | | | |
|---|---|---|---|
| yo | puedo | nosotros/as | podemos |
| tú | puedes | vosotros/as | podéis |
| Ud., él, ella | puede | Uds., ellos/as | pueden |

### pedir (e → i) *(to ask for, to order)*

| | | | |
|---|---|---|---|
| yo | pido | nosotros/as | pedimos |
| tú | pides | vosotros/as | pedís |
| Ud., él, ella | pide | Uds., ellos/as | piden |

Mi vecino no **dice** mucho, pero **empieza** a hablar más.
*My neighbor doesn't say much, but he's starting to talk more.*

Su esposa siempre **cuenta** chistes.
*His wife always tells jokes.*

**Empezamos** a pasar más tiempo juntos.
*We are starting to spend more time together.*

A veces ceno con él el viernes, y luego **vuelvo** a cenar con él el sábado.
*Sometimes I have dinner with him on Friday, and then I have dinner with him again on Saturday.*

## Adverbs

- Add **-mente** (*-ly*) to the end of the feminine form of adjectives to turn them into adverbs, maintaining any accent marks from the adjectives.

discreto/a → discretamente
emocional → emocionalmente

*discreet → discreetly*
*emotional → emotionally*

- As a general rule, place adverbs just after verbs or before adjectives or other adverbs they modify.

Tengo una vecina chismosa que habla **constantemente**.
*I have a gossipy neighbor who is constantly talking.*

Está **completamente** loca.
*She's completely crazy.*

SAM: 4-45 to 4-49

**EN UNA AGENCIA DE BIENES RAÍCES**

En este capítulo, aprendiste (*you learned*) a hablar de la casa y el barrio. Ahora vas a repasar lo que aprendiste con una simulación de la vida real trabajando como agente de bienes raíces (*real estate agent*) con clientes hispanos.

**4-37 ▸ Se vende.** Lee los siguientes anuncios de casas. ¿Cuál es el precio (*price*) de cada una? ¿De cuántos pies cuadrados (*square feet*) es cada una? ¿Cuáles son los números de teléfono?

| *La Mejor Revista Inmobiliaria* | *Verano* \| **VENTA CASA 21** 87 |
|---|---|

**1. VENTA CASA. Se vende casa parcialmente renovada** con 3 cuartos, 2 baños, sala y comedor. La casa tiene 1.084 pies cuadrados y el patio aproximadamente 1.900. Necesita reparaciones generales. No pierda esta oportunidad de vivir prácticamente en el centro del área metropolitana cerca de centros comerciales, restaurantes, escuelas, etc. con mucho terreno. Llamar al 990-7565, 990-4567, 635-2912. Precio: $211.500,00.

**2. Casa de 2.280 pies cuadrados** localizada en las afueras, 4 dormitorios, clóset grande en cuarto matrimonial, 2 baños, cocina recientemente renovada, sala, comedor, balcón y garaje para dos autos. $175.000 o mejor oferta, venta por dueños. Para más información o para visitar la propiedad, llamar al 793-7989 ó 545-5404.

**3. Casa céntricamente localizada** de 1.600 pies cuadrados y de reciente construcción, 3 cuartos y un baño, 2 cuartos con aire acondicionado y sistema de purificación por ósmosis. Relativamente cerca de centros comerciales, hospitales y campo de golf. Todo por $165.000,00. Para más información, llamar al 223-2992 ó 214-1112.

**4-38 ▸ Comparaciones.** En grupos, preparen por lo menos cinco comparaciones entre las casas de los anuncios anteriores.

Modelo   *La casa número uno tiene menos dormitorios que la casa dos, pero tiene tantos dormitorios como la casa tres.*

**4-39 ▸ En otras palabras.** Vuelve a leer los anuncios y haz (*make*) una lista de todos los adverbios con la terminación **-mente**.

**4-40 ▸ Este barrio.** Completa esta descripción de un barrio donde se vende una casa. Utiliza **hay** o formas de **ser** o **estar**.

Las casas (1) _____ nuevas y las calles (2) _____ limpias. (3) _____ un barrio seguro y las escuelas (4) _____ buenas. El barrio (5) _____ cerca de la universidad y las calles (6) _____ llenas de coches los días de clase, pero no (7) _____ mucho tráfico los fines de semana. (8) _____ muchos restaurantes y (9) _____ abiertos hasta tarde.

**4-41 ▶ Algunas preguntas.** Una familia piensa comprar una casa en el barrio donde vives. Completa cada pregunta con la forma correcta del verbo lógico entre paréntesis.

1. ¿ _____ jugar los niños afuera en la calle o en los parques sin problema? ¿ _____ muchos niños afuera? ¿ _____ a veces vagabundos (*vagrants*) en los parques? (jugar, dormir, poder)
2. ¿ _____ los autobuses el barrio? ¿A qué hora _____ a circular los autobuses? ¿Cuánto _____ el autobús? (costar, servir, empezar)
3. Generalmente, ¿ _____ los niños en la escuela o _____ (ellos) volver a casa para comer? ¿A qué hora _____ (ellos) de la escuela primaria al final del día? (almorzar, poder, volver)

**¿Y tú?** Ahora entrevista a otro/a estudiante con las preguntas anteriores sobre (*about*) el barrio donde vive.

**4-42 ▶ Ventajas y desventajas.** Hablas con un cliente de las ventajas y desventajas (*advantages and disadvantages*) de alquilar un apartamento en vez de (*instead of*) tener su propia casa. Prepara oraciones con el opuesto (*opposite*) de las palabras en letra cursiva.

Modelo  Si tiene su propia casa, tiene que pagar la luz *y* el agua.
        *Si alquila un apartamento, a veces no tiene que pagar ni la luz ni el agua.*

1. Si tiene su propia casa, tiene que cortar el césped *y* trabajar en el jardín.
2. Si tiene su propia casa, puede hacer *algunos* cambios (*changes*).
3. Si tiene su propia casa, casi *siempre* tiene la responsabilidad de reparar *algo*.
4. Si tiene su propia casa, *nunca* depende de *nadie* para arreglar *ningún* problema.

### ¡Hola! Entre profesionales

Whether you work in real estate here or you need to find lodging for a stay in a Spanish-speaking country, you will need to know the vocabulary to describe the housing options that are available and regional differences in terminology. Visit MySpanishLab for *Hoy día* to find more useful vocabulary, information, and activities such as the following one.

**Más anuncios.** Lee estos anuncios clasificados de viviendas en España, México y Puerto Rico. ¿Qué palabras se usan en cada anuncio para decir: *for rent, an apartment, a bedroom, parking, refrigerator*?

Se alquila piso, 3 dormitorios, 2 baños, sala, comedor y cocina, totalmente equipado con frigorífico y lavadora. Párquing incluido. 900€ con agua y luz. Teléfono: 91 377 51 07   (Barcelona, España)

Se renta departamento céntrico. Tres recámaras, dos baños, cuarto de estudio, comedor, cocina con refrigerador nuevo, estacionamiento para dos autos. $9.000 Teléfono: (55) 56 73 64 29   (Distrito Federal, México)

Se alquila: Apartamento, dos habitaciones, un baño, un estacionamiento, en buenas condiciones. Incluye agua y luz. Excelentes áreas recreativas con piscina, gimnasio y gacebo. Equipo: Estufa eléctrica, nevera, aire de ventana. 900$ Teléfono: 787 735 8991   (San Juan, Puerto Rico)

### La música, ¿símbolo de identidad?

SAM: 4-50
to 4-52

### Antes de leer

¿Cómo es el barrio donde vives? ¿Tiene la palabra *barrio* alguna connotación para ti en inglés? ¿Asocias tu barrio con algún ritmo musical? ¿Conoces (*Are you familiar with*) el ritmo musical del reggaetón? ¿Con qué ideas asocias este tipo de música?

> ▶ **Reading Strategy** *Predicting content*. Sometimes, the title of a reading or visuals that accompany it will trigger personal associations with the topic that allow you to think ahead about the information that will likely be discussed in the passage. Predicting the content of readings will allow you to anticipate new vocabulary you encounter in Spanish.

### Ahora tú

**4-43** ▶ **Relaciones.** Lee el título del artículo que aparece a continuación. ¿Qué palabras o ideas relacionadas con el tema crees que van a aparecer? ¿Crees que se van a mencionar distintos tipos de música? ¿La vida de los artistas? ¿Los temas y mensajes (*messages*) de las canciones? ¿Preferencias musicales?

## La música, ¿símbolo de identidad?

**A**rtistas de géneros musicales muy variados expresan con su música su forma de pensar, de sentir y de vivir[1]. Hay tipos de música considerados ofensivos por la letra[2], como el reggaetón. Pero los cantantes de reggaetón como Daddy Yankee piensan que la música también es una expresión de su identidad puertorriqueña, de su gente y de su vida en el barrio. Daddy Yankee quiere expresar el orgullo de su herencia[3] con su música. En algunas de sus canciones, como "Barrio fino", quiere transmitir un mensaje social y habla de cómo es crecer[4] y vivir en barrios amenazados[5] por la violencia de las pandillas[6]. Muchos cantantes cuentan historias personales con su música. Pero la música no define sólo a sus autores, sino[7] también a las personas que se identifican con ella.

**¿Qué piensas de las siguientes afirmaciones? ¿Estás de acuerdo[8]? ¿Sí o no?**

La música que escuchas habla de ti, de quién eres.
☐ Sí ☐ No

La música que prefieres refleja tus orígenes, tu ciudad, tu barrio.
☐ Sí ☐ No

La música es una cuestión de moda, y cambia con las generaciones.
☐ Sí ☐ No

La música es también un símbolo de tu identidad.
☐ Sí ☐ No

La música que escuchas puede condicionar tu forma de vestir[9] y también de pensar.
☐ Sí ☐ No

Con la tecnología, hoy la música está siempre contigo, nunca estás solo/a.
☐ Sí ☐ No

28

[1]*their way of thinking, feeling, and living* [2]*lyrics* [3]*pride of his heritage* [4]*to grow up* [5]*threatened* [6]*gangs* [7]*but* [8]*Do you agree?* [9]*way of dressing*

## Después de leer

👥 **4-44 ▶ Tus opiniones.** Comenta con un/a compañero/a tus respuestas a las afirmaciones del artículo. Explica por qué estás de acuerdo o no. Después entrevista a tu compañero/a con las siguientes preguntas.

**1.** ¿Qué música o canciones asocias con tu barrio?
**2.** ¿Hay algún tipo de música ofensivo para ti? ¿Cuál? ¿Por qué?
**3.** ¿Te gustan las canciones que tienen un mensaje social? ¿Por qué?
**4.** ¿Qué cantantes conoces (*do you know*) que hablen en sus canciones de su barrio o de sus orígenes?

**4-45 ▶ Las pandillas.** En muchas canciones de reggaetón, se habla de la influencia de las pandillas (*gangs*) en los barrios. Completa el siguiente texto con la forma correcta de **ser** o **estar**.

La violencia (1) _____ un problema grande en algunos barrios marginales. Muchos jóvenes (2) _____ solos, sin sus padres, todo el día, y no (3) _____ listos para tomar grandes responsabilidades o defenderse. El ambiente (*environment*) del barrio no siempre (4) _____ bueno para los jóvenes que no saben (*know*) muy bien qué destino seguir (*to follow*) y (5) _____ confundidos sobre su futuro. En algunos casos, sobrevivir (*to survive*) (6) _____ más importante que ir a clase y estudiar. Las pandillas (7) _____ grupos de jóvenes de barrios urbanos que, generalmente, (8) _____ juntos para ofrecerse protección. Pero sus actividades no (9) _____ siempre legales. La vida en muchos barrios no (10) _____ fácil.

**4-46 ▶ Un concierto de Daddy Yankee.** Teresa quiere ir a un concierto de Daddy Yankee y le pide a su amigo Ángel que la acompañe (*to accompany her*). Completa cada parte de su conversación con el verbo adecuado de la lista.

| cerrar | volver | querer | contar | poder |
|--------|--------|--------|--------|-------|

TERESA: Hay un concierto de Daddy Yankee el próximo sábado. ¿(1) _____ ir?
ÁNGEL: Ay, Teresa, no (2) _____. Tengo que trabajar el sábado y no (3) _____ a casa hasta la medianoche.
TERESA: ¿La medianoche?
ÁNGEL: Sí, el restaurante donde trabajo (4) _____ a las diez y después, mi jefe (*boss*) siempre (5) _____ conmigo para limpiar el lugar.

| dormir | jugar | querer | pensar | almorzar |
|--------|-------|--------|--------|----------|

TERESA: Y el domingo, ¿qué (6) _____ hacer?
ÁNGEL: Sabes que normalmente, los domingos (7) _____ hasta tarde, y a las tres (8) _____ en el parque con mi equipo de béisbol.
TERESA: Oh, sí, es cierto. Y el lunes, ¿(9) _____ con alguien en la universidad?
ÁNGEL: No, el lunes no almuerzo con nadie, ¿(10) _____ almorzar en la cafetería?
TERESA: Sí, en la cafetería está bien.
ÁNGEL: Perfecto, hasta el lunes. Diviértete (*Have fun*) en el concierto.

## 📖 Educadores de hoy

SAM: 4-53
to 4-55

### Antes de ver

La educación es una parte esencial del desarrollo (*development*) del individuo. El apoyo familiar (*family support*) y la educación que los jóvenes reciben en la escuela son la base para un buen futuro. Por eso, las escuelas son tan importantes para el barrio y pueden hacer una gran diferencia. En el video les presentamos a Pietro González y Bárbara Bonilla, dos maestros hispanos en Estados Unidos.

**4-47 ▶ Reflexiones.** ¿Crees que las minorías están bien representadas en las universidades norteamericanas? ¿Están bien representadas entre (*among*) los profesores y administradores también? ¿Qué porcentaje del alumnado (*student body*) en tu universidad es de origen hispano?

> ▶ **Listening Strategy** *Anticipating what people say*. To improve comprehension, think of specific questions that you think might be answered in the audio segment. These questions will help you stay focused during the listening process, and the responses you obtain will often correspond to the main ideas of the audio segment.

### Ahora tú

🎬 **4-48 ▶ Somos maestros.** En el video Bárbara y Pietro hablan de sus experiencias como maestros de español en escuelas públicas. Prepara unas preguntas que piensas que vas a poder contestar después de ver el video. Utiliza **quién, qué, cuándo, cómo, dónde** o **por qué** para crear las preguntas.

Modelo     *¿Qué enseña Bárbara?*
           *¿Qué enseña Pietro?*

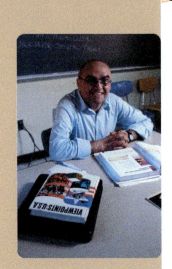

### Después de ver

**4-49 ▶ ¿Quién es quién?** Indica si las descripciones se refieren (*refer*) a Bárbara o a Pietro.

1. Es de origen chileno.
2. Es de origen cubano.
3. Enseña en una escuela pública bilingüe para niños hispanos.
4. Enseña todos los niveles (*levels*) de español, de Español 1 a Español 5.
5. Sus estudiantes hablan poco inglés.
6. Sus estudiantes estudian español.
7. Quiere enseñar a sus estudiantes que hay diferentes latinos.
8. Enseña porque hace algo importante por los jóvenes.

👥 **4-50 ▶ El futuro del español.** Escuchen otra vez las palabras del maestro Pietro al final de su testimonio y expliquen cuál es, según él (*according to him*), el futuro del español en Estados Unidos. Después, en grupos de tres, contesten las siguientes preguntas desde (*from*) su perspectiva personal.

1. En Estados Unidos, ¿crees que es más importante aprender español o alemán? ¿Por qué?
2. ¿Por qué estudias español? ¿Te gustaría estudiar otras lenguas? ¿Cuáles? ¿Por qué?
3. ¿Crees que está mejor preparada para el mercado de trabajo (*job market*) una persona que habla una lengua o una persona que habla varias? ¿Por qué?

## Un correo electrónico informal

SAM: 4-56

### Antes de escribir

Un estudiante hispano va a estudiar en tu universidad y vivir contigo. Tienes que escribirle (*to write him*) un correo electrónico con información sobre dónde vives y cómo es tu casa (apartamento o residencia). Lee la estrategia antes de escribir.

> ► **Writing strategy** *Using conventional phrases and logical organization.*
> It is common to use a casual style with a cordial tone when sharing personal information by e-mail. Your e-mail should also be organized logically. Before you begin to write, prepare some notes and organize them in a sequence that will add coherence to your message.
>
> Here are some conventional greetings and farewells you can use in Spanish to open and close e-mail messages.
>
> For opening your e-mail:
> **Hola ..., ¿qué tal?** *Hi ..., how are you?*
> **Querido/a ...** *(Dear ...)*
>
> For closing your e-mail:
> **Adiós** *Good-bye*
> **Hasta pronto** *See you soon*
> **Un saludo** *Greetings*
> **Un abrazo** *A hug*
> **Besos** *Kisses*

**4-51 ► ¡Prepárate!** Antes de empezar a escribir, anota ideas relacionadas con las cuatro categorías siguientes:

■ tu dirección y las partes de tu casa / apartamento / residencia
■ tu cuarto
■ el barrio y los vecinos
■ tu carácter y tus actividades en casa

### Ahora tú

**4-52 ► Tu correo electrónico informal.** Escribe ahora tu correo electrónico en cuatro párrafos correspondientes a las categorías mencionadas.

### Después de escribir

 **4-53 ► ¡Edita!** Intercambia (*Exchange*) tu correo electrónico con un/a compañero/a y revisa su texto. ¿Aparece toda la información relevante? Piensa en sugerencias para mejorar (*to improve*) la gramática y la organización del texto.

**4-54 ► ¡Revisa!** Revisa tu correo electrónico y asegúrate que contenga (*make sure it contains*) los siguientes elementos:

❏ el vocabulario apropiado para hablar de las partes de la casa
❏ los adjetivos para describir tu cuarto, tu barrio y tus vecinos
❏ el verbo **ser** para describir cómo son tu casa, tu cuarto, tu barrio y tus vecinos
❏ el verbo **estar** para indicar dónde está tu casa y cómo está normalmente tu cuarto
❏ los verbos para hablar de tus actividades en casa

**4-55 ► ¡Navega!** Busca programas para estudiar español en un país hispano y lee la descripción del alojamiento (*lodging*). ¿Hay más información para incorporar en tu correo? Visita la página web de *Hoy día* y usa los enlaces (*links*) sugeridos para esta actividad.

# 4 Vocabulario

## En casa

| | |
|---|---|
| las afueras | outskirts |
| el alquiler | rent |
| el animal | animal |
| el árbol | tree |
| el armario | wardrobe, closet |
| el baño | bathroom |
| el barrio | neighborhood |
| el campo | country |
| el centro | center, downtown |
| el coche (el carro) | car |
| la cocina | kitchen |
| el comedor | dining room |
| la dirección | address |
| el dormitorio | bedroom |
| la estufa | stove |
| la flor | flower |
| el garaje | garage |
| el jardín | garden, yard |
| el microondas | microwave oven |
| la nevera | refrigerator |
| la sala | living room |
| el sofá | sofa |
| el televisor | television set |
| el/la vecino/a | neighbor |

## Acciones

| | |
|---|---|
| alquilar | to rent |
| fumar | to smoke |
| pagar | to pay |

## Otras palabras y expresiones

| | |
|---|---|
| afuera | outside |
| agradable | pleasant, nice |
| caro/a | expensive |
| Me gustaría(n) . . . | I would like . . . |

*For numbers above 100, see page 102.*
*For indefinite and negative words, see page 104.*

## El cuarto, los muebles y los accesorios

| | |
|---|---|
| la alfombra | rug |
| la cómoda | chest (of drawers) |
| el espejo | mirror |
| la impresora | printer |
| la lámpara | lamp |
| los muebles | furniture |
| la pared | wall |
| la pintura | painting |
| el reproductor de DVD | DVD player |
| el suelo | ground, floor |

## Descripciones

| | |
|---|---|
| desordenado/a | messy |
| limpio/a | clean |
| listo/a | ready |
| lleno/a | full |
| muerto/a | dead |
| ordenado/a | neat, straightened up |
| propio/a | own |
| sucio/a | dirty |

## Los colores

| | |
|---|---|
| amarillo/a | yellow |
| anaranjado/a | orange |
| azul | blue |
| beige | beige |
| blanco/a | white |
| gris | gray |
| marrón (café) | brown |
| morado/a | purple |
| negro/a | black |
| rojo/a | red |
| rosado/a (rosa) | pink |
| verde | green |

## Otras palabras y expresiones

| | |
|---|---|
| dejar | to leave (something somewhere) |
| desafortunadamente | unfortunately |
| el dinero | money |
| la persona | person |
| por todos lados | everywhere |

*For a list of adjectives used with **estar**, see page 108.*

## Acciones

| | |
|---|---|
| almorzar (ue) | to eat / have lunch |
| cenar | to eat / have dinner |
| cerrar (ie) | to close |
| contar (ue) | to count, to tell |
| decir (i, yo digo) | to say, to tell |
| desayunar | to eat / have breakfast |
| dormir (ue) | to sleep |
| dormir (ue) la siesta | to take a nap |
| empezar (ie) | to begin |
| encontrar (ue) | to find |
| entender (ie) | to understand |
| jugar (ue) (a los videojuegos) | to play (video games) |
| pedir (i) | to ask for, to order |
| pensar (ie) | to think, to intend |
| perder (ie) | to lose, to miss |
| poder (ue) | to be able, can, may |
| preferir (ie) | to prefer |
| querer (ie) | to want |
| recordar (ue) | to remember |
| repetir (i) | to repeat |
| servir (i) | to serve |
| volver (ue) (a) | to return, to . . . again |

## Otras palabras y expresiones

| | |
|---|---|
| el desayuno | breakfast |
| Lo siento. | I'm sorry. |

## En la calle

| | |
|---|---|
| el autobús | bus |
| la basura | trash |
| el ruido | noise |
| el tráfico | traffic |
| el transporte público | public transportation |

## Los lugares

| | |
|---|---|
| la escuela | school |
| el estacionamiento | parking lot |
| la lavandería | laundromat |
| la parada de autobús | bus stop |

## Otros sustantivos

| | |
|---|---|
| el espacio | space |
| la privacidad | privacy |
| el quehacer doméstico | chore |
| el recibo de la luz (del agua, del gas) | light / electric (water, gas) bill |
| la responsabilidad | responsibility |

## Expresiones verbales

| | |
|---|---|
| andar en bicicleta | to ride a bicycle |
| arreglar | to fix, to straighten out / up |
| cortar el césped | to cut the grass |
| costar (ue) | to cost |
| esperar | to wait (for) |
| estacionar | to park |
| funcionar | to work (for machines, plans, or systems) |
| lavar | to wash |
| No conozco a | I don't know (a person) |
| sacar | to take out |

## Descripciones

| | |
|---|---|
| animado/a | lively |
| callado/a | quiet |
| chismoso/a | gossipy |
| cultural | cultural |
| hablador/a | talkative, chatty |
| práctico/a | practical |
| ruidoso/a | noisy |
| seguro/a | safe |

 Visit MySpanishLab for *Hoy día* for links to the mnemonic dictionary online for suggestions such as the following to help you remember vocabulary from this chapter, learn related words in Spanish, and use Spanish words to build your vocabulary in English.

### EXAMPLES

**pensar,** *to think:* The English adjective *pensive* means *deep in thought.* Related words: **el pensamiento,** *thought, thinking* and **pensativo/a,** *pensive.*

**lavar,** *to wash:* In English, you wash up in a *lavatory,* and you might use *Lava* soap. Related words: **un lavabo,** *a washbasin, a bathroom sink;* **un lavadero,** a laundry room; **una lavadora,** *a washing machine;* **un lavaplatos,** *a dishwasher;* **la lavandería,** *laundry, the laundromat.*

# 5 Los fines de semana

En el este capítulo, vas a aprender a hablar más de la rutina diaria, las actividades de tiempo libre y las fiestas.

Los españoles son en general gente activa, feliz y sociable, según un estudio del Centro de Investigaciones Sociales sobre relaciones interpersonales. Los jóvenes de 18 a 24 años prefieren divertirse (*to have fun*) con sus amigos para desconectar de la rutina diaria. Pero, los españoles de 35 a 44 años prefieren divertirse con su familia en su tiempo libre.

▶ ¿Prefieres divertirte con tu familia o con tus amigos?

▶ ¿Necesitas estar solo/a veces para desconectar?

Los españoles creen todavía en el matrimonio. Un 72,6% de los entrevistados no está de acuerdo con la frase, "El matrimonio es una institución pasada de moda (*outdated*)". Aproximadamente un 98% de los españoles cree que la fidelidad (*faithfulness*) y la tolerancia son factores muy importantes para el buen funcionamiento de un matrimonio.

▶ ¿Estás de acuerdo con la frase "el matrimonio es una institución pasada de moda"?

▶ ¿Cuáles crees que son los factores más importantes para el buen funcionamiento de un matrimonio?

# 📖 **Vocabulario**    La rutina diaria

SAM: 5-1 to 5-4

CD 2
Track 26

## ¿**Sabías** que...?

La siesta es una costumbre muy extendida en los países hispanos. Muchas personas vuelven a casa a la una y media o dos de la tarde para almorzar y descansan un rato (*a while*) después de comer. La siesta, según médicos especialistas, tiene muchos beneficios: aumenta la productividad y la creatividad y el trabajador se siente más predispuesto (*inclined*) a trabajar. También es beneficiosa para los estudiantes. Después de dormir una hora de siesta, los chicos y chicas se levantan más descansados y concentrados para aprender.

## ¡**Ojo!**

The verbs presented on this page have reflexive pronouns (**me, te . . .**) before them. In the following grammar explanation, you will learn when to include such pronouns. In this vocabulary presentation use them where they appear and focus on the meaning of the verbs.

Duermo hasta tarde.
Me despierto a las diez.

**Me quedo** un poco en la cama y **me levanto** a las diez y media.

**Me baño** o **me ducho** por la mañana y me lavo el pelo todos los días.

Me lavo los dientes.

**Me lavo la cara**, me maquillo y **me visto** para salir.

Me relajo en casa por la tarde.

**Me encuentro con** mis amigos en el centro. **Me divierto** mucho.

Cuando **me siento** cansada, vuelvo a casa y **me acuesto**.

---

**me quedo** *I stay*   **me levanto** *I get up*   **me baño** *I bathe*   **me ducho** *I shower*   **me lavo la cara** *I wash my face*   **me visto** *I get dressed*   **me encuentro con** *I meet up with, I get together with*   **me divierto** *I have fun*
**me siento** *I feel*   **me acuesto** *I go to bed*

Track 27

Una conversación. Dos amigos, Adán y Maite, hablan de su rutina de los sábados.

ADÁN: ¿Te despiertas tarde los sábados?

MAITE: No, me levanto a las seis y media. Trabajo a las ocho los sábados y me ducho antes de salir.

ADÁN: ¿Trabajas todo el día?

MAITE: No, vuelvo a casa a las dos.

ADÁN: ¿Qué haces por la tarde?

MAITE: Generalmente, me quedo en casa y me relajo. A veces duermo la siesta.

ADÁN: ¿Te quedas en casa por la noche también?

MAITE: Los sábados por la noche, prefiero salir con mis amigos a cenar o a bailar.

ADÁN: ¿Te acuestas tarde?

MAITE: Sí, casi siempre me acuesto tarde los sábados porque puedo dormir hasta tarde los domingos.

CD 2, Track 28

## ¡A escuchar!

Escuchen otra conversación en la cual dos amigos, Blanca y Gustavo, hablan de su rutina de los lunes. ¿Quién se levanta más temprano, él o ella? ¿Quién vuelve a casa primero? ¿A qué hora se acuesta cada uno?

**5-1 ▶ ¿Qué se hace primero?** Una estudiante habla de su rutina diaria. ¿En qué orden dice que hace las siguientes cosas?

Modelo  Me levanto. / Me despierto. / Desayuno.
*Me despierto, me levanto y luego desayuno.*

**1.** Me visto. / Me maquillo. / Me lavo la cara.

**2.** Me levanto. / Voy a la universidad. / Me visto.

**3.** Ceno. / Vuelvo a la casa. / Me acuesto después de estudiar.

**4.** Me levanto después de quince minutos. / Me despierto. / Me quedo un poco en la cama.

**5.** Me lavo los dientes. / Desayuno. / Me despierto.

**6.** Nos relajamos un poco después de comer. / Mis amigos y yo nos encontramos en la cafetería. / Almorzamos.

**5-2 ▶ Mi rutina.** Selecciona las palabras en letra cursiva que mejor describan tu rutina de los sábados o utiliza otra expresión para completar las oraciones.

**1.** Me despierto a *las ocho / las nueve / las diez / . . .* y me levanto *inmediatamente / después de quince minutos / . . .*

**2.** Me despierto *fácilmente / con dificultad.*

**3.** Me baño *por la mañana / por la tarde / por la noche.*

**4.** Me visto en *mi cuarto / el baño.*

**5.** Para relajarme, me gusta *escuchar música / leer una revista / . . .*

**6.** Generalmente, me quedo en casa *los sábados por la noche / los domingos por la tarde / todo el fin de semana / . . .*

**7.** Me divierto mucho cuando mis amigos y yo *vamos a bailar / vamos al café / jugamos al vóleibol / . . .*

**8.** No me divierto mucho cuando mis amigos y yo *vamos al centro comercial / hablamos de política / . . .*

**9.** Los sábados me acuesto a *las diez / las once / . . .*

**5-3 ▶ Otra conversación.** En parejas, vuelvan a leer *Una conversación* entre Adán y Maite. Luego, cambien la conversación para hablar de su rutina de los sábados.

# 📖 Gramática 1    Describing your routine: Reflexive verbs

SAM: 5-5 to 5-8

## Para averiguar

1. What is a reflexive verb?
2. What are two types of verbs that are often reflexive in Spanish, but not in English?
3. Which reflexive pronoun is used with each subject?
4. Where do you place reflexive pronouns with verbs conjugated in the present tense? Where do you place them with an infinitive after **antes de** or **después de**?
5. Will infinitives used after **antes de** or **después de** be translated by an infinitive in English?

■ Use reflexive verbs to describe actions that people do to or for themselves.

REFLEXIVE:    Adela se baña.
              *Adela is bathing (herself).*

NON-REFLEXIVE:    Adela baña al perro.
                  *Adela is bathing the dog.*

■ When conjugating reflexive verbs, remove the **se** from the infinitive and place the reflexive pronoun corresponding to the subject before the verb: **me** (*myself*), **te** (*yourself*), **nos** (*ourselves*), **os** (*yourselves*), **se** (*himself, herself, oneself, yourself, yourselves, themselves*).

### lavarse *(to wash oneself)*

| | | | | | |
|---|---|---|---|---|---|
| yo | **me** | lavo | nosotros/as | **nos** | lavamos |
| tú | **te** | lavas | vosotros/as | **os** | laváis |
| Ud., él, ella | **se** | lava | Uds., ellos/as | **se** | lavan |

■ Verbs used with reflexive pronouns in English (*myself, . . .*) are generally reflexive in Spanish (*to look at oneself* > **mirarse**). Verbs describing a change in mental or physical state or people doing something to their own body, including changing its position such as sitting down or standing up, are also generally reflexive in Spanish.

■ Some common reflexive verbs include the following. Note the stem-changing verbs indicated by **(ie)**, **(i)**, or **(ue)**.

| | | | |
|---|---|---|---|
| **aburrirse** | *to get bored* | **maquillarse** | *to put on make-up* |
| **acostarse (ue)** | *to lie down, to go to bed* | **ponerse (la ropa)** | *to put on (one's clothes)* |
| **bañarse** | *to bathe, to take a bath* | | |
| **despertarse (ie)** | *to wake up* | **presentarse** | *to introduce oneself* |
| **divertirse (ie)** | *to have fun* | **quedarse** | *to stay* |
| **ducharse** | *to take a shower* | **relajarse** | *to relax* |
| **enojarse** | *to get angry* | **sentarse (ie)** | *to sit down* |
| **irse** | *to go away, to leave* | **sentirse (ie)** | *to feel* |
| **lavarse (el pelo)** | *to wash (one's hair)* | **vestirse (i)** | *to get dressed* |
| **levantarse** | *to get up* | | |

— ¿A qué hora **te acuestas**?
— **Me acuesto** a la medianoche y **me despierto** a las cinco y media.
— ¿No **te sientes** cansado?
— Sí, necesito dormir más.

— *What time do you go to bed?*
— *I go to bed at midnight and I wake up at five thirty.*
— *Don't you feel tired?*
— *Yes, I need to sleep more.*

## ¡Ojo!

Generally, the definite article (**el, la, los, las**) is used instead of possessive adjectives (**mi, tu, su, nuestro/a**) with nouns naming a part of the body or clothing after a reflexive verb.

Me lavo **la** cara    I wash *my* face.

■ After prepositions like **para** (*in order to*), **después de** (*after*), or **antes de** (*before*), use the infinitive form of verbs, changing the reflexive pronoun to match the subject of the sentence. Note that in English, a different structure is used.

Me levanto inmediatamente **después de despertarme**.    { *I get up immediately after waking up.* / *I get up immediately after I wake up.* }

**5-4 ▶ La rutina diaria.** Completa las oraciones con la forma correcta de los verbos entre paréntesis en el orden lógico para describir la rutina diaria de Alejandro los lunes.

Modelo    Alejandro casi siempre *se despierta* a las seis, pero no *se levanta* inmediatamente. *Se queda* cinco o diez minutos en la cama después de despertarse. (quedarse, despertarse, levantarse)

1. Todas las mañanas _____ y _____ rápidamente en el baño. Luego, va a la cocina y _____ a la mesa a desayunar. (vestirse, ducharse, sentarse)

2. Después de desayunar, _____ los dientes, _____ la mochila y _____ para la universidad a las siete. (lavarse, ponerse, irse)

3. Alejandro siempre _____ cerca del profesor en todas sus clases. _____ con frecuencia en sus clases de música y francés, pero casi siempre _____ en su clase de historia porque el profesor es monótono. (divertirse, aburrirse, sentarse)

4. Los lunes, Alejandro _____ en la universidad siete horas y _____ del campus a las cuatro. Después de sus clases, _____ un poco con los amigos en un café. (quedarse, irse, divertirse)

5. Generalmente, Alejandro _____ cansado alrededor de (*around*) las once de la noche. Entonces, _____ el pijama y _____. (acostarse, ponerse, sentirse)

**¿Y tú?** Ahora, cambia las oraciones anteriores para describir tu rutina los días de clase y comparte la información con un/a compañero/a.

Modelo    *Casi siempre me despierto a las siete y media y me levanto inmediatamente. Casi nunca me quedo en la cama después de despertarme.*

**5-5 ▶ Mi rutina los fines de semana.** Expresa la misma idea sustituyendo un verbo de la lista por las palabras en letra cursiva en cada pregunta.

| | | | |
|---|---|---|---|
| aburrirse | irse | ponerse | relajarse |
| *despertarse (ie)* | levantarse | quedarse | sentirse (ie) |

Modelo    *¿Te levantas* temprano los sábados?
          *¿Te despiertas temprano los sábados?*

1. ¿A qué hora *te despiertas* los sábados?
2. ¿*Descansas* los sábados o tienes que trabajar?
3. Los sábados, ¿*sales* temprano de casa o *estás* en casa por la mañana?
4. ¿*Estás aburrido/a* o te diviertes cuando juegas a los videojuegos?
5. Normalmente, ¿*te vistes con* ropa elegante o ropa informal para salir con los amigos?
6. ¿*Estás* cansado/a los domingos por la mañana?

**¿Y tú?** Ahora, entrevista a un/a compañero/a de clase con las nuevas preguntas.

**5-6 ▶ En mi familia.** ¿Quién de tu familia hace las siguientes cosas?

Modelo    despertarse más temprano
          *Yo me despierto más temprano. / Todos nos despertamos a la misma hora.*

1. despertarse primero
2. levantarse más tarde
3. acostarse más tarde
4. bañarse por la mañana
5. quedarse más en casa
6. divertirse más

**Gramática 2**    Saying what you do for each other:
Reciprocal verbs

SAM: 5-9
to 5-11

### Para averiguar

1. What is a reciprocal verb?
2. Do reciprocal verbs in Spanish look different or have a different word order from reflexive verbs?
3. How would you say: My friends and I see (need, understand) each other?

■ Whereas reflexive verbs indicate that someone does something to or for oneself, reciprocal verbs indicate that two or more people do something to or for one another or each other.

■ Reciprocal verbs have the same pronouns (**nos, os, se**) and the same word order as reflexive verbs. Many verbs that you have already seen can be made reciprocal by adding the reciprocal pronouns.

| | |
|---|---|
| Mis vecinos nunca **se hablan**. | *My neighbors never talk to each other.* |
| **Nos vemos** con frecuencia. | *We see one another frequently.* |

■ Here are some reciprocal and reflexive verbs that are useful when describing relationships.

| | | | |
|---|---|---|---|
| **abrazarse** | *to hug each other* | **enamorarse (de)** | *to fall in love (with)* |
| **ayudarse** | *to help each other* | | |
| **besarse** | *to kiss each other* | **encontrarse (ue)** | *to meet up with each other* |
| **casarse (con)** | *to marry, to get married (to)* | **llevarse bien (con)** | *to get along well (with)* |
| **comunicarse** | *to communicate with each other* | **pelearse** | *to fight* |
| **divorciarse (de)** | *to divorce, to get divorced (from)* | **quererse (ie)** | *to love each other* |

Mi novio/a y yo **nos hablamos** por teléfono o **nos comunicamos** por correo electrónico varias veces al día.

**Nos vemos** casi todos los días. **Nos encontramos** en un café después del trabajo.

**Nos queremos** mucho y **nos vamos a casar** algún día.

**5-7 ▶ Mi mejor amigo y yo.**  ¿Describen las siguientes oraciones tu relación con tu mejor amigo/a? Contesta **cierto** o **falso** y corrige las oraciones falsas.

1. Nos hablamos por teléfono todos los días.
2. Nos comunicamos más por correo electrónico que por teléfono.
3. Nos vemos todos los días.
4. Nos encontramos a veces en un café.
5. Nos encontramos todos los días después de esta clase.
6. Nos abrazamos cuando nos vemos.
7. Nos ayudamos cuando hay problemas.
8. Nunca nos peleamos.

**5-8 ▶ Una pareja feliz.** Usen los verbos de la lista para contar una historia de amor entre Pablo y Felicia. Trabajen en grupos e incluyan todos los detalles (*details*) posibles. Luego, intercambien (*exchange*) su descripción con la de otro grupo para ver cuál es más completa e interesante.

Modelo    *Pablo y Felicia se ven por primera vez en un café. Se miran y Pablo se sienta en la mesa de al lado . . .*

| | | |
|---|---|---|
| verse por primera vez | no separarse hasta tarde | enamorarse |
| mirarse a los ojos | pedirse los números de teléfono | besarse |
| levantarse | abrazarse antes de irse | nunca pelearse |
| presentarse | hablarse por teléfono todos los días | quererse |
| hablarse por horas | encontrarse todos los días | casarse |

**5-9 ▶ Comparaciones culturales.** Lee el siguiente artículo sobre el rol de las mujeres en la sociedad hispana y contesta las preguntas.

Aunque (*Although*) la situación está cambiando en las nuevas generaciones, la mentalidad de muchas mujeres hispanas es diferente a la percepción que tiene la mujer norteamericana sobre el equilibrio laboral y familiar (*balance between work and family*). En muchos países de Latinoamérica la familia y la crianza (*raising*) de los hijos son prioridades para el individuo, y la mujer tiene un rol fundamental en estas sociedades. Las mujeres hispanas que optan por el matrimonio se casan generalmente entre los 20 y los 25 años. Las familias hispanas son a veces numerosas, y las responsabilidades de la mujer son muy grandes. Algunas mujeres hispanas son madres y esposas, se quedan en casa, se ocupan de (*take care of*) todos los quehaceres domésticos y se preocupan por el bienestar (*well-being*) de la familia. No hay tiempo para relajarse. El hombre generalmente trabaja fuera de la casa y se siente responsable de la economía familiar. El machismo es un estereotipo extendido en el mundo hispano, pero en realidad la mujer tiene un rol muy importante en la sociedad. Las mujeres hispanas entienden que ser madre es importante, pero también valoran (*value*) mucho prepararse en la escuela y en la universidad, y realizarse profesionalmente.

1. Identifica los verbos reflexivos en el texto e indica cuál es el infinitivo en cada caso.
2. ¿Cuáles son las prioridades del individuo en muchos países de Latinoamérica? ¿Son similares a las prioridades de la sociedad norteamericana?
3. Las mujeres hispanas que deciden casarse, ¿a qué edad se casan generalmente? ¿Tiene la mujer norteamericana responsabilidades similares a la mujer hispana? ¿Comparte estas responsabilidades con su pareja (*partner*)?
4. ¿Crees que la mujer norteamericana media (*average*) tiene tiempo para relajarse? ¿Qué hace la mujer norteamericana media para relajarse?

# 📖 **Vocabulario**   La ropa

SAM: 5-12 to 5-19

CD 2
Track 29

¿En qué tienda prefieres comprar ropa? ¿Es cara, **barata** o tiene **precios** razonables? **¿Gastas** mucho en ropa? ¿Qué **llevas** cuando vas a la playa? ¿Qué te pones para salir con los amigos?

## ¿**Sabías** que...?

En muchos países hispanos el sistema de tallas (*sizes*) en la ropa es diferente al de Estados Unidos. En España, por ejemplo, la talla más pequeña en ropa de mujer, equivalente a la talla 0 norteamericana, es la 34. También las tallas aumentan de dos en dos, así la talla 2 equivale a la 36, y así sucesivamente. Los números de los zapatos también cambian. En muchos países hispanos, el sistema que se usa también incluye dos dígitos.

## ¡Ojo!

Other commonly used words for **los tenis** include **los zapatos de tenis** and **las zapatillas de tenis**.

CD 2
Track 30

**Una conversación.** Una mujer compra un traje de baño.

DEPENDIENTA: ¿En qué puedo servirle?
CLIENTA: **Busco** un traje de baño.
DEPENDIENTA: ¿Qué color prefiere usted?
CLIENTA: Algo en amarillo o rosado si tiene. Llevo la **talla** 36.
DEPENDIENTA: ¿Le gustan éstos? **Están de moda.** Cuestan 415 pesos. ¿Es demasiado?
CLIENTA: No, es un buen precio. ¿**Me** puedo **probar ese** traje de baño amarillo?
DEPENDIENTA: Sí, **cómo no.** Los probadores están **por acá.**
*Después de probarse el traje de baño . . .*
DEPENDIENTA: ¿Le gusta ese traje de baño o desea probarse otro?
CLIENTA: **Me** voy a **llevar** éste.
DEPENDIENTA: ¿Cómo desea pagar, **en efectivo,** con cheque o con **tarjeta de débito o de crédito?**
CLIENTA: Con mi tarjeta de crédito.

🔊 CD 2, Track 31

## ¡A **escuchar!**

Escuchen otra conversación en la cual un hombre compra ropa. ¿Qué busca? ¿De qué color es la que compra? ¿Cuánto cuesta?

**barato/a** *cheap*   **el precio** *the price*   **gastar** *to spend*   **llevar** *to wear, to carry, to take*   **el dependiente / la dependienta** *the salesclerk*   **el cliente / la clienta** *the customer*   **buscar** *to look for*   **la talla** *size*   **estar de moda** *to be in fashion*   **probarse** *to try on*   **ese / esa (esos / esas)** *that (those)*   **cómo no** *of course*   **los probadores** *the fitting rooms*   **por acá** *over / through here*   **llevarse** *to take (away)*   **en efectivo** *in cash*   **una tarjeta** *a card*

**5-10 ▶ ¿Quién habla?** ¿Quién dice las siguientes cosas en una tienda, el cliente o el dependiente?

Modelo    ¿En qué puedo servirle?
             *el dependiente*

**1.** No quiero nada muy caro.
**2.** ¿Cuánto desea gastar?
**3.** ¿Tiene algo más barato?
**4.** ¿Qué talla lleva usted?

**5.** Quiero algo en azul o blanco.
**6.** ¿Me puedo probar esta camisa?
**7.** Los probadores están por acá.
**8.** ¿Necesita algo más o eso es todo?

**5-11 ▶ ¿Qué te pones?** ¿Qué ropa te pones en estas situaciones?

Modelo    Vas a la playa.
             *Me pongo un traje de baño.*

**1.** Vas a la montaña a esquiar.
**2.** Vas al lago a nadar.
**3.** Vas al parque a correr.
**4.** Sales a bailar con tus amigos.

**5.** Vas a una entrevista (*interview*) importante.
**6.** Te quedas en casa todo el día para relajarte.
**7.** Vas a la clase de español.
**8.** Vas a una boda (*wedding*).

 **5-12 ▶ Entrevista.** Entrevista a otro/a estudiante con estas preguntas.

**1.** ¿Qué tienda cerca de aquí tiene ropa cara / barata / bonita? ¿En qué tiendas compras mucha ropa?
**2.** Para ti, ¿qué es más importante, el precio o la calidad? ¿Cuál es tu tienda favorita?
**3.** Cuando sales con los amigos los sábados, ¿prefieres usar jeans o pantalones más elegantes? ¿En qué ocasiones te pones un traje / un vestido?

 **5-13 ▶ Otra conversación.** En parejas, vuelvan a leer *Una conversación* y preparen otra conversación lógica donde uno/a de ustedes quiere comprar un traje o un vestido en una tienda.

**5-14 ▶ Comparaciones culturales.** La moda es un aspecto muy importante de las culturas hispanas. Lee la siguiente información y contesta las preguntas.

En general, la mujer hispana se arregla mucho (*dresses up*) tanto para ir al trabajo como para salir de fiesta. Dependiendo de los países, hay una preferencia en la ropa por colores más vivos (*bright*) como en el Caribe, o colores más sobrios (*muted*) como en España y Argentina. La ropa de diseñadores hispanos como Isabel Toledo, Oscar de la Renta o Adolfo Domínguez se ve hoy también en las tiendas elegantes de Estados Unidos. ¿Cuál es tu color favorito para la ropa? ¿Qué tipo de ropa llevas para ir a clase o al trabajo? ¿Y para salir de fiesta?

    Los hombres hispanos, en general, son bastante clásicos en la ropa que usan. En los países del Caribe, donde el clima es muy caliente (*hot*), la ropa preferida por los hombres es de lino (*linen*) y la guayabera es muy típica de estos lugares, una camisa de lino que se lleva por fuera del (*untucked*) pantalón. Normalmente, los hombres no llevan pantalones cortos por la calle, sólo si van a la playa o de excursión. En Estados Unidos, ¿llevan los hombres pantalones cortos por la calle?

# Gramática 1

SAM: 5-20
to 5-21

## Pointing out people and things: Demonstrative adjectives and pronouns

### Para averiguar

1. How do you say *this / these* in Spanish?
2. How do you say *that / those*? What is the difference between **ese** and **aquel**?
3. How do you say *this one* instead of *this shirt*? Which may have a written accent mark, *this one* or *this shirt*?
4. When do you use the forms **esto, eso,** and **aquello**?

■ Use the following demonstrative adjectives to say *this / these* or *that / those*. There are two ways to say *that / those* in Spanish: **ese / esa / esos / esas** and **aquel / aquella / aquellos / aquellas**. **Aquel** is generally used to describe something at a greater distance than **ese**.

| **este** (this / these) | | **ese** (that / those) | | **aquel** (that / those) | |
|---|---|---|---|---|---|
| este sombrero | *this hat* | ese sombrero | *that hat* | aquel sombrero | *that hat* |
| esta falda | *this skirt* | esa falda | *that skirt* | aquella falda | *that skirt* |
| estos zapatos | *these shoes* | esos zapatos | *those shoes* | aquellos zapatos | *those shoes* |
| estas botas | *these boots* | esas botas | *those boots* | aquellas botas | *those boots* |

¿Te gustan **estos** zapatos?　　　　*Do you like these shoes?*
Me gusta **esa** blusa con **esa** falda.　*I like that blouse with that skirt.*
¿Puedo probarme **aquel** traje?　　　*May I try on that suit (over there)?*

■ The demonstrative pronouns look just like the demonstrative adjectives, except that the noun is omitted. Pronouns may have an optional accent mark on the stressed **e** to distinguish them from adjectives.

¿Te gustan estos zapatos?　　　　　*Do you like these shoes?*
No, prefiero **éstos**.　　　　　　　*No, I prefer these.*
Este reloj es más barato que **ése**.　*This watch is cheaper than that one.*

■ Use the neuter form of the demonstratives: **esto, eso,** or **aquello** to say *this* or *that* when referring to a general idea or a situation rather than to a specific noun, or when referring to a noun that has not yet been identified.

**Eso** es imposible.　　　　　*That is impossible.*
**Esto** es muy importante.　　*This is very important.*
¿Qué es **aquello**?　　　　　*What is that (over there)?*

**5-15 ▶ Preferencias.** Imagina que estás de compras con un/a amigo/a. Usando la forma correcta de los adjetivos demostrativos, pregúntale a un/a compañero/a de clase cuál de los artículos de ropa prefiere. Tu compañero/a debe contestar según sus gustos (*according to his/her tastes*).

Modelo　ESTE/A/OS/AS　　ESE/A/OS/AS　　AQUEL/AQUELLA/OS/AS
　　　　pantalones negros　jeans　　　　pantalones blancos
　　　E1: *¿Prefieres estos pantalones negros, esos jeans o aquellos pantalones blancos?*
　　　E2: *Prefiero los jeans.*

| ESTE/A/OS/AS | ESE/A/OS/AS | AQUEL/AQUELLA/OS/AS |
|---|---|---|
| 1. corbata roja | corbata azul | corbata verde |
| 2. camisa rosada | camisa negra | camisa blanca |
| 3. sandalias | tenis | botas |
| 4. falda corta | falda larga | vestido |
| 5. traje gris | traje negro | traje blanco |
| 6. camiseta de la universidad | camiseta multicolor | camiseta blanca o de un solo color |
| 7. blusa sin mangas (*sleeveless*) | blusa de manga larga | blusa de manga corta |

**5-16 ► De compras.** Estás en una tienda con una amiga que busca ropa nueva. Completa cada pregunta con **este / esta / estos / estas** y hazle la pregunta a otro/a estudiante. Tu compañero/a de clase debe contestar que es lo opuesto (*the opposite*) de lo que tú crees.

Modelo    E1: ¿Es demasiado largo *este* vestido?
          E2: *No, es demasiado corto.*

1. ¿Son demasiado grandes _____ zapatos?
2. ¿Es muy cara _____ camisa?
3. ¿Es demasiado larga _____ falda?
4. ¿Es feo _____ traje?
5. ¿Es demasiado corto _____ cinturón?
6. ¿Son muy caros _____ suéteres?
7. ¿Son de buena calidad (*quality*) _____ botas?
8. ¿Son muy altos _____ precios?

**5-17 ► Cumplidos.** En parejas, utilicen **ese / esa / esos / esas** con estos adjetivos para hacerles cumplidos (*to compliment*) a sus compañeros de clase. Pueden usar **parecer** para decir *to seem* o *to look* o **ser** (*to be*).

| | | | |
|---|---|---|---|
| agradable | cómodo | de última moda | nuevo |
| bonito | de buena calidad | elegante | práctico |
| caro | de un color bonito | fácil de lavar | versátil |

Modelos    *Mario, esos zapatos parecen muy cómodos.*
           *Anita, esa camiseta es muy bonita.*

**5-18 ► Mis favoritos.** Entrevista a tu compañero/a sobre sus cosas y personas favoritas. Después, reacciona a su respuesta con una de las expresiones de la lista y explica por qué te gusta o no.

| |
|---|
| Ese / Esa . . . también me gusta. |
| Ese / Esa . . . no me gusta. |
| No conozco (*I'm not familiar with*) ese / esa . . . |

Modelo    tu tienda favorita
          E1: *¿Cuál es tu tienda favorita?*
          E2: *Mi tienda favorita es Macy's.*
          E1: *Esa tienda también me gusta. Tiene ropa bonita. /*
              *Esa tienda no me gusta. Tiene precios altos. /*
              *No conozco esa tienda.*

1. tu restaurante favorito
2. tu película favorita
3. tu color favorito
4. tu actor favorito
5. tu actriz favorita
6. tu ciudad favorita
7. tu programa de televisión favorito
8. tu canción (*song*) favorita

**5-19 ► ¿Cuál prefieres?** En parejas, inventen una conversación entre estas amigas, Alicia y Elena.

Modelo    E1: *Alicia, ¿me debo comprar este vestido?*
          E2: *Ese vestido no me gusta mucho, Elena.*
              *Prefiero esta falda y cuesta menos.*
              *¿Te gusta esta falda anaranjada y negra?...*

#  Gramática 2

SAM: 5-22 to 5-25

## Saying what you intend to do: Using reflexive and reciprocal verbs in the infinitive

■ When a conjugated verb is followed by a reflexive / reciprocal verb in the infinitive, the reflexive / reciprocal pronoun may be placed either before the conjugated verb or attached to the end of the infinitive without changing the meaning of the sentence. The pronoun must correspond to the subject of the conjugated verb.

**Me** voy a levantar temprano.   }    *I'm going to get up early.*
Voy a levantar**me** temprano.

■ To say what someone just did, use **acabar de** followed by an infinitive. **Acabar** is conjugated as a regular **-ar** verb.

**Acabamos de** comer.      *We just ate.*
**Acabo de** levantarme.   }    *I just got up.*
Me **acabo de** levantar.

**5-20 ▶ ¿Y el sábado?** ¿Van a hacer estas personas las actividades indicadas entre paréntesis este sábado? Utiliza el pronombre reflexivo o recíproco lógico.

Este sábado . . .

**Modelo**    (Yo) . . . (levantarse antes de las seis de la mañana)
*(No) Voy a levantarme antes de las seis de la mañana. /*
*(No) Me voy a levantar antes de las seis de la mañana.*

1. (Yo) . . . (levantarse tarde, quedarse en casa por la mañana, relajarse por la tarde, ponerse un traje, casarse, acostarse después de la dos de la mañana)
2. Mi mejor amigo/a y yo . . . (verse, encontrarse en el centro, divertirse juntos/as, quedarse en el centro hasta muy tarde, relajarse juntos/as en mi casa)
3. Mi madre . . . (despertarse temprano, quedarse todo el día en casa, levantarse tarde, maquillarse, ponerse ropa formal para salir por la noche, relajarse por la noche)

**5-21 ▶ ¿Qué van a hacer?** Un hombre habla con su esposa sobre la familia y el trabajo. Completa cada oración con un infinitivo lógico de la lista. Cambia el pronombre reflexivo si es necesario.

| acostarse | divertirse | *levantarse* | ponerse | relajarse |
|---|---|---|---|---|
| despertarse | lavarse | maquillarse | quedarse | |

**Modelo**    Acabo de despertarme pero no quiero *levantarme* inmediatamente.

1. ¿Acabas de bañarte? ¿Vas a _____ antes de vestirte o después?
2. Los niños acaban de desayunar. Ahora, necesitan _____ los dientes antes de irse a la escuela.
3. Acabo de ponerme la camisa pero todavía (*still*) necesito _____ la corbata.
4. Son las diez y acabo de llegar a la oficina. Voy a _____ aquí hasta las seis.
5. Son las seis y acabo de salir del trabajo pero voy a _____ un poco con mis compañeros de trabajo en un café antes de volver a casa.
6. Los niños acaban de ponerse el pijama y tienen sueño. Van a _____.
7. Acabamos de trabajar todo el día. Ahora necesitamos _____. ¿Quieres ver un DVD?
8. Acabas de terminar una semana difícil. Mañana es sábado y puedes _____ tarde.

**5-22 ▶ Vacaciones de primavera (*Spring break*).** Vas a pasar las vacaciones con un/a compañero/a de clase y quieres saber si tiene la misma rutina diaria. Traduce el verbo entre paréntesis para completar las siguientes preguntas.

Cuando estás de vacaciones . . .

1. ¿Te gusta _____ (*to get up*) temprano o tarde?
2. ¿Necesitas café para _____ (*to wake up*) por la mañana?
3. ¿Prefieres _____ (*to bathe*) o _____ (*to shower*) por la mañana o por la noche?
4. ¿Cuánto tiempo necesitas para _____ (*to get dressed*) por la mañana?
5. ¿Qué te gusta hacer para _____ (*to have fun*)?
6. ¿Te gusta _____ (*to go to bed*) tarde?

**¿Y tú?** Ahora, usa las preguntas para entrevistar a otro/a estudiante sobre su rutina típica durante las vacaciones de primavera.

**5-23 ▶ Mis amigos y yo.** Pregúntale a un/a compañero/a de clase cuál es la rutina de las personas indicadas.

Modelo    (Tú) . . . poder / levantarse tarde / todos los días
          E1: *¿Puedes levantarte tarde todos los días? / ¿Te puedes levantar tarde todos los días?*
          E2: *Puedo levantarme tarde sólo los sábados. / Me puedo levantar tarde sólo los sábados. ¿Y tú?*
          E1: *Yo puedo levantarme tarde todos los días menos los martes y jueves. / Yo me puedo levantar tarde todos los días menos los martes y jueves.*

Tú . . .

1. preferir / vestirse antes de desayunar o después
2. tener que / levantarse temprano los sábados
3. poder / relajarse hoy después de clase

Tus padres . . .

4. tener que / levantarse temprano los sábados
5. preferir / acostarse tarde o temprano los sábados
6. preferir / quedarse en casa los domingos

Tu mejor amigo/a y tú . . .

7. preferir / encontrarse en un café o en la casa de uno/a de ustedes
8. ir a / verse mañana
9. preferir / comunicarse por correo electrónico, por SMS (*text messaging*) o por teléfono

**5-24 ▶ Entrevista.** Entrevista a otro/a estudiante con estas preguntas.

1. ¿A qué hora te vas a acostar esta noche? ¿Tienes que levantarte temprano mañana? ¿Vas a quedarte en casa mañana por la mañana? ¿A qué hora vas a irte de casa mañana?
2. ¿Puedes relajarte esta noche o tienes que estudiar o trabajar? ¿Qué haces para relajarte? ¿Escuchas música? ¿Lees un libro? ¿Ves la televisión?
3. ¿Qué haces para divertirte con los amigos? ¿Dónde prefieren encontrarse tus amigos y tú generalmente cuando salen? ¿Siempre se besan cuando se ven?

#  **Vocabulario**    Una fiesta

SAM: 5-26
to 5-27

CD 2
Track 32

¿Qué están haciendo en la fiesta?
¿Se están divirtiendo **los invitados**?

## ¿**Sabías** que...?

Hay distintas maneras de brindar
(*to toast*) en español. Algunos de los
brindis (*toasts*) más tradicionales son
**¡Salud!** (*To your health!*) y **¡Chinchín!**
(*Cheers!*). Otros brindis populares son:
**Arriba, abajo, al centro y adentro,**
donde la persona hace los gestos
indicados con la copa en la mano,
y también **Salud, dinero, amor y
tiempo para gozarlos** (*to enjoy
them*).

## ¡**Ojo**!

In this *Tema*, you will learn a new
verb form ending with **-ando** or
**-iendo** (*-ing*). Note how it is used
here to say what someone is do*ing*
at the moment. You will learn
more about using this verb form
in the next grammar section.

Está tocando la guitarra y cantando.

Está sacando una foto.

Están escuchando música y bailando.

Están viendo un DVD.

Están jugando a los videojuegos.

Están tomando y comiendo. Están hablando y contando **chistes**.

Están sirviendo comida.

Está durmiendo.

 CD 2, Track 34

## ¡**A escuchar**!

Ahora, escuchen otra conversación
telefónica entre dos amigos, Delia y
Javier. ¿Dónde está Javier? ¿Qué está
haciendo Delia?

CD 2
Track 33

**Una conversación.** Dos amigos hablan por teléfono.

MARÍA:    ¿Aló?
CARLOS:  ¿Puedo hablar con María, por favor?
MARÍA:    Soy yo. ¿Eres tú, Carlos?
CARLOS:  Hola, María. ¿Cómo estás?
MARÍA:    Bien, Carlos. ¿Y tú?
CARLOS:  Bien. ¿Estás ocupada? ¿Qué estás haciendo?
MARÍA:    Nada en especial. ¿Por qué?
CARLOS:  Mis amigos y yo estamos en el café El Rincón y después vamos
            a una fiesta a la casa de mi primo. ¿Quieres ir con nosotros?
MARÍA:    Sí, cómo no. Llego en veinte minutos.
CARLOS:  Está bien. Hasta luego.
MARÍA:    Chau.

**los invitados** *the guests*   **un chiste** *a joke*

**5-25 ▶ ¿Qué tal la fiesta?** ¿Es una fiesta divertida o aburrida si los invitados están haciendo estas cosas?

Modelo    Todos están hablando.
          *Es una fiesta divertida.*

**1.** Están hablando de política.
**2.** Están escuchando música hip-hop.
**3.** Todos están jugando a los videojuegos.
**4.** Están viendo videos de las vacaciones de tu mejor amigo/a.
**5.** Todos están contando chistes.
**6.** Están viendo el Superbowl en la tele.
**7.** Todos están bailando.
**8.** Todos están divirtiéndose.

**5-26 ▶ Una fiesta.** Estás en una fiesta en la casa de un amigo. ¿Qué están haciendo todos? Completa las oraciones con un verbo lógico de la lista.

| | | | |
|---|---|---|---|
| abrazándose | cantando | jugando | tomando |
| bailando | comiendo | *sirviendo* | viendo |
| besándose | durmiendo | tocando | |

Modelo    Mi amigo está *sirviendo* la comida.

**1.** Unos amigos y yo estamos _____ un video.
**2.** Yo estoy _____ limonada.
**3.** Dos novios están _____ un tango.
**4.** Alguien está _____ una siesta en el sofá.
**5.** Alguien está _____ el piano y _____ canciones.
**6.** El gato está _____ la comida de un invitado.
**7.** Unos invitados están _____ a los videojuegos.
**8.** Dos novios están _____ y _____ enfrente de todos.

**5-27 ▶ Otra conversación.** En parejas, vuelvan a leer *Una conversación* entre Carlos y María. Luego, cambien la conversación para invitar a su compañero/a de clase a hacer algo.

**5-28 ▶ Comparaciones culturales.** En los países hispanos, la música es un elemento esencial de su cultura y la variedad de ritmos es excepcionalmente rica (*rich*). Lee la información y contesta las preguntas.

■ La música del Caribe representa una combinación exuberante de ritmos africanos, europeos e indígenas. Una gran parte de los ritmos caribeños tiene su origen en la música de los esclavos traídos (*slaves brought*) de África. La salsa, el merengue, el danzón y el mambo son bailes típicos de Cuba, Puerto Rico, la República Dominicana y la costa de Colombia y Venezuela. En tu región, ¿hay música con influencias africanas, europeas o indígenas?

■ La música de mariachi es una representación del folklore mexicano. Los grupos de mariachis están formados generalmente por violines, trompetas y guitarras. Generalmente la música de mariachi expresa sentimientos de amor o describe la vida rural de México. En Estados Unidos y Canadá, ¿qué ritmos musicales representan el folklore o describen la vida rural de las distintas partes del país?

■ El tango, creado por los inmigrantes pobres de Buenos Aires entre 1850 y 1890, es un baile típicamente argentino lleno de pasión y con mucho contacto físico. Esto escandaliza a la sociedad conservadora de la época y el tango es prohibido. Pero la gente continúa bailando en secreto. En tu cultura, ¿hay música o bailes escandalosos para algunas personas? ¿Por qué son escandalosos?

Tango en el Barrio de San Telmo.

**Gramática 1** Describing what people are doing at the moment: The present progressive

SAM: 5-28 to 5-31

SAM: 5-28 to 5-31

 Para **averiguar**

1. What is the ending of the present participle of **-ar** verbs in Spanish? What is the ending of **-er** and **-ir** verbs? These endings correspond to what verb ending in English?
2. Which verb meaning *to be* do you use with present participles to say what is happening?
3. When does the **i** of the **-iendo** ending change to **y**?
4. Which category of verbs has stem changes in present participles: **-ar, -er,** or **-ir**? What do **o** and **e** become?
5. In the present progressive, what are the two possible placements of the reflexive pronoun? When the pronoun is attached to the end of the present participle, what do you write on the stressed syllable of the verb?
6. What are two cases in which the present progressive is used in English, but not in Spanish?

■ Use the present progressive to say what someone is in the process of doing at a particular moment.

■ The present progressive is composed of a conjugated form of **estar** followed by the present participle, which is the equivalent of the *-ing* form of the verb in English. The present participle is formed by replacing the **-ar** ending of infinitives with **-ando,** and **-er** or **-ir** with **-iendo.**

| | | | |
|---|---|---|---|
| hablar | → **hablando** | ¿Quién **está hablando**? | *Who is talking?* |
| comer | → **comiendo** | **Estamos comiendo.** | *We're eating.* |
| escribir | → **escribiendo** | ¿Qué **estás escribiendo**? | *What are you writing?* |

■ The initial **i** of the **-iendo** ending changes to **y** when it falls between two vowels. This occurs with **leer** (**leyendo**), **oír** (**oyendo**), and **creer** (**creyendo**).

| | | | |
|---|---|---|---|
| leer | → **leyendo** | ¿Qué **estás leyendo**? | *What are you reading?* |

■ There is no stem change in the present participle of **-ar** and **-er** stem-changing verbs.

| | | | |
|---|---|---|---|
| almorzar | → **almorzando** | ¿Estás **almorzando**? | *Are you having lunch?* |
| perder | → **perdiendo** | Estamos **perdiendo.** | *We're losing.* |

■ Stem-changing **-ir** verbs have the following changes in the present participle.

| | | | |
|---|---|---|---|
| o → u: dormir → **durmiendo** | Todos **están durmiendo.** | *Everyone is sleeping.* |
| e → i: servir → **sirviendo** | **Están sirviendo** la cena. | *They're serving dinner.* |

Other stem-changing **-ir** verbs you have seen include: **decir (diciendo), pedir (pidiendo), repetir (repitiendo), vestir (vistiendo),** and **divertir (divirtiendo).**

■ In the present progressive, reflexive pronouns may be placed either before the conjugated form of **estar** or attached to the end of the present participle. When attached to the end of the present participle, there is a written accent mark over the **a** or **e** of the **-ando** or **-iendo** ending.

**Se** están divirtiendo. /          *They are having fun.*
   Están divirti**é**ndo**se.**
**Me** estoy sirviendo café. /          *I'm serving myself some coffee.*
   Estoy sirvi**é**ndo**me** café.

■ In Spanish, the present progressive is rarely used with verbs that indicate coming and going. The simple present tense is used instead.

**Vamos** con ustedes.          *We're going with you.*
**Vienen** ahora.          *They're coming now.*

■ Do not use the present progressive to express future actions as you do in English. Use the immediate future (**ir a** + infinitive) instead.

**Voy a trabajar** este fin de semana.          *I'm working this weekend.*

■ Remember to use infinitives instead of present participles after **antes de** and **después de.**

antes de **dormir**          *before sleeping*
después de **levantarse**          *after getting up*

**5-29 ▶ ¿Dónde estás?** Estás en los siguientes lugares y alguien te llama (*calls you*) al celular. En parejas, preparen conversaciones para decir dónde estás y qué estás haciendo allí utilizando una actividad lógica de la lista.

| | | |
|---|---|---|
| *bailar con mis amigos* | dormir la siesta | tomar un café |
| buscar unos zapatos nuevos | estudiar | ver una exposición |
| cenar | hacer ejercicio | ver un partido de fútbol |
| comprar un libro | jugar al fútbol | americano |
| divertirse con los amigos | nadar | |

Modelo    en un club nocturno
E1: *¿Dónde estás?*
E2: *Estoy en un club nocturno.*
E1: *¿Qué estás haciendo?*
E2: *Estoy bailando con mis amigos.*

**1.** en un café
**2.** en la playa
**3.** en la biblioteca
**4.** en el parque

**5.** en una fiesta
**6.** en el centro comercial
**7.** en casa
**8.** en el gimnasio

**9.** en una librería
**10.** en un restaurante
**11.** en el estadio
**12.** en el museo

## 5-30 ▶ ¿Qué está haciendo?

¿Qué está haciendo Adela?

Modelo    *Está levantándose.*
*Se está levantando.*

**1.**

**2.**

**3.**

**4.**

**5.**

**6.**

**5-31 ▶ ¿En qué orden?** Un padre habla de lo que (*what*) acaba de hacer y lo que está haciendo ahora su familia. ¿Cuál es el orden lógico?

Modelo    yo (vestirse / bañarse)
*Acabo de bañarme. Ahora estoy vistiéndome.*
*(Me acabo de bañar. Ahora me estoy vistiendo.)*

**1.** yo (despertarse / preparar el desayuno)
**2.** mi esposa (bañarse / levantarse)
**3.** nosotros (almorzar / sentarse a comer)
**4.** mi esposa y yo (lavar los platos / comer)
**5.** mi esposa (sentarse en el sofá / dormir la siesta)
**6.** nuestra hija mayor (maquillarse para salir / bañarse)
**7.** nuestra hija mayor (salir para una fiesta / divertirse con los amigos)
**8.** nuestros hijos menores (acostarse / dormir)

# 📖 Gramática 2

SAM: 5-32
to 5-35

## Making plans and setting the date: Months and dates

Para **averiguar**

1. When do you use ordinal numbers (*first, second, third . . .*) and cardinal numbers (*one, two, three . . .*) with dates?
2. In English, there are two ways of giving dates, *May 1st* or *the 1st of May*. Which word order is similar to that in Spanish?

### ¡Ojo!

When referring to today's date, Spanish speakers will often omit **el** before the number: **Hoy es nueve de abril**. Note that it is never omitted when referring to when an event will take place: **El próximo examen es el veinte de abril**.

■ To give the date, use the ordinal number **primero** for the first of a month, but use the cardinal numbers (**dos, tres, cuatro . . . treinta y uno**) for the other days. The names of months are not capitalized in Spanish. As with days of the week, use **el** to say *on* a date.

El primero / dos / tres . . . de . . .

| | | | | | |
|---|---|---|---|---|---|
| **enero** | *January* | **mayo** | *May* | **septiembre** | *September* |
| **febrero** | *February* | **junio** | *June* | **octubre** | *October* |
| **marzo** | *March* | **julio** | *July* | **noviembre** | *November* |
| **abril** | *April* | **agosto** | *August* | **diciembre** | *December* |

— ¿Qué fecha es hoy?   — *What's the date today?*
— Es el veinte de diciembre.   — *It's December twentieth.*
— ¿Qué vas a hacer para la Navidad?   — *What are you going to do for Christmas?*

— Voy a estar en México. Voy a volver el primero de enero.   — *I'm going to be in Mexico. I'm going to return on January first.*

■ When talking about a period of several days or more, you can use **desde** to give the starting date and **hasta** to say *until when*.

Voy a estar de vacaciones **desde** el veintitrés de diciembre **hasta** el dos de enero.   *I'm going to be on vacation (starting) from the twenty-third of December until January second.*

**5-32** ▶ **¿Cuál es la fecha?**  ¿Con qué fecha de la lista asocias cada celebración? Adivina (*Guess*) si no estás seguro/a y tu profesor/a te dirá (*will tell you*) si la fecha correcta es antes o después hasta que tu respuesta sea correcta.

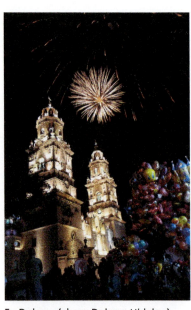

En Dolores (ahora Dolores Hidalgo), México, el cura (*priest*) Miguel Hidalgo inició la Guerra de Independencia en el año 1810 con el Grito de Dolores (*Cry from Dolores*). Cada 15 de septiembre un poco antes de la medianoche el presidente mexicano sale al balcón del Palacio Nacional para conmemorar este evento.

| | |
|---|---|
| el 27 de febrero | el 28 de julio |
| el 5 de mayo | el 15 de septiembre |
| el 4 de julio | el 16 de septiembre |
| el 5 de julio | el 12 de octubre |
| el 9 de julio | el 2 de noviembre |

1. el Día de la Independencia de México
2. la conmemoración de la victoria de los mexicanos contra los franceses en la batalla de Puebla
3. el Día de los Muertos en México
4. la Fiesta Nacional de Puerto Rico
5. la Fiesta Nacional de España
6. el Día de la Independencia de Costa Rica, El Salvador, Guatemala, Honduras y Nicaragua
7. el Día de la Independencia de la República Dominicana
8. el Día de la Independencia de Perú
9. el Día de la Independencia de Venezuela
10. el Día de la Independencia de Argentina

Originalmente creada para representar la clase social alta después de la revolución mexicana, la catrina es símbolo del Día de los Muerto, celebrado cada año el dos de noviembre.

**5-33 ▶ ¿Qué vas a hacer?** Pregúntale a otro/a estudiante si generalmente hace estas cosas en las fechas indicadas.

Modelo    el 31 de octubre / disfrazarse (*to dress up, to put on a costume*)
E1: *Generalmente, ¿te disfrazas el treinta y uno de octubre?*
E2: *A veces me disfrazo, pero otras veces no. ¿Y tú?*
E1: *Yo casi siempre me disfrazo.*

**1.** el 17 de marzo / ponerse ropa verde
**2.** el 25 de diciembre / pasar el día con la familia
**3.** el 31 de diciembre / salir con los amigos
**4.** el 1° de enero / levantarse temprano o tarde
**5.** el 14 de febrero / hacer algo especial
**6.** el 4 de julio / ver los fuegos artificiales (*fireworks*)

**5-34 ▶ Un calendario.**   ¿Qué planes tiene esta persona para este mes?

Modelo    *Va a visitar a su abuelita el primero de mayo.*

**5-35 ▶ Una fiesta.**   En parejas, hablen de una fiesta imaginaria que van a hacer para el cumpleaños de uno/a de ustedes. ¿Cuándo y dónde van a hacer la fiesta? ¿A quiénes van a invitar y qué van a hacer para divertirse? Preparen una conversación lógica.

#  Vocabulario

SAM: 5-36 to 5-42

## El tiempo y las estaciones

¿Cuál es tu **estación** favorita?

la primavera (20 de marzo – 21 de junio)
el verano (21 de junio – 22 de septiembre)
el otoño (22 de septiembre – 21 de diciembre)
el invierno (21 de diciembre – 20 de marzo)

**¿Qué tiempo hace?**

Hace sol. **El cielo** está **despejado**. Hace buen tiempo.

Hace (mucho) viento.

El cielo está nublado.

Llueve.

Nieva.

Hace (mucho) frío.

Hace fresco.

Hace (mucho) calor.

### ¿Sabías que...?

En los países de habla hispana, las temperaturas aparecen en grados centígrados y no en grados Fahrenheit. Para convertir los grados centígrados a grados Fahrenheit, multiplica por 9/5 y suma (*add*) 32.

### ¡Ojo!

The progressive forms **está lloviendo** (*it is raining*) and **está nevando** (*it is snowing*) are commonly used to say how the weather is at a particular moment. Use the infinitives **llover** and **nevar** to say how the weather is going to be in the near future: **Va a llover / nevar**. (*It's going to rain / snow.*)

**Una conversación.** Dos amigos, Lupe y Carlos, hablan de sus planes para mañana.

LUPE: ¿Qué vas a hacer mañana?
CARLOS: Tengo que trabajar por la mañana. Por la tarde, quiero ir al parque si hace buen tiempo. Si llueve, voy a estudiar. ¿Y tú? ¿Qué vas a hacer?
LUPE: Nada en especial. Si hace mal tiempo, voy a pasar el día en casa. Quiero dormir hasta tarde. Si hace buen tiempo, tengo ganas de ir de compras.

### ¡A escuchar!

CD 2, Track 37

Ahora, escuchen otra conversación en la cual Sonia va a visitar a Cristina, una amiga que vive muy lejos. ¿Cuándo va a llegar? ¿Qué tiempo hace esta semana? ¿Qué van a hacer si hace mal tiempo?

CD 2 Track 35

CD 2 Track 36

la estación *season*   ¿Qué tiempo hace? *What's the weather like?*   el cielo *the sky*   despejado/a *clear*

**5-36 ▶ ¿Es lógico?** Completa cada oración con la terminación lógica.

Modelo   Hace frío y *nieva* (hace calor, nieva).

En Taxco, México, cada día es como un día de primavera.

1. Hace calor y _____. (hace fresco, hace sol).
2. Llueve y _____. (hace mal tiempo, hace sol).
3. El cielo está nublado y _____. (llueve, hace sol).
4. El cielo está despejado y _____. (llueve, hace sol).
5. Hace sol y _____. (hace buen tiempo, nieva).

**5-37 ▶ Cuando . . .** ¿Qué te gusta hacer cuando hace el tiempo indicado?

| | | |
|---|---|---|
| comer en el patio | ir de compras | leer |
| dormir | ir al cine / lago / parque | nadar |
| esquiar | jugar a los videojuegos | quedarse en casa |
| ir a la playa | jugar al tenis | . . . |

Modelo   Cuando hace fresco, *me gusta correr por el parque.*

1. Cuando llueve . . .
2. Cuando nieva . . .
3. Cuando hace mucho frío . . .
4. Cuando hace mucho calor . . .
5. Cuando hace buen tiempo . . .

**5-38 ▶ ¿Qué te pones?** Describe la ropa que te pones cuando hace el tiempo indicado en la actividad anterior.

Modelo   Cuando hace fresco, *me pongo una camisa, un suéter y jeans.*

**5-39 ▶ Otra conversación.** En parejas, vuelvan a leer *Una conversación* entre Carlos y Lupe. Luego, preparen una conversación en la cual hablen de sus planes para este sábado si hace buen tiempo y si hace mal tiempo.

**5-40 ▶ Comparaciones culturales.** El clima afecta en cierta forma la personalidad de la gente y sus rutinas. Lee la siguiente información y contesta las preguntas.

El Caribe hispano, Cuba, Puerto Rico y la República Dominicana es un claro ejemplo de cómo el clima soleado (*sunny*) de todo el año influye en el carácter alegre (*joyful*) de las personas. Los caribeños tienen, en general, una actitud positiva ante la vida. Les gusta disfrutar de (*enjoy*) la vida y relajarse sin estrés ni prisas. El clima también afecta la actividad diaria de la gente. En climas cálidos (*warm*), como el Caribe, las personas socializan con frecuencia en la calle, porque hace buen tiempo y es agradable pasar tiempo al aire libre, en parques, plazas o junto (*by*) al mar. La luz del sol es fuente (*sunlight is a source*) de energía y vitalidad, y según los expertos, las personas que viven en climas cálidos son más sociables y abiertas que las personas que viven en climas fríos que son, generalmente, más reservadas.

1. ¿Crees que en las zonas cálidas de Estados Unidos la gente es más sociable y menos reservada que en las regiones más frías? ¿Crees que el clima es un factor en las diferencias de carácter?
2. ¿Cómo crees que influye el clima en la rutina y las diversiones de una persona que vive en Boston y una persona que vive en Miami?

# Resumen de gramática

SAM: 5-43
to 5-46

## Reflexive verbs

- Reflexive verbs describe actions that people do to or for themselves.

- In Spanish, verbs are also often reflexive when describing a change in mental or physical state: **aburrirse, despertarse (ie), divertirse (ie), enojarse, relajarse, sentirse (ie).**

  Reflexive verbs are also used when saying people do something to their own body: **acostarse (ue), bañarse, ducharse, lavarse (el pelo), levantarse, maquillarse, ponerse (la ropa), sentarse (ie), vestirse (i).**

- After reflexive verbs, the definite article (**el, la, los, las**) is used instead of possessive adjectives (*my, your, . . .*) with parts of the body or items of clothing.

- Reflexive pronouns are placed before the conjugated verb.

- With infinitives and present participles, they may be placed before the conjugated verb or attached to end of the infinitive or **-ando** / **-iendo** form of the verb.

- Note that after **antes de, después de**, or **para**, the reflexive pronoun must be placed at the end of an infinitive.

### Reflexive Pronouns

| | | | | |
|---|---|---|---|---|
| **me** | *myself* | | **nos** | *ourselves* |
| **te** | *yourself* | | **os** | *yourselves* |
| **se** | *yourself, oneself, himself, herself,* | | **se** | *yourselves, themselves* |

### **bañarse** *to bathe (oneself)*

| | | | | | | |
|---|---|---|---|---|---|---|
| yo | **me** | baño | | nosotros/as | **nos** | bañamos |
| tú | **te** | bañas | | vosotros/as | **os** | bañáis |
| Ud., él, ella | **se** | baña | | Uds., ellos/as | **se** | bañan |

—Generalmente, ¿dónde **te sientas** en clase? — *Generally, where do you sit in class?*

—**Me siento** cerca del profesor. — *I sit near the professor.*

—¿**Te aburres** en tus clases? — *Do you get bored in your classes?*

—**Me aburro** a veces, pero normalmente **me divierto**. — *I get bored sometimes, but normally I have fun.*

Me lavo **el** pelo todos los días. — *I wash **my** hair every day.*

**Me** visto en quince minutos. — *I get dressed in fifteen minutes.*

**Me** estoy visitiendo ahora. / Estoy vistiéndo**me** ahora. — *I'm getting dressed now.*

**Me** voy a vestir en el baño. / Voy a vestir**me** en el baño. — *I'm going to dress in the bathroom.*

**Me** maquillo después de vestir**me**. — *I put on my make-up after getting dressed.*

## Reciprocal verbs

- Reciprocal verbs indicate that two or more people do something to or for one another or each other. Reciprocal verbs have the same pronouns (**nos, os, se**) and the same placement rules as reflexive verbs.

—¿**Se** ven tu novia y tú todos los días? — *Do you and your girlfriend see each other every day?*

—Sí, **nos** encontramos después del trabajo para cenar. — *Yes, we meet each other after work for dinner.*

## *Acabar de*

- To say what someone just did, use **acabar de** + an infinitive. **Acabar** is a regular -**ar** verb.

**Acabamos de** levantarnos. — *We just got up.*
**Acabo de** lavarme el pelo. — *I just washed my hair.*
¿**Acabas de** llegar? — *Did you just arrive?*

## Demonstrative adjectives and pronouns

- Use the demonstrative adjectives to say *this / these* or *that / those.* There are two ways to say *that / those,* **ese** and **aquel**. **Aquel** is generally used to describe something at a greater distance than **ese**.

| **este** *(this / these)* | **ese** *(that / those)* | **aquel** *(that / those)* |
|---|---|---|
| este sombrero | ese sombrero | aquel sombrero |
| esta falda | esa falda | aquella falda |
| estos zapatos | esos zapatos | aquellos zapatos |
| estas botas | esas botas | aquellas botas |

- Demonstrative pronouns look like demonstrative adjectives, but they may have a written accent on the stressed **e**, and the noun is omitted.

¿Te gusta **este** traje o prefieres **ése** detrás de ti?

*Do you like this suit or do you prefer that one behind you?*

- Use the neuter forms: **esto, eso**, and **aquello** to refer to an idea or a situation rather than to a specific noun, or to refer to an unidentified noun.

**Eso** es imposible.
**Esto** es muy importante.

*That is impossible.*
*This is very important.*

## Present progressive

- Use the present progressive to describe actions in progress at a particular moment. It is composed of a conjugated form of **estar** and the present participle (**-ando** / **-iendo** form of the verb). The **i** of **-iendo** changes to **y** between vowels.

hablar → **hablando**
comer → **comiendo**
escribir → **escribiendo**

¿Quién está hablando?
Estamos comiendo.
¿Qué estás escribiendo?

*Who is talking?*
*We are eating.*
*What are you writing?*

leer → leyendo

¿Qué estás leyendo?

*What are you reading?*

- Stem changes occur only with **-ir** verbs in the present progressive. With these verbs **o** changes to **u** and **e** changes to **i**. There is no stem change for **-ar** and **-er** stem-changing verbs.

dormir → durmiendo

¿Está durmiendo el bebé?

*Is the baby sleeping?*

servir → sirviendo

¿Qué estás sirviendo?

*What are you serving?*

almorzar → almorzando

¿Estás almorzando?

*Are you having lunch?*

perder → perdiendo

Estamos perdiendo.

*We are losing.*

- In Spanish, the present progressive is rarely used with **ir** or **venir**. The simple present tense is used instead.

¿Adónde vas?
¿Vienen hoy?

*Where are you going?*
*Are they coming today?*

- Do not use the present progressive to express future actions as you do in English. Use the immediate future (**ir a** + infinitive) instead.

¿Qué vas a hacer esta noche?
Voy a quedarme en casa.

*What are you doing tonight?*
*I'm staying home.*

## Dates

- To give the date, use **primero** for the first of a month, but use the cardinal numbers (**dos, tres . . . treinta y uno**) for the other days. Months are not capitalized in Spanish.

Siempre voy a muchas fiestas **el treinta y uno de diciembre** y duermo todo el día **el primero de enero**.

*I always go to many parties on December thirty-first and sleep all day on January first.*

- When giving a range of dates, use **desde** to give the starting date and **hasta** to say *until* when.

Voy a estar de vacaciones **desde** el quince de agosto **hasta** el primero de septiembre.

*I'm going to be on vacation from August fifteenth until September first.*

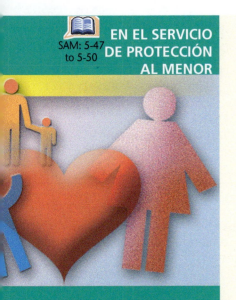

SAM: 5-47 to 5-50

**EN EL SERVICIO DE PROTECCIÓN AL MENOR**

En este capítulo, aprendiste (*you learned*) a hablar de la rutina diaria. Ahora vas a repasar lo que aprendiste con una simulación de la vida real trabajando para el Servicio de Protección al Menor (*Child Protective Services*).

**5-41 ▶ Custodia temporal.** Estás a cargo de (*in charge of*) dos hermanos, Diego y Lorenzo. Si se portan (*behave*) bien, ¿hacen las siguientes cosas o no?

Modelos   llevarse bien              irritarse todo el tiempo
          *Sí, se llevan bien.*      *No, no se irritan todo el tiempo.*

1. decirse cosas feas
2. hablarse con respeto
3. insultarse
4. pelearse
5. enojarse todo el tiempo
6. ayudarse

**5-42 ▶ ¿Ángel o diablito?** Lorenzo, el hermano mayor, se describe como un niño casi perfecto, pero dice que su hermano menor, Diego, tiene muchos problemas. ¿Qué dice Lorenzo que hace cada uno?

Modelo   levantarse de mal humor (*mood*) / levantarse de buen humor
         *Diego se levanta de mal humor pero yo me levanto de buen humor.*

1. despertarse muy poco durante la noche / despertarse mucho
2. enojarse con frecuencia / casi nunca enojarse
3. quedarse en la cama hasta muy tarde / casi siempre levantarse temprano
4. siempre lavarse los dientes / nunca lavarse los dientes
5. ponerse ropa sucia con frecuencia / siempre ponerse ropa limpia
6. acostarse temprano si hay clase al día siguiente / acostarse muy tarde

**¿Y tú?** Ahora pregúntale a otro/a estudiante si es más como Lorenzo o más como su hermano menor Diego.

Modelo   levantarse de mal humor (*mood*) / levantarse de buen humor
         E1: *¿Te levantas de mal humor o te levantas de buen humor?*
         E2: *Generalmente me levanto de buen humor.*

**5-43 ▶ ¿Qué están haciendo?** ¿Qué acaban de hacer los niños? ¿Qué están haciendo ahora? Utiliza los verbos en el orden lógico.

Modelo   desayunar / levantarse
         *Los niños acaban de levantarse. Ahora están desayunando.*

1. desayunar / lavarse los dientes
2. vestirse / bañarse
3. ponerse la chaqueta / vestirse
4. volver de la escuela / hacer su tarea
5. relajarse / terminar su tarea
6. enojarse / pelearse
7. acostarse / ponerse el pijama
8. acostarse / dormir

**5-44 ▶ ¿Qué tiempo hace?** Diles a los niños qué tiempo hace y qué ropa necesitan ponerse.

Modelo   *Hace mucho frío. Necesitan ponerse un abrigo y botas.*

1.
2.
3.
4.

**5-45 ▸ De compras.** Estás buscando ropa para los niños en el centro comercial. En grupos de tres, preparen una conversación en la cual hablan de varias prendas (*articles of clothing*). Utilicen **este / esta / estos / estas, ese / esa / esos / esas** y **aquel / aquella / aquellos / aquellas** en la conversación.

**5-46 ▸ Días feriados.** Utiliza las fechas de la lista y explica cuando hay vacaciones en la escuela de los niños. ¡Ojo! En español se escribe el día antes del mes.

Modelo    *Las vacaciones de Navidad son desde el dieciocho de diciembre hasta el primero de enero.*

| 15/1 | 16/2 | 13/3–22/3 | 26/5 | 1/9 | 21/11–26/11 | *18/12–1/1* |
|------|------|-----------|------|-----|-------------|-------------|

las vacaciones de Navidad
el Día del Trabajo
el Día de los Presidentes
las vacaciones de primavera

el Día de Conmemoración
    (*Memorial Day*)
el cumpleaños de Martin Luther King
las vacaciones de Acción de Gracias

¡Hola!  **Entre profesionales**

If you enjoy working with children, you might consider working in bilingual education. Visit MySpanishLab for *Hoy día* to find more useful vocabulary, information, and activities such as the following related to this field of work.

**5-47 ▸ Una junta con la directora.** La directora (*principal*) de una escuela bilingüe habla con un grupo de padres. Completa sus oraciones con el infinitivo lógico.

| ponerse | ofrecerse | familiarizarse | sentirse |
|---------|-----------|----------------|----------|
| comunicarse | reunirse (*to meet*) | presentarse | |

1. Para los padres es muy importante _____ parte de la escuela de sus hijos. Una buena manera de _____ con las actividades de la escuela y sus programas es _____ como voluntario.
2. Los padres deben _____ con los maestros varias veces al año para hablar sobre los progresos de sus hijos. Si vienen durante las horas de instrucción, es necesario _____ en la oficina para firmar (*to sign*) el registro.
3. Si tienen preguntas, deben _____ con el maestro de su hijo o _____ en contacto con el personal de la oficina.

## Pronóstico del tiempo

SAM: 5-51 to 5-52

### Antes de leer

¿Cómo es el clima en tu ciudad? ¿Miras el pronóstico del tiempo normalmente? ¿Te vistes de acuerdo con (*according to*) las predicciones del tiempo?

> ▶ **Reading Strategy** *Using standard formats.* Standard formats, like the weather forecast and other visual materials, facilitate the reading of certain texts when learning a foreign language. For example, when you look at a weather forecast, there are certain details accompanied by visuals that are used universally, no matter what the language is. When reading in a foreign language, take into account the non-textual information to help you gather information.

### Ahora tú

5-48 ▶ **Pronóstico semanal.** Observa con atención el gráfico del pronóstico del tiempo en Santiago, Chile. ¿Qué tiempo va a hacer cada día?

Modelo *El lunes, dos de agosto va a hacer viento y va a hacer fresco.*

DISFRUTA CHILE.COM

Destinos
Vuelos
Hoteles
Ocio
Guía de restaurantes

### El tiempo en Chile

Chile es un país de grandes contrastes y el clima refleja su variedad geográfica. El clima de Santiago, la capital, es mediterráneo. Las estaciones no están muy definidas y en realidad Santiago tiene una estación de lluvias y una estación seca[1]. Durante los meses de invierno, de mayo a septiembre, llueve bastante, pero generalmente no nieva mucho. El resto del año hace buen tiempo y las temperaturas son agradables. La temperatura media durante el invierno es de 8 grados centígrados aproximadamente, y la temperatura media durante el verano es de 19 grados centígrados.

**Pronóstico semanal de Santiago de Chile**

| | jueves 29 de julio | viernes 30 de julio | sábado 31 de julio | domingo 1 de agosto | lunes 2 de agosto | martes 3 de agosto | miércoles 4 de agosto |
|---|---|---|---|---|---|---|---|
| Mínima | 3° C | 0° C | 2° C | 6° C | 5° C | 4° C | 3° C |
| Máxima | 9° C | 5° C | 12° C | 13° C | 12° C | 11° C | 9° C |

[1] dry

## Después de leer

**5-49 ▶ Un viaje a Santiago.** Contesta las siguientes preguntas relacionadas con la lectura.

1. En Santiago, ¿están las estaciones del año bien definidas? ¿Cuántas estaciones hay?
2. ¿Cuándo es la estación de lluvias en Santiago? ¿Nieva también en la capital? Y en tu ciudad, ¿en qué estación llueve mucho? ¿Nieva algunas veces?
3. ¿Qué tiempo hace generalmente en agosto en tu ciudad? ¿Hace más frío o más calor que en Santiago, Chile?
4. Imagina que tus amigos y tú van a visitar Santiago de Chile, ¿en qué mes del año van a ir? ¿Por qué?
5. ¿Qué crees que hace la gente en Santiago durante los meses de julio y agosto? ¿Haces las mismas actividades en julio y agosto?

**5-50 ▶ ¿Qué tiempo está haciendo?** Contesta las siguientes preguntas utilizando el presente progresivo cuando sea apropiado.

1. ¿Cuál es tu estación favorita? ¿Qué tiempo está haciendo ahora en tu ciudad?
2. ¿Influye el clima en las actividades que tú y tus amigos están planeando? ¿Cómo?
3. ¿Crees que está cambiando el clima en tu ciudad a causa del calentamiento global (*global warming*)? Si crees que sí, ¿cómo está cambiando?
4. ¿Qué efectos notas que está teniendo el calentamiento global en Estados Unidos o en el mundo (*the world*)?

**5-51 ▶ Planes.** Completa la conversación de estas dos amigas con el verbo adecuado de la lista. Atención a los pronombres reflexivos.

| | | | |
|---|---|---|---|
| acostarse | encontrarse | llevarse | relajarse |
| divertirse | levantarse | quedarse | sentirse |

FÁTIMA: Lola, ¿qué vas a hacer durante las vacaciones de primavera?

LOLA: No sé, acabo de terminar los exámenes, y prefiero (1) _____ en casa y (2) _____ . Estoy muy cansada. ¿Y tú?

FÁTIMA: Voy a (3) _____ con mi hermana que está estudiando en Santiago, Chile.

LOLA: ¡Qué bueno! Ustedes van a (4) _____ mucho.

FÁTIMA: Sí, pero no voy a descansar nada. Mi hermana es muy activa, y seguro que vamos a (5) _____ todos los días temprano para ir de excursión, y vamos a (6) _____ tarde porque a ella le gusta mucho salir por la noche a bailar.

LOLA: Sí, pero ella va a (7) _____ muy contenta con tu visita.

FÁTIMA: Hmmm . . . eso es si podemos (8) _____ bien, porque cuando está aquí en casa, nos peleamos con frecuencia.

**5-52 ▶ Más pronósticos del tiempo.** Prepara un pronóstico del tiempo de tu ciudad para los próximos siete días. Utiliza como modelo el formato de las predicciones del tiempo en Santiago de Chile. Incluye las temperaturas en grados centígrados y en grados Fahrenheit.

## 📖 Mi gente, mi herencia

SAM: 5-53
to 5-55

### Antes de ver

Cada vez más las tradiciones y las culturas del mundo se encuentran y la identidad es cada vez más global. Pero todavía las personas se sienten orgullosas (*proud*) de sus raíces (*roots*) y viven su herencia (*heritage*) de una manera especial. Escucha los testimonios de varios hispanos en el video que describen cómo viven su herencia.

**5-53 ▶ Reflexiones.** Piensa en los distintos grupos étnicos que viven en Estados Unidos. ¿Cómo crees que viven su herencia en su rutina diaria? Y tú, ¿cómo vives tu herencia familiar?

> ▶ **Listening strategy** *Listening for words of the same family.* Adjectives that describe nationality derive from the name of the country of origin. In English, adjectives that describe nationality usually end in -*an*, -*ian*, -*n*. In Spanish, the most common endings for these adjectives are -**ano/a**, -**eño/a**, -**ino/a**, -**ol/a**, -**ayo/a**.
>
> de Perú → peru**ano/a**
> de Honduras → hondur**eño/a**
> de Argentina → argent**ino/a**
> de España → españ**ol/a**
> de Paraguay → paragu**ayo/a**

### Ahora tú

**5-54 ▶ Soy de . . .** Escucha a las personas en el video e identifica su país o región de origen y su nacionalidad como en el Modelo.

Modelo    *Héctor es de Costa Rica. Es costarricense.*

**1.** Analissa   **2.** Jorge   **3.** Itandehui   **4.** Edgar   **5.** Rosal

### Después de ver

**5-55 ▶ ¿Se sienten orgullosos?** Vuelve a escuchar con atención las palabras de las personas en el video que hablan sobre su herencia y sus raíces y responde de manera general a las siguientes preguntas.

**1.** ¿Se sienten orgullosos (*proud*) de su herencia?
**2.** ¿Se encuentran con gente de su mismo origen en la ciudad donde viven?
**3.** ¿Se divierten viviendo su herencia en su vida diaria? ¿Cómo se divierten?
**4.** ¿Cómo se sienten viviendo en Nueva York?

**5-56 ▶ Descripciones.** Describe a las siguientes personas del video e imaginen cómo es su rutina diaria y qué hacen cuando están con su familia y amigos.

**1.** Analissa Martínez, músico
**2.** Edgar Alcaraz, estudiante de administración de empresas
**3.** Hector Marín, pintor

# ESCRITORES EN ACCIÓN

## 📖 Confirmación de una visita

SAM: 5-56

### Antes de escribir

Un/a amigo/a va a visitarte (*to visit you*) el próximo fin de semana. Vas a escribirle para confirmar las fechas de su visita, y contarle qué van a hacer, qué tiempo va a hacer y la ropa que debe traer.

> ▶ **Writing strategies** *Sequencing actions.* When talking about your plans, you will generally need to sequence events and activities using words and expressions that will provide order to your text and make it flow more smoothly. Here are some examples:
>
> | | | | |
> |---|---|---|---|
> | **primero** | *first* | **durante** | *during* |
> | **luego** | *then, next, later* | **mientras tanto** | *meanwhile* |
> | **más tarde** | *later* | **en seguida** | *right away* |
> | **pronto** | *soon* | **desde . . . hasta** | *(starting)* |
> | **después** | *afterwards* | | *from . . . until* |

### ¡Ojo!

Remember to use infinitives instead of the *-ing* form or a conjugated form of a verb after **antes de** and **después de**.

Vamos a relajarnos un poco **antes de salir**.
*We are going to relax a little before going out.*
*We are going to relax a little before we go out.*

**5-57 ▶ ¡Prepárate!** Antes de escribir tu nota de confirmación, anota ideas relacionadas con las cuatro categorías siguientes:

- las fechas de la visita de tu amigo/a
- las actividades que van a realizar durante su visita
- el tiempo que va a hacer
- la ropa que él/ella debe traer

### Ahora tú

**5-58 ▶ Tu nota de confirmación.** Escribe ahora tu nota de confirmación incluyendo ideas de las categorías mencionadas y un saludo (*greeting*) y una despedida (*farewell*) de la página 127.

### Después de escribir

**5-59 ▶ ¡Edita!** Intercambia (*Exchange*) tu nota con un/a compañero/a y revisa el texto que él/ella ha escrito (*has written*). ¿Aparece toda la información relevante? Piensa en sugerencias para mejorar (*to improve*) la gramática y la organización del texto.

**5-60 ▶ ¡Revisa!** Revisa tu nota y asegúrate (*make sure*) que contenga los siguientes elementos:

- ❏ los verbos para hablar de actividades diarias
- ❏ el vocabulario para hablar del clima
- ❏ el vocabulario para hablar de la ropa
- ❏ las palabras y estructuras para indicar la secuencia de los eventos

**5-61 ▶ ¡Navega!** Visita la página web de *Hoy día* para encontrar enlaces de buscadores (*links for search engines*) en español. Selecciona uno e introduce el nombre de tu ciudad, el estado y la palabra "turismo". ¿Hay sitios en español con información sobre el turismo en tu ciudad? ¿Describen actividades o lugares interesantes para incluir en tus planes de visita de tu amigo/a? ¿Qué otra información útil aparece?

## La rutina diaria

| | |
|---|---|
| aburrirse | to get bored |
| acostarse (ue) | to lie down, to go to bed |
| bañarse | to bathe, to take a bath |
| despertarse (ie) | to wake up |
| divertirse (ie, i) | to have fun, to amuse yourself |
| ducharse | to shower, to take a shower |
| irse | to leave, to go away |
| lavarse el pelo / la cara | to wash your hair / your face |
| lavarse los dientes | to brush your teeth |
| levantarse | to get up |
| maquillarse | to put on make-up |
| ponerse (la ropa) | to put on (your clothes) |
| quedarse | to stay |
| relajarse | to relax |
| sentarse (ie) | to sit down |
| sentirse (ie, i) | to feel |
| vestirse (i, i) | to get dressed |

## Las interacciones personales

| | |
|---|---|
| abrazar(se) | to hug (each other) |
| ayudar(se) | to help (each other) |
| besar(se) | to kiss (each other) |
| casarse (con) | to marry, to get married (to) |
| comunicar (se) | to communicate (with each other) |
| divorciarse (de) | to divorce, to get divorced (from) |
| enamorarse (de) | to fall in love (with) |
| encontrarse (ue) (con) | to get together (with), meet up (with) |
| enojarse | to get angry |
| llevarse bien (con) | to get along well (with) |
| pelearse | to fight |
| presentarse | to introduce yourself |
| querer(se) (ie) | to love (each other) |

## La ropa

| | |
|---|---|
| el abrigo | overcoat |
| la blusa | blouse |
| la bolsa | purse |
| las botas | boots |
| los calcetines | socks |
| la camisa | shirt |
| la camiseta | T-shirt |
| la chaqueta | jacket |
| el cinturón | belt |
| la corbata | necktie |
| la falda | skirt |
| la gorra | cap |
| el impermeable | raincoat |
| los jeans | jeans |
| los pantalones | pants |
| los pantalones cortos | shorts |
| el pijama | pajamas |
| las sandalias | sandals |
| el sombrero | hat |
| la sudadera | sweatshirt |
| el suéter | sweater |
| los tenis | sneakers |
| el traje | suit |
| el traje de baño | swimsuit |
| el vestido | dress |
| los zapatos | shoes |

## De compras

| | |
|---|---|
| el cliente / la clienta | customer |
| el dependiente / la dependienta | salesclerk |
| el precio | price |
| los probadores | fitting rooms |
| la talla | size |

## Acciones

| | |
|---|---|
| buscar | to look for |
| gastar | to spend (money) |
| llevar | to take, to carry, to wear |
| llevarse | to take away |
| probarse (ue) | to try on |

## Descripciones

| | |
|---|---|
| aquel / aquella (aquellos/as) | that (those) (over there) |
| barato/a | cheap |
| ese / esa (esos/as) | that (those) |
| este / esta (estos/as) | this (these) |
| razonable | reasonable |

## Otras palabras y expresiones

| | |
|---|---|
| cómo no | of course |
| con cheque | with a check |
| con tarjeta de crédito / débito | with a credit / debit card |
| en efectivo | in cash |
| ¿En qué puedo servirle? | How may I help you? |
| estar de moda | to be in fashion |
| por acá | over / through here |

## La fecha

| | |
|---|---|
| ¿Qué fecha es? | *What is the date?* |
| Es (el) primero (dos, tres . . .) de . . . | *It's the first (second, third . . .) of . . .* |
| enero | *January* |
| febrero | *February* |
| marzo | *March* |
| abril | *April* |
| mayo | *May* |
| junio | *June* |
| julio | *July* |
| agosto | *August* |
| septiembre | *September* |
| octubre | *October* |
| noviembre | *November* |
| diciembre | *December* |

## Otras palabras

| | |
|---|---|
| ¿Aló? | *Hello? (on the telephone)* |
| Chau. | *Ciao., Bye.* |
| el chiste | *joke* |
| el/la invitado/a | *guest* |
| sacar una foto | *to take a picture* |

## El tiempo

| | |
|---|---|
| ¿Qué tiempo hace? | *What's the weather like?* |
| El cielo está despejado / nublado. | *The sky's clear / cloudy.* |
| Hace buen / mal tiempo. | *The weather's good / bad.* |
| Hace (mucho) calor. | *It's (very) hot.* |
| Hace fresco. | *It's cool.* |
| Hace (mucho) frío. | *It's (very) cold.* |
| Hace sol. | *It's sunny.* |
| Hace viento. | *It's windy.* |
| Llueve. | *It rains. It's raining.* |
| Nieva. | *It snows. It's snowing.* |
| Va a llover / nevar. | *It's going to rain / to snow.* |

## Las estaciones del año

| | |
|---|---|
| la primavera | *spring* |
| el verano | *summer* |
| el otoño | *autumn, fall* |
| el invierno | *winter* |

Visit MySpanishLab for *Hoy día* for links to the mnemonic dictionary online for suggestions such as the following to help you remember vocabulary from this chapter, learn related words in Spanish, and use Spanish words to build your vocabulary in English.

### EXAMPLES

**hacer calor,** *to be hot:* The body burns **calor,**ies for heat. Related words in Spanish: **calentar (ie),** *to heat;* **calentarse (ie),** *to get hot, to warm up;* **un clima cálido,** *a warm climate;* **un día caluroso,** *a hot day;* **un plato caliente,** *a hot plate.*

**hacer sol,** *to be sunny:* **Sol**ar energy comes from the sun and a **sol**stice refers to a shifting in the position of the sun with respect to the northern and southern hemispheres. Related words in Spanish: **solar,** *solar;* **un día soleado,** *a sunny day;* **el solsticio,** *the solstice.*

# 6 En Internet

En este capítulo, vas a hablar de las computadoras y los usos de Internet y repasar (*review*) el vocabulario y la gramática de los capítulos anteriores.

Terra Networks es el proveedor (*provider*) de servicios de Internet número uno en Latinoamérica y España y produce más contenido original digital para los hispanos en Estados Unidos que cualquier (*any*) otra compañía. Según un estudio de Terra Networks, el 75% de los internautas (*Internet users*) hispanos en Estados Unidos utiliza frecuentemente Internet y ve la televisión al mismo tiempo. El 44% de este 75% envía (*sends*) mensajes instantáneos o por correo electrónico sobre el programa que está mirando. El 40% dice que busca información en Internet de productos anunciados en televisión y el 35% visita el sitio web del programa que está viendo.

- ▸ ¿Ves la tele mientras navegas en la web?
- ▸ ¿Envías mensajes sobre los programas que ves?
- ▸ ¿Buscas información en Internet de los productos que ves anunciados en televisión?

# Vocabulario    Los procesadores de texto

SAM: 6-1
to 6-2

## ¿Sabías que...?

Con frecuencia se usan términos ingleses en español para hablar de las computadoras:

la web = la red

el email = el correo electrónico

el spam = el correo no deseado

el software = la aplicación informática / el programa informático

el hardware = los componentes físicos de una computadora

el comando = la orden

## ¡Ojo!

**Comprehension strategies.** Many words related to technology are cognates, and you can often guess the meanings of other words by basing them on the formats of similar software in English with which you are already familiar. You may wish to review the comprehension strategies *Recognizing cognates* and *Using standard formats* on pages 28 and 156.

En este capítulo vas a repasar el vocabulario y las estructuras gramaticales de los *Capítulos 1–5* en una simulación de la vida real dando clases de computación para mayores *(senior citizens)* en español en un centro comunitario. No se presenta gramática nueva.

CD 2, Track 49

¿Qué procesador de texto usas? ¿Qué se ve en la pantalla *(screen)* al abrir el programa?

CD 2
Track 50

**Una conversación.** Un voluntario de un centro comunitario habla con una señora mayor que no sabe *(doesn't know how)* usar la computadora pero quiere aprender.

EL VOLUNTARIO: ¿Qué desea aprender a hacer con la computadora?

LA SEÑORA: Sobre todo, quiero entender a mis hijos y a mis nietos cuando hablan de las computadoras y la tecnología, pues cuando estoy con ellos, no entiendo nada. Además, quiero comunicarme con ellos por email.

EL VOLUNTARIO: ¿Sabe usar un procesador de texto como *Microsoft Word*?

LA SEÑORA: No, no sé nada de computadoras, pero quiero aprender a navegar por Internet y usar el correo electrónico. Tengo una amiga que habla de sus viajes y otras experiencias virtuales. Tiene muchos amigos virtuales, ¡hasta un novio! No sé exactamente qué son los viajes ni los novios virtuales, pero me parecen interesantes para una persona mayor que vive sola como yo.

EL VOLUNTARIO: ¿Le gustaría crear una página o participar en una red social como *Facebook* o *MySpace*?

LA SEÑORA: No quiero mi propia página, pero me gustaría ver las páginas de mis nietos.

 CD 2, Track 51

## ¡A escuchar!

Ahora escuchen otra conversación en la cual un hombre mayor habla de por qué quiere aprender a navegar por la red. ¿Qué quiere aprender a hacer en Internet? ¿Qué sabe hacer ya *(already know how to do)*? ¿Qué necesita aprender a subir *(upload)*?

**6-1 ▶ Comandos.** Explícale a una persona con quien estás trabajando en qué menú de Microsoft Word **(Inicio, Insertar, Diseño de página** o **el botón de *Microsoft Office*)** debe hacer clic para realizar (*perform*) las siguientes acciones.

Modelo   Para crear un nuevo documento, se hace clic en *el botón de Microsoft Office.*

1. Para cambiar la fuente de cursiva a negrita (*bold*) se hace clic en . . .
2. Para encontrar formas como círculos o triángulos, se hace clic en . . .
3. Para insertar una tabla, se hace clic en . . .
4. Para cambiar la orientación de la página, se hace clic en . . .
5. Para insertar o cambiar un encabezado (*heading*) o un pie de página (*footer*), se hace clic en . . .
6. Para abrir un archivo (*file*), se hace clic en . . .
7. Para cambiar los márgenes de la página, se hace clic en . . .
8. Para copiar, cortar o pegar (*paste*) texto, se hace clic en . . .
9. Para insertar números de páginas, se hace clic en . . .
10. Para cambiar el número de columnas, se hace clic en . . .

**6-2 ▶ Comparaciones culturales.** Lee el siguiente artículo basado en un informe de la UNESCO sobre la brecha digital (*digital divide*) en el mundo y prepara una lista de los cognados que encuentres agrupados en las siguientes categorías: adjetivos, sustantivos (*nouns*) y verbos. Luego, contesta las preguntas que siguen al artículo.

Modelos   Adjetivos: *titulado*
Sustantivos: *sociedades*
Verbos: *alerta*

En un informe titulado "Hacia las sociedades del conocimiento", la Organización de las Naciones Unidas para la Educación, la Ciencia y la Cultura (UNESCO) alerta que el uso de Internet puede resultar en la desaparición de la mayoría de las 6.000 lenguas que se hablan hoy en el planeta. El documento mantiene que las nuevas tecnologías favorecen la homogeneización de la cultura y disminuyen la diversidad, señalando que "tres de cada cuatro páginas en Internet están escritas en inglés".

La organización reconoce que las nuevas tecnologías ofrecen muchos beneficios para las sociedades, pero también afirma que la disparidad en el acceso a las tecnologías de la información, la llamada "brecha digital", es un obstáculo entre los habitantes de muchas partes del mundo y los servicios ofrecidos por Internet. El 90% de la gente conectada a Internet vive en los países industrializados y usa un "club selecto" de lenguas vehiculares.

1. ¿Cuántas lenguas se hablan ahora en el planeta?
2. ¿Crees que es importante conservar esas lenguas?
3. De cada cuatro páginas web en Internet, ¿cuántas están escritas en inglés?
4. ¿Cómo se dice "la brecha digital" en inglés?
5. ¿Qué porcentaje de la gente que usa Internet vive en los países industrializados?

# 📖 Repaso 1

SAM: 6-3 to 6-4

## Expressing the verb to be:
## Ser, estar, and hay

Para **averiguar**

In the activities on this page, you will be reviewing the verbs *ser, estar,* and *hay.* Do you remember . . .
- whether you use the forms of **ser** or **estar** to say who people are? where they are from? where they are now? what they are like? how they are doing?
- how you say *there is, there are, is there,* and *are there*?
- what types of adjectives you use with **ser** to describe someone or something? what types of adjectives you use with **estar**?

See pages 12, 20, 40, and 108 or refer to the verb charts in the appendix or in *MySpanishLab* for review.

**6-3 ▶ Ansiedades.** Varias personas mayores hablan de su deseo y su miedo de aprender a usar una computadora. Empieza cada oración con **Somos . . .** o **Estamos . . .**

Modelo   poco acostumbrados (*accustomed*) a las nuevas tecnologías
*Estamos* poco acostumbrados a las nuevas tecnologías.

**1.** listos para aprender
**2.** mayores
**3.** como el loro (*parrot*) viejo que no aprende a hablar
**4.** interesados en la tecnología
**5.** nerviosos con las computadoras
**6.** estudiantes dedicados
**7.** preparados para la lección

**6-4 ▶ Primeros pasos.** Estás explicándole a alguien cómo se usa un procesador de texto. Completa las siguientes oraciones con **hay** o la forma correcta de **ser** o **estar**. Utiliza cada verbo sólo una vez en cada explicación.

Modelo   No *hay* por qué *estar* nervioso. *Es* fácil aprender a usar una computadora.

**1.** No _____ difícil usar este procesador de texto. _____ varios menús y los más importantes _____ en la barra de herramientas (*tool bar*).
**2.** La barra de herramientas _____ en la parte superior de la pantalla (*screen*). _____ la barra donde _____ varios iconos.
**3.** _____ algunos iconos que no _____ siempre visibles en la barra de herramientas porque _____ menos útiles.
**4.** _____ posible mover una selección de texto de una parte de un documento a otra, utilizando los dos botones "cortar" y "pegar" (*paste*) que _____ en la parte izquierda de la barra de herramientas. También _____ un botón para copiar texto.
**5.** Una fuente _____ un estilo de letra. _____ varias opciones como *Ariel* o *Tahoma* y la selección de fuentes _____ en este menú.
**6.** El comando "Ortografía y gramática" _____ útil si quiere ver si _____ errores gramaticales o errores de ortografía. _____ en el menú "Revisar".
**7.** _____ fácil crear un documento, ¿verdad? ¿ _____ preguntas o _____ todo claro por el momento?

**6-5 ▶ ¿Por qué vender por Internet?** Durante una lección sobre Internet, los participantes hablan de las tiendas en línea. Completa las siguientes oraciones con **hay** o con la forma correcta de **ser** o **estar**.

Modelo   *Hay* muchos beneficios de tener una tienda en Internet.

**1.** No _____ necesario tener mucho dinero para establecer una tienda en línea.
**2.** No _____ límite de posibilidades si su tienda _____ en Internet.
**3.** Sus productos _____ disponibles (*available*) para todo el mundo y no solamente en un área limitada.
**4.** La tienda puede _____ abierta las veinticuatro horas del día.
**5.** No _____ gastos (*expenses*) de alquiler ni de servicios públicos.
**6.** El correo electrónico _____ la mejor manera de promocionar los productos y no cuesta nada.
**7.** Las tiendas en Internet _____ muy competitivas y el servicio al cliente _____ muy importante.
**8.** Si los clientes no _____ satisfechos (*satisfied*), siempre _____ otras opciones para comprar por Internet.

# 📖 Repaso 2  Naming and describing people and things: Articles, nouns, and adjectives

SAM: 6-5 to 6-6

**6-6 ▶ Términos.** Completa las siguientes definiciones relacionadas con las computadoras con las formas correctas del artículo definido (**el, la, los, las**). Luego, indica qué expresión de la lista se explica en cada definición.

| la compresión de archivos | la extensión | la piratería |
|---|---|---|
| *la placa madre* | la informática | |

**Modelo**   Es *la* placa (*board*) principal de circuitos de *la* computadora.
Es *la placa madre*.

**1.** Es _____ grupo de tres letras que identifican _____ categoría de un archivo (*file*) como .doc para _____ documentos de *Microsoft Word* o .pdf para _____ archivos de *Adobe*.
**2.** Es _____ reducción del tamaño (*size*) de archivos para su transmisión vía Internet.
**3.** Es _____ tratamiento automático de _____ información por medio de computadoras.
**4.** Es _____ robo o _____ destrucción de un programa informático o de otro material protegido.

**6-7 ▶ Más términos.** Completa las siguientes definiciones con las formas correctas del artículo indefinido (**un, una**). Luego, indica qué expresión de la lista se explica en cada definición.

| una aplicación | un chat | un icono |
|---|---|---|
| un avatar | *una descarga* | un emoticono |

**Modelo**   Es *una* transferencia de datos por Internet.
Es *una descarga*.

**1.** Es _____ conversación en tiempo real por Internet.
**2.** Es _____ pequeño símbolo en la pantalla de _____ computadora que representa _____ programa.
**3.** Es _____ programa usado para realizar _____ tarea específica.
**4.** Es _____ símbolo como :-) o :-(que representa las emociones o los sentimientos de _____ persona en comunicaciones vía Internet.
**5.** Es _____ representación gráfica de _____ participante en _____ sala de chat o _____ foro.

**6-8 ▶ Emoticonos.** Dos amigas usan los siguientes emoticonos en lugar de adjetivos o sustantivos (*nouns*) en sus mensajes instantáneos. Cambia los emoticonos por la palabra española en la forma correcta.

| -_- | normal | :-( | triste | $-$ | rico/a |
|---|---|---|---|---|---|
| OwO | sorprendido/a | :-\ | disgustado/a | :-x | callado/a |
| <3 | enamorado/a | :-O | asustado/a (*scared*) | 0:-) | santo/a |
| :-) | feliz | :-m | pensativo/a | ò-ó | enojado/a |

DANIELA: Hola, Mónica. ¿Cómo estás?
MÓNICA: Estoy muy :-). Estoy <3 de un chico.
DANIELA: Estoy OwO. ¿Quién es? ¿Cómo es?
MÓNICA: Es un 0:-). Es un chico :-m y :-x pero muy guapo y tiene padres $-$. ¿Y tú? ¿Cómo estás?
DANIELA: Estoy un poco :-( y :-O. Mi novio está ò-ó conmigo.
MÓNICA: Es -_- tener problemas de vez en cuando, aún en las relaciones :-).

## 📖 Repaso 3 Saying how many: Numbers

SAM: 6-7
to 6-8

## Para averiguar

In the activities on this page, you will be reviewing numbers. Do you remember . . .

■ which numbers between 16 and 99 are written as single words? which must be written as three separate words?

■ when you use **cien** to say *one hundred*? when you use **ciento**?

■ which of these numbers does not change in plural forms: **cien/ciento, mil, un millón**? which has feminine plural forms?

■ when you use a period with numbers in Spanish? a comma?

See pages 14 and 102 for review.

**6-9 ▶ Los bloggers hispanos.** Completa las siguientes estadísticas de una encuesta (*survey*) de bitacoras.com sobre los bloggers hispanos con los números indicados.

Modelo   El *ochenta y uno* (81) por ciento de los bloggers son hombres y el *diecinueve* (19) por ciento son mujeres.

1. El _____ (38) por ciento de los bloggers tiene entre _____ (25) y _____ (34) años y el _____ (80) por ciento tiene entre _____ (19) y _____ (44) años.

2. El _____ (51) por ciento de los bloggers hispanos son españoles, el _____ (12) por ciento son argentinos, el _____ (9) por ciento mexicanos, el _____ (7) por ciento chilenos y el _____ (21) por ciento es de otras regiones hispanas.

3. El _____ (34) por ciento de los blogs tiene temas personales o autobiográficos, el _____ (11) por ciento es sobre las noticias (*news*) y la actualidad (*current issues*), el _____ (10) por ciento sobre cultura y sociedad, el _____ (6) por ciento sobre los medios de comunicación, el _____ (5) por ciento sobre historia, literatura y arte y el _____ (3) por ciento sobre tecnología.

4. El momento de la semana más activo en los blogs son los miércoles de _____ (16) a _____ (20) horas, es decir entre las _____ (4) y las _____ (8) de la tarde. El domingo es el día menos activo.

**6-10 ▶ ¿Cuál se usa más?** Compara el número de impactos (*hits*) en búsquedas por Internet para averiguar qué terminos son más comunes en español. Indica los números en español.

Modelo   "un sitio web" (14.800.000), "un sitio de Internet" (433.000)
*Hay catorce millones ochocientos mil para "un sitio web" y cuatrocientos treinta y tres mil para "un sitio de Internet".*

1. "página web" (145.000.000), "página de Internet" (546.000.000)
2. "navegar en la red" (69.100), "navegar en la web" (46.100)
3. "un buscador de Internet" (55.000), "un motor de búsqueda de Internet" (2.100.000)
4. "escribir un email" (46.800), "escribir un correo electrónico" (41.700)
5. "recibir spam" (40.400), "recibir correos no deseados" (212)
6. "una aplicación informática" (221.000), "un programa informático" (617.000)
7. "abrir un archivo" (188.000), "abrir un documento" (88.000)
8. "cargar una foto" (59.700), "subir una foto" (823.000)

## 📖 Repaso 4  Making comparisons: Comparatives

SAM: 6-9 to 6-10

**6-11 ▶ Más sobre los blogs.** Lee la siguiente información sobre los blogs y completa las oraciones con **más . . . que, menos . . . que** o **tanto . . . como**.

Modelo  El 86% de los bloggers escribe blogs en casa, el 38% en el trabajo, el 8% en un centro de estudios y el 7% en cibercafés. Los bloggers escriben *más* en casa *que* en el trabajo y casi *tantos* bloggers escriben donde estudian *como* en un cibercafé.

1. El 5% de los bloggers hispanos son peruanos, el 4% son colombianos y, el 3% son venezolanos. Hay _____ bloggers colombianos _____ venezolanos, pero hay _____ colombianos _____ peruanos.

2. El 22% dedica más de una hora todos los días a los blogs, el 24% una hora y el 23% media hora. Casi _____ personas pasan más de una hora en los blogs _____ las que pasan una hora o media hora en los blogs.

3. El 35% de los bloggers hispanos lee blogs en otras lenguas y un 65% lo hace sólo en español. _____ bloggers hispanos prefieren leer blogs sólo en español _____ en otras lenguas.

4. El 2% de los blogs es sobre temas humorísticos, el 1,9% sobre fotografía, el 1,9% sobre diseño y moda (*fashion*), el 1,8% sobre empleo y el 1,8% sobre música. Hay _____ blogs sobre fotografía _____ sobre diseño y moda, y hay _____ blogs sobre empleo _____ sobre música, pero hay _____ blogs sobre temas humorísticos _____ sobre cada uno de estos temas.

5. El 19% de los bloggers prefiere escribir por la noche, el 8% por la mañana y el 8% por la tarde. El 60% de los bloggers no tiene una hora preferida para escribir. _____ bloggers prefieren escribir por la mañana _____ por la tarde, pero _____ bloggers prefieren la mañana o la tarde _____ la noche.

**6-12 ▶ Correcciones.** Corrige las siguientes afirmaciones incorrectas usando **más . . . que** o **menos . . . que** en lugar de (*in place of*) **tan / tanto . . . como**.

Modelo  En Estados Unidos los adultos pasan *tanto* tiempo navegando en Internet *como* viendo la televisión.
*En Estados Unidos los adultos pasan más tiempo navegando en Internet que viendo la televisión.*

1. Las redes (*networks*) sociales son *tan* populares entre las personas mayores (*senior citizens*) *como* entre los jóvenes.
2. Internet es *tan* popular *como* los periódicos para informarse de las noticias (*news*).
3. Generalmente, la información publicada en Internet es *tan* fidedigna (*trustworthy*) *como* la información publicada en los libros.
4. Generalmente, se puede encontrar información *tan* reciente en Internet *como* en los libros.
5. Es *tan* fácil expresar su opinión en un blog *como* en la página editorial de un periódico.
6. Hay *tantas* páginas web en otras lenguas *como* en inglés.
7. La distribución de publicidad por televisión es *tan* cara *como* por email.
8. Las conexiones a Internet vía línea telefónica normal son *tan* rápidas *como* las conexiones vía fibra óptica.

Para **averiguar**

In the activities on this page, you will be reviewing comparatives. Do you remember . . .

■ how **más . . . que** and **menos . . . que** can be translated in English?
■ what **tan . . . como** means?
■ what **tanto . . . como** means? when **tanto** changes forms?
See page 110 for review.

**Vocabulario**  Los sitios web y las búsquedas

SAM: 6-11
to 6-12

CD 2
Track 52

Generalmente se pueden clasificar los sitios web en las siguientes categorías:

sitio buscador
sitio de comercio electrónico
sitio weblog (blog)
sitio de información
sitio de noticias
sitio de comunidad virtual

¿A qué categoría pertenece la página web que sigue?

**¡Ojo!**

**Comprehension strategy.** In order to find information efficiently on the Internet, it is necessary to skim web pages quickly to see whether they contain the information you are looking for. Skim the web page shown here to determine whether it is the homepage for a blog site, a company site, or a news site. What types of products does it offer? If you were looking for language textbooks, should you look further on this site or search for another one? See page 92 to review the comprehension strategy *Skimming*.

el encabezado

el punto c...al que llama más la atención

los menús de enlaces

el pie de página

**Una conversación.** Un voluntario que enseña diseño de páginas de Internet habla con un señor sobre el diseño de una página web.

EL VOLUNTARIO: ¿Qué tipo de página web le gustaría crear?

EL SEÑOR: Mi hijo es carpintero y quiero hacer una página para su compañía con información básica.

EL VOLUNTARIO: Bueno, primero vamos a hablar de la organización de la página principal. Normalmente hay cuatro secciones básicas en la página inicial. El encabezado tiene el nombre y el logo de la compañía. ¿Ya tienen un logo?

EL SEÑOR: Sí, es el nombre de la compañía, *Carpintería Reyes*, con dibujos de varias herramientas de carpintería.

EL VOLUNTARIO: Debajo del encabezado viene el contenido principal. Con frecuencia aquí hay una foto o una imagen como punto central para llamar la atención. A la derecha o a la izquierda del contenido principal está el menú de enlaces para navegar por otras páginas del sitio.

EL SEÑOR: ¿Como páginas con más fotos y una lista de precios?

EL VOLUNTARIO: Sí, así es. Finalmente está el pie de página. Frecuentemente contiene información como la dirección, el teléfono y la dirección de correo electrónico de la compañía.

CD 2, Track 54

## ¡A escuchar!

Ahora escuchen otra conversación en la cual dos personas hablan de una página de Internet de una agencia de viajes. ¿Cuáles son los aspectos positivos y cuáles los negativos del sitio?

**6-13 ▶ Comparaciones culturales.** Lee el siguiente artículo sobre el comercio electrónico en Latinoamérica. Luego indica si las afirmaciones que siguen el texto son ciertas o falsas. Corrige las oraciones falsas.

## El comercio electrónico en Latinoamérica

Hay varios obstáculos para el comercio electrónico en Latinoamérica: la baja conectividad, la desconfianza[1] de los consumidores y la poca disposición[2] al uso de tarjetas de crédito, pero las tiendas en línea empiezan a establecerse. Actualmente, el comercio electrónico crece[3] un 40% anualmente y las posibilidades de mantener esta expansión son buenas.

Chile es el país de Latinoamérica más activo en comercio electrónico y el 77% de los internautas[4] dice comprar en línea. Así mismo, los residentes de la capital chilena, Santiago, poseen más tarjetas de crédito que los de cualquier otra región de Latinoamérica. Argentina es el segundo país más activo con el 74% y México el tercero con el 71%. Los productos que más se venden por Internet son equipos electrónicos (50%), teléfonos u otros equipos de comunicación (28%) y libros (18%).

[1]mistrust  [2]willingness  [3]is growing  [4]Internet users

1. El uso de tarjetas de crédito es bajo en Latinoamérica y esto afecta al comercio electrónico de la región.
2. Menos consumidores compran en línea en Chile que en otras regiones de Latinoamérica.
3. Se gasta tanto en libros en línea como en equipos electrónicos.

## 📖 Repaso 1
SAM: 6-13
to 6-14

## Saying what people do: Conjugations of -ar, -er, and -ir verbs

**6-14 ▶ La generación multitarea (*multitasking*).** En el mundo moderno, todos tenemos que hacer varias cosas a la vez. Completa el siguiente artículo sobre la multitarea con las formas correctas de los verbos entre paréntesis.

Se dice que los jóvenes de hoy (1) _____ (pertenecer) a la "generación multitarea". (Ellos) (2) _____ (escuchar) música en su iPod, (3)_____ (participar) en un chat y (4) _____ (responder) a mensajes en su celular, todo mientras (5) _____ (estudiar) o (6) _____ (intentar [*to attempt*]) estudiar para un examen al día siguiente. La tecnología (7) _____ (permitir) hacer varias actividades a la vez, pero muchos expertos (8) _____ (creer) que la multitarea (9) _____ (reducir) la capacidad de aprendizaje y memoria. Según algunos estudios, una persona que (10) _____ (hacer) varias tareas a la vez, (11) _____ (comprender) menos porque no (12) _____ (entrar) profundamente en la materia. Esto (13) _____ (limitar) la capacidad de aprender en detalle porque no (14) _____ (dejar) suficiente tiempo para la consolidación de la materia en la memoria. Según un estudio de la Universidad de California, Los Ángeles, "las personas que (15) _____ (aprender) cosas utilizando la multitarea (16) _____ (utilizar) una parte diferente del cerebro que las personas que (17) _____ (estar) concentradas en una sola cosa." Además de causar problemas de aprendizaje, las investigaciones (18) _____ (indicar) que la multitarea (19) _____ (producir) más estrés y a veces (20) _____ (causar) problemas de salud (*health*).

**6-15 ▶ Cómo evitar la multitarea en la oficina.** La multitarea puede causar mucho estrés en la oficina. Aquí hay una descripción de cómo una empleada combate el estrés de la multitarea en el trabajo. Completa las descripciones de manera lógica con los verbos entre paréntesis en la forma **ella**.

Modelo    *Crea* listas organizadas de las cosas que *necesita* hacer. (crear, necesitar)

**1.** _____ los papeles en su escritorio en bandejas (*trays*) con el nombre del proyecto y así nunca _____ cosas perdidas en un escritorio desordenado. (buscar, organizar)

**2.** Cuando _____ a la oficina empieza con las tareas más difíciles. Dice que se siente más tranquila el resto del día si _____ ese trabajo primero. (llegar, terminar)

**3.** _____ y _____ a los correos electrónicos a intervalos predeterminados. (leer, responder)

**4.** _____ su correo electrónico a las nueve de la mañana, a la una y a las cinco de la tarde y siempre _____ respuestas a los correos electrónicos inmediatamente para no perder tiempo. (escribir, mirar)

**5.** _____ a intervalos regulares y _____ el tiempo para levantarse y hacer un poco de ejercicio. (usar, descansar)

**6.** Si es posible, no _____ todo el día enfrente de la computadora. _____ el trabajo en la computadora a tres horas seguidas (*in a row*). (limitar, pasar)

**7.** Cuando _____ a su casa, _____ el trabajo en la oficina. (dejar, regresar)

## 📖 Repaso 2   Requesting information: Question formation

SAM: 6-15 to 6-16

**6-16 ▶ Cuestionario.** Estás preparando un cuestionario para los participantes en cursos de informática de un centro comunitario. Completa las siguientes preguntas con la palabra interrogativa lógica.

Modelo     *¿Qué* desea aprender a hacer con la computadora? ¿Comunicarse por correo electrónico? ¿Navegar por Internet? ¿Usar un procesador de texto?

**1.** ¿ _____ quiere aprender a usar Internet? ¿Quiere buscar información? ¿Desea vender o comprar por Internet? ¿Quiere participar en una comunidad virtual?

**2.** ¿ _____ tipo de computadora prefiere usted? ¿Un Mac o un PC?

**3.** ¿ _____ experiencia tiene con las computadoras? ¿Ninguna? ¿Poca? ¿Mucha?

**4.** ¿ _____ va a usar la computadora? ¿En casa? ¿En casa de otra persona? ¿En la biblioteca municipal?

**5.** ¿ _____ puede ayudarle con la computadora en casa? ¿Un hijo? ¿Un nieto? ¿Un amigo? ¿Un vecino? ¿Nadie?

**6.** ¿ _____ horas a la semana puede usted dedicar a las lecciones de informática? ¿Dos o tres horas? ¿Cinco horas? ¿Más de cinco horas?

**7.** ¿ _____ es mejor ofrecer las lecciones en el centro comunitario? ¿Por la mañana? ¿Por la tarde? ¿Por la noche?

**8.** ¿ _____ es el mejor número de teléfono para comunicarnos con usted durante el día?

**6-17 ▶ Preguntas frecuentes.** Aquí hay una lista de respuestas a las preguntas más frecuentes sobre Internet. Escribe la pregunta lógica para cada respuesta usando las palabras subrayadas (*underlined*) con la palabra interrogativa lógica.

Modelo     Una cookie es un pequeño archivo de texto que un sitio web deja en la computadora de los visitantes.
           *¿Qué es una cookie?*

**1.** La diferencia entre Internet y una Intranet es que Internet se refiere a la conexión de computadoras a través de todo el mundo (*across the whole world*) y una Intranet es una conexión entre las computadoras de una sola organización.

**2.** Un dominio es el nombre de un sitio web.

**3.** Generalmente, la inscripción (*registration*) de un dominio lleva (*takes*) de 2 a 4 días.

**4.** Es posible determinar si un dominio está disponible (*available*) buscando el nombre en la base de datos *Whois* en Internet.

**5.** La inscripción de un dominio cuesta más o menos diez dólares al año.

**6.** Hay más de 100.000.000 sitios web en el mundo.

**7.** Hay más páginas web que sitios de Internet porque un sitio web puede contener miles de páginas.

**8.** Un motor de búsqueda es un software que busca texto según criterios determinados por el usuario.

**9.** Los motores de búsqueda más populares son *Google* y *Yahoo*.

**10.** Las oficinas centrales de *Google* y *Yahoo* están en California.

Para **averiguar**

In the activities on this page, you will be reviewing question formation. Do you remember . . .
■ where you generally place the subject with respect to the verb in a question?
■ how you say *who, what, which, where, when, why, how, how much, how many,* and *how often* in Spanish?
■ whether you use **qué** or **cuál** to translate *What is . . .?* or *What are . . .?* when asking for a definition? when asking for a selection out of a group of possibilities?
See page 46 for review.

## 📖 Repaso 3
SAM: 6-17
to 6-18

# Saying what people have:
# Tener and tener expressions

## Para averiguar

In the activities on this page, you will be reviewing **tener** and **tener** expressions. Do you remember . . .

- what the forms of **tener** are? what it means in English?
- how you say how old someone is? what you feel like doing? what you have to do?
- what **tener sed** means? what some other expressions with **tener** are that are translated by the verb *to be* in English?

See pages 72 and 78 or refer to the verb charts in the appendix or in *MySpanishLab* for review.

**6-18 ▶ En un café.** La mujer con la blusa morada describe a las personas en esta foto y el café donde pasa mucho tiempo. Completa las siguientes oraciones con el sujeto correcto de la lista y la forma correcta de **tener**.

| Yo | Mi novio | Todos | El café |
|----|----------|-------|---------|

Modelo    *Yo tengo* un a blusa
          morada.

1. _____ una camisa gris.
2. _____ una computadora portátil.
3. _____ *WiFi*.
4. _____ mucha sed.
5. _____ entre veinte y treinta años.
6. _____ mucho trabajo.

**6-19 ▶ ¿Qué tiene?** Una voluntaria que enseña una clase de informática habla con un señor mayor. Completa las oraciones de manera lógica con la forma correcta de **tener** en las expresiones entre paréntesis.

EL SEÑOR:    (Yo) (Modelo) *Tengo curiosidad* de aprender a usar la computadora pero (1) _____ de arruinar algo. (tener curiosidad, tener miedo)

LA VOLUNTARIA:    Todos (nosotros) (2) _____ cuando usamos una computadora por primera vez, pero usted necesita (3) _____ en sí mismo (*yourself*). ¿Con qué frecuencia ve usted a una persona arruinar una computadora? Nunca, ¿verdad? (tener ansiedad, tener confianza)

EL SEÑOR:    Sí, usted (4) _____. No es lógico. Necesita (5) _____ conmigo. No estoy acostumbrado a las nuevas tecnologías. (tener paciencia, tener razón)

LA VOLUNTARIA:    Le va a gustar mucho. Hoy día las computadoras (6) _____ de hacer cosas increíbles. (Nosotros) (7) _____ al mundo entero por Internet. (tener acceso, tener la capacidad)

EL SEÑOR:    Por fin voy a (8) _____ con quienes hablar. Mi esposa no (9) _____ hablar y prefiere ver la televisión. (tener amigos, tener ganas de)

LA VOLUNTARIA:    Pero, es importante (10) _____ en las relaciones en línea. Nunca debe dar información personal como su número de seguridad social ni información sobre sus cuentas bancarias porque algunas personas (11) _____. (tener precaución, tener malas intenciones)

EL SEÑOR:    (Yo) (12) _____ y (13) _____ con gente deshonesta. (tener mucha experiencia, tener ochenta años)

## Repaso 4  Saying what people do: Verbs with irregular **yo** forms

SAM: 6-19 to 6-20

**6-20 ► Costumbres.** Uno de los voluntarios del centro explica para qué usa Internet. Combina las frases de manera lógica usando la conjunción **cuando** con la primera o segunda parte de la oración y los verbos en la forma **yo**.

Modelos  verificar los horarios de las películas por Internet / salir al cine
*Verifico los horarios de las películas por Internet **cuando** salgo al cine.*

salir para el aeropuerto / verificar el estatus del vuelo (*flight*) en la web
***Cuando** salgo para el aeropuerto, verifico el estatus del vuelo en la web.*

1. oír una canción (*song*) que me gusta / descargar (*download*) la canción de *iTunes*
2. ver algo interesante en la tele / buscar más información por Internet sobre el tema del programa
3. hacer un viaje / reservar el hotel por Internet
4. subir mis fotos a mi álbum de fotos en línea / venir de vacaciones

**6-21 ► Tiendas en línea.** Estás hablando de los beneficios de las tiendas en línea. Completa las oraciones de manera lógica con la forma correcta de los verbos entre paréntesis.

Modelo  Si (yo) *oigo* un anuncio (*ad*) sobre un producto nuevo, *hago* una búsqueda por Internet para informarme sobre el producto. (hacer, oír)

1. Yo nunca _____ de casa para ir de compras. Siempre _____ todas mis compras por Internet. (hacer, salir)
2. Las tiendas virtuales _____ a su disposción toda clase de productos y generalmente _____ los mejores precios. (poner, tener)
3. (Yo) _____ productos en tiendas virtuales por todo el país antes de comprar y generalmente los productos _____ la misma garantía que en una tienda normal. (tener, ver)
4. En varios blogs, los clientes _____ qué productos y tiendas son los mejores y _____ recomendaciones. (decir, hacer)
5. Cuando los productos _____ de una tienda virtual, generalmente los clientes reciben un correo electrónico que _____ cuándo van a llegar. (decir, salir)
6. Un servicio de entrega (*delivery*) _____ las compras a casa y (yo) no _____ que perder tiempo manejando (*driving*) ni gastar gasolina. (tener, traer)

Para **averiguar**

In the activities on this page, you will be reviewing verbs with irregular **yo** forms. Do you remember . . .
- what the **yo** forms of the verbs **hacer, poner, traer, salir, venir,** and **ver** are?
- what the forms of the verb **oír** are? what **oír** means?
- what three idiomatic expressions with **hacer** are?
- which verb can be used to say that you *turn on* something?
See pages 72 and 82 or refer to the verb charts in the appendix or in *MySpanishLab* for review.

# 📖 Vocabulario   Usos de Internet

SAM: 6-21 to 6-22

🔊 ¿Para qué usas Internet?

CD 2
Track 55

escribir y recibir correos electrónicos

buscar información o leer noticias

chatear o participar en redes sociales

descargar música

ver videos o jugar a los videojuegos

CD 2
Track 56

Una conversación. Una voluntaria está explicándole a un novato (*beginner*) cómo hacer un CD de música descargada.

EL NOVATO: Tengo varias canciones descargadas que quiero grabar en un CD, pero no entiendo lo que tengo que hacer.

LA VOLUNTARIA: Bueno, es muy fácil. En el menú *Archivo* se selecciona "Nueva lista de reproducción" para crear una carpeta nueva con el nombre del CD que quiere grabar. Así es . . . muy bien . . . Ahora, con el ratón, puede arrastrar las canciones que quiere a esa lista de reproducción.

EL NOVATO: ¡Es muy fácil!

LA VOLUNTARIA: Sí, y rápido. Después de arrastrar todas las canciones, necesita hacer clic con el botón derecho sobre la lista de reproducción. En la ventana que aparece, puede configurar la grabación. Es mejor seleccionar la velocidad de grabación mínima, y yo prefiero dejar dos segundos entre las canciones.

CD 2, Track 57

## ¡A escuchar!

Ahora escuchen otra conversación en la cual un voluntario está explicándole a un novato como enviar un mensaje. ¿Qué palabras se usan para expresar *To, Subject, Attach* y *Send*?

**6-22 ▶ Correo electrónico.** Explica cómo se dice cada palabra en negrita (*boldface*) en los programas de correo electrónico de inglés.

Modelo    Se hace clic en **Redactar** para escribir un correo nuevo.
*Redactar significa "Write" o "Compose" en inglés.*

1. Se hace clic en **Recibidos** para ver los correos enviados a tu dirección de correo electrónico.
2. Se hace clic en **Destacados** para ver correos anteriores marcados como importantes.
3. Se hace clic en **Enviados** para ver correos enviados a otras personas.
4. Se hace clic en **Borradores** para ver correos anteriores no enviados.
5. Se hace clic en **Papelera** para ver los correos recientemente eliminados.

**6-23 ▶ Comparaciones culturales.** Lee el siguiente texto sobre el uso de Internet en Latinoamérica. Luego, selecciona las palabras correctas entre paréntesis para completar las oraciones que siguen al artículo.

Según un estudio de *Tendenciasdigitales.com,* los usos principales de Internet en Latinoamérica son en orden de importancia: enviar (*to send*) y recibir correos electrónicos (86% de los usuarios), buscar información (82%), chatear (69%), descargar archivos, software o música (57%), ver videos (53%), visitar redes sociales (52%), leer noticias (35%), realizar operaciones bancarias (34%), comprar productos o servicios (34%), realizar cursos o estudios (33%). Actualmente, los usos de Internet que crecen (*are growing*) más rápidamente son las redes sociales. La expansión reciente de las redes sociales es todo un fenómeno de masas. Entre sus usuarios el 71,2% participa en comunidades vituales para comunicarse, el 47,5% para ver fotos y el 35,3% para saber qué hacen sus amigos. Uno de los atractivos de las redes sociales es que facilita interacciones con terceras personas a través de (*third parties through*) una segunda porque los contactos de cada uno son visibles para todos los demás.

### ¡Ojo!

**Comprehension strategies.** In *Comparaciones culturales,* you are going to read about the most common uses of the Internet in Latin America and the growing importance of social networks (*redes sociales*). Begin to guess some of the information in the report by jotting down in English the ten most common things that you and others do on the Internet. Then, as you read, see which ones are mentioned. You can review the comprehension strategies *Anticipating content* and *Guessing meaning from context* on pages 30 and 60.

1. Los latinoamericanos usan Internet (*más, menos, tanto*) para descargar música (*que, como*) para buscar información.
2. Los latinoamericanos usan Internet (*más, menos, tanto*) para realizar operaciones bancarias (*que, como*) para comprar productos o servicios.
3. Los latinoamericanos usan redes sociales (*más, menos, tanto*) para hablar con la gente (*que, como*) para ver fotos.

## 📖 **Repaso 1**

SAM: 6-23 to 6-24

# Saying where you go and what you are going to do: **Ir, ir a** + infinitive

**6-24 ▶ Tecnologías del futuro.** ¿Crees que las siguientes tecnologías van a ser comunes en el futuro o que nunca van a existir? Completa cada oración con la forma correcta de **ir** para expresar tu opinión. Luego di (*say*) si crees que **es probable, es posible** o **es imposible**.

Modelo    Micrófonos conectados a computadoras *van* a traducir perfectamente de una lengua a otra en tiempo real.
*Es posible.*

1. Procesadores de texto _____ a escribir nuestros pensamientos (*thoughts*) directamente en un documento sin la necesidad de usar un teclado (*keyboard*).
2. En las tiendas, los clientes _____ a poder obtener información sobre productos y comparar precios usando el código de barras (*bar code*) y su teléfono celular conectado a Internet.
3. (Nosotros) _____ a sentirnos cómodos sin calor ni frío en todo momento gracias a ropa con computadoras ligeras (*light*), invisibles y flexibles.
4. Los doctores del futuro _____ a ser computadoras capaces (*capable*) de diagnosticar las enfermedades (*illnesses*) en segundos.
5. Los virus informáticos _____ a mutarse para poder infectar a los humanos.
6. (Nosotros) _____ a vivir en casas inteligentes sin la necesidad de hacer tareas domésticas.
7. Televisores inteligentes _____ a apagarse (*turn themselves off*) automáticamente si el televidente (*viewer*) se duerme durante un programa.
8. Papel inteligente en las paredes de los cuartos de una casa _____ a cambiar de color o diseño al pulsar (*upon pushing*) un botón.

**6-25 ▶ ¿Qué se hace primero?** ¿En qué orden dice alguien que va a hacer las siguientes cosas? Haz oraciones lógicas con **ir a** + infinitivo en la forma **yo**.

Modelo    consultar los sitios más interesantes / hacer una búsqueda
*Voy a hacer una búsqueda y voy a consultar los sitios más interesantes.*

1. comparar los precios / visitar varias tiendas en línea
2. comprar una nueva computadora / buscar la tienda más barata
3. abrir el procesador de texto / escribir un documento
4. escribir el texto / usar el corrector ortográfico (*spellcheck*)
5. corregir los errores / enviar el documento por correo electrónico
6. cerrar mi correo electrónico / leer los mensajes
7. descargar (*download*) varias canciones / hacer un CD
8. abrir una tienda en línea / comprar un dominio para un sitio web

## 📖Repaso 2   Indicating whose it is: Possessive adjectives

SAM: 6-25
to 6-26

**6-26 ▶ Explicaciones.** Combina los elementos de cada columna para explicar las siguientes cosas. Usa la forma correcta del verbo **ser** y la palabra **de** como en el Modelo.

Modelo   *Un dominio es el nombre de un sitio web.*

| | | |
|---|---|---|
| *un dominio* | el código de país (*country*) | un documento |
| la terminación ".doc" | una placa de circuitos | *un sitio web* |
| una URL | el sistema operativo | una organización |
| las letras "mx" | la extensión | la página inicial de un sitio |
| un dominio con ".org" | *el nombre* | una computadora |
| la placa (*board*) madre | un sitio | un sitio web mexicano |
| *Windows* | la dirección | muchas computadoras personales |

**6-27 ▶ Mensajes.** Completa los siguientes mensajes dejados en la página de una red social con los adjetivos posesivos indicados.

**La Bella**

29 jul   02:29 a.m.

Me gusta (1) _____ (*your*) página. (2) _____ (*My*) amigos y yo estamos interesados en el arte y la fotografía como tú. Todos los miembros de (3) _____ (*our*) comunidad tenemos páginas muy bonitas. (4) _____ (*My*) amigos son todos muy creativos y (5) _____ (*their*) páginas siempre tienen fotos nuevas e interesantes.

**Picasso**

30 jul   11:41 a.m.

Eres muy interesante y (6) _____ (*your*) página es sensacional. Me gustaría ser (7) _____ (*your*) amigo y chatear contigo. (8) _____ (*Our*) perfiles son muy parecidos. (9) _____ (*My*) intereses principales también son el arte y la fotografía. Chateo con (10) _____ (*your*) amigo Daniel B. con frecuencia. ¡(11) _____

(*His*) página es increíble! También me gustan (12) _____ (*his*) videos.

**6-28 ▶ Nuestro sitio web.** Estás preparando el texto para un sitio web de una nueva tienda electrónica. Completa las siguientes oraciones de manera lógica con la forma correcta de **nuestro/a/os/as** en uno de los espacios en blanco y **su/s** en el otro.

Modelo   Bienvenidos a *nuestro* sitio web. Somos *su* mejor opción para comprar equipos electrónicos.

**1.** Ofrecemos mejor selección que todos _____ competidores y _____ precios son más altos.

**2.** Estamos a _____ servicio y garantizamos todos _____ productos.

**3.** ¡_____ objetivo es _____ satisfacción!

**4.** _____ técnicos bilingües están listos para responder a todas _____ preguntas.

**5.** _____ departamento de servicio al cliente está abierto las veinticuatro horas del día para ajustarse a _____ horario.

**6.** _____ información personal está segura con nosotros. Nunca compartimos información de _____ clientes con terceros (*third parties*).

**7.** _____ opinión es importante para nosotros. _____ dirección de correo electrónico es Servicio@Electrogigante.com.

**8.** Gracias por _____ visita a _____ sitio web.

## 📖 Repaso 3    Pointing out which one: Demonstratives

SAM: 6-27
to 6-28

Para **averiguar**

In the activities on this page, you will be reviewing the demonstrative adjectives. Do you remember . . .

■ how you say *this* / *these* in Spanish?
■ how you say *that* / *those*?
■ what the difference between **ese** and **aquel** is?

See page 140 for review.

**6-29 ► ¿Este botón o aquel botón?** Completa las siguientes explicaciones con la forma correcta de **este / esta / estos / estas** en el primer espacio en blanco y **aquel / aquella / aquellos / aquellas** en el segundo.

**Modelo**    *Este* botón con **B** es para cambiar la fuente a negrita y *aquel* botón con *I* es para letra cursiva.

**1.** _____ botones con muchas líneas son para alinear o centrar el texto y _____ botones con puntos o números y líneas son para insertar viñetas (*bullets*) o números.

**2.** _____ botón con U es para subrayar texto y _____ botón con **abc** es para usar el corrector ortográfico.

**3.** _____ palabras subrayadas con rojo tienen errores ortográficos y _____ palabras subrayadas con verde tienen errores de gramática.

**4.** _____ hoja en blanco es para crear un documento nuevo y _____ carpeta (*folder*) abierta es para abrir un archivo que ya existe.

**5.** _____ icono con tijeras (*scissors*) es para cortar texto y _____ icono con dos hojas es para copiar texto.

**6.** _____ letra $X^2$ es para el superíndice (*superscript*) y _____ letra $X_2$ es para el subíndice.

**6-30 ► Más mensajes.** Completa los siguientes mensajes de una red social con los adjetivos demostrativos indicados.

**La Bella**

30 oct   01:41 a.m.

¡Hola! Me gusta mucho tu página nueva con (1) _____ (*these*) gráficos tan bonitos y (2) _____ (*these*) fotos con todos. ¿Quién es (3) _____ (*that*) hombre tan guapo contigo en la primera foto? Voy a cambiar mi página uno de (4) _____ (*these*) días también.

**Picasso**

03 nov   10:12 a.m.

¡Qué sorpresa ver (5) _____ (*that*) foto de todos nosotros en tu página! Recuerdo (6) _____ (*that*) día con nuestros amigos en (7) _____ (*that*) playa. ¿Quieres volver (8) _____ (*this*) fin de semana? No tengo que trabajar (9) _____ (*this*) sábado.

## 📖Repaso 4   Saying what people do: Stem-changing verbs

SAM: 6-29 to 6-30

**6-31 ▶ ¿Un usuario (*user*) o un motor de búsqueda?** Explica quién hace las siguientes cosas, un usuario o un motor de búsqueda.

Modelo    servir para buscar texto en sitios web
*Un motor de búsqueda sirve para buscar texto en sitios web.*

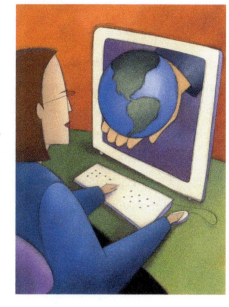

1. querer buscar algo
2. encontrar páginas web con el texto buscado
3. perder la concentración a veces
4. contar millones de sitios web en unos segundos
5. repetir la misma acción millones de veces en segundos
6. perder la paciencia con problemas técnicos
7. jugar a los videojuegos en la computadora para descansar
8. recordar la URL de millones de sitios web
9. entender los errores ortográficos
10. dormir si está cansado
11. servir a millones de usuarios
12. cerrar el motor de búsqueda después de terminar

**6-32 ▶ Bienvenido.** Estás preparando texto para un sitio web de una nueva tienda electrónica. Completa las siguientes oraciones con la forma correcta del verbo lógico entre paréntesis.

Modelo    (Nosotros) *Entendemos* que nuestros clientes *cuentan* con el mejor servicio. (contar, entender)

1. (Nosotros) _____ los productos que usted _____ a los mejores precios. (querer, tener)
2. (Nosotros) _____ a nuestros clientes con rapidez y dedicación. Usted nunca _____ su tiempo con nosotros. (perder, servir)
3. (Nosotros) _____ disculpas (*pardon*) a nuestros clientes si no _____ algo que buscan. (encontrar, pedir)
4. Si usted no _____ el producto que busca, (nosotros) _____ ayudarlo. (encontrar, poder)
5. (Nosotros) _____ que usted _____ tener preguntas. (entender, poder)
6. Usted _____ comprar las veinticuatro horas del día porque nuestra tienda en línea nunca _____. (cerrar, poder)
7. Nuestros clientes siempre _____ porque (nosotros) _____ en ellos como amigos. (pensar, volver)
8. Siempre escuchamos y _____ lo que nuestros clientes _____. (decir, recordar)

Para **averiguar**

In the activities on this page, you will be reviewing stem-changing verbs. Do you remember . . .
- in what forms of stem-changing verbs **e** becomes **ie** or **i**, and **o** or **u** becomes **ue**?
- in what two forms there is no stem change?
- which **-ar**, **-er**, and **-ir** verbs have stem changes?
- what the irregular **yo** form of **decir** is?
See page 114 or refer to the verb charts in the appendix or in *MySpanishLab* for review.

**Vocabulario**   Las comunidades en línea, los blogs y los foros

SAM: 6-31
to 6-32

 Aquí hay unos comentarios de blogs. ¿De qué tipo de blog son?

CD 2
Track 58

un blog personal o autobiográfico

un blog sobre noticias y actualidad

un blog sobre sociedad

un blog sobre deportes

un blog sobre cine o televisión

un blog sobre tecnología

un blog humorístico

un blog sobre juegos

### ¿Sabías que...?

Además de *MySpace* y *Facebook,* las redes sociales *Hi5* y *Sonico* son muy populares in Latinoamérica. *Sonico* es una red social basada en Argentina.

### ¡Ojo!

**Comprehension strategy.** In order to read blogs efficiently, it is necessary to be able to focus on the main idea of an entry or an opinion. See page 62 to review the comprehension strategy *Identifying the main idea*.

---

**Debes visitar este sitio si quieres divertirte con juegos de Bob Esponja. Me gusta mucho. Hay un juego en el cual Bob maneja un bus a Atlantis y tienes que usar el cursor para guiar el bus entre las medusas y las algas. En otro juego puedes vestir a Bob, poniéndole ropa de diferentes estilos. ¡Es muy divertido!**

---

Eres adicto a Internet cuando . . .

Dices que te llamas jgarcia@correo.com.
Tus hijos se llaman *Google* y *Yahoo*.
Tu perro tiene su propia página web.
Tu esposa pone su foto al lado del monitor para recordarte que existe.
Compras una casa de *Adobe*.
Le dices al taxista que tu dirección es: http://www.calleToledo.com/apto18.htm.

---

**Tanto en el aspecto tenístico como en el mental, las capacidades del "Gran Roger" son fuera de lo común. Es un genio, un virtuoso, sin puntos débiles, que nació para ser el mejor tenista de la historia. Tiene un extraordinario talento bajo presión, con una excelente tolerancia a la frustración y una incomparable capacidad de adaptación a todo tipo de situaciones.**

---

Algunos nunca leen blogs. Para otros los blogs son profetas de una nueva revolución de la información. Para mí, son una formidable herramienta para la libertad de expresión. En las sociedades donde existe censura y los medios de comunicación tradicionales están controlados por el gobierno, frecuentemente los bloggers son los auténticos periodistas.

CD 2
Track 59

Una conversación. Un hombre y una mujer recién casados están mirando un blog juntos y hacen comentarios sobre las entradas.

EL ESPOSO: Me gusta este sitio. Siempre tiene los mejores chistes. Vamos a leer los chistes sobre parejas. Escucha éste, "No desayuno porque pienso en ti. No almuerzo porque pienso en ti. No ceno porque pienso en ti. No duermo porque tengo hambre."

LA ESPOSA: Ah, mira ése, "Un anuncio en Match.com dice: Hombre invisible busca a mujer transparente para hacer cosas nunca vistas" . . . ¿Qué puede significar "cosas nunca vistas"? . . . Voy a leer el siguiente: "¿Por qué se casan las mujeres? Por falta de experiencia. ¿Por qué se divorcian? Por falta de paciencia. ¿Por qué se vuelven a casar? Por falta de memoria." . . . Pues yo tengo mucha paciencia, ¿verdad?

EL ESPOSO: ¡Claro que sí! Eres muy paciente . . . Bueno, vamos a leer el próximo chiste: "Tres hombres están en un bar y uno dice: De todas las películas de Disney mi esposa prefiere *Blancanieves y los siete enanitos*, y tenemos siete hijos. Otro hombre dice: Mi esposa prefiere *Los tres caballeros*, y tenemos tres hijos. El tercer hombre se levanta para irse y los otros le preguntan: ¿Por qué te vas? Y él contesta: Es que la película favorita de mi esposa es *101 Dálmatas*."

LA ESPOSA: Ahh . . . Me gusta esa película. ¡Es mi favorita de todas!

EL ESPOSO: ¿De verdad?

 CD 2, Track 60

## ¡A escuchar!

Ahora escuchen otra conversación en la cual una pareja habla de un blog. ¿Qué tipo de blog es? ¿De qué personas hablan?

6-33 ▶ **Comparaciones culturales.** Aquí hay tres respuestas a la pregunta "¿Son las redes sociales una pérdida de tiempo?" de un blog español. ¿Estás de acuerdo?

Yo estoy a favor de las redes sociales. Soy miembro de una red social y gracias a este sitio me comunico con amigos que viven muy lejos. También se encuentran grupos con intereses en común y el usuario tiene acceso a muchos foros que pueden ser educativos. Pero, entiendo que para muchos es una pérdida de tiempo. El factor determinante es el usuario.

En general las redes sociales no tienen ningún valor educativo. O por lo menos yo nunca aprendo nada viendo fotos de mis amigos y los amigos de los amigos de . . . o contestando cuestionarios de personalidad. Su propósito no es para educar sino que sirven para socializar, tal como lo indica su nombre. Sí, es verdad que pueden llegar a ser una pérdida de tiempo si se usan en exceso, pero no entiendo por qué hay que estar "a favor o en contra".

Tienen su utilidad, sobre todo para encontrarse o contactar con amigos. Incluso se usan para los negocios. Sin embargo, a mí no me gustan demasiado.

## 📖 Repaso 1

SAM: 6-33
to 6-34

# Saying what people do for themselves: Reflexive verbs

## Para averiguar

In the activities on this page, you will be reviewing reflexive verbs. Do you remember . . .

- what a reflexive verb is and how it is used?
- what reflexive pronoun is used for each subject?
- where you place reflexive pronouns with conjugated verbs?
- what the two possible placements of the reflexive pronoun are when you use a reflexive verb in the infinitive following a conjugated verb? whether the reflexive pronoun with infinitives changes to correspond to the subject of the conjugated verb?

See pages 134 and 142 or refer to the verb charts in the appendix or in *MySpanishLab* for review.

**6-34 ▶ Adicción a Internet.** Una esposa se queja (*is complaining*) porque su esposo es adicto a Internet y nunca pasa tiempo con ella. Completa sus oraciones para decir si hacen las cosas indicadas **siempre** o **nunca**.

Modelo    Mi esposo y yo . . . (divertirse juntos)
*Mi esposo y yo nunca nos divertimos juntos.*

1. Mi esposo . . . (quedarse toda la noche frente a la computadora)
2. Mi esposo . . . (acostarse hasta muy tarde)
3. Yo . . . (acostarse sola)
4. Mi esposo y yo . . . (comunicarse)
5. Mi esposo . . . (comunicarse con otras personas en línea)
6. Mi esposo . . . (enojarse si yo quiero usar la computadora)
7. Mi esposo y yo . . . (pelearse por la computadora)
8. Yo . . . (aburrirse sola)
9. Nosotros . . . (llevarse bien)
10. Un esposo y una esposa que . . . (divertirse juntos) . . . (divorciarse)

**6-35 ▶ Relaciones cibernéticas.** Completa cada sección del siguiente artículo sobre la infidelidad cibernética de manera lógica con la forma correcta de los verbos reflexivos entre paréntesis.

Modelo    El número de infieles *se multiplica* cada día en Internet. Millones de personas casadas *se inician* en relaciones sentimentales o románticas con desconocidos en sitios de conversación en Internet. (iniciarse, multiplicarse)

1. Usan el anonimato de sus computadoras para _____ en otra persona de otra edad y estado civil (*age and marital status*). _____ con conquistas virtuales, con la ayuda de cámaras de video, servicios de mensajería instantánea y mensajes electrónicos. (convertirse, divertirse)
2. Este tipo de relaciones es una adicción para algunas personas que _____ para ver quién está en línea después de que su pareja _____. (acostarse, conectarse)
3. Es el caso de Eduardo, ingeniero de 39 años. Todas las noches sigue la misma rutina: cena con su esposa y sus dos hijos, mira la televisión un rato y, a eso de las nueve _____ frente a la computadora y _____ en Don Juan, alias que usa para navegar por sitios de chat. (sentarse, transformarse)
4. Eduardo admite, "A veces, (yo) _____ en línea varias horas y no _____ hasta las dos o tres de la mañana". (acostarse, quedarse)
5. "(Yo) _____ como un jóven de veinte años cuando estoy chateando en línea," confiesa, "pero es difícil _____ al día siguiente". (levantarse, sentirse)

## Repaso 2    Saying what people do for each other: Reciprocal verbs

SAM: 6-35 to 6-36

**6-36 ▶ En una red social.** Un miembro de una red social habla de lo que hace con sus amigos virtuales. Forma oraciones con los verbos en la forma **nosotros** y la terminación lógica de la lista.

| | |
|---|---|
| grupos de discusión | *nuestra red social* |
| mensajería instantánea | auriculares (*headsets*) y micrófonos |
| el anonimato en Internet | una cámara web |

Modelo    hacerse amigos virtuales con . . .
*Nos hacemos amigos virtuales con nuestra red social.*

**1.** escribirse mensajes en tiempo real con . . .
**2.** verse con . . .
**3.** comunicarse sobre temas específicos con . . .
**4.** hablarse con chat de voz (*voice*) con . . .
**5.** protegerse de predadores en línea con . . .

**6-37 ▶ Chistes.** Encuentras los siguientes chistes en un blog humorístico. Completa cada chiste con la forma correcta de los verbos recíprocos o reflexivos de la lista correspondiente.

| | | | | | |
|---|---|---|---|---|---|
| acostarse | despertarse | escribirse | *hablarse* | levantarse | pelearse |

En este matrimonio el esposo y la esposa no *se hablan* (Modelo) después de
(1) _____ , sino que (*but instead*) (2) _____ una nota para comunicarse.
Una tarde después de una pelea, los dos se enojan y el esposo le escribe a su esposa, "¿Cuándo vamos a cenar?" y ella le escribe "La cena ya está lista". A la medianoche, todavía están enojados cuando (3) _____ . Él le escribe "Quiero despertarme a las 7:00" y ella le escribe "Está bien". Pasa la noche y cuando él
(4) _____ al día siguiente, ve que son las 10:30. Luego encuentra a su lado un papel que dice "Son las 7:00. Tienes que (5) _____ ."

| | | | |
|---|---|---|---|
| afeitarse | levantarse | ponerse | sentirse |
| casarse (3 veces) | mantenerse | quejarse (*to complain*) | |

Una chica (6) _____ indecisa, porque no sabe (*know*) con cuál de sus dos pretendientes debe (7) _____ . Uno es doctor, y el otro es militar. Le pregunta a su madre: ¿Con cuál de los dos debo (8) _____ , mamá?
— Inmediatamente su madre reponde: Debes (9) _____ con el militar, con él vas a ser más feliz.
— ¿Por qué dices eso, mamá?
— Mira, ellos (10) _____ temprano, (11) _____ todas las mañanas,
(12) _____ ropa limpia que lavan ellos mismos y (13) _____ en forma (*shape*). Además reciben órdenes sin (14) _____ .

| | | |
|---|---|---|
| acostarse | mirarse | preguntarse |

Dos pulgas (*fleas*) (15) _____ en el pelo de un perro, ven las estrellas (*the stars*), luego (16) _____ y (17) _____ : ¿crees que hay vida en otro perro?

Para **averiguar**

In the activities on this page, you will be reviewing reciprocal verbs. Do you remember . . .
■ what a reciprocal verb is?
■ whether reciprocal verbs in Spanish look different or have different word order from reflexive verbs?
■ where you place reciprocal pronouns with verbs conjugated in the present tense? where you place them with an infinitive after **antes de** or **después de**?
■ what the two possible placements of the reciprocal pronoun are when you use a reciprocal verb in the infinitive following a conjugated verb? whether the reciprocal pronoun with infinitives changes to correspond to the subject of the conjugated verb?
See pages 136 and 142 or refer to the verb charts in the appendix or in *MySpanishLab* for review.

## 📖 Repaso 3
SAM: 6-37
to 6-38

## Describing what is happening: The present progressive

### Para averiguar

In the activities on this page, you will be reviewing the present progressive. Do you remember . . .

■ what the ending of the present participle of **-ar** verbs in Spanish is? of **-er** and **-ir** verbs? to what verb ending in English these endings correspond?

■ which verb meaning *to be* you use with present participles to say what is happening?

■ when the **i** of the **-iendo** ending changes to **y**?

■ which category of verbs has stem changes in present participles: **-ar, -er,** or **-ir**? what **o** and **e** become?

■ what the two possible placements of reflexive / reciprocal pronouns are in the present progressive? what you write on the stressed syllable of the verb when the pronoun is attached to the end of the present participle?

See page 146 or refer to the verb charts in the appendix or in *MySpanishLab* for review.

**6-38 ▶ Por cámara web.** Estás viendo una calle peatonal en Buenos Aires, Argentina, mediante una cámara web en vivo. Escoge (*Choose*) la descripción que mejor describa lo que está pasando y complétala con el presente progresivo del verbo entre paréntesis.

**Modelo**     Mucha gente . . . / Nadie . . . (entrar y salir de tiendas)
*Mucha gente está entrando y saliendo de tiendas.*

1. Hace buen tiempo. No . . . / Hace mal tiempo y . . . (llover)
2. Todos . . . / Nadie . . . (pasear tranquilamente por la calle)
3. Dos niños . . . / Nadie . . . (correr)
4. Varias personas . . . / Nadie . . . (comer)
5. Un hombre . . . / Una mujer . . . (hablar por teléfono)
6. Un hombre con una chaqueta gris . . . / Una mujer con un abrigo marrón . . . (mirar hacia [*towards*] la cámara)
7. Un hombre con gafas de sol . . . / Una mujer con gafas de sol . . . (acompañar al hombre con la chaqueta gris)
8. Los dos hombres . . . / Sólo el hombre con las gafas del sol . . . (observar algo a la derecha)

**6-39 ▶ Chateando.** Dos amigos virtuales, Picasso y La Bella, están chateando en una red social. Completa su conversación de manera lógica con los verbos entre paréntesis en el presente progresivo.

**Modelo**     BELLA: Hola, Picasso. ¿Qué *estás haciendo* (tú)? ¿*Estás chateando* con alguien? (chatear, hacer)

1. PICASSO: Hola, Bella. No, (yo) no _____ con nadie en particular. _____ los perfiles de los amigos de mis amigos. (hablar, leer)
2. BELLA: Escucha, Picasso, ¡parece que (tú) _____ en grande en las fotos nuevas del parque de atracciones que tienes en tu página! ¿Quiénes son esas muchachas contigo? ¿_____ con una de ellas? (divertirse, salir)
3. PICASSO: Son mis primas. En las fotos (nosotros) _____ el cumpleaños de mi prima. Ella y yo _____ en la primera foto . . . Oye Bella, ¿por qué nunca estás conectada recientemente? (abrazarse, celebrar)
4. BELLA: Es que mis padres dicen que pierdo demasiado tiempo en línea, pero esta noche mi madre _____ la tele y mi padre ya _____. (dormir, ver)

# 📖Repaso 4   Describing how: Adverbs

SAM: 6-39
to 6-40

**6-40 ▶ Test de personalidad.** Estás preparando un test de personalidad llamado *¿Eres obsesivo compulsivo?* para un sitio web. En las siguientes preguntas, forma un adverbio sinónimo de las palabras en letra cursiva usando uno de los adjetivos entre paréntesis.

Modelo   ¿Haces ciertos gestos *una y otra vez*? (voluntario, repetitivo)
¿Haces ciertos gestos *repetitivamente*?

1. ¿Limpias *demasiado* las cosas? (excesivo, completo)
2. ¿*Siempre* te lavas las manos? (activo, constante)
3. ¿Revisas *varias veces* el gas, el agua, las luces y las cerraduras (*the lights and locks*) cuando sales de casa? (repetido, regular)
4. ¿Organizas *minuciosamente* tus viajes antes de salir? (breve, detallado)
5. ¿Sigues rutinas *sistemáticamente*? (metódico, relajado)
6. ¿Completas *escrupulosamente* todo tu trabajo? (meticuloso, rápido)
7. ¿Te vistes siempre *con ropa elegante* para salir con los amigos? (impecable, casual)
8. ¿Evitas (*Do you avoid*) *sin razón* ciertas cosas porque crees que traen mala suerte? (periódico, supersticioso)
9. ¿Piensas *con frecuencia* en problemas sin poder pensar en otra cosa? (frecuente, ilógico)
10. ¿Te sientes frustrado/a *con facilidad*? (fácil, reciente)

**6-41 ▶ Seguridad en Internet.** Aquí hay unas reglas importantes para proteger a los hijos en Internet. Completa cada una de manera lógica con adverbios formados a partir de los adjetivos entre paréntesis.

Es importante . . .

Modelo   vigilar *constantemente* los acciones de los hijos y hablar *abiertamente* con ellos. (abierto, constante)

1. estar _____ informado de los riesgos (*risks*) en Internet para hablar _____ con los hijos. (claro, suficiente)
2. usar seudónimos en vez de identificarse _____ porque los predadores buscan _____ víctimas inocentes en Internet. (constante, personal)
3. hablar _____ con los hijos de situaciones _____ peligrosas (*dangerous*) en Internet. (franco, potencial)
4. seleccionar una contraseña (*password*) _____ recordable por el usuario pero _____ descifrable por otros. (difícil, fácil)
5. cerrar _____ los sistemas de correo electrónico en computadoras de uso público después de terminar porque no se cierran _____ al abrir otra página. (automático, regular)
6. hacer preguntas si los hijos cambian _____ de pantalla (*screen*) cuando entras en su cuarto o si están _____ molestos por tus interrupciones. (inusual, rápido)
7. hablar _____ de problemas con los hijos sin reaccionar _____. (calmado, exagerado)
8. recordar que no se debe descargar _____ música o películas aun (*even*) navegando _____ en la web. (anónimo, ilegal)

**Para averiguar**

In the activities on this page, you will be reviewing the formation and use of adverbs. Do you remember . . .

■ what ending you use to form an adverb from an adjective in Spanish? whether you attach this ending to the masculine or feminine form of the adjective?
■ where you generally place adverbs with respect to verbs they modify? where you place them if they modify a whole sentence? if they modify an adjective?

See page 116 for review.

# Verb Charts

## Regular Verbs: Simple Tenses

| Infinitive<br>Present Participle<br>Past Participle | Indicative | | | | | Subjunctive | | Imperative |
|---|---|---|---|---|---|---|---|---|
| | **Present** | **Imperfect** | **Preterit** | **Future** | **Conditional** | **Present** | **Imperfect** | **Commands** |
| hablar<br>hablando<br>hablado | hablo<br>hablas<br>habla<br>hablamos<br>habláis<br>hablan | hablaba<br>hablabas<br>hablaba<br>hablábamos<br>hablabais<br>hablaban | hablé<br>hablaste<br>habló<br>hablamos<br>hablasteis<br>hablaron | hablaré<br>hablarás<br>hablará<br>hablaremos<br>hablaréis<br>hablarán | hablaría<br>hablarías<br>hablaría<br>hablaríamos<br>hablaríais<br>hablarían | hable<br>hables<br>hable<br>hablemos<br>habléis<br>hablen | hablara<br>hablaras<br>hablara<br>habláramos<br>hablarais<br>hablaran | habla (tú),<br>no hables<br>hable (usted)<br>hablemos<br>hablad (vosotros),<br>no habléis<br>hablen (Uds.) |
| comer<br>comiendo<br>comido | como<br>comes<br>come<br>comemos<br>coméis<br>comen | comía<br>comías<br>comía<br>comíamos<br>comíais<br>comían | comí<br>comiste<br>comió<br>comimos<br>comisteis<br>comieron | comeré<br>comerás<br>comerá<br>comeremos<br>comeréis<br>comerán | comería<br>comerías<br>comería<br>comeríamos<br>comeríais<br>comerían | coma<br>comas<br>coma<br>comamos<br>comáis<br>coman | comiera<br>comieras<br>comiera<br>comiéramos<br>comierais<br>comieran | come (tú),<br>no comas<br>coma (usted)<br>comamos<br>comed (vosotros),<br>no comáis<br>coman (Uds.) |
| vivir<br>viviendo<br>vivido | vivo<br>vives<br>vive<br>vivimos<br>vivís<br>viven | vivía<br>vivías<br>vivía<br>vivíamos<br>vivíais<br>vivían | viví<br>viviste<br>vivió<br>vivimos<br>vivisteis<br>vivieron | viviré<br>vivirás<br>vivirá<br>viviremos<br>viviréis<br>vivirán | viviría<br>vivirías<br>viviría<br>viviríamos<br>viviríais<br>vivirían | viva<br>vivas<br>viva<br>vivamos<br>viváis<br>vivan | viviera<br>vivieras<br>viviera<br>viviéramos<br>vivierais<br>vivieran | vive (tú),<br>no vivas<br>viva (usted)<br>vivamos<br>vivid (vosotros),<br>no viváis<br>vivan (Uds.) |

# Regular Verbs: Perfect Tenses

| Indicative | | | | | Subjunctive | |
| --- | --- | --- | --- | --- | --- | --- |
| Present Perfect | Past Perfect | Preterit Perfect | Future Perfect | Conditional Perfect | Present Perfect | Past Perfect |
| he<br>has<br>ha<br>hemos<br>habéis<br>han | había<br>habías<br>había<br>habíamos<br>habíais<br>habían | hube<br>hubiste<br>hubo<br>hubimos<br>hubisteis<br>hubieron | habré<br>habrás<br>habrá<br>habremos<br>habréis<br>habrán | habría<br>habrías<br>habría<br>habríamos<br>habríais<br>habrían | haya<br>hayas<br>haya<br>hayamos<br>hayáis<br>hayan | hubiera<br>hubieras<br>hubiera<br>hubiéramos<br>hubierais<br>hubieran |
| hablado comido vivido | hablado comido vivido | hablado comido vivido | hablado comido vivido | hablado comido vivido | hablado comido vivido | hablado comido vivido |

# Irregular Verbs

| Infinitive<br>Present Participle<br>Past Participle | Indicative | | | | | Subjunctive | | Imperative |
| --- | --- | --- | --- | --- | --- | --- | --- | --- |
| | Present | Imperfect | Preterit | Future | Conditional | Present | Imperfect | Commands |
| andar<br>andando<br>andado | ando<br>andas<br>anda<br>andamos<br>andáis<br>andan | andaba<br>andabas<br>andaba<br>andábamos<br>andabais<br>andaban | anduve<br>anduviste<br>anduvo<br>anduvimos<br>anduvisteis<br>anduvieron | andaré<br>andarás<br>andará<br>andaremos<br>andaréis<br>andarán | andaría<br>andarías<br>andaría<br>andaríamos<br>andaríais<br>andarían | ande<br>andes<br>ande<br>andemos<br>andéis<br>anden | anduviera<br>anduvieras<br>anduviera<br>anduviéramos<br>anduvierais<br>anduvieran | anda (tú),<br>no andes<br>ande (usted)<br>andemos<br>andad (vosotros),<br>no andéis<br>anden (Uds.) |
| caer<br>cayendo<br>caído | caigo<br>caes<br>cae<br>caemos<br>caéis<br>caen | caía<br>caías<br>caía<br>caíamos<br>caíais<br>caían | caí<br>caíste<br>cayó<br>caímos<br>caísteis<br>cayeron | caeré<br>caerás<br>caerá<br>caeremos<br>caeréis<br>caerán | caería<br>caerías<br>caería<br>caeríamos<br>caeríais<br>caerían | caiga<br>caigas<br>caiga<br>caigamos<br>caigáis<br>caigan | cayera<br>cayeras<br>cayera<br>cayéramos<br>cayerais<br>cayeran | cae (tú),<br>no caigas<br>caiga (usted)<br>caigamos<br>caed (vosotros),<br>no caigáis<br>caigan (Uds.) |
| dar<br>dando<br>dado | doy<br>das<br>da<br>damos<br>dais<br>dan | daba<br>dabas<br>daba<br>dábamos<br>dabais<br>daban | di<br>diste<br>dio<br>dimos<br>disteis<br>dieron | daré<br>darás<br>dará<br>daremos<br>daréis<br>darán | daría<br>darías<br>daría<br>daríamos<br>daríais<br>darían | dé<br>des<br>dé<br>demos<br>deis<br>den | diera<br>dieras<br>diera<br>diéramos<br>dierais<br>dieran | da (tú),<br>no des<br>dé (usted)<br>demos<br>dad (vosotros),<br>no deis<br>den (Uds.) |
| decir<br>diciendo<br>dicho | digo<br>dices<br>dice<br>decimos<br>decís<br>dicen | decía<br>decías<br>decía<br>decíamos<br>decíais<br>decían | dije<br>dijiste<br>dijo<br>dijimos<br>dijisteis<br>dijeron | diré<br>dirás<br>dirá<br>diremos<br>diréis<br>dirán | diría<br>dirías<br>diría<br>diríamos<br>diríais<br>dirían | diga<br>digas<br>diga<br>digamos<br>digáis<br>digan | dijera<br>dijeras<br>dijera<br>dijéramos<br>dijerais<br>dijeran | di (tú),<br>no digas<br>diga (usted)<br>digamos<br>decid (vosotros),<br>no digáis<br>digan (Uds.) |

# Irregular Verbs (continued)

| Infinitive Present Participle Past Participle | Indicative | | | | | Subjunctive | | Imperative |
|---|---|---|---|---|---|---|---|---|
| | Present | Imperfect | Preterit | Future | Conditional | Present | Imperfect | Commands |
| estar estando estado | estoy estás está estamos estáis están | estaba estabas estaba estábamos estabais estaban | estuve estuviste estuvo estuvimos estuvisteis estuvieron | estaré estarás estará estaremos estaréis estarán | estaría estarías estaría estaríamos estaríais estarían | esté estés esté estemos estéis estén | estuviera estuvieras estuviera estuviéramos estuvierais estuvieran | está (tú), no estés esté (usted) estemos estad (vosotros), no estéis estén (Uds.) |
| haber habiendo habido | he has ha hemos habéis han | había habías había habíamos habíais habían | hube hubiste hubo hubimos hubisteis hubieron | habré habrás habrá habremos habréis habrán | habría habrías habría habríamos habríais habrían | haya hayas haya hayamos hayáis hayan | hubiera hubieras hubiera hubiéramos hubierais hubieran | |
| hacer haciendo hecho | hago haces hace hacemos hacéis hacen | hacía hacías hacía hacíamos hacíais hacían | hice hiciste hizo hicimos hicisteis hicieron | haré harás hará haremos haréis harán | haría harías haría haríamos haríais harían | haga hagas haga hagamos hagáis hagan | hiciera hicieras hiciera hiciéramos hicierais hicieran | haz (tú), no hagas haga (usted) hagamos haced (vosotros), no hagáis hagan (Uds.) |
| ir yendo ido | voy vas va vamos vais van | iba ibas iba íbamos ibais iban | fui fuiste fue fuimos fuisteis fueron | iré irás irá iremos iréis irán | iría irías iría iríamos iríais irían | vaya vayas vaya vayamos vayáis vayan | fuera fueras fuera fuéramos fuerais fueran | ve (tú), no vayas vaya (usted) vamos, no vayamos id (vosotros), no vayáis vayan (Uds.) |
| oír oyendo oído | oigo oyes oye oímos oís oyen | oía oías oía oíamos oíais oían | oí oíste oyó oímos oísteis oyeron | oiré oirás oirá oiremos oiréis oirán | oiría oirías oiría oiríamos oiríais oirían | oiga oigas oiga oigamos oigáis oigan | oyera oyeras oyera oyéramos oyerais oyeran | oye (tú), no oigas oiga (usted) oigamos oíd (vosotros), no oigáis oigan (Uds.) |

# Irregular Verbs (continued)

| Infinitive / Present Participle / Past Participle | Indicative | | | | | Subjunctive | | Imperative |
|---|---|---|---|---|---|---|---|---|
| | Present | Imperfect | Preterit | Future | Conditional | Present | Imperfect | Commands |
| poder<br>pudiendo<br>podido | puedo<br>puedes<br>puede<br>podemos<br>podéis<br>pueden | podía<br>podías<br>podía<br>podíamos<br>podíais<br>podían | pude<br>pudiste<br>pudo<br>pudimos<br>pudisteis<br>pudieron | podré<br>podrás<br>podrá<br>podremos<br>podréis<br>podrán | podría<br>podrías<br>podría<br>podríamos<br>podríais<br>podrían | pueda<br>puedas<br>pueda<br>podamos<br>podáis<br>puedan | pudiera<br>pudieras<br>pudiera<br>pudiéramos<br>pudierais<br>pudieran | |
| poner<br>poniendo<br>puesto | pongo<br>pones<br>pone<br>ponemos<br>ponéis<br>ponen | ponía<br>ponías<br>ponía<br>poníamos<br>poníais<br>ponían | puse<br>pusiste<br>puso<br>pusimos<br>pusisteis<br>pusieron | pondré<br>pondrás<br>pondrá<br>pondremos<br>pondréis<br>pondrán | pondría<br>pondrías<br>pondría<br>pondríamos<br>pondríais<br>pondrían | ponga<br>pongas<br>ponga<br>pongamos<br>pongáis<br>pongan | pusiera<br>pusieras<br>pusiera<br>pusiéramos<br>pusierais<br>pusieran | pon (tú),<br>no pongas<br>ponga (usted)<br>pongamos<br>poned (vosotros),<br>no pongáis<br>pongan (Uds.) |
| querer<br>queriendo<br>querido | quiero<br>quieres<br>quiere<br>queremos<br>queréis<br>quieren | quería<br>querías<br>quería<br>queríamos<br>queríais<br>querían | quise<br>quisiste<br>quiso<br>quisimos<br>quisisteis<br>quisieron | querré<br>querrás<br>querrá<br>querremos<br>querréis<br>querrán | querría<br>querrías<br>querría<br>querríamos<br>querríais<br>querrían | quiera<br>quieras<br>quiera<br>queramos<br>queráis<br>quieran | quisiera<br>quisieras<br>quisiera<br>quisiéramos<br>quisierais<br>quisieran | quiere (tú),<br>no quieras<br>quiera (usted)<br>queramos<br>quered (vosotros),<br>no queráis<br>quieran (Uds.) |
| saber<br>sabiendo<br>sabido | sé<br>sabes<br>sabe<br>sabemos<br>sabéis<br>saben | sabía<br>sabías<br>sabía<br>sabíamos<br>sabíais<br>sabían | supe<br>supiste<br>supo<br>supimos<br>supisteis<br>supieron | sabré<br>sabrás<br>sabrá<br>sabremos<br>sabréis<br>sabrán | sabría<br>sabrías<br>sabría<br>sabríamos<br>sabríais<br>sabrían | sepa<br>sepas<br>sepa<br>sepamos<br>sepáis<br>sepan | supiera<br>supieras<br>supiera<br>supiéramos<br>supierais<br>supieran | sabe (tú),<br>no sepas<br>sepa (usted)<br>sepamos<br>sabed (vosotros),<br>no sepáis<br>sepan (Uds.) |
| salir<br>saliendo<br>salido | salgo<br>sales<br>sale<br>salimos<br>salís<br>salen | salía<br>salías<br>salía<br>salíamos<br>salíais<br>salían | salí<br>saliste<br>salió<br>salimos<br>salisteis<br>salieron | saldré<br>saldrás<br>saldrá<br>saldremos<br>saldréis<br>saldrán | saldría<br>saldrías<br>saldría<br>saldríamos<br>saldríais<br>saldrían | salga<br>salgas<br>salga<br>salgamos<br>salgáis<br>salgan | saliera<br>salieras<br>saliera<br>saliéramos<br>salierais<br>salieran | sal (tú),<br>no salgas<br>salga (usted)<br>salgamos<br>salid (vosotros),<br>no salgáis<br>salgan (Uds.) |

# Irregular Verbs (continued)

| Infinitive / Present Participle / Past Participle | Indicative | | | | | Subjunctive | | Imperative |
| --- | --- | --- | --- | --- | --- | --- | --- | --- |
| | Present | Imperfect | Preterit | Future | Conditional | Present | Imperfect | Commands |
| ser<br>siendo<br>sido | soy<br>eres<br>es<br>somos<br>sois<br>son | era<br>eras<br>era<br>éramos<br>erais<br>eran | fui<br>fuiste<br>fue<br>fuimos<br>fuisteis<br>fueron | seré<br>serás<br>será<br>seremos<br>seréis<br>serán | sería<br>serías<br>sería<br>seríamos<br>seríais<br>serían | sea<br>seas<br>sea<br>seamos<br>seáis<br>sean | fuera<br>fueras<br>fuera<br>fuéramos<br>fuerais<br>fueran | sé (tú),<br>no seas<br>sea (usted)<br>seamos<br>sed (vosotros),<br>no seáis<br>sean (Uds.) |
| tener<br>teniendo<br>tenido | tengo<br>tienes<br>tiene<br>tenemos<br>tenéis<br>tienen | tenía<br>tenías<br>tenía<br>teníamos<br>teníais<br>tenían | tuve<br>tuviste<br>tuvo<br>tuvimos<br>tuvisteis<br>tuvieron | tendré<br>tendrás<br>tendrá<br>tendremos<br>tendréis<br>tendrán | tendría<br>tendrías<br>tendría<br>tendríamos<br>tendríais<br>tendrían | tenga<br>tengas<br>tenga<br>tengamos<br>tengáis<br>tengan | tuviera<br>tuvieras<br>tuviera<br>tuviéramos<br>tuvierais<br>tuvieran | ten (tú),<br>no tengas<br>tenga (usted)<br>tengamos<br>tened (vosotros),<br>no tengáis<br>tengan (Uds.) |
| traer<br>trayendo<br>traído | traigo<br>traes<br>trae<br>traemos<br>traéis<br>traen | traía<br>traías<br>traía<br>traíamos<br>traíais<br>traían | traje<br>trajiste<br>trajo<br>trajimos<br>trajisteis<br>trajeron | traeré<br>traerás<br>traerá<br>traeremos<br>traeréis<br>traerán | traería<br>traerías<br>traería<br>traeríamos<br>traeríais<br>traerían | traiga<br>traigas<br>traiga<br>traigamos<br>traigáis<br>traigan | trajera<br>trajeras<br>trajera<br>trajéramos<br>trajerais<br>trajeran | trae (tú),<br>no traigas<br>traiga (usted)<br>traigamos<br>traed (vosotros),<br>no traigáis<br>traigan (Uds.) |
| venir<br>viniendo<br>venido | vengo<br>vienes<br>viene<br>venimos<br>venís<br>vienen | venía<br>venías<br>venía<br>veníamos<br>veníais<br>venían | vine<br>viniste<br>vino<br>vinimos<br>vinisteis<br>vinieron | vendré<br>vendrás<br>vendrá<br>vendremos<br>vendréis<br>vendrán | vendría<br>vendrías<br>vendría<br>vendríamos<br>vendríais<br>vendrían | venga<br>vengas<br>venga<br>vengamos<br>vengáis<br>vengan | viniera<br>vinieras<br>viniera<br>viniéramos<br>vinierais<br>vinieran | ven (tú),<br>no vengas<br>venga (usted)<br>vengamos<br>venid (vosotros),<br>no vengáis<br>vengan (Uds.) |
| ver<br>viendo<br>visto | veo<br>ves<br>ve<br>vemos<br>veis<br>ven | veía<br>veías<br>veía<br>veíamos<br>veíais<br>veían | vi<br>viste<br>vio<br>vimos<br>visteis<br>vieron | veré<br>verás<br>verá<br>veremos<br>veréis<br>verán | vería<br>verías<br>vería<br>veríamos<br>veríais<br>verían | vea<br>veas<br>vea<br>veamos<br>veáis<br>vean | viera<br>vieras<br>viera<br>viéramos<br>vierais<br>vieran | ve (tú),<br>no veas<br>vea (usted)<br>veamos<br>ved (vosotros),<br>no veáis<br>vean (Uds.) |

# Stem-Changing and Orthographic-Changing Verbs

| Infinitive / Present Participle / Past Participle | Indicative | | | | | Subjunctive | | Imperative |
|---|---|---|---|---|---|---|---|---|
| | Present | Imperfect | Preterit | Future | Conditional | Present | Imperfect | Commands |
| almorzar (z, c) almorzando almorzado | almuerzo almuerzas almuerza almorzamos almorzáis almuerzan | almorzaba almorzabas almorzaba almorzábamos almorzabais almorzaban | almorcé almorzaste almorzó almorzamos almorzasteis almorzaron | almorzaré almorzarás almorzará almorzaremos almorzaréis almorzarán | almorzaría almorzarías almorzaría almorzaríamos almorzaríais almorzarían | almuerce almuerces almuerce almorcemos almorcéis almuercen | almorzara almorzaras almorzara almorzáramos almorzarais almorzaran | almuerza (tú) no almuerces almuerce (usted) almorcemos almorzad (vosotros) no almorcéis almuercen (Uds.) |
| buscar (c, qu) buscando buscado | busco buscas busca buscamos buscáis buscan | buscaba buscabas buscaba buscábamos buscabais buscaban | busqué buscaste buscó buscamos buscasteis buscaron | buscaré buscarás buscará buscaremos buscaréis buscarán | buscaría buscarías buscaría buscaríamos buscaríais buscarían | busque busques busque busquemos busquéis busquen | buscara buscaras buscara buscáramos buscarais buscaran | busca (tú) no busques busque (usted) busquemos buscad (vosotros) no busquéis busquen (Uds.) |
| corregir (g, j) corrigiendo corregido | corrijo corriges corrige corregimos corregís corrigen | corregía corregías corregía corregíamos corregíais corregían | corregí corregiste corrigió corregimos corregisteis corrigieron | corregiré corregirás corregirá corregiremos corregiréis corregirán | corregiría corregirías corregiría corregiríamos corregiríais corregirían | corrija corrijas corrija corrijamos corrijáis corrijan | corrigiera corrigieras corrigiera corrigiéramos corrigierais corrigieran | corrige (tú) no corrijas corrija (usted) corrijamos corregid (vosotros) no corrijáis corrijan (Uds.) |
| dormir (ue, u) durmiendo dormido | duermo duermes duerme dormimos dormís duermen | dormía dormías dormía dormíamos dormíais dormían | dormí dormiste durmió dormimos dormisteis durmieron | dormiré dormirás dormirá dormiremos dormiréis dormirán | dormiría dormirías dormiría dormiríamos dormiríais dormirían | duerma duermas duerma durmamos durmáis duerman | durmiera durmieras durmiera durmiéramos durmierais durmieran | duerme (tú) no duermas duerma (usted) durmamos dormid (vosotros) no durmáis duerman (Uds.) |
| incluir (y) incluyendo incluido | incluyo incluyes incluye incluimos incluís incluyen | incluía incluías incluía incluíamos incluíais incluían | incluí incluiste incluyó incluimos incluisteis incluyeron | incluiré incluirás incluirá incluiremos incluiréis incluirán | incluiría incluirías incluiría incluiríamos incluiríais incluirían | incluya incluyas incluya incluyamos incluyáis incluyan | incluyera incluyeras incluyera incluyéramos incluyerais incluyeran | incluye (tú), no incluyas incluya (usted) incluyamos incluid (vosotros), no incluyáis incluyan (Uds.) |

# Stem-Changing and Orthographic-Changing Verbs (continued)

| Infinitive / Present Participle / Past Participle | Indicative — Present | Imperfect | Preterit | Future | Conditional | Subjunctive — Present | Imperfect | Imperative — Commands |
|---|---|---|---|---|---|---|---|---|
| llegar (g, gu) llegando llegado | llego llegas llega llegamos llegáis llegan | llegaba llegabas llegaba llegábamos llegabais llegaban | llegué llegaste llegó llegamos llegasteis llegaron | llegaré llegarás llegará llegaremos llegaréis llegarán | llegaría llegarías llegaría llegaríamos llegaríais llegarían | llegue llegues llegue lleguemos lleguéis lleguen | llegara llegaras llegara llegáramos llegarais llegaran | llega (tú), no llegues llegue (usted) lleguemos llegad (vosotros), no lleguéis lleguen (Uds.) |
| pedir (i, i) pidiendo pedido | pido pides pide pedimos pedís piden | pedía pedías pedía pedíamos pedíais pedían | pedí pediste pidió pedimos pedisteis pidieron | pediré pedirás pedirá pediremos pediréis pedirán | pediría pedirías pediría pediríamos pediríais pedirían | pida pidas pida pidamos pidáis pidan | pidiera pidieras pidiera pidiéramos pidierais pidieran | pide (tú), no pidas pida (usted) pidamos pedid (vosotros), no pidáis pidan (Uds.) |
| pensar (ie) pensando pensado | pienso piensas piensa pensamos pensáis piensan | pensaba pensabas pensaba pensábamos pensabais pensaban | pensé pensaste pensó pensamos pensasteis pensaron | pensaré pensarás pensará pensaremos pensaréis pensarán | pensaría pensarías pensaría pensaríamos pensaríais pensarían | piense pienses piense pensemos penséis piensen | pensara pensaras pensara pensáramos pensarais pensaran | piensa (tú), no pienses piense (usted) pensemos pensad (vosotros), no penséis piensen (Uds.) |
| producir (zc) produciendo producido | produzco produces produce producimos producís producen | producía producías producía producíamos producíais producían | produje produjiste produjo produjimos produjisteis produjeron | produciré producirás producirá produciremos produciréis producirán | produciría producirías produciría produciríamos produciríais producirían | produzca produzcas produzca produzcamos produzcáis produzcan | produjera produjeras produjera produjéramos produjerais produjeran | produce (tú), no produzcas produzca (usted) produzcamos producid (vosotros), no produzcáis produzcan (Uds.) |
| reír (i, i) riendo reído | río ríes ríe reímos reís ríen | reía reías reía reíamos reíais reían | reí reíste rio reímos reísteis rieron | reiré reirás reirá reiremos reiréis reirán | reiría reirías reiría reiríamos reiríais reirían | ría rías ría riamos riáis rían | riera rieras riera riéramos rierais rieran | ríe (tú), no rías ría (usted) riamos reíd (vosotros), no riáis rían (Uds.) |

# Stem-Changing and Orthographic-Changing Verbs (continued)

| Infinitive Present Participle Past Participle | Indicative | | | | | Subjunctive | | Imperative |
|---|---|---|---|---|---|---|---|---|
| | Present | Imperfect | Preterit | Future | Conditional | Present | Imperfect | Commands |
| seguir (i, i) (ga) siguiendo seguido | sigo sigues sigue seguimos seguís siguen | seguía seguías seguía seguíamos seguíais seguían | seguí seguiste siguió seguimos seguisteis siguieron | seguiré seguirás seguirá seguiremos seguiréis seguirán | seguiría seguirías seguiría seguiríamos seguiríais seguirían | siga sigas siga sigamos sigáis sigan | siguiera siguieras siguiera siguiéramos siguierais siguieran | sigue (tú), no sigas siga (usted) sigamos seguid (vosotros), no sigáis sigan (Uds.) |
| sentir (ie, i) sintiendo sentido | siento sientes siente sentimos sentís sienten | sentía sentías sentía sentíamos sentíais sentían | sentí sentiste sintió sentimos sentisteis sintieron | sentiré sentirás sentirá sentiremos sentiréis sentirán | sentiría sentirías sentiría sentiríamos sentiríais sentirían | sienta sientas sienta sintamos sintáis sientan | sintiera sintieras sintiera sintiéramos sintierais sintieran | siente (tú), no sientas sienta (usted) sintamos sentid (vosotros), no sintáis sientan (Uds.) |
| volver (ue) volviendo vuelto | vuelvo vuelves vuelve volvemos volvéis vuelven | volvía volvías volvía volvíamos volvíais volvían | volví volviste volvió volvimos volvisteis volvieron | volveré volverás volverá volveremos volveréis volverán | volvería volverías volvería volveríamos volveríais volverían | vuelva vuelvas vuelva volvamos volváis vuelvan | volviera volvieras volviera volviéramos volvierais volvieran | vuelve (tú), no vuelvas vuelva (usted) volvamos volved (vosotros), no volváis vuelvan (Uds.) |

# Spanish-English Glossary

The **Spanish-English Glossary** presents all active vocabulary presented in *Hoy día,* as well as all words used in the readings, except for exact cognates. Numbers following entries indicate the chapter where words are introduced. All translations separated by commas before a number are considered active in that chapter. Gender of nouns in Spanish is indicated by *(m)* for masculine and *(f)* for feminine. Nouns referring to people that have both masculine and feminine forms are indicated by *(m/f)*, and those that are generally used in the prural are followed by *(pl)*.

## A

**a** to; **a causa de** because of; **a continuación** next; **a la derecha de** to the right of 2; **a la izquierda de** to the left of 2; **a la parrilla** grilled; **a la una, a las dos** at one o'clock, at two o'clock 2; **a pesar de que** despite, in spite of; **a petición** upon request 11; **A qué hora?** At what time? 2; **a través de** across; **a veces** sometimes 4; at times 2; **al** + *infinitivo* as soon as you + verb 7; **al** + *infinitivo* upon verb + *-ing* 7; **al aire libre** outdoors 2; **al este de** east of 2; **al fondo de** at the end of, at the back of 7; **al horno** baked; **al lado de** next to 2; **al norte de** north of 2; **al oeste de** west of 2; **al principio** at the beginning 8; **al sur de** south of 2; **al vapor** steamed

**abajo** down
**abandonar** abandon
**abierto/a** open 2, 4
**abogado/a** *(m/f)* lawyer 8
**abono** *(m)* fertilizer
**abordar** board 7
**abrazar(se)** hug (each other) 5
**abrazo** *(m)* hug
**abrigo** *(m)* coat; overcoat 5
**abril** April 5
**abrir** open 3
**abrocharse el cinturón** buckle your seatbelt 7
**absolutamente** absolutely
**absurdo/a** absurd 10
**abuela** *(f)* grandmother 3
**abuelo** *(m)* grandfather 3
**abuelos** *(mpl)* grandparents 3
**aburrido/a** bored 2, 4; boring 1
**aburrirse** get bored 5
**abuso** *(m)* abuse
**acá** here 5; **por acá** over / through here 5
**acabar de** have just
**acampar** camp 7
**acceder** accede
**acceso** *(m)* access 11

**accesorio** *(m)* accessory 4
**accidente** *(m)* accident 10
**acción** *(f)* action
**acelerar** accelerate, speed up
**aceptar** accept
**acerca de** about 8
**aclarar** clarify
**acompañar** accompany
**aconsejar** advise 10
**acontecimiento** *(m)* event 8
**acostarse (ue)** lie down, go to bed 5
**acostumbrado/a** accustomed
**acostumbrar** accustom
**actitud** *(f)* attitude
**actividad** *(f)* activity 2
**activista** *(m/f)* activist
**activo/a** active
**actor** *(m)* actor 8
**actriz** *(f)* actress 8
**actualidad** *(f)* current event
**actualmente** currently, presently
**actuar** act
**acusación** *(f)* accusation
**adaptación** *(f)* adaptation
**adaptar** adapt
**adecuado/a** appropriate
**además** besides 11
**adentro** inside
**adicción** *(f)* addiction
**adicional** additional
**adicto/a** *(m/f)* addict
**Adiós.** Good-bye. 1
**adivinar** guess
**adjetivo** *(m)* adjective
**administración** *(f)* administration; **administración de empresas** *(f)* business administration
**administrador/a** *(m/f)* administrator
**admirador/a** *(m/f)* admirer
**admirar** admire
**admitir** admit
**adobado/a** marinated
**adolescencia** *(f)* adolescence
**adónde** (to) where 2
**adoptar** adopt
**adquisitivo/a** purchasing

**adulto/a** *(m/f)* adult
**adverbio** *(m)* adverb
**advertencia** *(f)* warning
**advertir** warn
**aerolínea** *(f)* airline 7
**aeropuerto** *(m)* airport 7
**afectar** affect
**afeitarse** shave
**afirmación** *(f)* affirmation
**africano/a** African
**afuera** outside 4
**afueras** *(fpl)* outskirts 4
**agencia** *(f)* agency
**agencia de viajes** *(f)* travel agency 7
**agente** *(m/f)* agent
**agitación** *(f)* agitation 12
**agosto** August 5
**agradable** agreeable; pleasant, nice 4
**agresivo/a** aggressive
**agrícolo/a** agricultural
**agricultor/a** *(m/f)* farmer 8
**agricultura** *(f)* agriculture
**agua** *(f, el)* water 4
**ahora** now
**ahorrar** save 11
**ahumado/a** smoked
**aire** *(m)* air; **aire acondicionado** air conditioning; **al aire libre** outdoors 2
**ajustarse a** adjust to
**alarma** *(f)* alarm
**alarmado/a** alarmed
**alcoba** *(f)* bedroom
**alcohólico/a** alcoholic
**aldredor de** around
**alegrarse de que** be happy that 11
**alemán** *(m)* German
**alergia** *(f)* allergy 10
**alertar** alert
**alfombra** *(f)* rug 3, 4
**alga** *(f)* seaweed
**álgebra** *(f)* algebra
**algo** something 4
**alguien** someone 4
**alguno/a(s)** some, any 4
**alimenticio/a** nourishing
**alimento** *(m)* food

alinear align
aliviar alleviate
allí there
almorzar (ue) eat / have lunch 4
almuerzo (ligero) (m) (light) lunch 9
Aló. Hello. (on the telephone) 5
alojamiento (m) lodging
alojarse en stay at (on a trip), lodge at 7
alquilar rent 4
alquiler (m) rent 4
alternativo/a alternative
alto/a tall, high 3
alumno/a (m/f) pupil, student 8
ama de casa (f, el) housewife 8
amable lovable
amarillo/a yellow 4
ambiente (m) atmosphere;
    environment 11
amigo/a (m/f) friend; mejor amigo/a (m/f)
    best friend 1
amistoso/a friendly 3
amor (m) love
amueblado/a furnished
analgésico (m) analgesic
anaranjado/a orange 4
andar en bicicleta ride a bicycle 4
ángel (m) angel
animación (f) animation
animado/a lively 4
animal (m) animal 4
ánimo (m) courage; dar ánimo a alguien
    cheer someone up 10; levantarle el
    ánimo lift someone's spirits 10
anoche last night 7
anonimato (m) anonymity
anónimo/a anonymous
anotar note, write down
ansiedad (f) anxiety
antes before; antes de before 2; lo antes
    posible as soon as possible
antibióticos (mpl) antibiotics 10
anticipar anticipate
antidepresivo (m) antidepressant
antiguo/a old
antiinflamatorio (m) anti-inflammatory
antipático/a unpleasant 1
antónimo (m) antonym
anual annual
anualmente annually
anunciante (m/f) advertiser
anunciar announce, advertise
anuncio (m) advertisement
anuncio clasificado (m) classified ad
año (m) year 1; al año per year 1;
    tener . . . años be . . . years old 3
apagar turn off 11
aparecer appear
apartamento (m) apartment

apasionado/a passionate
apellido (m) last name 11
aplicación informática (f) software 6
aplicar apply
apoyo (m) support
apreciar appreciate
aprender learn (to) 3
aprendizaje (m) learning
apropriado/a appropriate
aproximadamente approximately
aproximar approximate
aquel / aquella (aquellos as) that (those)
    (over there) 5
aquí here 1
árbol (m) tree 4
archivador (m) filing cabinet 11
archivar file 11
archivero (m) filing cabinet
archivo (m) archive 6
área (f) area
área recreativa (f) recreation area
argentino/a (m/f) Argentine
armario (m) wardrobe, closet 4
armas (fpl) arms (military)
armoniosamente harmoniously
arqueológico/a archeological
arquitectura (f) architecture
arrastrar drag
arreglar fix, straighten out / up 4
arrestar arrest
arriba up
arroz (m) rice 9
arruinar ruin
arte (m) art
artículo (m) article; artículos de oficina
    (mpl) office supplies 11
artista (m/f) artist
artritis (f) arthritis 10
arvejas (fpl) peas
asado/a roasted
asalto (m) assault
ascender go up, climb
ascensor (m) elevator 7
asco (m) disgust, revulsion 9; dar asco
    be revolting, be unable to stand 9
asegurar assure
asesinar murder
así thus; ¡Así es! that's right 9
asiento (m) seat 7
asignar assign
asistencia (f) assistance
asistente de vuelo (m/f) flight attendant 7
asistir (a) attend 3
asma (f) asthma
asociar associate
aspecto (m) aspect 11
aspecto físico physical appearance 3
aspirina (f) aspirin 10

asunto (m) matter, subject
asustado/a frightened, scared 8
ataque (m) attack
atención (f) attention
atender (ie) attend to, wait on 11
atentamente sincerely
aterrizar land 7
atlántico/a Atlantic
atleta (m/f) athlete
atmósfera (f) atmosphere
atracción (f) attraction
atractivo/a attractive
atraer attract
atún (m) tuna
audiencia (f) audience
aumentar increase
aumento (m) increase; raise 11
aún even
aunque although
ausente absent
autenticidad (f) authenticity
auténtico/a authentic
auto (m) automobile, auto, car
autobiográfico/a autobiographical
autobús (m) bus 4
autodisciplina (f) self-discipline
automáticamente automatically
automático/a automatic
automedicación (f) self-medication
automedicarse self-medicate
automóvil (m) automobile, auto, car
autor/a (m/f) author
autoridad (f) authority
autorretrato (m) self-portrait
avance (m) advance
aventurero/a adventurous
averiguar investigate
avión (m) airplane 7
ayer yesterday 7
ayuda (f) help; ayuda alimentaria (f)
    food assistance; ayuda humanitaria
    (f) humanitarian aid 12
ayudar(se) help (each other) 5
azúcar (m) sugar 9
azul blue 3, 4

## B

bailar dance 2
baile (m) dance
bajar de get off / out of, get down from 7
bajar de peso lose weight 9
bajo/a short (in height), low 3
balcón (m) balcony 7
banana (f) banana
banano (m) banana
banca (f) banking 11
banco (m) bank 7

banquete *(m)* banquet
bañarse bathe, take a bath 5
baño *(m)* bathroom 4
bar *(m)* bar
barato/a inexpensive, cheap 5
barba *(f)* beard 3
barra de herramientas *(f)* tool bar
barrio *(m)* neighborhood 4
basar base
base de datos *(f)* database 11
básico/a basic
básquetbol *(m)* basketball
bastante enough
basura *(f)* trash 4
bebé *(m)* baby
bebedero *(m)* drinking fountain
beber drink 3
bebible drinkable
bebida *(f)* drink 9; **bebida alcohólica** *(f)*
    alcoholic drink 9
beige beige 4
béisbol *(m)* baseball 8
beisbolista *(m/f)* baseball player 8
bellas artes *(fpl)* fine arts
belleza *(f)* beautiful
bello/a beautiful
beneficiar benefit
beneficio *(m)* benefit 11
beneficioso/a beneficial
besar(se) kiss (each other) 5
beso *(m)* kiss
biblioteca *(f)* library 1
bicicleta *(f)* bicycle 4; **andar en bicicleta**
    ride a bicycle 4
bien well 1, 4; **muy bien** very well 1
bienes raíces *(mpl)* real estate
bienestar *(m)* well-being
bienvenido/a welcome 7
bigote *(m)* mustache 3
bilingüe bilingual
billete *(m)* bill 11; ticket 7
biología *(f)* biology
bistec *(m)* steak 9
blanco *(m)* space
blanco/a white 4
bloqueador solar *(m)* sunblock
blusa *(f)* blouse 5
boca *(f)* mouth 10
boda *(f)* wedding 8
bodega *(f)* wine shop
boleto *(m)* ticket 7
bolígrafo *(m)* pen
bolsa *(f)* purse 5
bombero/a *(m/f)* firefighter 8
bonito/a handsome / pretty 1
borrador eraser; delete button
bosque *(m)* woods, forest 7
botánico/a *(m/f)* herbalist
botas *(fpl)* boots 5

botella *(f)* bottle 9
botón button 6
botones *(m)* bellboy
Brasil Brazil
brazada *(f)* stroke (swimming)
brazo *(m)* arm 10
breve brief
brillante brilliant
brócoli *(m)* broccoli 9
bronquitis *(f)* bronchitis
brusco/a brusque
Buenas noches. Good evening.
    Good night. 1
Buenas tardes. Good afternoon. 1
bueno/a good 1
Buenos días. Good morning. 1
buscador *(m)* search engine
buscar look for 5; search
búsqueda *(f)* search; **motor de búsqueda**
    *(m)* search engine
buzón de voz *(m)* voice mailbox 11

## C

cabeza *(f)* head 10
cada each 1
cada vez every time
cadena *(f)* chain; channel, chain
caer a fall into 8; **caerse** fall 10
café *(adj.)* brown 3
café *(m)* coffee 2; **café solo** *(m)* black
    coffee 9
cafeína *(f)* caffeine 9
cafetería *(f)* cafeteria 1
cajero/a *(m/f)* teller, cashier 11; **cajero**
    **automático** *(m)* ATM machine 11
cajón *(m)* drawer 11
calabacín *(m)* squash 9
calabaza *(f)* pumpkin, gourd
calcetines *(mpl)* socks 5
calculadora *(f)* calculator 1
calcular calculate 11
calendario *(m)* calendar
calentar(se) (ie) heat; *refl* get hot,
    warm up
calidad *(f)* quality
cálido/a warm
caliente hot
calificado/a qualified
callado/a quiet 4; silent 6
calle *(f)* street 4
calmado/a calm
calor *(m)* heat; **Hace (mucho) calor.** It's
    (very) hot. 5; **tener calor** be hot 3
calorías *(fpl)* calories 9
caluroso/a warm
cama *(f)* bed 1; **cama doble** *(f)* double
    bed 7

cámara *(f)* room; **cámara de comercio** *(f)*
    chamber of commerce
camarero/a *(m/f)* waiter
camarones *(mpl)* shrimp 9
cambiar change / exchange 7
cambio *(m)* change; **cambios climáticos**
    *(m)* climate change
camello *(m)* camel
caminar walk 10
camisa *(f)* shirt 5
camiseta *(f)* T-shirt 5
campaña *(f)* campaign
campeonato *(m)* championship 8
campo *(m)* country 4
campus *(m)* campus
Canadá Canada
canal *(m)* channel
cancelar cancel
cancha de tenis *(f)* tennis court
canción *(f)* song
candidato/a *(m/f)* candidate
canoso/a gray-haired, white-haired 3
cansado/a tired 4
cantante *(m/f)* singer 8
cantar sing 2
cantidad *(f)* quantity
capacidad *(f)* capacity
capítulo *(m)* chapter
captar capture
cara *(f)* face 10
carácter *(m)* character 3
característica *(f)* characteristics
carbohidratos *(mpl)* carbohydrates 9
cárcel *(f)* prison
cargar fotos take photographs
cargo *(m)* charge 11
Caribe Caribbean
caribeño/a Caribbean
cariñoso/a loving, affectionate 3
carne *(f)* meat 9
carne de cerdo *(m)* pork
caro/a expensive 4
carpeta *(f)* file (folder) 11
carpintería *(f)* carpentry
carpintero/a *(m/f)* carpenter
carrera *(f)* career; **hacer la carrera de . . .**
    get a degree in . . . 8
carretera *(f)* highway
carro *(m)* car 4
carta *(f)* letter; menu 9
casa *(f)* house; **en casa** at home 4
casado/a married 3, 4
casarse (con) marry, get married (to) 5
casi almost 2
caso *(m)* case
castaño brown 3
catarata *(f)* cataract; waterfall
catarro *(m)* cold 10
catedral *(f)* cathedral

categoría (f) category
católico/a Catholic
causar cause
cebolla (f) onion 9
celebración (f) celebration
celebrar celebrate
celular (m) cell phone
cena (f) dinner 2
cenar eat / have dinner 4
censo (m) census
censura (f) censure
centavo (m) cent 9
centígrado (m) centigrade
centralizado/a centralized
centrar center
céntrico/a central
centro (m) center, downtown 4; centro
    comercial (m) shopping center,
    mall 2; centro comunitario (m)
    community center
Centroamérica Central America
centroamericano/a (m/f) Central
    American
cerca (de) near 2
cercana/o close, near
cerdo/a (m/f) pig
cereales (mpl) cereal 9
cerebro (m) brain 10
ceremonia (f) ceremony
cerrado/a closed 2
cerrar (ie) close 4
cerveza (f) beer 9
césped (m) grass, lawn 4
chaqueta (f) jacket 5
chatear chat 6
Chau. Ciao, Bye. 5
chau see you later
chelo (m) cello
cheque de viaje (m) traveler's check 7
chequeo (m) checkup
chequera (f) checkbook 11
chica (f) girl
chícharos (mpl) peas 9
chico (m) boy
chile (m) chile pepper 9; chile relleno
    (m) stuffed pepper 9
chileno/a Chilean
chino (m) Chinese
chisme (m) gossip
chismoso/a gossipy 4
chiste (m) joke 5
chistoso/a funny, likes to joke around 3
choclo (m) corn
chuleta de cerdo (f) pork chop 9
cibercafé (m) cybercafé
cibernético/a cybernetic
cien(to) hundred
ciencia (f) science
ciencias políticas (fpl) political science

ciencias sociales (fpl) social sciences
científico/a (m/f) scientist 8
cierto/a certain; true
cifra (f) number, figure
cigarrillo (m) cigarette
cine (m) cinema 2
cinturón (m) belt 5; seat belt
circuito (m) circuit
circulación (f) circulation
circular circulate, drive
círculo (m) circle
circunstancia (f) circumstance
cirugía (f) surgery 10
cirujano/a (m/f) surgeon 10
cita (f) appointment 10; date
ciudad (f) city 2; ciudad natal (f)
    hometown
civilización (f) civilization
claramente clearly
claro/a clear
clase (f) class 1; clase (de español) (f)
    (Spanish) class 1; compañero/a de
    clase (m/f) classmate 1; ¿Qué clases
    tienes? What classes do you have? 1;
    salón de clase (m) classroom 1
clásico/a classical 2
clasificados (mpl) classified ads
clasificar classify
claúsula (f) clause
cliente / clienta (m/f) customer 5
clientela (f) clientele
clima (m) climate
clóset (m) closet
club nocturno (m) night club 2
cobrar cash (a check), charge (a fee) 11
coche (m) car, automobile 3
cocina (f) kitchen 4
cocinar cook 2
código (m) code
cognado (m) cognate
coherente coherent
colapsar collapse
colega (m/f) colleague 11
colegio (m) college, school; high school 8
colesterol (m) cholesterol 9, 10
coliflor (m) cauliflower 9
colocar place, put
colombiano/a Colombian
colonizador/a (m/f) colonizer
coloquial colloquial
color (m) 4
columna (f) column
comando (m) order 6
combatir combat
combinación (f) combination
combinar combine
comedero (m) bird / animal feeder
comedia (f) comedy
comedor (m) dining room 4

comentar comment
comentario (m) commentary 6
comenzar (ie) begin, start 10
comer eat 2; comer fuerte eat heavily 9
comercial commercial
comercio (m) commerce
comestible edible
cometer commit
cómico/a comic
comida (f) food 1; meal 9; comida
    basura (f) junk food 9
comienzo (m) beginning
comisión (f) commission
comité (f) committee
¿cómo? how? 2; ¿Cómo es . . . ? How
    is . . . ?, What's . . . like? 1; ¿Cómo está
    usted? How are you? (form.) 1; ¿Cómo
    estás? How are you? (fam.) 1; cómo no
    of course 5; ¿Cómo se dice . . . en
    inglés? How do you say . . . in
    English? 1; ¿Cómo se escribe? How is
    that written? 1; ¿Cómo se llama
    usted? What is your name? (form.) 1;
    ¿Cómo te llamas? What is your
    name? (fam.) 1
como like, as 1; tan . . . como as . . . as 4;
    tan pronto como as soon as 11;
    tanto/a/os/as . . . como as much . . . as,
    as many . . . as 4
cómoda (f) chest (of drawers) 4
cómodo/a comfortable
compañero/a (m/f) companion 1;
    compañero/a de casa (m/f) house-
    mate; compañero/a de clase (m/f)
    classmate 1; compañero/a de cuarto
    (m/f) roommate 1
compañía (f) company 11
comparación (f) comparison
comparar compare
compartimento (m) compartment
compartir share 3
compatibilidad (f) compatibility 11
compatriota (m/f) compatriot 12
competición (f) competition
competir compete
competitivo/a competitive
complejo (m) complex
complementar complement
complemento directo / indirecto (m)
    direct / indirect object
completamente completely
completar complete
completo/a full, complete 11
complicado/a complicated
cómplice (m/f) accomplice
componentes físicos (m) hardware 6
comprar buy 2
comprender understand 3; No
    comprendo. I don't understand. 1

**comprensivo/a** understanding 3
**compresión** *(f)* compression 6
**comprometer** commit
**computación** *(f)* computing
**computador** *(m)* computer
**computadora** *(f)* computer 1
**común** common 10
**comunicación** communication
**comunicar(se)** communicate (with each other) 5
**comunidad** *(f)* community; **centro comunitario** *(m)* community center
**comunitario/a** community (adj.)
**con** with 2; **con / sin acento** with / without an accent 1; **con antelación** in advance 7; **con atención** with attention 8; **con cheque** with a check 5; **con frecuencia** frequently 2; **¿con qué frecuencia?** how often? 2; **con regularidad** regularly 10; **con retraso** with a delay, late 7; **con tarjeta de crédito / débito** with a credit / debit card 5; **con vistas a . . .** with a view of . . . , overlooking 7
**concentración** *(f)* concentration
**concentrado/a** concentrated
**concentrarse** concentrate 10
**concepto** *(m)* concept
**concientización pública** *(f)* public awareness
**concierto** *(m)* (classical music) concert 2
**conciso/a** concise
**concreto/a** concrete
**concursante** *(m/f)* contestant, competitor
**concurso** *(m)* game show, competition
**condado** *(m)* county
**condenar** condemn
**condición** *(f)* condition
**condicional** conditional
**condicionar** condition
**condimento** *(m)* condiment
**conducir** drive
**conectar** connect 8
**conectividad** *(f)* connectivity
**conexión** *(f)* connection
**conferencia** *(f)* conference
**confesar** confess
**confianza** *(f)* confidence
**confiar** have confidence in, trust
**configurar** configure
**confirmación** *(f)* confirmation
**confirmar** confirm
**confundido/a** confused 2, 4
**confusión** *(f)* confusion
**congestión** *(f)* congestion 10
**congestionado/a** congested 10
**congresista** *(m/f)* congressman / woman
**Congreso** *(m)* Congress 12
**conjunción** *(f)* conjunction

**conmemorar** commemorate
**conmigo** with me 2
**connotación** *(f)* connotation
**conocer** know, be familiar with, be acquainted with, meet 7; **conocido/a** known; **No conozco a . . .** I don't know . . . (a person) 4
**conocimiento** *(m)* knowledge
**conquista** *(f)* conquest
**conquistar** conquer
**consecuencia** *(f)* consequence
**consejero/a** *(m/f)* counselor 8
**consejo** *(m)* advice, counsel
**conservador/a** conservative 3
**conservar** conserve
**consideradamente** considerately
**consistir** consist
**consonante** *(f)* consonant
**constantemente** constantly
**construcción** *(f)* construction 8
**consulado** *(m)* consulate
**consulta** *(f)* consultation
**consultar** consult
**consumerismo** *(m)* consumerism
**consumidor/a** *(m/f)* consumer
**consumo** *(m)* consumption
**contabilidad** *(f)* accounting
**contactar** contact
**contacto** *(m)* contact
**contador/a** *(m/f)* accountant 8, 11
**contaminación** *(f)* contamination
**contaminar** contaminate
**contar (ue)** count, tell 4
**contenedor** *(m)* container
**contener** contain
**contenido** *(m)* content
**contento/a** happy, glad 2; **estar contento/a de que** be happy that 11
**contestar** answer 2
**contexto** *(m)* context
**contigo** with you 3
**continuar** continue
**contra** against
**contrario** *(m)* contrary
**contraseña** *(f)* password
**contraste** *(m)* contrast
**contratar** hire 11
**contribución** *(f)* contribution
**contribuir** contribute
**control de seguridad** *(m)* security check 7
**controlar** control 10
**conversación** *(f)* conversation
**convertir** convert
**cooperación** *(f)* cooperation
**copa** *(f)* stemmed glass, wine glass 9
**copia** *(f)* copy; **sacar una copia** make a copy 11
**copiar** copy

**corazón** *(m)* heart 10
**corbata** *(f)* necktie 5
**cordialmente** cordially
**corrección** *(f)* correction
**correcto/a** right, correct 7
**corregir** correct
**correo** *(m)* mail; **correo electrónico** *(m)* e-mail 3; **correo no deseado** *(m)* spam 6; **oficina de correos** *(f)* post office 7
**correr** run 3
**corresponder** correspond
**correspondiente** corresponding
**corriente** running
**corrupción** *(f)* corruption
**cortar(se)** cut (oneself) 10; **cortar el césped** cut the grass 4; **cortarse el pelo** cut one's hair 7
**corte** *(f)* court
**Corte Suprema** *(f)* Supreme Court
**cortesía** *(f)* courtesy
**corto/a** short 3
**cosa** *(f)* thing 1
**cosmopolito/a** cosmopolitan
**costa** *(f)* coast
**costar (ue)** cost 4
**costarricense** Costa Rican
**costo** *(m)* cost
**costo de vida** *(m)* cost of living
**costoso/a** costly
**costumbre** *(f)* custom
**crear** create
**creatividad** *(f)* creativity
**crecer** grow
**creciente** growing
**crédito** *(m)* credit
**creer (en / que)** believe (in / that) 3
**crema** *(f)* cream 9
**crimen** *(m)* crime
**criminalidad** *(f)* crime (in general) 12
**cristal** crystal
**criterios** *(mpl)* criteria
**criticar** criticize
**crítico/a** *(m/f)* critic
**cruce** *(m)* intersection
**cuaderno** *(m)* notebook 1; **cuaderno de ejercicios** *(m)* workbook 1
**cuadra** *(f)* (city) block 7
**cuál(es)** which, what 2
**cualidad** *(f)* quality
**cualquier** any
**¿cuándo?** when? 2
**¿cuánto/a?** how much 2; **¿cuántos/as?** how many 2; **¿Cuánto cuesta(n) . . . ?** How much does it (do they) cost?
**cuarto** *(m)* 4; room 1
**cuarto/a** fourth
**cubano/a** Cuban
**cubismo** *(m)* cubism
**cuchara** *(f)* spoon 9

**cuchillo** (*m*) knife 9
**cuello** (*m*) neck 10
**cuenta** (*f*) account, bill 11; check 9;
    **cuenta bancaria** (*f*) bank account;
    **cuenta corriente / de ahorros** (*f*)
    checking / savings account 11
**cuento** (*m*) story, tale 8
**cuerpo** (*m*) body 10
**cuestión** (*f*) question
**cuestionario** (*m*) questionnaire
**cuidado** (*m*) care; **cuidado de niños** (*m*)
    childcare; **cuidado prenatal** (*m*)
    prenatal care 10; **tener cuidado** be
    careful 10
**cuidar(se)** take care of (oneself) 10
**culinario/a** culinary
**cultivable** arable
**cultivar** cultivate
**cultivo** (*m*) crop
**cultura** (*f*) culture
**cultural** cultural 4
**cumpleaños** (*m*) birthday 2
**cumplido** (*m*) compliment
**cumplir** turn (an age), carry out 8
**curación** (*f*) healing
**curativo/a** curative
**curiosidad** (*f*) curiosity 12; **tener**
    **curiosidad** be curious
**currículum vitae** (*m*) curriculum vitae,
    résumé 11
**cursivo/a** cursive
**curso** (*m*) course; **curso universitario**
    (*m*) university course
**cursor** (*m*) cursor 6

### D

**dama** (*f*) lady
**danza** (*f*) dance
**dar** give 9; **dar ánimo a alguien** cheer
    someone up 10; **dar asco** be revolting,
    be unable to stand 9; **dar hambre**
    make hungry 9; **dar la bienvenida**
    welcome; **dar miedo** scare; **dar sed**
    make thirsty 9
**datar de** date from
**datos** (*mpl*) data; **datos personales** (*mpl*)
    personal data 11
**de** of, from 1; **de . . . a . . .** from . . . to . . .
    2; **de carácter** personality-wise 3; **de**
    **compras** shopping 5; **¿De dónde**
    **eres?** Where are you from? (*fam.*) 1;
    **¿De dónde es usted?** Where are you
    from? (*form.*) 1; **de habla inglesa**
    English-speaking; **de la mañana** in
    the morning 2; **de la noche** in the
    evening / night 2; **de la tarde** in the
    afternoon 2; **de mediana edad**

middle-aged 3; **de niño/a** as a child 8;
**de (no) fumadores** (non-)smoking 7;
**de seguridad** security 7; **de tu madre**
**/ padre** your mother's / father's side
3; **de última moda** latest fashion; **de**
**vacaciones** on vacation 7; **¿De veras?**
Really? 11; **de vez en cuando** once in
a while
**de compras: ir de compras** go
    shopping 2
**debajo de** below, under 2
**debatir** debate
**deber** must / should 3
**debido a** due to
**débil** weak
**debilitar** debilitate
**débito** (*m*) debit
**década** (*f*) decade
**decidir** decide 7
**décimo/a** tenth
**decir (i)** say, tell 4; **¿Cómo se dice . . .**
    **en inglés?** How do you say . . . in
    English? 1
**decisión** (*f*) decision
**declarar** declare
**dedicación** (*f*) dedication
**dedicar** dedicate; **dedicarse a** do (for a
    living), devote oneself to 8
**dedos** (*mpl*) fingers 10
**deducir** deduce
**defender** defend
**déficit** (*m*) deficit
**definar** define
**definición** (*f*) definition
**definido/a** defined
**deforestación** (*f*) deforestation 12
**dejar** leave (something somewhere) 4;
    **dejar de** (+ *infinitive*) stop . . . -*ing* 10
**delante de** ahead of, in front of 2
**delantero/a** front
**delegación** (*f*) delegation
**delgado/a** thin 3
**delicioso/a** delicious
**demanda** (*f*) demand
**demás** (*mpl*) the rest
**demasiado** too, too much 2, 5
**demócrata** (*m/f*) Democrat
**democratización** (*f*) democratization
**demostrativo/a** demonstrative
**dentista** (*m/f*) dentist 10
**dentro de** within
**denunciar** denounce
**departamento** (*m*) department 11
**depender (de)** depend
**dependiente / dependienta** salesclerk 5
**deportes** (*mpl*) sports 2
**deportista** athletic, fond of sports 8
**deportista** (*m/f*) athlete 8
**depositar** deposit 11

**depósito (directo)** (*m*) (direct) deposit 11
**depresión** (*f*) depression 10
**deprimido/a** depressed
**derecha** (*f*) right; **a la derecha de** to the
    right of 2
**derecho** (*m*) right
**derivado** (*m*) derivative
**desafortunadamente** unfortunately 4
**desaparición** (*f*) disappearance
**desarrollar** develop 10
**desarrollo** (*m*) development 11
**desastre** (*m*) disaster
**desastroso/a** disastrous
**desayunar** eat / have breakfast 4
**desayuno** (*m*) breakfast 4, 7
**descafeinado/a** decaffeinated
**descansar** rest 2
**descarga** (*f*) data transfer 6
**descargar** download 6
**descender** descend
**descifrable** decipherable
**desconectado/a** disconnected
**desconectar** disconnect
**desconocer** not to know
**desconocido/a** unknown 2
**desconocido/a** (*m/f*) stranger
**describir** describe
**descripción** (*f*) description
**desde . . . hasta** (starting) from . . . until
**desear** want; wish, desire 2
**desempleado/a** unemployed
**desempleo** (*m*) unemployment
**desequilibrio** (*m*) imbalance
**desesperanza** (*f*) despair 10
**desfile** (*m*) parade
**deshonesto/a** dishonest
**desnutrición** (*f*) malnutrition
**desordenado/a** disordered; messy 4
**desorganizado/a** disorganized
**despacio** slow, slowly
**despedida** (*f*) farewell
**despedir (i, i)** fire 11; **despedirse (i)** say
    goodbye
**despegar** take off 7
**despejado/a** clear 5
**despejar** clear 5
**despertarse (ie)** wake up 5
**después (de)** after 2
**destacar** highlight
**destino** (*m*) destination
**destruir** destroy
**desventaja** (*f*) disadvantage
**detalle** (*m*) detail
**detener** detain
**deteriorarse** deteriorate
**determinante** determining
**detrás de** behind 2
**devastación** (*f*) devastation
**devolver (ue)** return to 11

día (m) day 2; **Buenos días.** Good
  morning. 1; **días laborales** work days;
  **hoy día** nowadays; **mediodía** noon 2;
  **todo el día** all day; **todos los días**
  every day 2
diabetes (f) diabetes 10
diablo (m) devil
diagnosticar diagnose
diálogo (m) dialogue
diario/a daily 2
dibujar draw 11
dibujo (m) picture
dibujos animados (mpl) cartoon
diccionario (m) dictionary 1
diciembre December 5
diente (m) tooth
dieta (f) diet 9
diferencia (f) difference
diferente different
difícil difficult 1
dificultad (f) difficulty 10
digestión (f) digestion
dígito (m) digit
dimensión (f) dimension
dinámica (f) dynamic
dinero (m) money 4; **dinero en efectivo**
  (m) cash 11
dirección (f) address 4
directo/a direct
director/a (m/f) director 11
dirigir direct
disciplina (f) discipline
discoteca (f) discotheque
discretamente discreetly
discreto/a discreet
discriminatorio/a discriminatory
¡Disculpe! Excuse me! Pardon me! 7
discurso (m) speech
discusión (f) discussion
discutir discuss
diseñador/a (m/f) designer; **diseñador/a**
  **de software** (m/f) software designer 8;
  **diseñador/a gráfico/a** (m/f) graphic
  artist 11
diseñar design 11
diseño (m) design 6; **diseño de páginas**
  **web** (m) web page design 11; **diseño**
  **gráfico** (m) graphic design
disfrutar enjoy
disgustado/a disgusted 6
disidente (m/f) dissident
disminuir diminish
disparidad (f) disparity
disponibilidad (f) availability 7
disponible available 7, 11
distancia (f) distance
distinguido/a distinguished
distinto/a different, distinct
distribución (f) distribution

distribuir distribute 11
distrito (m) district
diversidad (f) diversity
diversión (f) diversion
divertido/a fun 1
divertir(se) (ie, i) amuse, entertain; refl
  have fun, amuse oneself 5
divisa (f) currency
divorciado/a divorced 3, 4
divorciarse (de) divorce, get divorced
  (from) 5
divorcio (m) divorce
doble double
doctorado (m) doctoral degree
documento (m) document 11
dólar (m) dollar 11
doler (ue) hurt, ache 9
dolor (m) pain, ache 10
dolorido/a sore 10
doméstico/a domestic
domingo Sunday 2
dominicano/a Dominican
dominio (m) domain
dónde where? 2
dormir (ue) sleep 4; **dormir (ue) una**
  **siesta** take a nap 4
dormitorio (m) bedroom 4
dosis (f) dose
droga (f) drug
ducha (f) shower 7
ducharse shower, take a shower 5
dudar doubt 10
dueño/a (m/f) owner
dulces (mpl) sweets 9
duración (f) length
durante during 3
durar last 7

### E

ecológico/a ecological
economía (f) economy 12
económico/a economic
economista (m/f) economist
ecoturismo (m) ecotourism 7
edad (f) age 8
edificio (m) building 1
editar edit
educación (f) education
educado/a polite
educador/a (m/f) educator
educar educate
educativo/a educative
efectivo (m) cash 11
efectivo/a effective
efecto (m) effect
eficacia (f) efficacy
egoísta selfish 3

ejemplo (m) example
ejercicio (m) exercise 1; **cuaderno de**
  **ejercicios** (m) workbook 1
ejotes (mpl) green beans 9
él he
elección (f) election 12
electricidad (f) electricity
electrónico/a electronic
elegante elegant
elemento (m) element
elevador (m) elevator
eliminar eliminate
ella she
ellos/as they
elocuente eloquent
elote (m) corn
elusivo/a elusive
embarazada pregnant; **estar embarazada**
  be pregnant 10
embarazo (m) pregnancy 10
embarque (m) boarding
emergencia (f) emergency
emisión (f) emission
emoción (f) emotion 11
emocionado/a excited 8
emocional emotional
emocionante moving, exciting, thrilling
emoticono (m) emoticon 6
emperador (f) emperor
empezar (ie) start, begin 4
empleado/a (m/f) employee 11
empleador/a (m/f) employer
empleo (m) employment, job 10; **empleo**
  **a tiempo completo / parcial** (m)
  full-time / part-time job 11
empresa (f) company, enterprise,
  business 11
empresario/a (m/f) businessman/woman
en at, in, on 1; **en casa** at home 4; **en**
  **cuanto a** as for 9; **en efectivo** in cash;
  **en el trabajo** at work 2; **en ese caso**
  in that case 7; **en forma** in shape 10;
  **en general** in general; **en la calle . . .**
  on . . . Street 2; **en la oficina** at the
  office 2; **en línea** online; **¿En qué**
  **puedo servirle?** How may I help
  you? 5; **en seguida** right away; **en**
  **vez de** instead of 9; **en vías de**
  **desarrollo** developing; **en vivo** live
enamorado/a in love, enamored 6
enamorarse (de) fall in love (with) 5
encabezado heading, headline
encantador/a enchanting
encantar love 9
encargado/a (m/f) person in charge,
  employer 7
encender (ie) turn on 11
enchiladas (fpl) enchiladas 9
encierro (m) running of the bulls

**encima de** on top of 2
**encontrar(se) (ue)** find 4; *refl* get together, meet up 5
**encuesta** *(f)* survey
**encuestador/a** *(m/f)* surveyor
**endorfina** *(f)* endorphin
**energía** *(f)* energy 9
**enero** January 5
**enfermarse** become ill; get sick 10
**enfermedad** *(f)* illness 10
**enfermero/a** *(m/f)* nurse 8
**enfermo/a** sick, ill 1, 4
**enfrentar** face; **enfrentarse (con)** confront
**enfrente de** across from, facing 2
**enlace** *(m)* link
**enojado/a** angry 2
**enojarse** get angry 5
**ensalada** *(f)* salad 9
**ensayo** *(m)* essay, paper 3
**enseguida** right away
**enseñar** teach
**entender (ie)** understand 4
**entero/a** entire, whole 9
**entonces** so, then, next 2
**entrada** *(f)* entrance 7; entry
**entre** among, between
**entrenar** train 11
**entretenemiento** *(m)* entertainment 12
**entrevista** *(f)* interview 11
**entrevistado/a** *(m/f)* interviewee
**entrevistador/a** *(m/f)* interviewer
**entrevistar** interview
**envejecimiento** *(m)* aging
**enviar** send 6, 7
**enzima** *(f)* enzyme
**epidemia** *(f)* epidemic
**episodio** *(m)* episode
**época** *(f)* epoch
**equilibrado/a** balanced 9
**equipado/a** equipped
**equipaje** *(m)* luggage
**equipar** equip
**equipo** *(m)* equipment; team 8
**equitativo/a** equitable
**equivalente** equivalent
**equivaler** amount to, be equivalent to
**equivocado/a** wrong, mistaken 11
**erradicación** *(f)* eradication
**escala** *(f)* scale; stopover; **hacer escala** make a stopover 7
**escalera** *(f)* stairs, staircase 7
**escalfado/a** poached
**escandalizar** scandalize
**escándolo** *(m)* scandal
**escandaloso/a** scandalous
**escanear** scan 11
**escáner** *(m)* scanner 11
**escena** *(f)* scene
**esclavo/a** *(m/f)* slave

**escribir** write 3; **¿Cómo se escribe?** How is that written? 1
**escritor/a** *(m/f)* writer
**escritorio** *(m)* desk 1
**escrupulosamente** scrupulously
**escuchar** listen (to) 2
**escuela** *(f)* school 4; **escuela normal** *(f)* elementary school 11; **escuela primaria** *(f)* elementary school 8, 11; **escuela secundaria** *(f)* secondary school 8
**ese / esa (esos / esas)** that (those) 3, 5
**esencial** essential
**eslogan** *(m)* slogan
**espacio** *(m)* space 4
**espaguetis** *(mpl)* spaghetti
**espalda** *(f)* back 10
**España** Spain
**español** *(m)* Spanish 1
**español/a** Spanish
**español/a** *(m/f)* Spaniard
**espárragos** *(mpl)* asparagus 9
**especial** special
**especialista** *(m/f)* specialist 10
**especializar** specialize
**especialmente** especially
**específico/a** specific
**espejo** *(m)* mirror 4
**esperar** hope 10; wait (for) 7
**espinacas** *(fpl)* spinach 9
**espíritu** *(m)* spirit
**espiritual** spiritual
**esposo/a** *(m/f)* spouse
**esquiar** ski 2
**esquina** *(f)* corner 7
**esta noche** tonight
**esta semana** this week 2
**estabilidad** *(f)* stability
**estabilizar** stabilize
**establecer** establish
**establecimiento** *(m)* establishment
**estación** *(f)* season 5; station; **estación de servicio** *(f)* service station, gas station 7
**estacionamiento** *(m)* parking lot 4
**estacionar** park 4
**estadio** *(m)* stadium
**estado** *(m)* state
**estados físicos** *(mpl)* physical states 10
**Estados Unidos** *(mpl)* United States
**estadounidense** American
**estampilla** *(f)* stamp
**estante** *(m)* shelf 1, 4
**estar** be 1; **estar a disposición** be available; **estar contento/a de que** be happy that 11; **estar de acuerdo** agree; **estar de buen / mal humor** be in a good / bad mood 11; **estar de moda** be in fashion 5; **estar embarazada** be pregnant 10; **estar en ayunas** fast; **estar**

**encargado/a de** be in charge of 11; **estar seguro/a** be sure 10; **estar triste de que** be sad that 11
**estatua** *(f)* statue
**estatura mediana** medium height 3
**este / esta (estos / estas)** this 2; this (these) 5
**este** *(m)* east 2; **al este de** east of 2
**estéreo** *(m)* stereo 1
**estereotipo** *(m)* stereotype
**esteroides** *(mpl)* steroids
**estilo** *(m)* style
**estimación** *(f)* estimation
**estimado/a** esteemed
**estimar** estimate
**estimulante** stimulating
**estimular** stimulate
**estímulo** *(m)* stimulus
**estómago** *(m)* stomach 10
**estornudar** sneeze 10
**estrategia** *(f)* strategy
**estrella** *(f)* star
**estrés** *(m)* stress 10
**estresante** stressful
**estricto/a** strict 3
**estructura** *(f)* structure
**estudiante** *(m/f)* student 1
**estudiar** study 2
**estudiar en el extranjero** study abroad
**estudio** *(m)* study
**estudios** *(mpl)* studies
**estufa** *(f)* stove 4
**estupendo/a** stupendous
**eterno/a** eternal
**ética** *(f)* ethics
**etiqueta** *(f)* etiquette
**étnico/a** ethnic
**europeo/a** European
**evaluación** *(f)* evaluation
**evaluar** evaluate 11
**evento** *(m)* event 3; **evento deportivo** sports event 3
**evidente** evident
**evitar** avoid 9
**exagerado/a** exaggerate
**examen** *(m)* exam; **examen parcial** *(m)* mid-term exam
**examinar** examine 10
**excelente** excellent
**excepcionalmente** exceptionally
**excesivamente** excessively
**excesivo/a** excessive
**exceso** *(m)* excess
**excursión** *(f)* excursion; **ir de excursión** go on an outing, go on a hike 7
**excusa** *(f)* excuse
**exhalar** exhale
**exhausto/a** exhausted
**existir** exist

**éxito** *(m)* success; **tener éxito** be successful
**exótico/a** exotic
**expansión** *(f)* expansion
**expedición** *(f)* expedition
**experiencia** *(f)* experience; **experiencia profesional** *(f)* professional experience 11
**experto/a** *(m/f)* expert
**explicación** *(f)* explanation
**explicar** explain 9
**explotación** *(f)* exploitation
**exposición** exhibition
**expresar** express
**expresión** *(f)* expression
**exquisito/a** exquisite
**extender** extend
**extendido/a** extensive
**extensión** *(f)* extension 6
**extracto** *(m)* extract
**extranjero/a** foreign
**extraño/a** strange
**extraordinario/a** extraordinary
**extrovertido/a** outgoing, extroverted 1
**exuberante** exuberant

## F

**fábrica** *(f)* factory
**fabricar** make, manufacture
**fácil** easy 1
**facilidad** *(f)* facility
**facilitar** facilitate
**fácilmente** easily
**factura** *(f)* bill
**facturar el equipaje** check one's luggage 7
**facultad (de medicina)** *(f)* school (of medicine)
**falda** *(f)* skirt 5
**fallar** fail, be down 11
**falsamente** falsely
**falso/a** false
**falta** *(f)* lack; **falta de concentración / de interés** *(f)* lack of concentration / of interest 10
**faltar (a)** be absent, be missing, be needed 8
**fama** *(f)* fame
**familia** *(f)* family
**familiar** family member, relative 3; pertaining to family
**famoso/a** famous 8
**fanático/a** fanatic
**farmacia** *(f)* pharmacy 7
**fascinante** fascinating
**fastidiar** bother, annoy
**fatiga** *(f)* fatigue
**favorecer** favor

**favorito/a** favorite
**febrero** February 5
**fecha** *(f)* date 5; **fecha de nacimiento** *(f)* birthday
**feliz** happy
**feminino/a** feminine
**fenómeno** *(m)* phenomenon
**feo/a** ugly 1
**feria** *(f)* festival
**ferrocarril** *(m)* railway
**fervor** *(m)* fervor
**festivo/a** festive
**fibra** *(f)* fiber 9; **fibra óptica** *(f)* fiber optic
**ficticio/a** fictitious
**fiebre** *(f)* fever 10
**fiesta** *(f)* party 3; **fiesta de cumpleaños** *(f)* birthday party 8; **hacer una fiesta** have a party 3
**filosofía** *(f)* philosophy
**fin de semana** *(m)* weekend 2
**final** *(m)* end
**finalmente** finally
**financiación** *(f)* financing
**financiar** finance
**financiero/a** financial
**firma** *(f)* signature, firm, company
**firmante** *(m/f)* signer
**firmar** sign 11
**física** *(f)* physics
**físicamente** physically 3
**físico/a** physical
**flan** *(m)* flan 9
**flexible** flexible 3
**flor** *(f)* flower 4
**floreciente** flourishing
**fluido/a** fluid
**flúor** *(m)* fluoride
**folleto** *(m)* brochure
**fondo** *(m)* end, back; **al fondo de**
**forma** *(f)* forma; **en forma** in shape 10
**formación académica** *(f)* education 11
**formar** form
**formato** *(m)* format
**formulario** *(m)* form
**foro** *(m)* forum
**fortuna** *(f)* fortune
**fosfato** *(m)* phosphate
**foto** *(f)* photograph; **sacar una foto** take a picture 5
**fotocopiadora** *(f)* photocopier 11
**fotografía** *(f)* photography
**fracción** *(f)* fraction
**francés** *(m)* French
**franco/a** frank
**frase** *(f)* phrase
**frecuencia** *(f)* frequency
**frecuente** frequent
**frenético/a** frenetic
**fresas** *(fpl)* strawberries 9

**fresco/a** cool; fresh; **Hace fresco.** It's cool. 5
**frigorífico** *(m)* refrigerator
**frijoles** *(mpl)* beans 9
**frío** *(m)* cold; **Hace (mucho) frío.** It's (very) cold; 5 **tener frío** be cold 3
**frío/a** cold 3
**frito/a** fried
**frívolo/a** frivolous
**frontera** *(f)* border
**frustración** *(f)* frustration
**fruta** *(f)* fruit 9
**frutillas** *(fpl)* strawberries
**fuente** *(f)* font; source
**fuera** outside
**fuerte** strong 8
**fuerza** *(f)* force 12; strength 10
**fumador/a** *(m/f)* smoker
**fumar** smoke 4
**funcionamiento** *(m)* functioning
**funcionar** function; work (for machines, plans, or systems) 4
**fundar** found
**furioso/a** furious
**fútbol** soccer (football) 2; **fútbol americano** football 2
**futbolista** *(m/f)* soccer player 8
**futuro** *(m)* future

## G

**gafas** *(fpl)* glasses 3; **gafas de sol** *(fpl)* sunglasses
**galería** *(f)* gallery
**galleta** *(f)* cookie 9
**galón** *(m)* gallon
**ganar** earn; win 8
**ganas** *(fpl)*: **tener ganas de** feel like
**garaje** *(m)* garage 4
**garantía** *(f)* guarantee
**garantizar** guarantee
**garganta** *(f)* throat 10
**gas** *(m)* gas 4; **gasolina** *(f)* gasoline 7
**gasolinera** *(f)* service station, gas station 7
**gastar** spend (money) 5
**gasto** *(m)* expense
**gástrico/a** gastric
**gastronomía** *(f)* gastronomy
**gato/a** *(m/f)* cat
**generación** *(f)* generation
**generalmente** generally 2
**generar** generate
**género** *(m)* genre
**generoso/a** generous 3
**genético/a** genetic
**genio/a** *(m/f)* genius
**gente** *(f)* people 2

**geografía** (f) geography
**gerente de fábrica** (m/f) factory manager 8
**gesto** (m) gesture 8
**gimnasio** (m) gym(nasium) 1
**globalización** (f) globalization
**globalizar** globalize
**gobernabilidad** (f) governability
**gobernador/a** (m/f) governor
**gobierno** (m) government
**gol** (m) goal 8
**golpear** hit, strike 8
**gordo/a** fat 3
**gorra** (f) cap 5
**gozar** enjoy
**grabación** recording
**grabar** record
**gracias** thank you 1; **gracias a** thanks to
**grado** (m) degree; grade 8
**graduación** (f) graduation 8
**graduarse** graduate 8
**gráfico** (m) figure; **diseñador/a gráfico/a** (m/f) graphic artist 11; **diseño gráfico** (m) graphic design; graphic design program 11
**grafiti** (m) graffiti
**gramática** (f) grammar; grammatic
**gramatical** grammatical
**gramo** (m) gram
**gran / grande** big 1; large
**grano** (m) grain 9
**grasa** (f) fat 9
**gratis** free
**gratuito/a** free
**grave** serious, grave 10
**gripe** (f) flu
**gris** gray 3, 4
**gritar** yell
**grupo** (m) group
**guapo/a** good-looking, handsome 3
**guardar** keep; **guardar cama** stay in bed 10
**guardia** (m/f) guard
**gubernamental** governmental
**guerillero/a** (m/f) guerrilla 12
**guerra** (f) war
**guía** (f) guide; **guía (turística)** (f) (tourist) guidebook 7; **guía (turístico/a)** (m/f) (tourist) guide 7
**guiar** guide, drive
**guineo** (m) banana
**guisantes** (mpl) peas
**guitarra** (f) guitar 2
**gustar** be pleasing to, please 2; **Me gusta(n) . . .** I like; **Me gustaría(n)** I would like . . . 4; **(No) me gusta** (+ *singular noun*) I (don't) like . . . 1; **¿Te gusta** (+ *singular noun*)? Do you like . . . ? 1; **¿Te gustan** (+ *plural noun*)? Do you like . . . ? 1
**gusto** (m) taste

## H

**habichuelas** (mpl) beans
**habilidad** (f) ability
**habitación** (f) room 7; bedroom; **habitación sencilla/doble** (f) single / double room 7
**habitante** (m/f) inhabitant
**hábito** (m) habit; **hábitos alimenticios** (mpl) eating habits
**hablador/a** talkative, chatty 4
**hablar** speak, talk 2
**hace . . . . . . ** ago 7
**hacer** do, make 2; **Hace buen / mal tiempo.** The weather's good / bad. 5; **Hace fresco.** It's cool. 5; **Hace (mucho) calor.** It's (very) hot. 5; **Hace (mucho) frío.** It's (very) cold. 5; **Hace sol.** It's sunny. 5; **Hace viento.** It's windy. 5; **hacer clic** click; **hacer ejercicio** exercise 2; **hacer escala** make a stopover 7; **hacer esquí acuático** waterski 2; **hacer la carrera de . . .** get a degree in . . . 8; **hacer la maleta** pack one's suitcase 7; **hacer sol** be sunny; **hacer una fiesta** have a party 3; **hacer una pregunta** ask a question 3; **hacer un viaje** take a trip 3
**Haití** (f) Haiti
**hambre** (f) hunger; **dar hambre** make hungry 9; **tener hambre** be hungry 3
**hamburguesa** (f) hamburger 9
**harina** (f) flour 9
**hasta** until 2; **desde . . . hasta** (starting) from . . . until; **Hasta luego.** See you later. 1; **Hasta mañana.** See you tomorrow. 1; **Hasta pronto.** See you soon.; **hasta que** until 11
**hay** there is, there are / is there, are there 1
**hecho** (m) fact
**helado (de vainilla)** (m) (vanilla) ice cream 9
**hemisferio** (m) hemisphere
**herencia** (f) heritage
**hermana** (f) sister 3
**hermanastro/a** (m/f) stepbrother / sister
**hermano** (m) brother 3
**hermanos** (mpl) siblings 3
**herramienta** (f) tool
**híbrido/a** hybrid
**hidratación** (f) hydration
**hidrógeno** (m) hydrogen
**hierba** (f) herb
**hija** (f) daughter 3

**hijo** (m) son 3
**hijos** (mpl) children 3
**hinchado/a** swollen 10
**hispano/a** (m/f) Hispanic
**historia** (f) history; story
**histórico/a** historical
**hogar** (m) household
**hoja de cálculo** (f) spreadsheet 11
**Hola.** Hi. 1
**hombre** (m) man; **hombre de negocios** (m) businessman / woman 8
**homeopatía** (f) homeopathy
**homogeneización** (f) homogenization
**honesto/a** honest
**hora** (f) hour, time; 2; **¿A qué hora?** At what time? 2; **horas de oficina** office hours
**horario** (m) schedule 2
**hormona** (f) hormone
**horóscopo** (m) horoscope
**hospedar** lodge
**hospicio** (m) hospice
**hospitalidad** (f) hospitality
**hostal** (m) hostel
**hotel** (m) hotel 7
**hoy** today 1, 2
**hoy día** nowadays
**hueso** (m) bone 10
**huésped** (m/f) guest 7
**huevo** (m) egg 9
**humanidades** (fpl) humanities
**humanitario/a** humanitarian
**humano** (m) human being
**humor** (m) mood; **estar de buen / mal humor** be in a good / bad mood 11
**humorístico/a** humorous
**huracán** (m) hurricane

## I

**icono** (m) icon 6
**ida** (f) outward flight 7
**idea** (f) idea 2, 8
**idéntico/a** identical
**identidad** (f) identity
**identificable** identifiable
**identificación** (f) identification 7
**identificar** identify
**idioma** (m) language 11
**idiomático/a** idiomatic
**iglesia** (f) church 2
**igual** equal
**igualdad** (f) equality
**Igualmente.** Likewise. 1
**ilegal** illegal
**ilógico/a** illogical
**ilustración** (f) illustration 4

**imagen** *(f)* image
**imaginar** imagine
**imaginario/a** imaginary
**imbécil** *(m/f)* idiot
**(im)paciente** (im)patient 1
**impacto** *(m)* impact
**impecable** impeccable
**imperfecto** *(m)* imperfect tense
**impermeable** *(m)* raincoat 5
**implicar** imply
**imponer** impose
**importancia** *(f)* importance
**importante** important
**importar** be important, matter 9
**imposible** impossible 10
**impresión** *(f)* impression
**impresionante** impressive
**impresora** *(f)* printer 4, 11
**imprimir** print 11
**impuestos** *(mpl)* taxes 11
**impulsar** drive, propel
**impulso** *(m)* impulse
**incendio** *(m)* fire
**incidente** *(m)* incident
**incluido/a** included 7
**incluir** include
**incluso** even; including
**incorporar** incorporate
**incorrecto/a** incorrect
**increíble** incredible
**incrementar** increase
**indefenso/a** defenseless
**independencia** *(f)* independence
**independiente** independent
**independizarse** become independent
**indicación** *(f)* indication
**indicador** *(m)* indicator
**indicar** indicate
**indicativo/a** indicative
**índice** *(m)* index
**indiferente** indifferent
**indígeno/a** indigenous
**indignación** *(f)* indignation 12
**individuo** *(m)* individual
**indocumentado/a** undocumented
**industria** *(f)* industry
**industrializar** industrialize
**infancia** *(f)* childhood
**infantil** children's
**infectado/a** infected 10
**infectar** infect
**infidelidad** *(f)* infidelity
**infiel** *(m/f)* unfaithful person, infidel
**infinitivo** *(m)* infinitive
**inflación** *(f)* inflation
**influencia** *(f)* influence
**influir (en)** influence 10

**información** *(f)* information 11
**informar(se)** report, inform; *refl* inform oneself
**informática** *(f)* computer science; computing 11; information technology 6
**informativo/a** informative
**informe** *(m)* report
**ingeniería** *(f)* engineering
**ingeniero/a** *(m/f)* engineer 8
**inglés** *(m)* English
**ingrediente** *(m)* ingredient
**inhalación** *(f)* inhalation
**inhumano/a** inhumane
**inicial** initial
**iniciar** initiate; start
**iniciativa** *(f)* initiative
**inicio** *(m)* start
**injusticia** *(f)* injustice
**inmediatamente** immediately
**inmersión** *(f)* immersion
**inmigración** *(f)* immigration 12
**inmigrante** *(m/f)* immigrant 8
**inmigrar** immigrate
**inmunológico/a** immunological
**innecesario/a** unnecessary
**inocente** innocent
**inquieto/a** worried
**insertar** insert 6
**insignificante** insignificant
**insistir (en)** insist (on) 10
**insomnio** *(m)* insomnia 10
**inspirar** inspire
**instalar** install
**instantáneamente** instantaneously
**instantáneo/a** instantaneous
**institución** *(f)* institution
**instituto** *(m)* high school
**instrucción** *(f)* instruction
**instrumento** *(m)* instrument
**insuficiente** insufficient
**insultar** insult
**integral** whole-grain 9
**intelectual** *(m)* intellectual 1
**inteligente** intelligent 1
**intención** *(f)* intention
**intenso/a** intense
**interacción** *(f)* interaction
**interactivo/a** interactive
**interactuar** interact
**intercambiar** exchange
**interés** *(m)* interest
**interesado/a** interested (in)
**interesante** interesting 1
**interesar** interest 9
**internacional** international
**interrogativo/a** interrogative

**interrogatorio** *(m)* interrogation
**interrupción** *(f)* interruption
**intervalo** *(m)* interval
**íntimo/a** intimate
**intriga** *(f)* intrigue
**introducir** introduce
**introducir datos** input data 11
**inundación** *(f)* flood 12
**inusual** unusual
**invasión** *(f)* invasion 12
**investigación** *(f)* investigation, research
**investigar** investigate
**invierno** *(m)* winter 5
**invitado/a** *(m/f)* guest 5
**invitar** invite 8
**inyección** *(f)* injection 10; shot
**ir** go 2; **ir a** + *infinitive* be going to + *verb* 2; **ir de compras** go shopping 2; **ir de excursión** go on an outing, go on a hike 7; **ir de vacaciones** go on vacation 7
**irresponsable** irresponsible 1
**irritabilidad** *(f)* irritability 10
**irritar** irritate
**irse** leave, go away 5
**isla** *(f)* island
**italiano/a** Italian
**itinerante** traveling
**itinerario** *(m)* itinerary 7
**izquierda** *(f)* left; **a la izquierda de** to the left of 2

**J**

**jamón** *(m)* ham 9
**japonés** *(m)* Japanese
**jaqueca** *(f)* migraine
**jardín** *(m)* garden, yard 4
**jeans** *(mpl)* jeans 5
**jefe/a** *(m/f)* boss 11
**joven** young 3
**joven** *(m/f)* youth
**jubilación** *(f)* retirement 8; **pensión de jubilación** *(f)* retirement pension 11
**jubilarse** retire 8
**judías verdes** *(fpl)* green beans
**jueves** Thursday 2
**juez** *(m/f)* justice, judge
**jugar (ue)** play 4
**jugo** *(m)* juice; **jugo de naranja** *(m)* orange juice 9
**julio** July 5
**junio** June 5
**junto a** next to 7
**juntos/as** together 2
**justicia** *(f)* justice 12
**justo/a** right, correct

## K

**kilo** *(m)* kilogram 9

## L

**la** the, it
**laboral** pertaining to work
**laboratorio** *(m)* laboratory; **laboratorio de biología** *(m)* biology laboratory; **laboratorio de lenguas** *(m)* language laboratory 1
**lado** *(m)* side; **al lado de** next to 2; **por todos lados** everywhere 4
**lago** *(m)* lake 2
**lamentar** lament
**lámpara** *(f)* lamp 4
**lápiz** *(m)* pencil 1
**largo/a** long 3
**lasaña** *(f)* lasagna
**lastimar(se)** hurt (oneself) 10
**lateralmente** sideways
**latino/a** *(m/f)* Latino
**Latinoamérica** Latin America
**lavabo** washbasin
**lavadero** laundry room
**lavadora** washing machine
**lavandería** *(f)* laundry, laundromat 4
**lavaplatos** dishwasher
**lavar** wash 4; **lavarse el pelo / la cara** wash one's hair / one's face 5; **lavarse los dientes** brush one's teeth 5
**le** (to, for) you *(sing. / form.)*, him, her 6; **Le gusta(n) . . .** You like . . . ; He / She likes . . . 1; **Le gustaría . . .** He / She / You would like . . .
**lección** *(f)* lesson
**leche** *(f)* milk 9
**lechuga** *(f)* lettuce 9
**lector/a** *(m/f)* reader
**lectura** *(f)* reading
**leer** read 3
**legislación** *(f)* legislation
**legumbres** *(fpl)* legumes 9
**lejos (de)** far (from) 2
**lengua** *(f)* language
**lenguaje** *(m)* language
**lentamente** slowly
**letra** *(f)* letter
**levantar** lift, raise; **levantar pesas** lift weights 2; **levantarle el ánimo** lift someone's spirits 10; **levantarse** get up 5
**ley** *(f)* law 12
**leyenda** *(f)* legend
**liberal** liberal 3

**liberar** free
**libertad** *(f)* liberty, freedom
**libre** free
**librería** *(f)* bookstore 2
**libro** *(m)* book 1; **libro de texto** *(m)* textbook 3
**licencia** *(f)* license
**licenciatura** *(m)* degree
**liceo** *(m)* high school
**líder** *(m/f)* leader 6
**liga** *(f)* league
**ligero/a** light 9
**limitar** limit
**limón** *(m)* lemon 9
**limonada** *(f)* lemonade 9
**limpiar** clean 2
**limpio/a** clean 4
**línea** *(f)* line 11; **en línea** online
**líquido** *(m)* liquid
**lista** *(f)* list
**listo/a** ready 4
**literatura** *(f)* literature
**litro** *(m)* liter
**llamada** *(f)* call 7
**llamado/a** so-called
**llamar(se)** call; *refl* be named, called 3; **¿Cómo se llama usted?** What is your name? *(form.)* 1; **¿Cómo te llamas?** What is your name? *(fam.)* 1; **Me llamo . . .** My name is . . . 1
**llave** *(f)* key 7
**llegada** *(f)* arrival 7
**llegar** arrive 2
**lleno/a** full 4
**llevar(se)** take, carry, wear 5; *refl* take away 5; **llevarse bien (con)** get along well (with) 5
**llorar** cry 8
**llover** rain 5; **Llueve.** It rains. It's raining. 5
**lluvia** *(f)* rain
**lo** it; **lo antes posible** as soon as possible 11; **lo que** what, that which 8; **Lo siento.** I'm sorry. 4
**localizar** locate
**loco/a** crazy
**lógica** *(f)* logic
**lógico/a** logical
**lograr** achieve
**los** the 1; you, them; **los (lunes . . . )** on (Mondays) 1
**luchar** fight
**luego** next, then, later; **Hasta luego.** See you later. 1
**lugar** *(m)* place 4, 7
**lunes** Monday 2
**luz** *(f)* electricity, light 4

## M

**madrastra** *(f)* stepmother
**madre** *(f)* mother 3
**maestría** *(f)* master's degree
**maestro/a** *(m/f)* teacher 8
**magnífico/a** magnificent
**maíz** *(m)* corn 9
**mal** bad(ly) 1
**maleta** *(f)* suitcase 7; **hacer la maleta** pack one's suitcase 7
**malo/a** bad 1
**mamá** *(f)* mama
**mandato** *(m)* command
**mandón / mandona** bossy 3
**manejar** drive 10; handle, manage
**manera** *(f)* way, manner
**manga** *(f)* sleeve
**mango** *(m)* mango 9
**manicura** *(f)* manicure
**mano** *(f)* hand 10
**mantenamiento** *(m)* maintenance
**mantener(se)** maintain 11; *refl* keep (oneself) 10
**mantequilla** *(f)* butter 9
**manzana** *(f)* apple 9
**mañana** *(f)* morning 2; tomorrow; **de la mañana** in the morning 2; **Hasta mañana.** See you tomorrow. 1; **por la mañana** in the morning 2
**mapa** *(m)* map
**maquillarse** put on make-up 5
**mar** *(m)* sea 7
**maravilloso/a** marvelous
**marca** *(f)* brand
**marcar un gol** score a goal 8
**mareado/a** dizzy, queasy 10
**margen** *(m)* margin
**mariscos** *(mpl)* seafood; shellfish 9
**marrón (color café)** brown 3
**martes** Tuesday 2
**marxista** Marxist
**marzo** March 5
**más** more, plus 1; **más . . . que** more . . . than 4; **más de + *number*** more than + *number* 7; **más tarde** later; **más vale que . . .** one had better . . . 10
**masa** *(f)* mass
**masaje** *(m)* massage
**mascota** *(f)* pet 3
**masivo/a** massive
**masticar** chew
**matemática** *(f)* mathematics
**materia** *(f)* material
**material de oficina** *(m)* office supplies 11
**materialista** materialistic
**materno/a** maternal

**matrimonio** (m) matrimony, marriage
**máximo/a** maximum
**mayo** May 5
**mayor** older, oldest 3
**mayoría** (f) majority
**mayormente** mostly
**me** me, myself; (to, for) me 6; **Me gusta(n)** . . . I like; **Me gustaría(n)** . . . I would like . . . 4; **No me gusta(n)** . . . I don't like . . . 1
**media hermana** (f) half sister
**medianoche** (f) midnight 2
**mediante** by means of
**medicamiento** (m) medicine, medication 7, 10
**medicina** (f) medicine; **medicina preventiva** (f) preventive medicine 10
**médico/a** medical
**médico/a** (m/f) doctor, physician 8, 10
**medida** (f) measure
**medio/a** half
**medio ambiente** (m) environment 12
**medio hermano** (m) half brother
**medio oeste** (m) the midwest
**mediodía** noon 2
**medios de comunicación** (mpl) means of communication 3
**mediterráneo/a** Mediterranean
**medusa** (f) jellyfish
**megáfono** (m) megaphone
**mejor** better, best 3; **mejor amigo/a** (m/f) best friend 1
**melodramático/a** melodramatic
**melón** (m) melon 9
**memoria** (f) memory
**memorizar** memorize
**mencionar** mention
**menor** younger, youngest 3
**menor** (m/f) minor
**menos** minus, less, except 1; till 2; **menos . . . que** less . . . than 4
**mensaje** (m) message 7
**mensajería instantánea** (f) instant messaging
**mensual** monthly
**mentalidad** (f) mentality
**mente** (f) mind
**menú** (m) daily specials; menu
**mercado** (m) market; **mercado de trabajo** (m) job market
**mes** (m) month 2; **al mes** per month 2
**mesa** (f) table 1
**mesero/a** (m/f) server 9
**meticuloso/a** meticulous
**metódico/a** methodical
**método** (m) method
**métrico/a** metric
**metropolitano/a** metropolitan

**mexicano/a** Mexican 2
**México** Mexico
**mezquita** (f) mosque 2
**mí** me 2
**micrófono** (m) microphone
**microondas** (m) microwave oven 4
**miedo** (m) fear; **dar miedo** scare, frighten; **tener miedo (de)** be afraid of, fear 3; **tener miedo de que** be afraid that 11
**miel** (f) honey
**miembro** (m) member
**mientras** as 8; while, as long as 8, 11; **mientras tanto** meanwhile
**miércoles** Wednesday 2
**migraña** (f) migraine
**migratorio/a** migratory
**mil** (m) thousand
**militar** (m/f) soldier
**millonario/a** (m/f) millionaire
**millón** (m) million
**mínimo/a** minimum 11
**ministerio** (m) ministry
**minoría** (f) minority
**minuto** (m) minute
**mío/a** mine 9
**mirar** look at, watch 2
**mi(s)** my 1, 3
**misión** (f) mission
**mismo/a** same 1
**mitad** (f) half
**mixto/a** mixed
**mochila** (f) bookbag, backpack 1
**moda** (f) fashion; **estar de moda** be in fashion 5
**modalidad** (f) modality
**modelo** (m) model
**moderar** moderate
**modernidad** (f) modernity
**moderno/a** modern 1
**modificación** (f) modification
**molestar** bother 9, 11
**molestia** (f) discomfort
**molesto/a** upset, bothered 2, 4
**momentáneo/a** momentary
**momento** (m) moment
**moneda** (f) coin, money 11
**monitor** (m) monitor 11
**monolingüe** monolingual
**montaña** (f) mountain 2
**montar** mount
**monumento** (m) monument
**morado/a** purple 4
**moreno/a** dark-complexioned 3
**morir (ue, u)** die 8
**mortalidad** (f) mortality
**motivación** (f) motivation
**motivo** (m) reason 11
**moto** (f) motorcycle 8
**motociclista** (m/f) biker 8

**motor de búsqueda** (m) search engine
**mover** mover
**móvil** mobile
**movimiento** (m) movement
**muchacha** (f) girl 2
**muchacho** (m) boy, guy 2
**mucho/a/os/as** much, many, a lot of 1; **Mucho gusto.** Pleased to meet you. 1
**mudarse** move (residence), relocate 8
**muebles** (mpl) furniture 4
**muerte** (f) death 8
**muerto/a** dead 4
**mujer** (f) woman; **mujer de negocios** (f) businesswoman; **mujer policía** (m/f) policewoman 8
**muletas** (fpl) crutches 10
**multiplicar** multiply
**multitarea** (f) multitasking
**mundial** worldwide 6
**mundo** (m) world
**músculo** (m) muscle
**musculoso/a** muscular
**museo** (m) museum 2
**música** (f) music 2
**músico** (m/f) musician 8
**musulmán** Muslim
**mutarse** mutate
**muy** very; **muy bien** very well 1

### N

**nacer** be born 8
**naciente** nascent, new
**nacimiento** (m) birth, Nativity scene 8; **fecha de nacimiento** birthday
**nación** (f) nation
**nacional** national
**nacionalidad** (f) nationality
**Naciones Unidas** United Nations 12
**nada** nothing, (not) anything 3, 4; **nada en especial** nothing in particular, nothing special 3
**nadar** swim 2
**nadie** no one; nobody, (not) anyone 4
**naranja** (f) orange 9
**narcotraficante** (m/f) drug trafficker
**narcotráfico** (m) drug trafficking
**nariz** (f) nose 10
**narración** (f) narration 8
**natal** native
**nativo/a** native
**naturaleza** (f) nature 7
**navegar** navigate
**Navidad** (f) Christmas
**necesario/a** necessary
**necesidad** (f) necessity 7
**necesitar** need 2, 10
**negativo/a** negative

negligencia *(f)* negligence
negociación *(f)* negotiation
negocio *(m)* business
negro/a black 3, 4
nervioso/a nervous 2, 4
nevar snow 5; **Nieva.** It snows. It's
   snowing. 5
nevera *(f)* refrigerator 4
ni nor 2; **ni . . . ni . . .** neither . . . nor 4; **ni
   un/a solo/a** not a single 8
nicaragüense Nicaraguan
nicotina *(f)* nicotine
nieta *(f)* granddaughter 3
nieto *(m)* grandson 3
nietos *(mpl)* grandchildren 3
ninguno / ninguna (ningún) no, none,
   not any 4
niñez *(f)* childhood 8
niño/a *(m/f)* boy / girl; child
nivel *(m)* level
no fumador/a *(m/f)* non-smoker
noche *(f)* evening, night 2; **de la noche** in
   the evening/night 2; **por la noche** in
   the evening/night 2
nocturno/a nocturnal
no-hispano/a non-Hispanic
nombrar name
nombre *(m)* name 11
normal normal 3
normalmente normally
noroeste *(m)* northeast
norte *(m)* north; **al norte de** north of 2
norteamericano/a *(m/f)* (North)
   American
nos us; (to, for) us; ourselves, each other,
   one another 6
nosotros/as we
nota *(f)* note
notablemente notably
notar note
noticias *(fpl)* news
noticiero *(m)* news provider 12
novato/a *(m/f)* beginner
novela *(f)* novel
noveno/a ninth
noviembre November 5
novio/a *(m/f)* boyfriend/girlfriend;
   fiancé(e) 1
nublado/a cloudy 5
nuestro/a(s) our 3; ours 9
Nueva Jersey New Jersey
Nueva York New York
nuevo/a new 1
Nuevo México New Mexico
número *(m)* number; **número de
   seguridad social** *(m)* social security
   number; **número de teléfono** *(m)*
   telephone number
numeroso/a numerous

nunca never 2
nutrición *(f)* nutrition
nutricional nutritional

### O

o or 4
obesidad *(f)* obesity
objetivo *(m)* objective
objetivo/a objective
objeto *(m)* object
obligación *(f)* obligation
obligar obligate
obligatorio/a obligatory
obra *(f)* work
obrero/a *(m/f)* worker; **obrero/a de
   fábrica** *(m/f)*, factory worker 8;
   **obrero/a de la construcción** *(m/f)*,
   construction worker 8
observar observe
obstáculo *(m)* obstacle
obstetra *(m/f)* obstetrician 10
obtener obtain 11
ocasión *(f)* occasion
ocio *(m)* leisure
octavo/a eighth
octubre October 5
ocupado/a busy 1
ocurrir occur
oeste *(m)* west; **al oeste de** west of 2
ofensivo/a offensive
oferta *(f)* offer; **oferta de empleo** *(f)* job
   offer 11
oficina *(f)* office 2, 11; **en la oficina** at the
   office 2; **horas de oficina** office hours;
   **material de oficina** *(m)* office supplies
   11; **oficina de correos** *(f)* post office 7
ofrecer offer 9
oído *(m)* inner ear 10
oír hear 3
Ojalá que . . . Let's hope that . . . 10
ojo watch out
ojo *(m)* eye 3
oliva *(f)* olive
onza *(f)* ounce
opción *(f)* option
operación *(f)* operation 10
opinar think, have an opinion
opinión *(f)* opinion
oportunidad *(f)* opportunity 11
oposición *(f)* opposition
optimista optimistic 1
oración *(f)* sentence 1
orden *(m)* order
ordenado/a neat, straightened up 4
ordenador *(m)* computer
ordenar order
ordinario/a ordinary

orégano *(m)* oregano
oreja *(f)* ear 10
organismo *(m)* body
organización *(f)* organization
organizar organize 11
orgullo *(m)* pride
orgulloso/a proud 8
orientación orientation
oriente *(m)* orient
origen *(m)* origin
originalmente originally
orquesta *(f)* orchestra; **orquesta sinfónica**
   *(f)* symphonic orchestra
ortografía *(f)* spelling
oscuro/a dark
ósmosis *(m)* osmosis
otoño *(m)* autumn, fall 5
otro/a other, another 1
oxígeno *(m)* oxygen
ozono *(m)* ozone

### P

paciencia *(f)* patience
paciente patient 1
paciente *(m/f)* patient 10
padrastro *(m)* stepfather
padre *(m)* father 3
padres *(mpl)* parents 3
pagar pay 4
página *(f)* page; **página web** *(f)* web page
pago *(m)* pay 11
país *(m)* country
país extranjero *(m)* foreign country 7
palabra *(f)* word 1
palacio *(m)* palace
pan *(m)* bread 9
pandilla *(f)* gang
pánico *(m)* panic
pantalla *(f)* screen 11
pantalones *(mpl)* pants 5; **pantalones
   cortos** *(mpl)* shorts 5
papa *(f)* potato; **papa al horno / frita** *(f)*
   baked / fried potato 9; **papas fritas**
   *(fpl)* French fries
papel *(m)* (piece of) paper 1; role
papelera *(f)* waste basket
papitas *(fpl)* potato chips 9
paquete *(m)* package 7; packet
para for 1; by, in order to, to; in order to
   (+ *infinitive*) 8
parada de autobús *(f)* bus stop 4
paralización *(f)* paralysis
paramédico/a *(m/f)* paramedic 8
parcial partial 11
parecido/a similar
pared *(f)* wall 4
pareja *(f)* couple; pair

**paréntesis** *(m)* parenthesis(es)
**parque** *(m)* park
**párquing** parking
**párrafo** *(m)* paragraph
**parrilla** *(f)* grill; **a la parrilla** grilled
**parte** *(m)* part
**participación** *(f)* participation
**participante** *(m/f)* participant
**participar** participate 6
**participio** *(m)* participle
**partido** *(m)* game 2
**partisano/a** partisan 12
**pasado/a** past 7
**pasaje** *(m)* plane ticket 7
**pasajero/a** *(m/f)* passenger 7
**pasaporte** *(m)* passport 7
**pasar** happen 8; pass, spend (time) 2
**pasatiempo** *(m)* pastime 2
**pasear** walk, stroll
**pasillo** *(m)* aisle, hall 7
**pasión** *(f)* passion
**paso** *(m)* step
**pastel (de chocolate)** *(m)* (chocolate) cake 9
**pastilla** *(f)* tablet, pill 10
**patata** *(f)* potato
**paterno/a** paternal
**pausa** *(f)* pause
**peatonal** pedestrian
**pecho** *(m)* chest 10
**pedir (i, i)** ask for, order 4; order; request 10
**pelea** *(f)* fight
**pelearse** fight 5
**película** *(f)* film, movie 2
**peligroso/a** dangerous
**pelirrojo/a** red-haired 3
**pelo** *(m)* hair 3
**peluquería** *(f)* barber shop, hair salon 7
**penicilina** *(f)* penicillin
**pensamiento** thought
**pensar (ie)** think, intend 4; **pensar (en)** think (about) 4
**pensativo/a** pensive 6
**pensión de jubilación** *(f)* retirement pension 11
**peor** worse 4
**pequeño/a** little, small 1
**percepción** *(f)* perception
**perder (ie)** lose, miss 4
**pérdida** *(f)* loss
**perdido/a** lost
**perezoso/a** lazy 1
**perfeccionar** perfect
**perfeccionista** perfectionist
**perfecto/a** perfect 2
**perfil** *(m)* profile
**periódico** *(m)* newspaper 3; **periódico internacional** *(m)* international

newspaper 7; **quiosco de periódicos** *(m)* newsstand 7
**periodista** *(m/f)* journalist 12
**permanecer** remain
**permanente** permanent
**permisivo/a** permissive
**permiso** *(m)* permission 8
**permitir** permit, allow 7; **¿Me permite . . . ?** May I see . . . ? 7
**pero** but 1
**perro/a** *(m/f)* dog 3
**persecución** *(f)* persecution
**persona** *(f)* person 4
**personaje** *(m)* character
**personalidad** *(f)* personality
**perspectiva** *(f)* perspective
**pertenecer** belong; pertain
**Perú** Peru
**pescado** *(m)* fish 9
**pescar** fish 7
**pesimista** pessimistic 1
**peso** *(m)* peso 9
**petróleo** *(m)* petroleum
**pie** *(m)* foot 10; **pie de página** *(m)* footer
**piel** *(f)* skin 10
**pierna** *(f)* leg 10
**pijama** *(m)* pajamas 5
**pimienta** *(f)* pepper 9
**pimiento verde** *(m)* green pepper 9
**pintar** paint 11
**pintor/a** *(m/f)* painter 8
**pintoresco/a** picturesque
**pintura** *(f)* painting 4
**piña** *(f)* pineapple 9
**pirámide** *(f)* pyramid
**piratería** *(f)* piracy 6
**piscina** *(f)* pool; swimming pool 2
**piso** *(m)* floor
**pizarra** *(f)* blackboard 1; chalkboard
**placa madre** *(f)* motherboard 6
**planear** plan
**planeta** *(f)* planet
**planificar** plan
**plano** *(m)* map 7
**planta** *(f)* plant 1
**planta baja** *(f)* ground floor 7
**plástico/a** plastic
**plátano** *(m)* banana 9
**plato** *(m)* plate, dish 9; **plato hondo** *(m)* soup dish 9; **plato (llano)** *(m)* plate 9; **plato principal** *(m)* main dish, entrée 9; **plato regional** *(m)* regional dish 7
**playa** *(f)* beach 2
**población** *(f)* population
**pobreza** *(f)* poverty
**poco** *(m)* little, bit
**poco/a/os/as** little, few 1; **un poco cansado/a** a little tired 1
**poder** *(m)* power

**poder (ue)** be able to, can 4
**poderoso/a** powerful
**poema** *(m)* poem
**policía / mujer policía** *(m/f)* police officer 8
**política** *(f)* politics
**político/a** political
**político/a** *(m/f)* politician
**pollo (asado)** *(m)* (roasted) chicken 9
**poner** put, place, set 3; **poner la radio** turn on the radio 3; **ponerle una inyección a alguien** give someone a shot 10; **ponerse (la ropa)** put on (clothing)
**popular** popular 7
**por** for, on account of, because of, by, by way of, via, during; **por acá** over / through here 5; **por ciento** percent; **por ejemplo** for example; **por encima** above; **por eso** so, that's why, therefore, for that reason 8; **por favor** please 1; **por la mañana** in the morning 2; **por la noche** in the evening / night 2; **por la tarde** in the afternoon 2; **por parte de mi madre (padre)** on my mother's (father's) side 3; **por separado** separately; **por teléfono** on the telephone 11; **por todos lados** everywhere 4
**¿por qué?** why 2
**porcentaje** *(m)* percentage
**porque** because 2, 8
**portarse** behave 8
**poseer** possess
**posesión** *(f)* possession
**posesivo/a** possessive
**posibilidad** *(f)* possibility
**posible** possible 10
**posición** *(f)* position
**positivo/a** positive
**posponer** postpone
**postal** *(f)* postcard
**postre** *(m)* dessert 9
**potencial** potential
**potenciar** make possible
**práctica** *(f)* practice
**prácticamente** practically
**practicar** practice
**práctico/a** practical 4, 11
**precaución** *(f)* precaution
**precio** *(m)* price 5
**precioso/a** precious; lovely, beautiful
**predador** *(m)* predator
**predeterminado/a** predetermined
**predicción** *(f)* prediction
**predominar** predominate
**preferencia** *(f)* preference
**preferible** preferable 10
**preferido/a** favorite 9; preferred
**preferir (ie, i)** prefer 2, 4, 10

**pregunta** *(f)* question 3; **hacer una pregunta** ask a question 3
**preguntar** ask 9
**prematuramente** prematurely
**prematuro/a** premature
**premio** *(m)* prize
**prender** turn on
**prensa** *(f)* press
**preocupado/a** worried 8
**preocupar(se)** preoccupy; *refl* worry 10
**prepa** *(f)* high school
**preparación** *(f)* preparation
**preparar** prepare 2
**preparativo** *(m)* preparation
**preparatoria** *(f)* high school 11
**presencia** *(f)* presence
**presentación** *(f)* introduction; presentation
**presentador/a** *(m/f)* news anchor 12; presenter 12
**presentar** introduce; present; **presentarse** show up; be present; introduce oneself 5
**presente indicativo** *(m)* present indicative
**presente progresivo** *(m)* present progressive
**preservación** *(f)* preservation
**presidente/a** *(m/f)* president 12
**presión** *(f)* pressure; **presión arterial** *(f)* blood pressure 10
**préstamo** *(m)* loan 11
**prestar** lend 9
**prestigio** *(m)* prestige
**presumido/a** stuck-up 3
**presupuestario/a** estimated
**pretendiente** *(m/f)* suitor
**pretérito** *(m)* preterit tense
**prevenir** prevent
**previamente** previously
**previo/a** previous
**primario/a** primary
**primavera** *(f)* spring 5
**primer(o)/a** first; **Es (el) primero de . . .** It's the first of . . . 5
**primo/a** *(m/f)* cousin 3
**principio** *(m)* beginning; **al principio** at the beginning 8
**prioridad** *(f)* priority
**prisa** *(f)* hurry; **tener prisa** be in a hurry 3
**privacidad** *(f)* privacy 4
**privado/a** private
**probabilidad** *(f)* probability
**probadores** *(mpl)* fitting rooms 5
**probar(se) (ue)** try 7; *refl* try on 5
**problema** *(m)* problem
**procesador de texto** *(m)* word processor 6, 11
**proceso** *(m)* process
**producción** *(f)* production

**producir** produce
**productividad** *(f)* productivity
**producto** *(m)* product
**productor/a** *(m/f)* producer
**profesión** *(f)* profession
**profesional** professional 8
**profesional** *(m/f)* professional
**profesor/a** *(m/f)* professor
**profundo/a** deep 10; profound
**programa** *(m)* program; **programa de diseño gráfico** *(m)* graphic design program 11; **programa informática** *(f)* software 6
**programación** *(f)* programming
**programador/a** *(m/f)* programmer 8, 11
**programar** program 11
**progreso** *(m)* progress
**prohibir** forbid 10; prohibit
**promedio** *(m)* average
**promedio/a** average
**prometador/a** promising
**prometer** promise
**prominente** prominent
**promoción** *(f)* promotion
**promocionar** promote
**promover** promote
**pronombre** *(m)* pronoun 12
**pronóstico del tiempo** *(m)* weather forecast 12
**pronto** soon
**pronunciar** pronounce
**propiedad** *(f)* property
**propio/a** own 4
**propósito** *(m)* goal; resolution
**propuesta** *(f)* proposal 12
**protección** *(f)* protection
**proteger** protect
**proteína** *(f)* protein 9
**protesta** *(f)* protest
**protocolo** *(m)* protocol
**proverbio** *(m)* proverb
**provocar** provoke, cause
**próximo/a** next 1
**proyecto** *(m)* project
**(p)sicología** *(f)* psychology
**psiquiatra** *(m/f)* psychiatrist 10
**psiquiatría** *(f)* psychiatry
**publicación** publication
**publicado/a** published 11
**públicamente** publicly
**publicar** publish
**publicidad** *(f)* advertisement 11; advertising 11; publicity
**publicitar** publicize
**público** *(m)* public
**público/a** public; **concientización pública** *(f)* public awareness
**pueblo** *(m)* people
**puerta** *(f)* door 1; gate 7

**puertorriqueño/a** Puerto Rican
**pues** so 1; well
**puesto** *(m)* position 11
**pulmones** *(mpl)* lungs 10
**pulmonía** *(f)* pneumonia
**punto** *(m)* point
**pupitre** *(m)* student desk 1
**puré** purée(d), mashed
**purificación** *(f)* purification

## Q

**¿qué?** what 2; **¿Qué clases tienes?** What classes do you have? 1; **¿Qué estudias?** What are you studying? 1; **¿Qué fecha es?** What is the date? 5; **¿Qué significa . . . en inglés?** What does . . . mean in English? 1; **¿Qué tal . . . ?** How is / are / was / were . . . ? 7; **¿Qué te pasa?** What's wrong with you? 10; **¿Qué tiempo hace?** What's the weather like? 5
**que** than; that 1
**quedarse** stay 5
**quehacer** *(m)* task; **quehacer doméstico** *(m)* chore 4
**quemar(se)** burn (oneself) 10
**querer(se) (ie)** love, want 2, 4, 10; *refl* love (each other) 5
**Querido/a . . .** Dear . . .
**queso** *(m)* cheese 9
**quién(es)** who, whom 2
**química** *(f)* chemistry
**químico/a** chemical
**quinceañera** *(f)* fifteenth birthday celebration
**quinto/a** fifth
**quiosco de periódicos** *(m)* newsstand 7
**quizás** perhaps, maybe 10

## R

**rábano** *(m)* radish 9
**radio** *(f)* radio 3
**radiografía** *(f)* X-ray 10
**raíz** *(f)* root
**ranchero/a** *(m/f)* rancher
**rápidamente** rapidly
**rapidez** *(f)* rapidity
**rápido/a** rapid
**raro/a** weird 3
**rato** *(m)* while
**ratón** *(m)* mouse 11
**ratos libres** free time
**razón** *(f)* reason 3; **tener razón** be right 3
**razonable** reasonable 5
**reacción** *(f)* reaction 11
**reaccionar** react; reaction

**realidad** (f) reality
**realista** down-to-earth 3; realistic
**realizarse** come true; realize oneself
**realmente** really
**recado** (m) message 11
**recámara** (f) bedroom
**recepción** (f) front desk 7
**recepcionista** (m/f) receptionist 7
**recesión** (f) recession
**receta** (f) prescription 10
**recetar** prescribe 10
**recibir** receive 3
**recibo de la luz** (m) light bill 4
**recién casados** (mpl) newlyweds
**reciente** recent
**recipiente** (m/f) recipient
**recíproco/a** reciprocal
**recoger** pick up, gather 7
**recomendación** (f) recommendation
**recomendar (ie)** recommend 7, 10
**recompensa** (f) compensation
**reconocer** recognize
**reconversión** (f) reconversion
**recordable** memorable
**recordar (ue)** remember 4
**recreo** (m) recess 8; recreation
**recuerdo** (m) memory 8; souvenir 7
**recurso** (m) resource; **recursos humanos** (mpl) human resources 11
**red** (f) network; web 6
**redacción** (f) writing, composition
**redactar** write
**reducción** (f) reduction
**reducir** reduce
**referencia** (f) reference 11
**referir** refer
**reflejar** reflect
**reflexión** (f) reflection
**reflexivo/a** reflexive
**reforma** (f) reform
**refresco** (m) soft drink 9
**refrigerador** (m) refrigerator
**refugio** (m) refuge
**regalar** give as a gift 9
**regalo** (m) gift, present 2
**reggaetón** (m) reggae
**régimen** (m) regime
**región** (f) region
**registrar** register
**regla** (f) rule
**regresar** return 2
**regulación** (f) regulation
**regular** as usual 1
**regularidad** (f) regularity
**regularmente** regularly
**relación** (f) relationship
**relacionar** relate
**relajado/a** easy-going 3
**relajarse** relax 5

**relativamente** relatively
**relatividad** (f) relativity
**relevante** relevant
**religioso/a** religious
**relleno/a** stuffed
**reloj** (m) clock, watch 1
**remedio** (m) remedy
**remedio casero** (m) home remedy
**rendir** yield, give
**renovable** renewable
**renovar** renovate
**renta** (f) rent
**rentar** rent
**reparación** (f) repair
**reparar** repair
**repasar** review
**repetir (i)** repeat 4
**repetitivamente** repetitively
**repetitivo/a** repetitive
**reportaje** (m) report
**reportero/a** (m/f) reporter 12
**represalia** (f) reprisal
**representante** (m/f) representative
**representar** represent
**reproducción** (f) reproduction
**reproductor de DVD** (m) DVD player 4
**República Dominicana** (f) Dominican Republic
**republicano/a** (m/f) Republican
**reputación** (f) reputation
**requerir (ie)** require
**reseña** (f) review
**reserva** (f) reservation
**reservado/a** reserved 3; shy
**reservar** reserve 7
**resfriado/a** chilled, with a cold 10
**resfriarse** catch a cold 10
**residencia** (f) dormitory 1; residence hall 1
**residente** (m/f) resident
**resistencia** (f) resistance
**resolución** (f) resolution
**resolver (ue)** resolve 11
**respaldo** (m) back
**respecto a** with respect to
**respetar** respect
**respeto** (m) respect
**respetuoso/a** respectful
**respirar** breathe 10
**respiratorio/a** respiratory
**responder** respond
**responsabilidad** (f) responsibility 4
**responsable** responsible 1
**responsable** (m/f) person in charge 11
**respuesta** (f) answer, response 1
**restaurante** (m) restaurant 2, 9
**resto** (m) remainder, rest
**restricción** (f) restriction
**resultado** (m) result
**resultar** result

**resumen** (m) summary
**retener** retain
**retirar** remove; retire 11; withdraw 11
**retiro** (m) withdrawal 11
**retraso** (m) delay
**retrato** (m) portrait
**reunir** meet
**revisar** review
**revisión dental** (f) dental check-up 10
**revista** (f) magazine 3
**revolución** (f) revolution
**revolucionario/a** (m/f) revolutionary
**rey** (m) king
**rezar** pray 2
**rico/a** rich 6
**ritmo** (m) rhythm
**robo** (m) robbery
**rodilla** (f) knee 10
**rojo/a** red 3
**rol** (m) role
**romántico/a** romantic
**romper(se) (el brazo)** break (one's arm) 10
**ropa** (f) clothes 2, 5; **ponerse (la ropa)** put on (clothing)
**rosa** pink
**rosado/a (rosa)** pink 4
**rubio/a** blond 3
**rueda** (f) wheel
**ruido** (m) noise 4
**ruidoso/a** noisy 4
**ruina** (f) ruin
**ruinas** (fpl) ruins 7
**rutina** (f) routine; **rutina diaria** (f) daily routine 5

## S

**sábado** Saturday 2
**saber** know, find out 7; **No sé.** I don't know. 1;
**sacar** take, take (out), get 7; **sacar una copia** make a copy 11; **sacar una foto** take a picture 5
**sal** (f) salt 9
**sala** (f) living room 4; room; **sala de chat** (f) chat room; **sala de espera** (f) waiting room; **sala de urgencia** (f) emergency room 10
**salario** (m) salary 11
**salida** (f) departure 7; outing
**salir** go out 2; leave 3; **salir en velero** go sailing 7
**salmón** (m) salmon
**salón** (m) hall, room; **salón de clase** (m) classroom 1
**salsa** (f) sauce
**salteado/a** sautéed
**salud** (f) health 9, 10

**saludable** healthy
**saludar** greet 8
**saludo** (*m*) greeting
**salutación** (*f*) salutation
**salvadoreño/a** Salvadoran
**salvar** save
**salvo/a** safe
**sandalias** (*f*) sandals 5
**sangre** (*f*) blood 10
**sanidad** (*f*) sanity
**sano/a** healthy 9
**santo/a** saintly 6
**santo/a** (*m/f*) saint
**satisfacción** (*f*) satisfaction
**satisfacer** satisfy
**sazón** (*m*) seasoning
**se** himself, herself, yourself, yourselves, themselves, each other, one another 5; to you, to him, to her, to you, to them 8; **¿Cómo se dice ... en inglés?** How do you say ... in English? 1; **¿Cómo se escribe?** How is that written? 1; **¿Cómo se llama usted?** What is your name? (*form.*) 1; **Se escribe ...** It's written ... 1; **Se llama(n) ...** His / Her name is ... (Their names are ...); **se parece a ...** He / She looks like ... 3; **se puede** one can ... 6
**sección** (*f*) section
**secretario/a** (*m/f*) secretary 8
**secreto** (*m*) secret
**secuencia** (*f*) sequence
**sed** (*f*) thirst; **dar sed** make thirsty 9; **tener sed** be thirsty 3
**seducir** seduce
**segmento** (*m*) segment
**seguir (i, i)** follow, continue 9
**según** according to
**segundo/a** second
**seguridad** (*f*) security 7; **número de seguridad social** (*m*) social security number
**seguro/a** safe 4; secure; **estar seguro/a** be sure 10
**seguro médico** (*m*) medical insurance 11
**seleccionar** select
**sello** (*m*) stamp 7
**semana** (*f*) week 2; **fin de semana** (*m*) weekend 2; **la semana pasada** (*f*) last week 7; **la semana que viene** (*f*) the coming week 2
**semanal** weekly
**semestre** (*m*) semester
**Senado** (*m*) Senate
**senador/a** (*m/f*) senator
**sencillo/a** single
**sensación** (*f*) sensation
**sensacional** sensational
**sentarse (ie)** sit down 5

**sentimiento** (*m*) feeling; sentiment
**sentir (ie, i)** feel 5; **Lo siento.** I'm sorry. 4; **sentir que** be sorry that 11
**señalar** signal
**señor** Mr., sir 1
**señora (Sra.)** Mrs., Mme. 1
**señorita (Srta.)** Miss 1
**separado/a** separate; **por separado** separately
**septiembre** September 5
**séptimo/a** seventh
**ser** be 1; **¡Así es!** that's right 9 **¿Cómo es ... ?** How is ... ?, What's ... like? 1; **¿Cuántos son en ... ?** How many are there in ... ?; **¿De dónde eres?** Where are you from? (*fam.*) 2; **¿De dónde es?** Where are you from? (*form.*) 2; **ser operado/a** be operated on, have an operation 10; **son** equals; **Son las dos (tres).** It's one (two) o'clock. 2; **Soy ...** I am, I'm ... 1; **Soy de ...** I'm from ... 1
**serenidad** (*f*) serenity
**serie policíaca** (*f*) police series
**serio/a** serious 1, 3
**servicio** (*m*) service
**servicio técnico** (*m*) technical service 11
**servilleta** (*f*) napkin 9
**servir (i, i)** help 5; serve 4; **¿En qué puedo servirle?** How may I help you? 5
**sesión** session
**sesionar** meet, be in session
**seudónimo** (*m*) pseudonym
**severo/a** severe
**sexismo** (*m*) sexism
**sexto/a** sixth
**sicología** (*f*) psychology
**siempre** always 2, 4
**siesta** (*f*) nap
**significado** (*m*) significance
**significar** mean; **¿Qué significa ... en inglés?** What does ... mean in English? 1
**siguiente** following 1
**silla** (*f*) chair 1, 4
**símbolo** (*m*) symbol
**similitud** (*f*) similarity
**simpático/a** nice 1; pleasant
**simulación** (*f*) simulation
**simultáneamente** simultaneously
**sin** without 2; **sin embargo** nevertheless; **sin hogar** homeless 12
**sinagoga** (*f*) synagogue 2
**síndrome** (*m*) syndrome
**sinónimo** (*m*) synonym
**sinónimo/a** synonymous
**síntoma** (*m*) symptom 10
**sistema** (*m*) system 11

**sistemáticamente** systematically
**sitio** (*m*) site; **sitio histórico / turístico** (*m*) historic / tourist site 7; **sitio web** (*m*) web site
**situación** (*f*) situation
**situar** situate, locate
**sobre** over, about, on 9; **sobre todo** above all 8
**sobrevivir** survive
**sobrina** (*f*) niece 3
**sobrino** (*f*) nephew 3
**socializar** socialize
**socialmente** socially
**sociedad** (*f*) society
**sociología** (*f*) sociology
**sofá** (*m*) sofa 4
**sofisticado/a** sophisticated
**sol** (*m*) sun; **gafas de sol** (*fpl*) sunglasses; **Hace sol.** It's sunny. 5
**soleado/a** sunny
**solicitar** request
**solicitud de empleo** (*f*) job application 11
**solidaridad** (*f*) solidarity 12
**sólo** only 1
**solo/a** alone 2, 4
**solsticio** (*m*) solstice
**soltero/a** single 3
**solución** (*f*) solution
**sombrero** (*m*) hat 5
**sonrisa** (*f*) smile 8
**soñar (ue) con** dream of / about 8
**sopa** (*f*) soup 9
**sorprender** surprise 11
**sorprendido/a** surprised 2, 4, 6
**sorpresa** (*f*) surprise
**sospechoso/a** (*m/f*) suspect
**subir a** get on / in, go up 7
**su(s)** your (*sing. / form.*), your (*pl.*), his, her, its, their 3
**súbito/a** sudden
**subjuntivo** (*m*) subjunctive
**subrayar** underline
**suburbano/a** suburban
**sucesivamente** succesively
**sucio/a** dirty 4
**sucursal** (*f*) branch office 11
**sudadera** (*f*) sweatshirt 5
**Sudamérica** South America
**sueldo** (*m*) wage, salary 11
**suelo** (*m*) ground, floor 4
**sueño** (*m*) dream 8; sleep; **tener sueño** be sleepy
**suerte** (*f*) luck; **tener suerte** be lucky 3
**suéter** (*m*) sweater 5
**suficiente** sufficient
**sufrir** suffer
**sugerencia** (*f*) suggestion
**sugerir (ie, i)** suggest 10
**superar** overtake

**superior** higher
**supermercado** (*m*) supermarket
**supersticioso/a** superstitious
**supervisor/a** (*m/f*) supervisor 11
**suplemento** (*m*) supplement
**sur** (*m*) south; **al sur de** south of 2; south
**suspenso** (*m*) suspense
**sustancia** (*f*) substance
**sustantivo** (*m*) noun 4
**sustituir** substitute
**suyo/a** his, hers, yours (*pl.*), yours (*form. / sing.*) theirs 9

## T

**tabaco** (*m*) tabacco
**tabaquismo** (*m*) smoking
**tabla** (*f*) table (graphic)
**tal** such; **¿Qué tal . . . ?** How is / are / was / were . . . ? 7; **tal vez** maybe, perhaps 10
**talento** (*m*) talent
**talla** (*f*) size 5
**también** also, too 1
**tampoco** neither 4
**tan** so; **tan . . . como** as . . . as 4; **tan pronto como** as soon as 11
**tanto** so much 10
**tanto/a/os/as . . . como** as much . . . as, as many . . . as 4
**tarde** late 2; **más tarde** later
**tarde** (*f*) afternoon 2; **de la tarde** in the afternoon 2; **por la tarde** in the afternoon 2
**tarea** (*f*) homework 1
**tarifa** (*f*) tariff
**tarjeta** (*f*) card; **tarjeta de débito** (*f*) debit card; **tarjeta de embarque** (*f*) boarding pass 7; **tarjeta telefónica** (*f*) phone card 7
**tasa** (*f*) rate; **tasa de interés** (*f*) interest rate 11
**tatuaje** (*m*) tatoo
**taxi** (*m*) taxi 7
**taxista** (*m/f*) taxi driver
**taza** (*f*) cup 9
**te** you, yourself (*fam.*) 1; **¿Te gusta** (+ *singular noun*)**?** Do you like . . . ? 1; **¿Te gustan** (+ *plural noun*)**?** Do you like . . . ? 1; **¿Te parece bien?** Does that seem okay to you? 2; **Te veo. . . .** You look . . . to me. 10
**té** tea; **té helado / caliente** (*m*) iced / hot tea 9
**teatro** (*m*) theater 2
**teclado** (*m*) keyboard 11
**técnica** (*f*) technique
**técnico/a** technical

**tecnología** (*f*) technology
**telefonía** telephony
**telefónico/a** telephonic
**teléfono** (*m*) telephone 2; **número de teléfono** (*m*) telephone number; **por teléfono** on the telephone 11; **teléfono público** (*m*) public telephone 7
**telenovela** (*f*) soap opera
**teletrabajar** telecommute
**teletrabajo** (*m*) telecommuting
**televidente** (*m/f*) television viewer
**televisión** (*f*) television
**televisión (tele)** (*f*) television (TV) 2
**televisor** (*m*) television; television set 1, 4
**tema** (*m*) theme
**temático/a** thematic
**temer (que)** fear (that) 11
**temperamental** moody 3
**temperatura** (*f*) temperature 10
**temporal** temporary
**temprano** early 2
**tendencia** (*f*) tendency
**tenedor** (*m*) fork 9
**tener** have 3; **(No) tengo . . .** I (don't) have . . . 1; **tener . . . años** be . . . years old 3; **tener calor** be hot 3; **tener cuidado** be careful 10; **tener curiosidad** be curious; **tener éxito** be successful; **tener frío** be cold 3; **tener ganas de** feel like; **tener hambre** be hungry 3; **tener miedo (de)** be afraid of, fear 3; **tener miedo de que** be afraid that 11; **tener prisa** be in a hurry 3; **tener que** have to, must; **tener razón** be right 3; **tener sed** be thirsty 3; **tener sueño** be sleepy; **tener suerte** be lucky 3; **Tengo . . .** I have . . . 1
**tenis** (*m*) tennis
**tenis** (*mpl*) sneakers 5; tennis shoes
**tenista** (*m/f*) tennis player
**teoría** (*f*) theory
**terapeuta** (*m/f*) therapist 10
**terapia** (*f*) therapy 10; **terapia de grupo** (*f*) group therapy 10
**tercero/a** third
**terco/a** stubborn 3
**terminación** (*f*) ending
**terminar** finish
**término** (*m*) term
**terraza** (*f*) terrace
**terreno** (*m*) land, terrain
**territorio** (*m*) territory
**terrorismo** (*m*) terrorism
**terrorista** (*m/f*) terrorist 12
**testigo/a** (*m/f*) witness
**testimonio** (*m*) testimony
**texto** (*m*) text
**ti** you 2
**tía** (*f*) aunt 3

**tiempo** (*m*) time; weather 5; **Hace buen / mal tiempo.** The weather's good / bad. 5; **pronóstico del tiempo** (*m*) weather forecast; **tiempo completo** (*m*) full-time 11; **tiempo libre** (*m*) free time 2; **tiempo parcial** (*m*) part-time 11; **tiempo verbal** (*m*) verb tense
**tienda** (*f*) store 2
**tierra** (*f*) land
**timbre postal** (*m*) stamp
**tímido/a** shy, timid 1
**tío** (*m*) uncle 3
**típico/a** typical
**tipo** (*m*) type
**titular** (*m*) headline
**título** (*m*) title
**tocar** play (music, musical instruments) 2
**todavía** still
**todavía no** not yet 11
**todo/a/os/as** all, every 1; **por todos lados** everywhere 4; **todo el día** all day 2; **todos** everyone 4; **todos los días** every day 2
**Tokio** Tokyo
**tolerancia** (*f*) tolerance
**tomar** drink, take 2; **tomar asiento** take a seat; **tomar el sol** sunbathe 2; **tomar una decisión** make a decision 10
**tomate** (*m*) tomato 9
**tono** (*m*) tone, beep 11
**tonto/a** foolish; stupid, silly 1
**tortilla (de maíz / de harina)** (*f*) corn / flour tortilla 9
**tos** (*f*) cough 10
**toser** cough 10
**totalitario/a** totalitarian
**totalmente** totally
**trabajador/a** hardworking 1
**trabajador/a social** (*m/f*) social worker 8
**trabajar** work 2
**trabajo** (*m*) job, work 2; **en el trabajo** at work 2
**tradición** (*f*) tradition
**tradicional** traditional
**tradicionalismo** (*m*) traditionalism
**traducción** (*f*) translation
**traducir** translate
**traer** bring 3
**tráfico** (*m*) traffic 4
**tragedia** (*f*) tragedy
**traje** (*m*) suit 5; **traje de baño** (*m*) swimsuit 5
**trámite** (*m*) transaction 11
**tranquilidad** (*f*) tranquility
**tranquilo/a** calm 3
**transformación** (*f*) transformation
**transformar** transform
**transición** (*f*) transition
**transmisión** (*f*) transmission

**transmitir** transmit
**transparente** transparent
**transporte** *(m)* transportation
**transporte público** *(m)* public transportation 4
**tratamiento** *(m)* treatment 10
**tratar (de)** treat, try (to) 8
**trato** *(m)* dealings
**travieso/a** mischievous 8
**tren** *(m)* train
**triángulo** *(m)* triangle
**tribunal** *(m)* jury
**trigo** *(m)* wheat
**trimestre** *(m)* trimester
**triste** sad 2, 4, 10; **estar triste de que** be sad that 11
**tristeza** *(f)* sadness 10
**trompeta** *(f)* trumpet
**tú** you *(sing. / fam.)*
**tu(s)** your *(sing. / fam.)* 1, 3
**tuna** university band
**tuno** university band member
**turbulencia** *(f)* turbulence
**turismo** *(m)* tourism
**turista** *(m/f)* tourist
**tuyo/a** yours *(sing. / fam.)* 9

**U**

**u** or (before words beginning with o)
**ubicación** *(f)* location 11
**último/a** last, latest 7
**un/a** a, an 1
**una vez** once 2
**unido/a** united
**uniforme** *(m)* uniform
**unión** *(f)* union
**universidad** *(f)* university 1
**universitario/a** university 8
**unos/as** some 1
**urbano/a** urban
**urgente** urgent 10
**usar** use 2
**usario/a** *(m/f)* user
**usted** you *(sing. / form.)*
**ustedes** you *(pl.)*
**útil** useful 1
**utilidad** *(f)* utility
**utilización** *(f)* use, utilization
**utilizar** use
**uvas** *(fpl)* grapes 9

**V**

**vacaciones** *(fpl)* vacation, holiday; **ir de vacaciones** go on vacation 7
**valor** *(m)* value
**valoración** *(f)* valuation
**valorar** value
**vapor** *(m)*: **al vapor** steamed
**variado/a** varied
**variedad** *(f)* variety
**varios/as** several 1
**varón** male
**vaso** *(m)* glass 9
**vecindario** *(m)* neighborhood 7
**vecino/a** *(m/f)* neighbor 4
**vegetariano/a** vegetarian
**vehículo** *(m)* vehicle
**velero** *(m)* sailboat 7
**velocidad** *(f)* velocity
**vendedor/a** *(m/f)* seller
**vender** sell 3
**venir** come 3
**venta** *(f)* sale
**ventaja** *(f)* advantage
**ventana** *(f)* window 1, 4
**ventanilla** *(f)* counter window 11; window (of a vehicle or box office) 7
**ver** see 2
**verano** *(m)* summer 5
**verbo** *(m)* verb
**verdad** true
**verdadero/a** true
**verde** green 3, 4
**verduras** *(fpl)* vegetables 9
**verificar** verify
**versátil** versatile
**versión** *(f)* version
**vestido** *(m)* dress 5
**vestigio** *(m)* vestige
**vestirse (i, i)** get dressed 5
**vez** *(f)*: **en vez de** instead of 9
**vía** via
**viajar** travel 7
**viaje** *(m)* trip 3; **hacer un viaje** take a trip 3
**viajero/a** *(m/f)* traveler
**viceversa** vice versa
**víctima** *(f)* victim
**victoria** *(f)* victory
**vida** *(f)* life 8; **vida nocturna** *(f)* night life
**videojuego** *(m)* videogame

**viejo/a** old 1, 4
**viento** *(m)* wind; **Hace viento.** It's windy. 5
**viernes** Friday 2
**vigilar** watch, be vigilant
**vinagre** *(m)* vinegar
**vino** *(m)* wine; **vino tinto / blanco** *(m)* red / white wine 9
**viñeta** *(f)* comic strip
**violencia** *(f)* violence
**virtuoso/a** *(m/f)* virtuouso
**visita** *(f)* visit
**visitante** *(m/f)* visitor
**visitar** visit 7
**vista** *(f)* view
**vitalidad** *(f)* vitality
**vitaminas** *(fpl)* vitamins 9
**vivienda** *(f)* housing, dwelling
**vivir** live 3
**vivo** live; **en vivo** live
**vocabulario** *(m)* vocabulary
**vocal** *(f)* vowel
**voluntariamente** voluntarily
**voluntario/a** voluntary
**voluntario/a** *(m/f)* volunteer
**volver (ue) (a)** return, . . . again 4
**vomitar** vomit, throw up 10
**vosotros/as** you *(pl. / fam.)*
**votante** *(m/f)* voter
**votar** vote
**voz** *(f)* voice
**vuelo** *(m)* flight 7
**vuelta** *(f)* returning flight 7
**vuestro/a(s)** your *(pl./ fam.)* 3

**Y**

**y** and 4
**ya** already 7
**ya no** no longer, not any more 10
**yo** I
**yogur** *(m)* yogurt

**Z**

**zanahoria** *(f)* carrot 9
**zapatillas de tenis** *(mpl)* tennis shoes
**zapatos** *(mpl)* shoes 5
**zona** *(f)* zone

# English-Spanish Glossary

The **English-Spanish Glossary** includes all active vocabulary presented in *Hoy día*, as well as other high frequency words. Numbers following entries indicate the chapter where words are introduced. All translations separated by commas before a number are considered active in that chapter. Gender of nouns in Spanish is indicated by *(m)* for masculine and *(f)* for feminine. Nouns referring to people that have both masculine and feminine forms are indicated by *(m/f)*, and those that are generally used in the plural are followed by *(pl)*.

## A

**a** un/a 1
**a lot of** mucho/a/os/as 1
**abandon** abandonar
**ability** habilidad *(f)*
**able: be able to** poder (ue) 4, 7
**about** acerca de 8; sobre 9
**above** por encima
**above all** sobre todo 8
**absent** ausente; **be absent** faltar (a) 8
**absolutely** absolutamente
**absurd** absurdo/a 10
**abuse** abuso *(m)*
**accede** acceder
**accelerate** acelerar
**accent** acento 3; **with an accent** con acento 1; **without an accent** sin acento 1
**accept** aceptar
**access** acceso *(m)* 11
**accessory** accesorio *(m)* 4
**accident** accidente *(m)* 10
**accompany** acompañar
**accomplice** cómplice *(m/f)*
**according to** según
**account** cuenta *(f)* 11
**accountant** contador/a *(m/f)* 8, 11
**accounting** contabilidad *(f)*
**accusation** acusación *(f)*
**accustom** acostumbrar
**accustomed** acostumbrado/a
**ache** doler (ue) 9; dolor *(m)* 10
**achieve** lograr
**across** a través de; **across from** enfrente de 2
**act** actuar
**action** acción *(f)*
**active** activo/a
**activist** activista *(m/f)*
**activity** actividad *(f)* 2
**actor** actor *(m)* 8
**actress** actriz *(f)* 8
**ad: classified ad** anuncio clasificado *(m)*
**adapt** adaptar
**adaptation** adaptación *(f)*
**addict** adicto/a *(m/f)*

**addiction** adicción *(f)*
**additional** adicional
**address** dirección *(f)* 4
**adjective** adjetivo *(m)*
**adjust to** ajustarse a
**administration** administración *(f)*
**administrator** administrador/a *(m/f)*
**admire** admirar
**admirer** admirador/a *(m/f)*
**admit** admitir
**adolescence** adolescencia *(f)*
**adopt** adoptar
**adult** adulto/a *(m/f)*
**advance** avance *(m)*
**advantage** ventaja *(f)*
**adventurous** aventurero/a
**adverb** adverbio *(m)*
**advertise** anunciar
**advertisement** anuncio *(m)*; publicidad *(f)* 11
**advertiser** anunciante *(m/f)*
**advertising** publicidad *(f)* 11
**advice** consejo *(m)*
**advise** aconsejar 10
**affect** afectar
**affectionate** cariñoso/a 3
**affirmation** afirmación *(f)*
**afraid: be afraid (of)** tener miedo (de) 3; **be afraid that** tener miedo de que 11
**African** africano/a
**after** después 2; después (de) que 11
**afternoon** tarde *(f)* 2
**afterwards** después
**again** otra vez
**against** contra
**age** edad *(f)* 8
**agency** agencia *(f)*
**agent** agente *(m/f)*
**aggressive** agresivo/a
**aging** envejecimiento *(m)*
**agitation** agitación *(f)* 12
**ago** hace . . . 7
**agree** estar de acuerdo
**agreeable** agradable
**agricultural** agrícolo/a
**agriculture** agricultura *(f)*

**ahead of** delante de 2
**air conditioning** aire acondicionado *(m)*
**airline** aerolínea *(f)* 7
**airplane** avión *(m)* 7
**airport** aeropuerto *(m)* 7
**aisle** pasillo *(m)* 7
**alarm** alarma *(f)*
**alarmed** alarmado/a
**alcoholic** alcohólico/a
**alcoholic drink** bebida alcohólica *(f)* 9
**alert** alertar
**algebra** álgebra *(f)*
**align** alinear
**all** todo/a/os/as 1; **all day** todo el día 2
**allergy** alergia *(f)* 10
**alleviate** aliviar
**allow** permitir 10
**almost** casi 2
**alone** solo/a 2, 4
**already** ya 7
**also** también 1
**alternative** alternativo/a
**although** aunque
**always** siempre 2, 4
**American** estadounidense; (norte)americano/a *(m/f)*
**among** entre
**amount to** equivaler
**amuse** divertir
**amuse yourself** divertirse (ie, i) 5
**an** un/a
**analgesic** analgésico *(m)*
**and** y 4
**angel** ángel *(m)*
**angry** enojado/a 2
**angry: get angry** enojarse 5
**animal** animal *(m)*
**animal feeder** comedero *(m)*
**animation** animación *(f)*
**announce** anunciar
**annoy** fastidiar
**annual** anual
**anonymity** anonimato *(m)*
**anonymous** anónimo/a
**another** otro/a 1
**answer** contestar 2

**answer** respuesta (f) 1
**antibiotics** antibióticos 10
**anticipate** anticipar
**antidepressant** antidepresivo (m)
**anti-inflammatory** antiinflamatorio (m)
**antonym** antónimo (m)
**anxiety** ansiedad (f)
**any** alguno/a(s) 4; cualquier
**apartment** apartamento (m)
**appear** aparecer
**apple** manzana (f) 9
**application** aplicación (f) 6; **job application** solicitud de empleo (f) 11
**apply** aplicar
**appointment** cita (f) 10
**appreciate** apreciar
**appropriate** apropiado/a
**approximate** aproximar
**April** abril 5
**arable** cultivable
**archeological** arqueológico/a
**architecture** arquitectura (f)
**archive** archivo (m) 6
**Are there . . . ?** ¿Hay . . . ? 1
**area** área (f)
**Argentine** argentino/a (m/f)
**arm** brazo (m) 10
**arms (military)** armas (fpl)
**around** aldredor de
**arrest** arrestar
**arrival** llegada (f) 7
**arrive** llegar 2
**art** arte (m)
**arthritis** artritis (f) 10
**article** artículo (m)
**artist** artista (m/f)
**as** como 1; mientras 8; **as . . . as** tan . . . como 4; **as for** en cuanto a 9; **as long as** mientras 11; **as many . . . as** tanto/a/os/as . . . como 4; **as much . . . as** tanto/a . . . como 4; **as soon as** tan pronto como 11; **as soon as possible** lo antes posible 11; **as usual** regular 1
**ask** pedir (i, i) 10; preguntar 9; **ask a question** hacer una pregunta 3; **ask for** pedir (i, i) 4
**asparagus** espárragos 9
**aspect** aspecto (m) 11
**aspirin** aspirina (f) 10
**assault** asalto (m)
**assign** asignar
**assistance** asistencia (f); ayuda; **food assistance** ayuda alimentaria (f)
**associate** asociar
**assure** asegurar
**asthma** asma (f)
**at** en, a 1; **at the back of** al fondo de 7; **at**

**the beginning** al principio 8; **at the end of** al fondo de 7; **at times** a veces 2; **At what time?** ¿A qué hora? 2; **at work** en el trabajo 2
**athlete** atleta (m/f); deportista (m/f) 8
**athletic** deportista (adj.) 8
**Atlantic** atlántico/a
**ATM** cajero automático (m) 11
**atmosphere** ambiente (m); atmósfera (f)
**attack** ataque (m)
**attend** asistir (a) 3; **attend to** atender (ie) 11
**attention** atención (f)
**attitude** actitud (f)
**attract** atraer
**attraction** atracción (f)
**attractive** atractivo/a
**audience** audiencia (f)
**August** agosto 5
**aunt** tía (f) 3
**authentic** auténtico/a
**authenticity** autenticidad (f)
**author** autor/a (m/f)
**authority** autoridad (f)
**autobiographical** autobiográfico/a
**automatic** automático/a
**automobile** auto (m); automóvil (m); carro (m); coche (m)
**autumn** otoño (m) 5
**availability** disponibilidad (f) 7
**available** disponible 7, 11; **be available** estar a disposición
**average** promedio (m); promedio/a
**avoid** evitar 9
**away: take away** llevarse 5

### B

**baby** bebé (m)
**back** espalda (f) 10; respaldo (m)
**backpack** mochila (f) 1
**bad** malo/a 1
**bad(ly)** mal 1
**baked / fried potato** al horno 9
**balanced** equilibrado/a 9
**balcony** balcón (m) 7
**banana** banana (f); banano (m); guineo (m); plátano (m) 9
**bank** banco (m) 7
**bank account** cuenta bancaria (f)
**banking** banca (f) 11
**banquet** banquete (m)
**bar** bar (m) 3
**barber shop** peluquería (f) 7
**base** basar
**baseball** béisbol (m) 8
**baseball player** beisbolista (m/f) 8
**basic** básico/a
**basketball** básquetbol (m)

**bath: take a bath** bañarse 5
**bathe** bañarse 5
**bathroom** baño (m) 4
**be** estar; ser 1; **be able to** poder (ue) 4, 7; **be absent** faltar (a) 8; **be acquainted with** conocer 7; **be afraid of** tener miedo (de) 3; **be afraid that** tener miedo de que 11; **be available** estar a disposición; **be born** nacer 8; **be called** llamarse 3; **be careful** tener cuidado 10; **be cold** tener frío 3; **be curious** tener curiosidad; **be down** fallar 11; **be equivalent** equivaler; **be familiar with** conocer 7; **be happy that** alegrarse de que 11; estar contento/a de que 11; **be hot** tener calor 3; **be hungry** tener hambre 3; **be important** importar 9; **be in a good / bad mood** estar de buen / mal humor 11; **be in a hurry** tener prisa 3; **be in charge of** estar encargado/a de 11; **be in fashion** estar de moda 5; **be in session** sesionar; **be lucky** tener suerte 3; **be missing** faltar 9; faltar (a); **be named** llamarse 3; **be needed** faltar 9; **be operated on** ser operado/a 10; **be pleasing to** gustar 2; **be pregnant** estar embarazada 10; **be revolting** dar asco 9; **be right** tener razón 3; **be sad (that)** estar triste de (que) 11; **be sleepy** tener sueño; **be sorry that** sentir (ie, i) que 11; **be successful** tener éxito; **be sunny** hacer sol; **be sure** estar seguro/a 10; **be thirsty** tener sed 3; **be unable to stand** dar asco 9; **be vigilant** vigilar; **be . . . years old** tener . . . años 3; **How is . . . ?** ¿Cómo es . . . ? 1
**beach** playa (f) 2
**beans** frijoles (mpl) 9; habichuelas (mpl)
**beard** barba (f) 3
**beautiful** bello/a; precioso/a
**beauty** belleza (f)
**because** porque 2, 8; **because of** a causa de, por
**bed** cama (f) 1
**bedroom** alcoba (f); dormitorio (m) 4; habitación (f); recámara (f)
**beep** tono (m) 11
**beer** cerveza (f) 9
**before** antes (de)
**begin** comenzar (ie) 10; empezar (ie) 4
**beginner** novato/a (m/f)
**beginning** comienzo (m)
**behave** portarse 8
**behind** detrás de 2
**believe (in / that)** creer (en / que) 3, 10
**bellboy** botones (m)
**belong** pertenecer

**below** debajo de 2
**belt** cinturón (m) 5
**beneficial** beneficioso/a
**benefit** beneficiar
**benefit** beneficio (m) 11
**besides** además 11
**best** mejor 3; **best friend** mejor
amigo/a (m/f) 1
**better** mejor 3
**between** entre 1, 2
**bicycle** bicicleta (f) 4; **ride a bicycle**
andar en bicicleta 4
**big** grande 1
**biker** motociclista (m/f) 8
**bilingual** bilingüe
**bill** billete (m) 11; cuenta (f) 9, 11; factura (f)
**biology** biología (f)
**biology laboratory** laboratorio de
biología (m)
**bird feeder** comedero (m)
**birth** nacimiento (m) 8
**birthday** cumpleaños (m); fecha de
nacimiento (f) 2; **birthday party**
fiesta de cumpleaños (f) 8
**bit** poco (m)
**black** negro/a 3, 4
**blackboard** pizarra (f) 1
**block (in a city)** cuadra (f) 7
**blond** rubio/a 3
**blood** sangre (f) 10
**blood pressure** presión arterial (f) 10
**blouse** blusa (f) 5
**blue** azul 3, 4
**board** abordar 7
**boarding** embarque (m)
**boarding pass** tarjeta de embarque (f) 7
**bodily** corporal
**body** cuerpo (m) 10; organismo (m)
**bone** hueso (m) 10
**book** libro (m) 1
**bookbag** mochila (f) 1
**bookstore** librería (f) 2
**boots** botas (fpl) 5
**border** frontera (f)
**bored** aburrido/a 2, 4; **get bored**
aburrirse 5
**boring** aburrido/a 1
**boss** jefe/a (m/f) 11
**bossy** mandón / mandona 3
**bother** fastidiar; molestar 9, 11
**bothered** molesto/a 2, 4
**bottle** botella (f) 9
**boy** chico (m); muchacho (m) 2; niño (m)
**boyfriend** novio/a (m/f) 1
**brain** cerebro (m) 10
**branch office** sucursal (f) 11
**brand** marca (f)
**Brazil** Brasil

**bread** pan (m) 9
**break (one's arm)** romper(se) (el brazo) 10
**breakfast** desayuno (m) 4
**breathe** respirar 10
**brief** breve
**brilliant** brillante
**bring** traer 3
**broccoli** brócoli (m) 9
**brochure** folleto (m)
**bronchitis** bronquitis (f)
**brother (m)** hermano (m) 3
**brown** café 3; castaño 3; marrón 3, 4
**brush one's teeth** lavarse los dientes 5
**brusque** brusco/a
**buckle one's seatbelt** abrocharse el
cinturón 7
**building** edificio (m) 1
**burn (onseself)** quemar(se) 10
**bus** autobús (m) 4
**bus stop** parada de autobús (f) 4
**business** empresa (f); negocio (m)
**business administration** administración
de empresas (f)
**businessman/woman** empresario/a (m/f);
hombre / mujer de negocios (m) 8
**busy** ocupado/a 1
**but** pero 1
**butter** mantequilla (f) 9
**button** botón 6
**buy** comprar 2
**by** para; por; **by means of** mediante; **by**
**way of** por
**Bye.** Chau.; Ádios. 5

## C

**café** café (m) 2
**cafeteria** cafetería (f) 1
**caffeine** cafeína (f) 9
**cake** pastel (m) 9
**calculate** calcular 11
**calculator** calculadora (f) 1
**calendar** calendario (m)
**call** llamada (f) 7
**call** llamar
**calm** calmado/a; tranquilo/a 3
**calories** calorías 9
**camel** camello (m)
**camp** acampar 7
**campaign** campaña (f)
**campus** campus (m)
**can** poder (ue) 4, 7
**Canada** Canadá
**cancel** cancelar
**candidate** candidato/a (m/f)
**cap** gorra (f) 5
**capacity** capacidad (f)
**capture** captar

**car** auto (m); automóvil (m); carro (m) 4;
coche (m) 3, 4
**carbohydrates** carbohidratos 9
**care** cuidado (m); **take care of (oneself)**
cuidar(se) 10
**career** carrera (f)
**careful: be careful** tener cuidado 10
**Caribbean** caribeño/a
**carpenter** carpintero/a (m/f)
**carpentry** carpintería (f)
**carpet** alfombra (f)
**carrot** zanahoria (f) 9
**carry** llevar 5
**carry out** cumplir 8
**cartoon** dibujos animados (mpl)
**case** caso (m)
**cash: in cash** en efectivo 5
**cash (a check)** cobrar 11
**cashier** cajero/a (m/f) 11
**cat** gato/a (m/f)
**cataract** catarata (f)
**category** categoría (f)
**cathedral** catedral (f)
**Catholic** católico/a
**cauliflower** coliflor (m) 9
**cause** causar; provocar
**celebrate** celebrar
**celebration** celebración (f)
**cell phone** celular (m)
**cello** chelo (m)
**censure** censura (f)
**census** censo (m)
**cent** centavo (m) 9
**center** centro (m) 4
**center** centrar
**centigrade** centígrado (m)
**central** céntrico/a
**Central America** Centroamérica
**Central American** centroamericano/a (m/f)
**centralized** centralizado/a
**cereal** cereales 9
**ceremony** ceremonia (f)
**certain** cierto/a
**chain** cadena (f)
**chair** silla (f) 1, 4
**chalkboard** pizarra (f)
**chamber of commerce** cámara de
comercio (f)
**championship** campeonato (m) 8
**change** cambio (m)
**change** cambiar
**channel** cadena (f); canal (m)
**chapter** capítulo (m)
**character** carácter (m) 3; personaje (m)
**characteristic** característica (f)
**charge** cargo (m) 11
**charge (a fee)** cobrar 11
**chat** chatear 6; **chat room** sala de chat (f)

**chatty** hablador/a 4
**cheap** barato/a 5
**check** cheque (*m*) 5; cuenta (*f*) 9
**check one's luggage** facturar el equipaje
**checkbook** chequera (*f*) 11
**checking / savings account** cuenta
    corriente / de ahorros (*f*) 11
**checkup** chequeo (*m*)
**cheer someone up** dar ánimo a alguien 10
**cheese** queso (*m*) 9
**chemical** químico/a
**chemistry** química (*f*)
**chest** pecho (*m*) 10
**chest (of drawers)** cómoda (*f*) 4
**chew** masticar
**chicken** pollo (*m*) 9
**child** niño/a (*m/f*); **as a child** de niño/a 8
**childcare** cuidado de niños (*m*)
**childhood** infancia (*f*); niñez (*f*) 8
**children** hijos (*mpl*) 3
**children's** infantil
**chile pepper** chile (*m*) 9
**Chilean** chileno/a
**chilled** resfriado/a 10
**Chinese** chino (*m*)
**cholesterol** colesterol (*m*) 10
**chore** quehacer doméstico (*m*) 4
**Christmas** Navidad (*f*)
**church** iglesia (*f*) 2
**Ciao.** Chau. 5
**cigarette** cigarrillo (*m*)
**cinema** cine (*m*) 2
**circle** círculo (*m*)
**circuit** circuito (*m*)
**circulate** circular
**circulation** circulación (*f*)
**circumstance** circunstancia (*f*)
**city** ciudad (*f*) 2
**city map** plano de la ciudad (*m*) 7
**civilization** civilización (*f*)
**clarify** aclarar
**class** clase (*f*) 1; **classmate** compañero/a
    de clase (*m/f*); **classroom** salón de
    clase (*m*) 1
**classical** clásico/a 2
**classified ad** anucio clasificado (*m*)
**classify** clasificar
**clause** cláusula (*f*)
**clean** limpio/a 4
**clean** limpiar
**clear** claro/a; despejado/a 5
**clear** despejar 5
**click** hacer clic
**client** cliente (*m*)
**clientele** clientela (*f*)
**climate** clima (*m*); **climate change**
    cambios climáticos (*m*)
**climb** ascender
**clock** reloj (*m*) 1

**close** cercana/o
**close** cerrar (ie) 4
**closed** cerrado/a 2
**closet** armario (*m*) 4; clóset (*m*)
**clothing** ropa (*f*) 2, 5
**cloudy** nublado/a 5
**coast** costa (*f*)
**coat** abrigo (*m*)
**code** código (*m*)
**coffee** café 3; **black coffee** café solo (*m*) 9
**cognate** cognado (*m*)
**coherent** coherente
**coin** moneda (*f*) 11
**cold** frío/a 3; frío (*m*); catarro (*m*) 10;
    **be cold** tener frío 3; **catch a cold**
    resfriarse 10; **It's (very) cold.** Hace
    (mucho) frío. 5
**collapse** colapsar
**colleague** colega (*m/f*) 11
**college** colegio (*m*)
**colloquial** coloquial
**Colombian** colombiano/a (*m/f*)
**colonizer** colonizador/a (*m/f*)
**color** color (*m*) 4; **What color is it?**
    ¿De qué color es?
**column** columna (*f*)
**combat** combatir
**combination** combinación (*f*)
**combine** combinar
**come** venir 3; **come true** realizarse
**comedy** comedia (*f*)
**comfortable** cómodo/a
**comic** cómico/a
**comic strip** viñeta (*f*)
**command** mandato (*m*)
**commemorate** conmemorar
**comment** comentar
**commentary** comentario (*m*) 6
**commerce** comercio (*m*); **chamber of**
    **commerce** cámara de comercio (*f*)
**commercial** comercial
**commission** comisión (*f*)
**commit** cometer; comprometer
**committee** comité (*f*)
**common** común 10
**communicate (with each other)**
    comunicar(se) 5
**communication** comunicación
**community** comunidad (*f*)
**community (adj.)** comunitario/a
**community center** centro comunitario (*m*)
**companion** compañero/a (*m/f*)
**company** compañía (*f*) 11; empresa (*f*) 11;
    firma (*f*)
**compare** comparar
**comparison** comparación (*f*)
**compartment** compartimento (*m*)
**compatibility** compatibilidad (*f*) 11
**compatriot** compatriota (*m/f*) 12

**compensation** recompensa (*f*)
**compete** competir
**competition** competición (*f*); concurso (*m*)
**competitive** competitivo/a
**competitor** concursante (*m/f*)
**complement** complementar
**complete** completo/a 11
**complete** completar
**complex** complejo (*m*)
**complicated** complicado/a
**compliment** cumplido (*m*)
**composition** redacción (*f*)
**compression** compresión (*f*) 6
**computer** computador (*m*);
    computadora (*f*) 1; ordenador (*m*)
**computer science** informática (*f*)
**computing** computación (*f*);
    informática (*f*) 11
**concentrate** concentrarse 10
**concentrated** concentrado/a
**concentration** concentración (*f*)
**concept** concepto (*m*)
**concert** concierto (*m*) 2
**concise** conciso/a
**concrete** concreto/a
**condemn** condenar
**condiment** condimento (*m*)
**condition** condición (*f*)
**condition** condicionar
**conditional** condicional
**conference** conferencia (*f*)
**confess** confesar
**confidence** confianza (*f*); **have**
    **confidence in** confiar
**configure** configurar
**confirm** confirmar
**confirmation** confirmación (*f*)
**confront** enfrentarse (con)
**confused** confundido/a 2
**confusion** confusión (*f*)
**congested** congestionado/a 10
**congestion** congestión (*f*) 10
**Congress** Congreso (*m*) 12
**congressman/woman** congresista (*m/f*)
**conjunction** conjunción (*f*)
**connect** conectar 8
**connection** conexión (*f*)
**connectivity** conectividad (*f*)
**connotation** connotación (*f*)
**conquer** conquistar
**conquest** conquista (*f*)
**consequence** consecuencia (*f*)
**conservative** conservador/a 3
**conserve** conservar
**consist** consistir
**consonant** consonante (*f*)
**construction** construcción (*f*) 8;
    **construction worker** obrero/a de la
    construcción (*m/f*) 8

**consulate** consulado *(m)*
**consult** consultar
**consultation** consulta *(f)*
**consumer** consumidor/a *(m/f)*
**consumerism** consumerismo *(m)*
**consumption** consumo *(m)*
**contact** contacto *(m)*
**contact** contactar
**contain** contener
**container** contenedor *(m)*
**contaminate** contaminar
**contamination** contaminación *(f)*
**content** contenido *(m)*
**contestant** concursante *(m/f)*
**context** contexto *(m)*
**continue** continuar; seguir (i, i)
**contrary** contrario *(m)*
**contrast** contraste *(m)*
**contribute** contribuir
**contribution** contribución *(f)*
**control** controlar 10
**conversation** conversación *(f)*
**convert** convertir
**cook** cocinar 2
**cookie** galleta *(f)* 9
**cool** fresco/a; **It's cool.** Hace fresco. 5
**cooperation** cooperación *(f)*
**copy** copiar; **make a copy** sacar una copia 11
**cordially** cordialmente
**corn** choclo *(m)*; elote *(m)*; maíz *(m)* 9
**corn / flour tortilla** tortilla (de maíz / de harina) *(f)* 9
**corner** esquina *(f)* 7
**correct** correcto/a; justo/a 7
**correct** corregir
**correction** corrección *(f)*
**correspond** corresponder
**corresponding** correspondiente
**corruption** corrupción *(f)*
**cosmopolitan** cosmopolito/a
**cost** costo *(m)*; **cost of living** costo de vida *(m)*
**cost** costar (ue) 4
**Costa Rican** costarricense
**costly** costoso/a
**cough** tos *(f)* 10
**cough** toser 10
**counsel** consejo *(m)*
**counselor** consejero/a *(m/f)* 8
**count** contar (ue) 4
**country** campo *(m)* 4; país *(m)*
**county** condado *(m)*
**couple** pareja *(f)*
**course** curso *(m)*
**court** corte *(f)*
**courtesy** cortesía *(f)*
**cousin** primo/a *(m/f)* 3
**crazy** loco/a

**cream** crema *(f)* 9
**create** crear
**creativity** creatividad *(f)*
**credit** crédito *(m)*
**credit card** tarjeta de crédito *(f)*
**crime** crimen *(m)*; criminalidad *(f) (in general)* 12
**criteria** criterios *(mpl)*
**critic** crítico/a *(m/f)*
**criticize** criticar
**crop** cultivo *(m)*
**crutches** muletas *(fpl)* 10
**cry** llorar 8
**crystal** cristal
**Cuban** cubano/a
**cubism** cubismo *(m)*
**culinary** culinario/a
**cultivate** cultivar
**cultural** cultural 4
**culture** cultura *(f)*
**cup** taza *(f)* 9
**curative** curativo/a
**curiosity** curiosidad *(f)* 12
**curious: be curious** tener curiosidad
**currency** divisa *(f)*
**current event** actualidad *(f)*
**currently** actualmente
**curriculum vitae** currículum vitae *(m)* 11
**cursive** cursivo/a
**cursor** cursor *(m)* 6
**custom** costumbre *(f)*
**customer** cliente / clienta *(m/f)* 5
**cut** cortar; **cut one's hair** cortarse el pelo 7; **cut the grass** cortar el césped 4; **cut (yourself)** cortar(se) 10
**cybercafé** cibercafé *(m)*
**cybernetic** cibernético/a

### D

**daily** diario/a 2
**daily routine** rutina diaria *(f)* 5
**daily specials** menú *(m)*
**dance** baile *(m)*; danza *(f)*
**dance** bailar 2
**dangerous** peligroso/a
**dark** oscuro/a
**dark-complexioned** moreno/a 3
**data** datos *(mpl)*
**data transfer** descarga *(f)* 6
**database** base de datos *(f)* 11
**date** cita *(f)*; fecha *(f)* 5; **What is the date?** ¿Qué fecha es? 5
**date from** datar de
**daughter** hija *(f)* 3
**day** día *(m)* 2; **all day** todo el día 2; **every day** todos los días 2; **work days** días laborales

**dead** muerto/a 4
**dealings** trato *(m)*
**Dear . . .** Querido/a . . .
**death** muerte *(f)* 8
**debate** debatir
**debilitate** debilitar
**debit** débito *(m)*
**debit card** tarjeta de débito 5; tarjeta de débito *(f)*
**decade** década *(f)*
**decaffeinated** descafeinado/a
**December** diciembre 5
**decide** decidir 7
**decipherable** descifrable
**decision** decisión *(f)*; **make a decision** tomar una decisión 10
**declare** declarar
**dedicate** dedicar
**dedication** dedicación *(f)*
**deduce** deducir
**deep** profundo/a 10
**defend** defender
**defenseless** indefenso/a
**deficit** déficit *(m)*
**define** definar
**defined** definido/a
**definition** definición *(f)*
**deforestation** deforestación *(f)* 12
**degree** grado *(m)*; licenciatura *(m)*; **get a degree in . . .** hacer la carrera de . . . 8
**delay** retraso *(m)* 7
**delegation** delegación *(f)*
**delete button** borrador *(m)*
**delicious** delicioso/a
**demand** demanda *(f)*
**Democrat** demócrata *(m/f)*
**democratization** democratización *(f)*
**demonstrative** demonstrativo/a
**denounce** denunciar
**dental check-up** revisión dental *(f)* 10
**dentist** dentista *(m/f)* 10
**department** departamento *(m)* 11
**departure** salida *(f)* 7
**depend** depender (de)
**deposit** depositar 11
**deposit** depósito *(m)* 11
**depressed** deprimido/a
**depression** depresión *(f)* 10
**derivative** derivado *(m)*
**descend** descender
**describe** describir
**description** descripción *(f)* 4
**design** diseño *(m)* 6; **graphic design** diseño gráfico *(m)*; **graphic design program** programa de diseño gráfico *(m)* 11
**design** diseñar 11
**designer** diseñador/a *(m/f)*
**desire** desear 2

**desk** escritorio *(m)* 1; pupitre *(m)*
**despair** desesperanza *(f)* 10
**despite** a pesar de que
**dessert** postre *(m)* 9
**destination** destino *(m)*
**destroy** destruir
**detail** detalle *(m)*
**detain** detener
**deteriorate** deteriorarse
**determining** determinante
**devastation** devastación *(f)*
**develop** desarrollar 10
**developing** en vías de desarrollo
**development** desarrollo *(m)* 11
**devil** diablo *(m)*
**devote oneself to** dedicarse a 8
**diabetes** diabetes *(f)* 10
**diagnose** diagnosticar
**dialogue** diálogo *(m)*
**dictionary** diccionario *(m)* 1
**die** morir (ue, u) 8
**diet** dieta *(f)* 9
**difference** diferencia *(f)*
**different** diferente; distinto/a
**difficult** difícil 1
**difficulty** dificultad *(f)* 10
**digestion** digestión *(f)*
**digit** dígito *(m)*
**dimension** dimensión *(f)*
**diminish** disminuir
**dining room** comedor *(m)* 4
**dinner** cena *(f)* 2
**direct** directo/a
**direct** dirigir
**direct deposit** depósito directo *(m)* 11
**direct / indirect object** complemento directo / indirecto *(m)*
**direction** dirección *(f)*
**director** director/a *(m/f)* 11
**dirty** sucio/a 4
**disadvantage** desventaja *(f)*
**disappearance** desaparición *(f)*
**disaster** desastre *(m)*
**disastrous** desastroso/a
**discipline** disciplina *(f)*
**discomfort** molestia *(f)*
**disconnect** desconectar
**discotheque** discoteca *(f)*
**discreet** discreto/a
**discreetly** discretamente
**discriminatory** discriminatorio/a
**discuss** discutir
**discussion** discusión *(f)*
**disgusted** disgustado/a 6
**dish** plato *(m)*
**dishonest** deshonesto/a
**dishwasher** lavaplatos
**disordered** desordenado/a

**disorganized** desorganizado/a
**disparity** disparidad *(f)*
**dissident** disidente *(m/f)*
**distance** distancia *(f)*
**distinct** distinto/a
**distinguished** distinguido/a
**distribute** distribuir 11
**distribution** distribución *(f)*
**district** distrito *(m)*
**diversion** diversión *(f)*
**diversity** diversidad *(f)*
**divorce** divorcio *(m)*; **get divorced from** divorciarse (de) 5
**divorced** divorciado/a 3, 4
**dizzy** mareado/a 10
**do** hacer 2; **do (for a living)** dedicarse a 8
**doctor** médico/a *(m/f)* 8, 10
**doctoral degree** doctorado *(m)*
**document** documento *(m)* 11
**dog** perro *(m/f)* 3
**dollar** dólar *(m)*
**domain** dominio *(m)*
**domestic** doméstico/a
**Dominican** dominicano/a
**Dominican Republic** República Dominicana *(f)*
**door** puerta *(f)*
**dormitory** residencia *(f)* 1
**dose** dosis *(f)*
**double** doble; **double bed** cama doble *(f)* 7; **double room** habitación doble *(f)* 7
**doubt** dudar 10
**down** abajo; **get down from** bajar de 7
**download** descargar 6
**down-to-earth** realista 3
**downtown** centro *(m)* 4
**drag** arrastrar
**draw** dibujar 11
**drawer** cajón *(m)* 11
**dream** sueño *(m)* 8; **dream of / about** soñar (ue) con 8
**dress** vestido *(m)* 5; **get dressed** vestirse (i, i) 5
**drink** bebida *(f)* 9
**drink** beber 3; tomar 2
**drinkable** bebible
**drinking fountain** bebedero *(m)*
**drive** circular; conducir; guiar; impulsar; manejar 10
**drug** droga *(f)*
**drug trafficker** narcotraficante *(m/f)*
**drug trafficking** narcotráfico *(m)*
**due to** debido a
**during** durante 3; por
**DVD player** reproductor de DVD *(m)* 4
**dwelling** vivienda *(f)*
**dynamic** dinámica *(f)*

## E

**each** cada 1
**ear** oreja *(f)* 10
**ear (inner)** oído *(m)* 10
**early** temprano 2
**earn** ganar
**easily** fácilmente
**east** este; **east of** al este de 2
**easy** fácil 1
**easy-going** relajado/a 3
**eat** comer 2; **eat / have breakfast** desayunar 4; **eat / have dinner** cenar 4; **eat / have lunch** almorzar (ue) 4; **eat heavily** comer fuerte 9
**eating habits** hábitos alimenticios *(mpl)*
**ecological** ecológico/a
**economic** económico/a
**economist** economista *(m/f)*
**economy** economía *(f)* 12
**ecotourism** ecoturismo *(m)* 7
**edible** comestible
**edit** editar
**educate** educar
**education** educación *(f)*; formación académica *(f)* 11
**educative** educativo/a
**educator** educador/a *(m/f)*
**effect** efecto *(m)*
**effective** efectivo/a
**efficacy** eficacia *(f)*
**egg** huevo *(m)* 9
**eighth** octavo/a
**election** elección *(f)* 12
**electricity** electricidad *(f)*; luz *(f)* 4
**electronic** electrónico/a
**elegant** elegante
**element** elemento *(m)*
**elementary school** escuela primaria *(f)* 8
**elevator** ascensor *(m)* 7; elevador *(m)*
**eliminate** eliminar
**eloquent** elocuente
**elusive** elusivo/a
**e-mail** correo electrónico *(m)* 3
**emergency** emergencia *(f)*
**emergency room** sala de urgencia *(f)* 10
**emission** emisión *(f)*
**emoticon** emoticono *(m)* 6
**emotion** emoción *(f)* 11
**emotional** emocional
**emperor** emperador *(f)*
**employee** empleado/a *(m/f)*
**employer** empleador/a *(m/f)*; encargado/a *(m/f)* 7
**employment** empleo *(m)* 10
**enamored** enamorado/a 6
**enchanting** encantador/a
**end** final *(m)*

**ending** terminación (f)
**endorphine** endorfina (f)
**energy** energía (f) 9
**engineer** ingeniero/a (m/f) 8
**engineering** ingeniería (f)
**English** inglés (m); **English-speaking** de habla inglesa
**enjoy** disfrutar; gozar
**enough** bastante
**enterprise** empresa (f) 11
**entertain** divertir
**entertainment** entretenemiento (m) 12
**entire** entero/a 9
**entrance** entrada (f) 7
**entrée** plato principal (m) 9
**entry** entrada (f)
**environment** ambiente (m) 11; medio ambiente (m) 12
**enzyme** enzima (f)
**epidemic** epidemia (f)
**episode** episodio (m)
**epoch** época (f)
**equal** igual
**equality** igualdad (f)
**equip** equipar
**equipment** equipo (m)
**equipped** equipado/a
**equitable** equitativo/a
**equivalent: be equivalent** equivaler; equvalente
**eradication** erradicación (f)
**eraser** borrador
**especially** especialmente
**essay** ensayo (m) 3
**essential** esencial
**establish** establecer
**establishment** establicimiento (m)
**esteemed** estimado/a
**estimate** estimar
**estimated** presupuestario/a
**estimation** estimación (f)
**eternal** eterno/a
**ethics** ética (f)
**ethnic** étnico/a
**etiquette** etiqueta (f)
**European** europeo/a
**evaluate** evaluar 11
**evaluation** evaluación (f)
**even** aún; incluso
**evening** noche (f) 2
**event** acontecimiento (m) 8; evento (m) 3
**every** todo/a/os/as 1
**every day** todos los días 2
**every time** cada vez
**everyone** todos 4
**everywhere** por todos lados 4
**evident** evidente
**exaggerate** exagerado/a

**exam** examen (m); **mid-term exam** examen parcial (m)
**examine** examinar 10
**example** ejemplo (m)
**excellent** excelente
**except** menos 1, 2
**exceptionally** excepcionalmente
**excess** exceso (m)
**excessive** excesivo/a
**excessively** excesivamente
**exchange** cambiar 7; intercambiar
**excited** emocionado/a 8
**exciting** emocionante
**excursion** excursión (f)
**excuse** excusa (f)
**Excuse me!** ¡Disculpe! 7
**exercise** ejercicio (m); **cuaderno de ejercicios** workbook 1
**exercise** hacer ejercicio 2
**exhale** exhalar
**exhausted** exhausto/a
**exhibition** exposición
**exist** existir
**exotic** exótico/a
**expansion** expansión (f)
**expedition** expedición (f)
**expense** gasto (m)
**expensive** caro/a 4
**experience** experiencia (f)
**expert** experto/a (m/f)
**explain** explicar 9
**explication** explicación (f)
**exploitation** explotación (f)
**express** expresar
**expression** expresión (f)
**exquisite** exquisito/a
**extend** extender
**extension** extensión (f) 6
**extensive** extendido/a
**extract** extracto (m)
**extraordinary** extraordinario/a
**extroverted** extrovertido/a 1
**exuberant** exuberante
**eye** ojo (m) 3

**F**

**face** cara (f) 10
**face** enfrentarse (con) 7
**facilitate** facilitar
**facility** facilidad (f)
**facing** enfrente de 2
**fact** hecho (m)
**factory** fábrica (f)
**factory manager** gerente de fábrica (m/f) 8
**factory worker** obrero/a de fábrica (m/f) 8
**fail** fallar 11
**fall** otoño (m) 5

**fall** caer(se) 10; **fall into** caer a 8
**fall in love (with)** enamorarse (de) 5
**false** falso/a (m)
**fame** fama (f)
**familiar: be familiar with** conocer 7
**family** familia (f)
**family member** familiar 3
**famous** famoso/a 8
**fanatic** fanático/a
**far (from)** lejos (de) 2
**farewell** despedida (f)
**farmer** agricultor/a (m/f) 8
**fascinating** fascinante
**fashion** moda (f); **latest fashion** de última moda
**fast** estar en ayunas
**fat** gordo/a 3
**fat** grasa (f) 9
**father** padre (m) 3
**fatigue** fatiga (f)
**favor** favorecer
**favorite** favorito/a; preferido/a
**fear** temer 11; tener miedo (de) 3; **fear that** temer que 11
**fear** miedo (m)
**February** febrero 5
**feel** sentirse (ie, i) 5; **feel like** tener ganas de
**feeling** sentimiento (m)
**feminine** feminino/a
**fertilizer** abono (m)
**fervor** fervor (m)
**festival** feria (f)
**festive** festivo/a
**fever** fiebre (f) 10
**few** poco/a/os/as 1
**fiancé(e)** novio/a (m/f)
**fiber** fibra (f) 9; **fiber optic** fibra óptica
**fictive** ficticio/a
**fifth** quinto/a
**fight** pelea (f)
**fight** luchar; pelearse 5
**figure** cifra (f); gráfico (m)
**file** archivar 11
**file (folder)** carpeta (f) 11
**filing cabinet** archivador (m) 11; archivero (m)
**film** película (f)
**finally** finalmente
**finance** financiar
**financial** financiero/a
**financing** financiación (f)
**find** encontrar (ue) 4
**find out** saber 7
**fine arts** bellas artes (fpl)
**fingers** dedos 10
**finish** terminar
**fire** despedir (i, i) 11; incendio (m)
**firefighter** bombero/a (m/f) 8

**firm** firma *(f)*

**first** primer(o)/a; **It's the first of . . .** Es (el) primero de . . . 5

**fish** pescado *(m)* 9

**fish** pescar 7

**fit** en forma

**fitting rooms** probadores *(mpl)* 5

**fix** arreglar 4

**flexible** flexible 3

**flight** vuelo *(m)* 7

**flight attendant** asistente de vuelo *(m/f)* 7

**flood** inundación *(f)* 12

**floor** piso *(m)*; suelo *(m)* 4

**flour** harina *(f)*

**flourishing** floreciente

**flower** flor *(f)* 4

**flu** gripe *(f)*

**fluid** fluido/a

**fluoride** flúor *(m)*

**follow** seguir (yo sigo) 9

**following** siguiente 1

**font** fuente *(f)*

**food** alimento *(m)*; comida *(f)* 2, 9; **food assistance** ayuda alimentaria *(f)*

**foolish** tonto/a

**foot** pie *(m)* 10

**football** fútbol americano 2

**footer** pie de página *(m)*

**for** para 1; por; **for that reason** por eso

**for example** por ejemplo

**for that reason** por eso

**forbid** prohibir 10

**force** fuerza *(f)* 10, 12

**forecast** pronóstico *(m)*

**foreign** extranjero/a

**foreign country** país extranjero *(m)* 7

**forest** bosque *(m)* 7

**fork** tenedor *(m)* 9

**form** forma *(f)*; formulario *(m)*

**form** formar

**format** formato *(m)*

**fortune** fortuna *(f)*

**forum** foro *(m)*

**found** fundar

**fourth** cuarto/a

**fraction** fracción *(f)*

**frank** franco/a

**free** gratis; gratuito/a; libre

**free** liberar

**free time** ratos libres; tiempo libre *(m)* 2

**freedom** libertad *(f)*

**French** francés *(m)*

**French fries** papas fritas *(fpl)*

**frenetic** frenético/a

**frequency** frecuencia *(f)*

**frequent** frecuente

**frequently** con frecuencia 2

**fresh** fresco/a

**Friday** viernes 2

**fried** frito/a

**friend** amigo/a *(m/f)*

**friendly** amistoso/a 3

**frightened** asustado/a 8

**frivolous** frívolo/a

**from** de 1; **from . . . to** de . . . a . . . 2; **from . . . until** desde . . . hasta; **I'm from . . .** Soy de . . . 1

**front** delantero/a

**front desk** recepción *(f)* 7

**fruit** fruta *(f)* 9

**frustration** frustración *(f)*

**full** completo/a 11; lleno/a 4

**full-time job** empleo a tiempo completo *(m)* 11

**fun** divertido/a 1; **have fun** divertirse (ie, i) 5

**function** funcionar

**functioning** funcionamiento *(m)*

**funny** chistoso/a 3

**furious** furioso/a

**furnished** amueblado/a

**furniture** muebles *(mpl)* 4

**future** futuro *(m)*

**G**

**gallery** galería *(f)*

**gallon** galón *(m)*

**game** partido *(m)* 2

**game show** concurso *(m)*

**gang** pandilla *(f)*

**garage** garaje *(m)* 4

**garden** jardín *(m)* 4

**gas station** estación de servicio *(f)* 7; gasolinera *(f)* 7

**gasoline** gas *(m)* 4; gasolina *(f)* 7

**gastric** gástrico/a

**gastronomy** gastronomía *(f)*

**gate** puerta *(f)* 7

**gather** recoger 7

**general: in general** en general

**generally** generalmente 2

**generate** generar

**generation** generación *(f)*

**generous** generoso/a 3

**genetic** genético/a

**genius** genio/a *(m/f)*

**genre** género *(m)*

**geography** geografía *(f)*

**German** alemán *(m)*

**gesture** gesto *(m)* 8

**get** obtener, sacar 7; **get a degree in . . .** hacer la carrera de . . . 8; **get along well (with)** llevarse bien (con) 5; **get angry** enojarse 5; **get bored** aburrirse 5; **get divorced from** divorciarse (de) 5; **get down from** bajar de 7; **get dressed** vestirse (i, i) 5; **get hot** calentarse (ie); **get married (to)** casarse (con) 5; **get off / out of** bajar de 7; **get on / in** subir a 7; **get sick** enfermarse 10; **get together** encontrarse (ue) 5; **get up** levantarse 5

**gift** regalo *(m)* 2

**girl** chica *(f)*; muchacha *(f)* 2; niña *(f)*

**girlfriend** novia *(m/f)* 1

**give** dar 9; rendir; **give as a gift** regalar 9; **give someone a shot** ponerle una inyección 10

**glad** contento/a 2

**glass** copa *(f)* 9; vaso *(m)* 9

**glasses** gafas *(fpl)* 3; **sunglasses** gafas de sol *(fpl)* 3

**globalization** globalización *(f)*

**globalize** globalizar

**go** ir 2; **go away** irse 5; **go on a hike** ir de excursión 7; **go on an outing** ir de excursión 7; **go on vacation** ir de vacaciones 7; **go out** salir; **go sailing** salir en velero 7; **go shopping** ir de compras 2; **go to bed** acostarse (ue) 5; **go up** ascender; subir a 7

**goal** gol *(m)* 8; propósito *(m)*

**going to + *verb*** ir a + *infinitive* 5; **It's going to rain / snow.** Va a llover / nevar. 5

**good** bueno/a

**Good afternoon.** Buenas tardes. 1

**Good evening.** Buenas noches. 1

**Good morning.** Buenos días. 1

**Good night.** Buenas noches. 1

**Good-bye.** Adiós. 1

**good-looking** guapo/a 3

**gossip** chisme *(m)*

**gossipy** chismoso/a 4

**gourd** calabaza *(f)*

**governability** gobernabilidad *(f)*

**government** gobierno *(m)*

**governmental** gubernamental

**governor** gobernador/a *(m/f)*

**grade** grado *(m)* 8

**graduate** graduarse 8

**graduation** graduación *(f)* 8

**graffiti** grafiti *(m)*

**grain** grano *(m)* 9

**gram** gramo *(m)*

**grammar** gramática *(f)*

**grammatical** gramatical

**grandchildren** nietos *(mpl)* 3

**granddaughter** nieta *(f)* 3

**grandfather** abuelo *(m)* 3

**grandmother** abuela *(f)* 3

**grandparents** abuelos *(mpl)* 3

**grandson** nieto *(m)* 3

**grapes** uvas 9

**graphic artist** diseñador/a gráfico/a *(m/f)* 11

**graphic design** diseño gráfico (m)

**graphic design program** programa de diseño gráfico (m) 11

**grass** césped (m) 4

**grave** grave 10

**gray** gris 3, 4

**gray-haired** canoso/a 3

**green** verde 3, 4

**green beans** ejotes (mpl); judías verdes (fpl)

**greet** saludar 8

**greeting** saludo (m)

**grill** parrilla (f); **grilled, on the grill** a la parrilla

**ground** suelo (m) 4

**ground floor** planta baja (f) 7

**group** grupo (m)

**group therapy** terapia de grupo (f) 10

**grow** crecer

**growing** creciente

**guarantee** garantía (f)

**guarantee** garantizar

**guard** guardia (m/f)

**guerrilla** guerillero/a (m/f) 12

**guess** adivinar

**guest** huésped (m/f) 7; invitado/a (m/f) 5

**guide** guía (f); guiar

**guitar** guitarra (f) 2

**guy** muchacho (m) 2

**gym(nasium)** gimnasio (m) 1

H

**habit** hábito (m)

**hair** pelo (m) 3

**hair salon** peluquería (f) 7

**Haiti** Haití (f)

**half** medio/a; mitad (f)

**half brother** medio hermano (m)

**half sister** media hermana (f)

**hall** pasillo (m) 7; salón (m)

**ham** jamón (m) 9

**hamburger** hamburguesa (f) 9

**hand** mano (f) 10

**handle** manejar

**handsome** bonito/a; guapo/a 3

**happen** pasar 8

**happy** contento/a 2; feliz; **be happy that** alegrarse de que 11; estar contento/a de que 11

**hardware** componentes físicos (m) 6

**hard-working** trabajador/a 1

**harmoniously** armoniosamente

**hat** sombrero (m) 5

**have** tener 3; **have a party** hacer una fiesta 3; **have an opinion** opinar; **have confidence in** confiar; **have fun** divertirse (ie, i) 5; **have just** acabar de; **have to** tener que ; **He has a mustache /**

beard. Tiene bigote / barba.; **He / She has glasses.** Tiene gafas. 3; **I have . . .** tengo . . . 1; **What classes do you have?** ¿Qué clases tienes? 1

**he** él

**head** cabeza (f) 10

**heading** encabezado (m)

**headline** encabezado (m); titular (m)

**healing** curación (f)

**health** salud (f) 9, 10

**healthy** saludable; sano/a 9

**hear** oír 3

**heart** corazón (m) 10

**heat** calentar (ie); calor (m)

**height** estatura 3; **medium height** estatura mediana 3

**Hello. (on the telephone)** Aló. 5

**help** ayuda (f)

**help** ayudar; servir (i) 5; **help (each other)** ayudar(se) 5; **How may I help you?** ¿En qué puedo servirle? 5

**hemisphere** hemisferio (m)

**her** ella 2; la; su(s) 1, 3, **(to, for) her** le, se

**herb** hierba (f)

**herbalist** botánco/a (m/f)

**here** acá; aquí 1; **over here** por acá

**heritage** herencia (f)

**hers** suyo/a 9

**herself** se 6

**Hi.** Hola. 1

**high** alto/a 3

**high school** colegio (m) 8; instituto (m); liceo (m); prepa (f); preparatoria (f) 11

**higher** superior

**highlight** destacar

**highway** carretera (f)

**him** él 1; lo; **(to, for) him** le, se

**himself** se 6

**his** su(s) 1; suyo/a 9

**Hispanic** hispano (m/f)

**historic / tourist site** sitio histórico / turístico (m) 7

**historical** histórico/a

**history** historia (f)

**hit** golpear 8

**holiday** vacaciones

**home remedy** remedio casero (m)

**homeless** sin hogar 12

**homeopathy** homeopatía (f)

**hometown** ciudad natal (f)

**homework** tarea (f) 1

**homogenization** homogeneización (f)

**honest** honesto/a

**honey** miel (f)

**hope** esperar 10

**hormone** hormona (f)

**horoscope** horóscopo (m)

**hospice** hospicio (m)

**hospitality** hospitalidad (f)

**hostel** hostal (m)

**hot** caliente; **be hot** tener calor 3; **get hot** calentarse (ie) **It's (very) hot.** Hace (mucho) calor. 5

**hotel** hotel (m) 7

**hour** hora (f) 2

**house** casa (f) 4

**household** hogar (m)

**housemate** compañero/a de casa (m/f)

**housewife** ama de casa (f) 8

**housing** vivienda (f)

**How?** ¿Cómo? 2; **How are you?** (fam.) ¿Cómo estás? 1; **How are you?** (form.) ¿Cómo está usted? 1; **How do you say . . . in English?** ¿Cómo se dice . . . en inglés? 1; **How is / are / was / were . . . ?** ¿Qué tal . . . ? 7; **How is . . . ?** ¿Cómo es . . . ? 1; **How is it going?** ¿Qué tal?; **How is that written?** ¿Cómo se escribe? 1; **How many?** ¿Cuántos/as? 2; **How may I help you?** ¿En qué puedo servirle? 5; **How much?** ¿Cuánto/a? 2; **How often?** ¿Con qué frecuencia? 2

**hug** abrazo (m)

**hug (each other)** abrazar (se) 5

**human being** humano (m)

**human resources** recursos humanos (mpl) 11

**human rights** derechos humanos (mpl)

**humanitarian** humanitario/a

**humanitarian aid** ayuda humanitaria (f) 12

**humanities** humanidades (fpl)

**humorous** humorístico/a

**hundred** cien(to)

**hunger** hambre (f)

**hungry be hungry** tener hambre 3; **make hungry** dar hambre 9

**hurricane** huracán (m)

**hurry: be in a hurry** tener prisa 3

**hurt** doler (ue) 9; **hurt (yourself)** lastimar(se) 10

**hybrid** híbrido/a

**hydration** hidratación (f)

**hydrogen** hidrógeno (m)

I

**I** yo; **I (don't) have . . .** (no) tengo . . . 1; **I don't know** No conozco a 4; **I don't know.** No sé. 1; **I (don't) like . . .** (No) me gusta / (+ singular noun) 1; (No) me gustan / (+ plural noun) 1; **I don't understand.** No comprendo. 1; **I have . . .** tengo . . . 1; **I like** Me gusta(n) **I need . . .** Necesito . . . 1;

**I would like . . .** Me gustaría(n) . . . 4;
**I'm doing very well, thank you.**
Estoy muy bien, gracias.; **I'm from . . .**
Soy de . . . 1; **I'm sorry.** Lo siento. 4;
**I'm studying . . .** Estudio . . . 1
**ice cream** helado (m) 9
**icon** icono (m) 6
**idea** idea (f) 2, 8
**identical** idéntico/a
**identifiable** identificable
**identification** identificación (f) 7
**identify** identificar
**identity** identidad (f)
**idiomatic** idiomático/a
**idiot** imbécil (m/f)
**ill** enfermo/a 1, 4; **become ill** enfermarse
**illegal** ilegal
**illness** enfermedad (f) 10
**illogical** ilógico/a
**illustration** ilustración (f) 4
**image** imagen (f)
**imaginary** imaginario/a
**imagine** imaginar
**imbalance** desequilibrio (m)
**immediately** inmediatamente
**immersion** inmersión (f)
**immigrant** inmigrante (m/f) 8
**immigrate** inmigrar
**immigration** inmigración (f) 12
**immunological** inmunológico/a
**impact** impacto (m)
**impatient** impaciente 1
**impeccable** impecable
**imperfect tense** imperfecto (m)
**imply** implicar
**importance** importancia (f)
**important** importante; **be important**
importar 9
**impose** imponer
**impossible** imposible 10
**impression** impresión (f)
**impressive** impresionante
**impulse** impulso (m)
**in** en 1, 2; **in advance** con antelación 7;
**in cash** en efectivo; **in front of**
delante de 2; **in general** en general;
**in love** enamorado/a 6; **in order to**
para + infinitive 8; **in spite of** a pesar
de que; **in that case** en ese caso 7
**in order to** para
**in shape** en forma 10
**in that case** en ese caso 7
**incident** incidente (m)
**include** incluir
**included** incluido/a 7
**including** incluso
**incorporate** incorporar
**incorrect** incorrecto/a
**increase** aumento (m)

**increase** aumentar; incrementar
**incredible** increíble
**independence** independencia (f)
**independent** independiente; **become**
**independent** independizarse
**independently** independientemente
**index** índice (m)
**indicate** indicar
**indication** indicación (f)
**indicative** indicativo/a
**indicator** indicador (m)
**indifferent** indiferente
**indigenous** indígeno/a
**indignation** indignación (f) 12
**individual** individuo (m)
**industrialize** industrializar
**industry** industria (f)
**inexpensive** barato/a
**infect** infectar
**infected** infectado/a 10
**infidel** infiel (m/f)
**infidelity** infidelidad (f)
**infinitive** infinitivo (m)
**inflation** inflación (f)
**influence** influencia (f)
**influence** influir (en) 10
**inform** informar; **inform oneself**
informarse
**information** información (f) 11
**information technology** informática (f) 6
**informative** informativo/a
**ingredient** ingrediente (m)
**inhabitant** habitante (m/f)
**inhalation** inhalación (f)
**inhumane** inhumano/a
**initial** inicial
**initiate** iniciar
**initiative** iniciativa (f)
**injection** inyección (f) 10
**injustice** injusticia (f)
**innocent** inocente
**input data** introducir datos 11
**insert** insertar 6
**inside** adentro
**insignificant** insignificante
**insist (on)** insistir (en) 10
**insomnia** insomnio (m) 10
**inspire** inspirar
**install** instalar
**instant messaging** mensajería
instantánea (f)
**instantaneous** instantáneo/a
**instead of** en vez de 9
**institution** institución (f)
**instruction** instrucción (f)
**instrument** instrumento (m)
**insufficient** insuficiente
**insult** insultar
**insurance** seguro (m) 11

**intellectual** intelectual 1
**intelligent** inteligente 1
**intend** pensar (ie) 4
**intense** intenso/a
**intention** intención (f)
**interact** interactuar
**interaction** interacción (f)
**interactive** interactivo/a
**interest** interés (m)
**interest** interesar 9
**interest rate** tasa de interés (f) 11
**interested (in)** interesado/a
**interesting** interesante 1
**international** internacional
**interrogation** interrogatorio (m)
**interrogative** interrogativo/a
**interruption** interrupción (f)
**intersection** cruce (m)
**interval** intervalo (m)
**interview** entrevista (f) 11
**interview** entrevistar
**interviewee** entrevistado/a (m/f)
**interviewer** entrevistador/a (m/f)
**intimate** íntimo/a
**intrigue** intriga (f)
**introduce** introducir; presentar;
**introduce oneself** presentarse 5
**introduction** presentación (f)
**invasion** invasión (f) 12
**investigate** averiguar; investigar
**investigation** investigación (f)
**invite** invitar 8
**irresponsible** irresponsable 1
**irritability** irritabilidad (f) 10
**irritate** irritar
**Is there . . . ?** ¿Hay . . . ? 1
**island** isla (f)
**it** lo, la; **It rains. It's raining.** Llueve. 5; **It
snows. It's snowing.** Nieva. 5; **It's
cool.** Hace fresco. 5; **It's going to rain /
to snow.** Va a llover / nevar. 5; **It's
sunny.** Hace sol. 5; **It's the first of . . .**
Es (el) primero de . . . 5; **It's (very)
cold.** Hace (mucho) frío. 5; **It's (very)
hot.** Hace (mucho) calor. 5; **It's windy.**
Hace viento. 5
**Italian** italiano/a
**itinerary** itinerario (m) 7
**its** su(s) 3

## J

**jacket** chaqueta (f) 5
**January** enero 5
**Japanese** japonés (m)
**jeans** jeans (mpl) 5
**jellyfish** medusa (f)
**job** empleo (m) 11; trabajo (m) 2; **full-**

**time job** empleo a tiempo completo *(m)* 11; **job application** solicitud de empleo *(f)* 11; **job market** mercado de trabajo *(m)*; **job offer** oferta de empleo *(f)* 11; **part-time job** empleo a tiempo parcial *(m)* 11
**joke** chiste *(m)* 5
**journalist** periodista *(m/f)* 12
**judge** juez *(m/f)*
**juice** jugo *(m)*
**July** julio 5
**June** junio 5
**junk food** comida basura *(f)* 9
**jury** tribunal *(m)*
**justice** juez *(m/f)*; justicia *(f)* 12

**keep** guardar; **keep (yourself)** mantenerse 10
**key** llave *(f)* 7
**keyboard** teclado *(m)* 11
**kilogram** kilo *(m)* 9
**king** rey *(m)*
**kiss** beso *(m)*
**kiss (each other)** besar (se) 5
**kitchen** cocina *(f)* 4
**knee** rodilla *(f)* 10
**knife** cuchillo *(m)* 9
**know** conocer 7; saber 7; **I don't know.** No conozco a 4; **I don't know.** No sé. 1
**knowledge** conocimiento *(m)*
**known** conocido/a

**laboratory** laboratorio *(m)*; **biology laboratory** laboratorio de biología *(m)*; **language laboratory** laboratorio de lenguas *(m)*
**lack** falta *(f)*; **lack of concentration / of interest** falta de concentración / de interés *(f)* 10
**lady** dama *(f)*
**lake** lago *(m)* 2
**lament** lamentar
**lamp** lámpara *(f)* 4
**land** terreno *(m)*; tierra *(f)*
**land** aterrizar 7
**language** idioma *(m)* 11; lengua *(f)*; lenguaje *(m)*
**large** grande
**lasagna** lasaña *(f)*
**last** último/a 7
**last** durar 7
**last name** apellido *(m)* 11
**last night** anoche 7

**last week** semana pasada *(f)* 7
**late** con retraso 7; tarde 2
**later** luego; más tarde
**latest** último/a
**Latin America** Latinoamérica
**Latino** latino/a *(m/f)*
**laundromat** lavandería *(f)* 4
**laundry** lavandería *(f)*
**laundry room** lavadero
**law** ley *(f)* 12
**lawn** césped *(m)* 4
**lawyer** abogado/a *(m/f)* 8
**lazy** perezoso/a 1
**leader** líder *(m/f)* 6
**league** liga *(f)*
**learn (to)** aprender 3
**learning** aprendizaje *(m)*
**leave** dejar 4; irse 5; salir 3
**left: to the left of** a la izquierda de 2
**leg** pierna *(f)* 10
**legend** leyenda *(f)*
**legislation** legislación *(f)*
**legumes** legumbres *(fpl)* 9
**leisure** ocio *(m)*
**lemon** limón *(m)* 9
**lemonade** limonada *(f)* 9
**lend** prestar 9
**length** *(time)* duración *(f)*
**less** menos 1; **less . . . than** menos . . . que 4
**lesson** lección *(f)*
**Let's hope that . . .** Ojalá que . . . 10
**letter** carta *(f)*; letra *(f)*
**lettuce** lechuga *(f)* 9
**level** nivel *(m)*
**liberal** liberal 3
**liberty** libertad *(f)*
**library** biblioteca *(f)* 1
**license** licencia *(f)*
**lie down** acostarse (ue) 5
**life** vida *(f)* 8
**lift someone's spirits** levantarle el ánimo 10
**lift weights** levantar pesas 2
**light** ligero/a 9
**light** luz *(f)*
**like: I (don't) like . . .** (No) me gusta (+ singular noun) 1; (No) me gustan (+ plural noun) 1; **I would like . . .** Me gustaría(n) . . . 4
**like** como 1
**likes to joke around** chistoso/a 3
**Likewise.** Igualmente. 1
**limit** limitar
**line** línea *(f)* 11
**link** enlace *(m)*
**liquid** líquido *(m)*
**list** lista *(f)*
**listen (to)** escuchar 2
**liter** litro *(m)*

**literature** literatura *(f)*
**little** poco/a/os/as 1; **a little** poco *(m)*
**little** pequeño/a 1
**live** vivo; en vivo
**live** vivir 3
**lively** animado/a 4
**living room** sala *(f)* 4
**loan** préstamo *(m)* 11
**locate** localizar; situar
**location** ubicación *(f)* 11
**lodge** alojarse 7; hospedar
**lodging** alojamiento *(m)*
**logic** lógica *(f)*
**logical** lógico/a
**logically** lógicamente
**long** largo/a 3
**look: look at** mirar 2; **look for** buscar 5
**lose** perder (ie) 4
**lose weight** bajar de peso 9
**loss** pérdida *(f)*
**lost** perdido/a
**love** encantar 9; 11; **love (each other)** amor *(m)*; querer (se) (ie) 5 querer (ie) 10; **in love** enamorado/a 6
**lovable** amable
**lovely** precioso/a
**loving** cariñoso/a 3
**low** bajo/a 3
**luck:** suerte *(f)*
**lucky: be lucky** tener suerte 3;
**luggage** equipaje *(m)*
**lunch** almuerzo *(m)* 9
**lungs** pulmones 10

**magazine** revista *(f)* 3
**magnificent** magnifico/a
**mail** correo
**main dish** plato principal *(m)* 9
**maintain** mantener 11
**maintenance** mantenamiento *(m)*
**majority** mayoría *(f)*
**make** fabricar; hacer 2; **make a copy** sacar una copia 11; **make a decision** tomar una decisión 10; **make a stopover** hacer escala 7; **make hungry** dar hambre 9; **make possible** potenciar; **make thirsty** dar sed 9
**male** varón
**mall** centro comercial *(m)* 2
**malnutrition** desnutrición *(f)*
**mama** mamá *(f)*
**man** hombre *(m)*
**manage** manejar
**mango** mango *(m)* 9
**manicure** manicura *(f)*
**manner** manera *(f)*

**manufacture** fabricar
**many** mucho/a/os/as 1
**map** mapa (m); plano (m)
**March** marzo 5
**margin** margen (m)
**marinated** adobado/a
**market** mercado (m) 9; **job market** mercado de trabajo (m)
**marriage** matrimonio (m)
**married** casado/a 3, 4
**marry: get married (to)** casarse (con) 5
**marvelous** maravilloso/a
**Marxist** marxista
**mashed** puré
**mass** masa (f)
**massage** masaje (m)
**massive** masivo/a
**master's degree** maestría (f)
**material** materia (f)
**materialistic** materialista
**maternal** materno/a
**mathematics** matemática (f)
**matrimony** matrimonio (m)
**matter** asunto (m)
**matter** importar 9
**maximum** máximo/a
**May** mayo 5
**May I see . . . ?** Me permite . . . ? 7
**maybe** quizás 10; tal vez 10
**me** me; mí 2
**meal** comida (f) 9
**mean** significar; **What does . . . mean in English?** ¿Qué significa . . . en inglés?
**meanwhile** mientras tanto
**measure** medida (f)
**meat** carne (f) 9
**medical** médico/a
**medical insurance** seguro médico (m) 11
**medication** medicamiento (m) 10
**medicine** medicamiento (m) 7; medicina (f)
**medios de comunicación** means of communication 3
**Mediterranean** mediterráneo/a
**medium height** estatura mediana 3
**meet** conocer 7; reunir; sesionar; **meet up** encontrarse (ue) 5
**megaphone** megáfono (m)
**melodramatic** melodramático/a
**melon** melón (m) 9
**member** miembro (m)
**memorable** recordable
**memorize** memorizar
**memory** memoria (f); recuerdo (m) 8
**mental states** estados mentales (m) 10
**mentality** mentalidad (f)
**mention** mencionar
**menu** carta (f) 9
**message** mensaje (m) 7; recado (m) 11
**messy** desordenado/a 4

**method** método (m)
**methodical** metódico/a
**meticulous** meticuloso/a
**metric** métrico/a
**metropolitan** metropolitano/a
**Mexican** mexicano/a 2
**Mexico** México
**microphone** micrófono (m)
**microwave oven** microondas (m) 4
**middle-aged** de mediana edad 3
**midnight** medianoche (f) 2
**mid-term exam** examen parcial (m)
**midwest** medio oeste (m)
**migraine** jaqueca (f); migraña (f)
**migratory** migratorio/a
**milk** leche (f) 9
**million** millón (m)
**millionaire** millonario/a (m/f)
**mind** mente (f)
**mine** mío/a 9
**minimum** mínimo/a 11
**ministry** ministerio (m)
**minor** menor (m/f)
**minority** minoría (f)
**minus** menos 1, 2
**minute** minuto (m)
**mirror** espejo (m) 4
**mischievous** travieso/a 8
**miss** perder (ie) 4
**Miss** señorita (Srta.) 1
**missing: be missing** faltar (a) 9
**mission** misión (f)
**mistaken** equivocado/a 11
**mixed** mixto/a
**Mme.** señora (Sra.) 1
**mobile** móvil
**modality** modalidad (f)
**model** modelo (m)
**moderate** moderar
**modern** moderno/a 1
**modernity** modernidad (f)
**modification** modificación (f)
**moment** momento (m)
**momentary** momentáneo/a
**Monday** lunes 2
**money** dinero (m) 4; moneda (f) 11; **(money in) cash** (dinero en) efectivo (m) 11
**monitor** monitor (m) 11
**monolingual** monolingüe
**month** mes 2; **per month** al mes 2
**monthly** mensual
**monument** monumento (m)
**mood** humor 11; **be in a good / bad mood** estar de buen / mal humor 11
**moody** temperamental 3
**more** más; **more . . . than** más . . . que 4; **more than + number** más de + number 7

**morning** mañana (f) 2; **in the morning** de / por la mañana 2
**mortality** mortalidad (f)
**mosque** mezquita (f) 2
**mostly** mayormente
**mother** madre (f) 3
**motherboard** placa madre (f) 6
**motivation** motivación (f)
**motor** motor (m)
**motorcycle** moto (f) 8
**mount** montar
**mountain** montaña (f) 2
**mouse** ratón (m) 11
**mouth** boca (f) 10
**move** mover
**move (residence)** mudarse 8
**movement** movimiento (m)
**movie** película (f) 2
**moving** emocionante
**Mr.** señor 1
**Mrs.** señora (Sra.) 1
**much** mucho/a/os/as 1; **as much . . . as** tanto/a/ . . . como 4
**multiply** multiplicar
**multitasking** multitarea (f)
**murder** asesinar
**muscle** músculo (m)
**muscular** musculoso/a
**museum** museo (m) 2
**music** música (f) 2
**musician** músico (m/f) 8
**Muslim** musulmán
**must** deber 3; tener que
**mustache** bigote (m) 3
**mutate** mutarse
**my** mi(s) 1, 3; **My name is . . .** Me llamo . . . 1
**myself** me 6

## N

**name** nombre (m) 11
**name** nombrar; **What is your name?** (fam.) ¿Cómo te llamas? 1; **What is your name?** (form.) ¿Cómo se llama usted? 1
**nap** siesta (f); **take a nap** dormir (ue) una siesta 4
**napkin** servilleta (f) 9
**narration** narración (f) 8
**nascent** naciente
**nation** nación (f)
**national** nacional
**nationality** nacionalidad (f)
**native** natal; nativo/a
**Nativity scene** nacimiento (m)
**nature** naturaleza (f) 7
**navigate** navegar

**near** cerca; cerca de 2; cercana/o
**neat** ordenado/a 4
**necessary** necesario/a
**necessity** necesidad (f)
**neck** cuello (m) 10
**necktie** corbata (f) 5
**need** necesitar 2; **I need . . .** Necesito . . . 1
**needed: be needed** faltar 9
**negative** negativo/a
**negligence** negligencia (f)
**negotiation** negociación (f)
**neighbor** vecino/a (m/f) 4
**neighborhood** barrio (m) 4; vecindario (m) 7
**neither** tampoco 4; **neither . . . nor** ni . . . ni . . . 4
**nephew** sobrino (f) 3
**nervous** nervioso/a 2, 4
**network** red (f)
**never** nunca 2
**nevertheless** sin embargo
**new** naciente; nuevo/a 1
**New Jersey** Nueva Jersey
**New Mexico** Nuevo México
**New York** Nueva York
**newlyweds** recién casados
**news** noticias (fpl)
**news anchor** presentador/a (m/f) 12
**news provider** noticiero (m) 12
**newspaper** periódico (m) 3
**newsstand** quiosco de periódicos (m) 7
**next** a continuación; entonces; luego 8; próximo/a 1; **next to** al lado de 2; junto a 7
**Nicaraguan** nicaragüense
**nice** agradable 4; simpático/a 1
**nicotine** nicotina (f)
**niece** sobrina (f) 3
**night** noche (f); **last night** anoche 7
**night club** club nocturno (m) 2
**night life** vida nocturna (f)
**ninth** noveno/a
**no** no; ninguno / ninguna (ningún) 1
**no longer** ya no 10
**no one** nadie
**nobody** nadie 4
**nocturnal** nocturno/a
**noise** ruido (m) 4
**noisy** ruidoso/a 4
**none** ninguno / ninguna (ningún) 4
**non-Hispanic** no-hispano/a
**non-smoker** no fumador/a (m/f)
**noon** mediodía 2
**nor** ni 2
**normal** normal 3
**normally** normalmente
**north** norte; **north of** al norte de 2
**(North) American** norteamericano/a (m/f)

**northeast** noroeste (m)
**nose** nariz (f) 10
**not** no; **not a single** ni un/a solo/a 8; **not . . . any** ningún / ninguna 1, 4; **not any more** ya no 10; **not a single** ni un/a solo/a 8; **not yet** todavía no 11
**not to know** desconocer
**notably** notablemente
**note** anotar; notar
**note** nota (f)
**notebook** cuaderno (m) 1
**nothing** nada 3, 4; **nothing in particular** nada en especial 3; **nothing special** nada en especial 3
**noun** nombre (m) 4; sustantivo (m)
**nourishing** alimenticio/a
**novel** novela (f)
**November** noviembre 5
**now** ahora
**nowadays** hoy día
**number** cifra (f); número (m)
**numerous** numeroso/a
**nurse** enfermero/a (m/f) 8
**nutrition** nutrición (f)
**nutritional** nutricional

## O

**obesity** obesidad (f)
**object** objeto (m)
**objective** objetivo (m)
**objective** objetivo/a
**obligate** obligar
**obligation** obligación (f)
**obligatory** obligatorio/a
**observe** observar
**obstacle** obstáculo (m)
**obstetrician** obstetra (m/f) 10
**obtain** obtener 11
**occasion** ocasión (f)
**occur** ocurrir
**October** octubre 5
**of** de 1
**of course** cómo no 5
**offensive** ofensivo/a
**offer** oferta (f); **job offer** oferta de empleo (f) 11
**offer** ofrecer 9
**office** oficina (f) 2, 11; **at the office** en la oficina 2; **office hours** horas de oficina; **office supplies** artículos de oficina (mpl) 11; material de oficina (m) 11
**often: How often?** ¿Con qué frecuencia? 2
**old** antiguo/a; viejo/a 1, 4
**older** mayor 3
**oldest** mayor 3
**olive** oliva (f)
**on** en 1, 2; sobre 9

**on account of** por
**on top of** encima de 2
**once** una vez 2
**once in a while** de vez en cuando
**one had better . . .** más vale que . . . 10
**oneself** se 6
**onion** cebolla (f) 9
**online** en línea
**only** solamente; sólo 1
**open** abierto/a 2, 4
**open** abrir 3
**operation** operación (f) 10
**opinion: have an opinion** opinar; opinión (f)
**opportunity** oportunidad (f) 11
**opposition** oposición (f)
**optimistic** optimista 1
**option;** opción (f)
**or** o 4; u
**orange** anaranjado/a 4; naranja (f) 9
**orange juice** jugo de naranja (m) 9
**orchestra** orquesta (f)
**order** comando (m) 6; orden (m); **in order to** para
**order** ordenar; pedir (i, i) 4
**ordinary** ordinario/a
**oregano** orégano (m)
**organization** organización (f)
**organize** organizar 11
**orient** oriente (m)
**orientation** orientación
**origin** origen (m)
**originally** originalmente
**osmosis** ósmosis (m)
**other** otro/a 1
**ounce** onza (f)
**our** nuestro/a(s) 3
**ours** nuestro/a(s) 9
**ourselves** nos 6
**outdoors** al aire libre 2
**outgoing** extrovertido/a 1
**outing** salida (f)
**outside** afuera 4; fuera
**outskirts** afueras (m/f) 4
**outward flight** ida (f) 7
**over** sobre 9
**over here** por acá 5
**overcoat** abrigo (m) 5
**overlooking** con vistas a . . . 7
**overtake** superar
**own** propio/a 4
**owner** dueño/a (m/f)
**oxygen** oxígeno (m)
**ozone** ozono (m)

## P

**pack one's suitcase** hacer la maleta 7
**package** paquete (m) 7

**packet** paquete *(m)*
**page** página *(f)* 1
**pain** dolor *(m)* 10
**paint** pintar 11
**painter** pintor/a *(m/f)* 8
**painting** pintura *(f)* 4
**pair** pareja *(f)*
**pajamas** pijama *(m)* 5
**palace** palacio *(m)*
**panic** pánico *(m)*
**pants** pantalones *(mpl)* 5
**paper** ensayo *(m)* 3; *(piece of)* papel *(m)* 1
**parade** desfile *(m)*
**paragraph** párrafo *(m)*
**paralysis** paralización *(f)*
**paramedic** paramédico/a *(m/f)* 8
**Pardon me!** ¡Disculpe! 7
**parenthesis(es)** paréntesis *(mpl)*
**parents** padres *(mpl)* 3
**park** parque *(m)*
**park** estacionar 4
**parking** párquing
**parking lot** estacionamiento *(m)* 4
**part** parte *(m)*
**partial** parcial 11
**participant** participante *(m/f)*
**participate** participar 6
**participation** participación *(f)*
**participle** participio *(m)*
**partisan** partisano/a 12
**part-time** tiempo parcial *(m)* 11
**part-time job** empleo a tiempo parcial *(m)* 11
**party** fiesta *(f)* 3; **birthday party** fiesta de cumpleaños *(f)* 8; **have a party** hacer una fiesta 3
**pass** pasar 2
**passenger** pasajero/a *(m/f)* 7
**passion** pasión *(f)*
**passionate** apasionado/a
**passport** pasaporte *(m)* 7
**password** contraseña *(f)*
**past** pasado/a 7
**pastime** pasatiempo *(m)* 2
**paternal** paterno/a
**patience** paciencia *(f)*
**patient** paciente *(m/f)* 10
**patient** paciente
**pause** pausa *(f)*
**pay** pago *(m)* 11
**pay** pagar 4
**peas** arvejas *(fpl)*; chícharos *(mpl)* 9; guisantes *(mpl)*
**pedestrian** peatonal
**pen** bolígrafo *(m)* 1
**pencil** lápiz *(m)* 1
**penicillin** penicilina *(f)*
**pensive** pensativo/a 6

**people** gente *(f)* 2; pueblo *(m)*
**pepper** pimienta *(f)* 9; pimiento *(m)* 9
**per month / per year** al mes / al año 2
**percent** por ciento
**percentage** porcentaje *(m)*
**perception** percepción *(f)*
**perfect** perfeccionar; perfecto/a 2
**perfectionist** perfeccionista
**perfectly** perfectamente
**perhaps** quizás 10; tal vez 10
**permanent** permanente
**permission** permiso *(m)* 8
**permissive** permisivo/a
**permit** permitir 7, 10
**persecution** persecución *(f)*
**person** persona *(f)* 4
**person in charge** encargado/a *(m/f)* 7; responsable *(m/f)* 11
**personal data** datos personales *(mpl)* 11
**personality** personalidad *(f)*
**personality-wise** de carácter 3
**perspective** perspectiva *(f)*
**pertain** pertenecer
**Peru** Perú
**peso** peso *(m)* 9
**pessimistic** pesimista 1
**pet** mascota *(f)* 3
**petroleum** petróleo *(m)*
**pharmacy** farmacia *(f)* 7
**phenomenon** fenómeno *(m)*
**philosophy** filosofía *(f)*
**phone card** tarjeta telefónica *(f)* 7
**phosphate** fosfato *(m)*
**photocopier** fotocopiadora *(f)* 11
**photograph** foto *(f)*
**photographs; take photographs** cargar fotos, sacar fotos
**photography** fotografía *(f)*
**phrase** frase *(f)*
**physical** físico/a
**physical appearance** aspecto físico 3
**physical states** estados físicos *(mpl)* 10
**physically** físicamente 3
**physician** médico/a *(m/f)* 8
**physics** física *(f)*
**pick up** recoger 7
**picture** dibujo *(m)*; **take a picture** sacar una foto 5
**picturesque** pintoresco/a
**pig** cerdo/a *(m/f)*
**pill** pastilla *(f)* 10
**pineapple** piña *(f)* 9
**pink** rosa; rosado/a (rosa) 4
**piracy** piratería *(f)* 6
**place** colocar; lugar *(m)* 4, 7; poner 3
**plan** planear; planificar
**plane ticket** pasaje; boleto *(m)* 7
**planet** planeta *(f)*

**plant** planta *(f)* 1
**plastic** plástico/a
**plate** plato *(m)* 9
**play** jugar 4; *(music)* tocar
**pleasant** agradable 4; simpático/a
**please** por favor 1
**please, be pleasing to** gustar 2
**Pleased to meet you.** Mucho gusto. 1
**plus** más 1
**pneumonia** pulmonía *(f)*
**poached** escalfado/a
**poem** poema *(m)*
**point** punto *(m)*
**police officer** policía / mujer policía *(m)* 8
**police series** serie policíaca *(f)*
**polite** educado/a
**political** político/a
**political science** ciencias políticas *(fpl)*
**politician** político/a *(m/f)*
**politics** política *(f)*
**pool** piscina *(f)*
**popular** popular 7
**population** población *(f)*
**pork** carne de cerdo *(m)*
**pork chop** chuleta de cerdo *(f)* 9
**portrait** retrato *(m)*
**position** posición *(f)*; puesto *(m)* 11
**positive** positivo/a
**possess** poseer
**possession** posesión *(f)*
**possessive** posesivo/a
**possibility** posibilidad *(f)*
**possible** posible 10; **make possible** potenciar
**postcard** postal *(f)*
**post office** oficina de correos *(f)* 7
**postpone** posponer
**potato** patata *(f)*
**potato chips** papitas *(fpl)* 9
**potential** potencial
**poverty** pobreza *(f)*
**power** poder *(m)*
**powerful** poderoso/a
**practical** práctico/a 4, 11
**practice** práctica *(f)*
**practice** practicar
**pray** rezar 2
**precaution** precaución *(f)*
**precious** precioso/a
**predator** predador *(m)*
**predetermined** predeterminado/a
**prediction** predicción *(f)*
**predominate** predominar
**prefer** preferir (ie, i) 2, 4, 10
**preferable** preferible 10
**preference** preferencia *(f)*
**preferred** preferido/a 9
**pregnancy** embarazo *(m)* 10

**pregnant** embarazada; **be pregnant** estar embarazada 10
**premature** prematuro/a
**prenatal care** cuidado prenatal (m) 10
**preoccupy** preocupar
**preparation** preparación (f)
**prepare** preparar 2
**prescribe** recetar 10
**prescription** receta (f) 10
**presence** presencia (f)
**present** presentar; regalo (m) 2
**present indicative** presente indicativo (m)
**present progressive** presente progresivo (m)
**presentation** presentación (f)
**presenter** presentador/a (m/f) 12
**presently** actualmente
**preservation** preservación (f)
**president** presidente/a (m/f) 12
**press** prensa (f)
**pressure** presión (f)
**prestige** prestigio (m)
**preterit tense** pretérito (m)
**pretty** bonito/a 1
**prevent** prevenir
**preventive medicine** medicina preventiva (f) 10
**previous** previo/a
**price** precio (m) 5
**pride** orgullo (m)
**primary** primario/a
**primary school** escuela normal (f) 11; escuela primaria (f) 11
**print** imprimir 11
**printer** impresora (f) 4, 11
**priority** prioridad (f)
**prison** cárcel (f)
**privacy** privacidad (f) 4
**private** privado/a
**prize** premio (m)
**probability** probabilidad (f)
**problem** problema (m)
**process** proceso (m)
**produce** producir
**producer** productor/a (m/f)
**product** producto (m)
**production** producción (f)
**productivity** productividad (f)
**profession** profesión (f)
**professional** profesional (m/f) 8
**professional experience** experiencia profesional (f) 11
**professor** profesor/a (m/f)
**profile** perfil (m)
**profound** profundo/a
**profoundly** profundamente
**program** programa (m); programar 11

**programmer** programador/a (m/f) 8, 11
**programming** programación (f)
**progress** progreso (m)
**prohibit** prohibir 10
**project** proyecto (m)
**prominent** prominente
**promise** prometer
**promising** prometedor/a
**promote** promocionar; promover
**promotion** promoción (f)
**pronoun** pronombre (m)
**pronounce** pronunciar
**propel** impulsar
**property** propiedad (f)
**proposal** propuesta (f) 12
**protect** proteger
**protection** protección (f)
**protein** proteína (f) 9
**protest** protesta (f)
**protocol** protocolo (m)
**proud** orgulloso/a 8
**proverb** proverbio (m)
**provoke** provocar
**pseudonym** seudónimo (m)
**psychiatrist** psiquiatra (m/f) 10
**psychiatry** psiquiatría (f)
**psychology** (p)sicología (f)
**public** público (m)
**public** público/a
**public awareness** concientización pública (f)
**public transportation** transporte público (m) 4
**publication** publicación
**publicity** publicidad (f)
**publicize** publicitar
**publicly** públicamente
**publish** publicar
**published** publicado/a 11
**Puerto Rican** puertorriqueño/a
**pumpkin** calabaza (f)
**pupil** alumno/a (m/f) 8
**purchasing** adquisitivo/a
**purée(d)** puré
**purification** purificación (f)
**purple** morado/a 4
**purse** bolsa (f) 5
**put** colocar; poner 3; **put on (clothing)** ponerse (la ropa); **put on make-up** maquillarse 5; **put on (one's clothes)** ponerse (la ropa) 5
**pyramid** pirámide (f)

## Q

**qualified** calificado/a
**quality** calidad (f); cualidad (f)
**quantity** cantidad (f)

**queasy** mareado/a 10
**question** cuestión (f); pregunta (f) 3
**questionnaire** cuestionario (m)
**quiet** callado/a 4

## R

**radish** rábano (m) 9
**railway** ferrocarril (m)
**rain** lluvia (f)
**rain** llover 5; **It rains. It's raining.** Llueve. 5; **It's going to rain / snow.** Va a llover / nevar. 5
**raincoat** impermeable (m) 5
**raise** aumento (m) 11
**rancher** ranchero/a (m/f)
**rapid** rápido/a
**rapidity** rapidez (f)
**rapidly** rápidamente
**rate** tasa (f)
**react** reaccionar
**reaction** reacción (f) 11
**read** leer 3
**reader** lector/a (m/f)
**reading** lectura (f)
**ready** listo/a 4
**real estate** bienes raíces (mpl)
**realistic** realista
**reality** realidad (f)
**realize oneself** realizarse
**Really?** ¿De veras? 11
**really** realmente
**reason** motivo (m) 11
**reasonable** razonable 5
**receipt** recibo (m) 4
**receive** recibir 3
**recent** reciente
**recently** recientemente
**receptionist** recepcionista (m/f) 7
**recess** recreo (m) 8
**recession** recesión (f)
**recipient** recipiente (m/f)
**reciprocal** recíproco/a
**recognize** reconocer
**recommend** recomendar (ie) 7, 10
**recommendation** recomendación (f)
**reconversion** reconversión (f)
**record** grabar
**recording** grabación
**recourse** recurso (m)
**recreation** recreo (m)
**recreation area** área recreativa (f)
**red** rojo/a 3, 4
**red-haired** pelirrojo/a 3
**reduce** reducir
**reduction** reducción (f)
**refer** referir
**reference** referencia (f) 11

reflect reflejar
reflection reflexión (f)
reflexive reflexivo/a
reform reforma (f)
refrigerator frigorífico; nevera (f) 4; refrigerador (m)
refuge refugio (m)
reggae reggaetón (m)
regime régimen (m)
region región (f)
regional dish plato regional (m) 7
register facturar; registrar
regularity regularidad (f)
regularly con regularidad 10; regularmente
regulation regulación (f)
relate relacionar
relation relación
relationship relación (f)
relative familiar 3
relatively relativamente
relativity relatividad (f)
relax relajarse 5
relevant relevante
religious religioso/a
relocate mudarse
remain permanecer
remainder resto (m)
remedy remedio (m)
remember recordar (ue) 4
remove retirar
renewable renovable
renovate renovar
rent alquiler (m) 4; renta (f)
rent alquilar 4; rentar
repair reparación (f)
repair reparar
repeat repetir (i) 4
repetitive repetitivo/a
repetitively repetitivamente
report informe (m); reportaje (m)
report informar
reporter reportero/a (m/f) 12
represent representar
representative representante (m/f)
reprisal represalia (f)
reproduction reproducción (f)
Republican republicano/a (m/f)
repulse dar asco 9
reputation reputación (f)
request pedir (i, i) 10; solicitar
require requerir
research investigación (f)
reservation reserva (f)
reserve reservar 7
reserved reservado/a 3
residence hall residencia 1
resident residente (m/f)

resistance resistencia (f)
resolution propósito (m); resolución (f)
resolve resolver (ue) 11
respect respetar; respeto (m)
respectful respetuoso/a
respiratory respiratorio/a
respond responder
responsability responsabilidad (f)
response respuesta (f) 1
responsibility responsabilidad (f) 4
responsible responsable
rest (los) demás; resto (m)
rest descansar 2
restaurant restaurante (m) 2, 9
restriction restricción (f)
result resultado (m)
result resultar
résumé currículum vitae (m) 11
retain retener
retire jubilarse 8; retirar 11
retirement jubilación (f) 8
retirement pension pensión de jubilación (f) 11
return devolver (ue) 11; regresar 2; volver (ue) 4
returning flight vuelta (f) 7
review repasar; revisar
review reseña (f)
revolution revolución (f)
revolutionary revolucionario/a (m/f)
revulsion asco (m) 9
rhythm ritmo (m)
rice arroz (m) 9
rich rico/a 6
ride a bicycle andar en bicicleta 4
right correcto/a 7; justo/a; be right tener razón 3; to the right of a la derecha de 2
right away enseguida
right (legal) derecho (m)
roasted asado/a
robbery robo (m)
role papel (m); rol (m)
romantic romántico/a
room cuarto (m) 1, 4; sala (f); salón (m); double room habitación doble (f); single room habitación sencilla (f)
roommate compañero/a de cuarto (m/f)
root raíz (f)
rope ropa (f)
routine rutina (f)
rug alfombra (f) 4
ruin arruinar; ruina (f)
ruins ruinas 7
rule regla (f)
run correr 3
running corriente
running of the bulls encierro (m)

## S

sad triste 2, 4, 10; be sad that estar triste de que 11
sadness tristeza (f) 10
safe salvo/a; seguro/a 4
sailboat velero (m) 7
saint santo/a (m/f)
saintly santo/a 6
salad ensalada (f) 9
salary salario (m) 11; sueldo (m) 11
sale venta (f)
salesclerk dependiente / dependienta 5
salmon salmón (m)
salt sal (f) 9
salutation salutación (f)
Salvadoran salvadoreño/a
same mismo/a 1
sandals sandalias (f) 5
sanity sanidad (f)
satisfaction satisfacción (f)
satisfy satisfacer
Saturday sábado 2
sauce salsa (f)
sautéed salteado/a
save ahorrar 11; salvar
say decir (i) 4; How do you say . . . in English? ¿Cómo se dice . . . en inglés? 1
saying goodbye despedidas
scale escala (f)
scan escanear 11
scandal escándolo (m)
scandalize escandalizar
scandalous escandaloso/a
scanner escáner (m) 11
scare dar miedo
scared asustado/a 8
scene escena (f)
schedule horario (m) 2
school colegio (m); escuela (f) 4
school of medicine facultad de medicina (f)
science ciencia (f)
scientist científico/a (m/f) 8
score a goal marcar un gol 8
screen pantalla (f) 11
scrupulously escrupulosamente
sea mar (m) 7
seafood mariscos (mpl)
search buscar; búsqueda (f)
search engine buscador (m); motor de búsqueda (m)
seasoning sazón (m)
seasons estaciones (fpl) 5
seat asiento (m) 7; take a seat tomar asiento
seat belt cinturón (m)
seaweed alga (f)

second segundo/a
secondary school escuela secundaria (f) 8
secret secreto (m)
secretary secretario/a (m/f) 8
section sección (f)
secure seguro/a
security seguridad (f) 7
security check control de seguridad (m) 7
seduce seducir
see ver 2
See you later. Chau.; Ádios.; Hasta luego. 1
See you soon. Hasta pronto.
See you tomorrow. Hasta mañana. 1
seem parecer 2
segment segmento (m)
select seleccionar
self-discipline autodisciplina (f)
selfish egoísta 3
self-medicate automedicarse
self-medication automedicación (f)
self-portrait autorretrato (m)
sell vender 3
seller vendedor/a (m/f)
semester semestre (m)
Senate Senado (m)
senator senador/a (m/f)
send enviar 6, 7
sensation sensación (f)
sensational sensacional
sentence oración (f) 1
sentiment sentimiento (m)
separate separado/a; separar
separately por separado
September septiembre 5
sequence secuencia (f)
serenity serenidad (f)
serious grave 10; serio/a 1, 3
serve servir (i, i) 4, 5
server mesero/a (m/f) 9
service servicio (m)
service station estación de servicio
    (f) 7; gasolinera (f) 7
session sesión
set poner 3
seventh séptimo/a
several varios/as 1
severe severo/a
sexism sexismo (m)
share compartir 3
shave afeitarse
she ella
shelf estante (m) 1, 4
shellfish mariscos 9
shirt camisa (f) 5
shoes zapatos (mpl) 5
shopping de compras 5
shopping center centro comercial (m) 2
short corto/a 3

short (in height), low bajo/a 3
shorts pantalones cortos (mpl) 5
shot inyección (f) 10
shower ducha (f) 7
shower ducharse 5; take a shower
    ducharse 5
shrimp camarones 9
shy reservado/a; tímido/a 1
siblings hermanos (mpl) 3
sick enfermo/a 1, 4; get sick
    enfermarse 10
side lado (m); on my mother's / father's
    side por parte de mi madre / padre 3
sideways lateralmente
sign firmar 11
signal señalar
signature firma (f)
signer firmante (m/f)
significance significado (m)
silent callado/a 6
silly tonto/a 1
similar parecido/a
similarity similitud (f)
simple sencillo/a
simulation simulación (f)
simultaneously simultáneamente
sincerely atentamente
sing cantar 2
singer cantante (m/f) 8
single sencillo/a; soltero/a 3
sir señor 1
sister hermana (f) 3
sit down sentarse (ie) 5
site sitio (m)
situate situar
situation situación (f)
sixth sexto/a
size talla (f) 5
ski esquiar 2
skin piel (f) 10
skirt falda (f) 5
slave esclavo/a (m/f)
sleep sueño (m)
sleep dormir (ue) 4
sleepy: be sleepy tener sueño
sleeve manga (f)
slogan eslogan (m)
slow despacio
slowly lentamente, despacio
sluggishly perezosamente
small pequeño/a 1
smile sonrisa (f) 8
smoke fumar 4
smoked ahumado/a
smoker fumador/a (m/f)
smoking tabaquismo (m)
sneakers tenis (mpl) 5
sneeze estornudar 10

snow nevar 5; It snows. It's snowing.
    Nieva. 5; It's going to snow. Va a
    nevar. 5
so pues 1; entonces 2; por eso 8; tan
so much tanto 10
soap opera telenovela (f)
so-called llamado/a
soccer (football) fútbol 2
soccer player futbolista (m/f) 8
sociable sociable 3
social sciences ciencias sociales (fpl)
social security number número de
    seguridad social (m)
social worker trabajador/a social (m/f) 8
socialize socializar
socially socialmente
society sociedad (f)
sociology sociología (f)
socks calcetines (mpl) 5
sofa sofá (f) 4
soft drink refresco (m) 9
software aplicación informática (f) 6;
    programa informática (f) 6
software designer diseñador/a de
    software (m/f) 8
soldier militar (m/f)
solidarity solidaridad (f) 12
solstice solsticio (m)
solution solución (f)
some alguno/a(s) 4; unos/as 1
someone alguien 4
something algo 2, 4
sometimes a veces 2, 4
son hijo (m) 3
song canción (f)
soon pronto
sophisticated sofisticado/a
sore dolorido/a 10
sorry: be sorry that sentir (ie, i) que 11;
    I'm sorry. Lo siento. 4
soup sopa (f) 9
soup dish plato hondo (m) 9
source fuente (f)
south sur (m); south of al sur de 2
South America Sudamérica
souvenir recuerdo (m) 7
space blanco (m); espacio (m) 4
spaghetti espaguetis (mpl)
Spain España
spam correo no deseado (m) 6
Spaniard español/a (m/f)
Spanish español (m) 1
Spanish español/a
Spanish class clase de español (f) 1
speak hablar 2
special especial
specialist especialista (m/f) 10
specialize especializar

**specific** específico/a

**speech** discurso (m)

**speed up** acelerar

**spelling** ortografía (f)

**spend (money)** gastar 5

**spend (time)** pasar 2

**spinach** espinacas (f) 9

**spirit** espíritu (m)

**spiritual** espiritual

**spoon** cuchara (f) 9

**sports** deportes (mpl) 2; **fond of sports** deportista (adj.) 8; **sports event** evento deportivo 3

**spouse** esposo/a (m/f)

**spreadsheet** hoja de cálculo (f) 11

**spring** primavera (f) 5

**squash** calabacín (m) 9

**stability** estabilidad (f)

**stabilize** estabilizar

**stadium** estadio (m)

**staircase** escalera (f) 7

**stairs** escalera (f) 7

**stamp** estampilla (f); sello (m) 7; timbre postal (m)

**star** estrella (f)

**start** comenzar (ie) 10; empezar (ie); iniciar

**start** inicio (m)

**state** estado (m)

**station** estación (f)

**statue** estatua (f)

**stay** quedarse 5; **stay at (on a trip)** alojarse en 7; **stay in bed** guardar cama 10

**steak** bistec (m) 9

**steamed** al vapor

**stemmed glass** copa (f) 9

**step** paso (m)

**stepbrother** hermanastro (m)

**stepfather** padrastro (m)

**stepmother** madrastra (f)

**stepsister** hermanastra (f)

**stereo** estéreo (m) 1

**stereotype** estereotipo (m)

**steroids** esteroides (mpl)

**still** todavía

**stimulate** estimular; estímulo (m)

**stimulating** estimulante

**stomach** estómago (m) 10

**stop . . . -ing** dejar de + infinitive 10

**stopover** escala (f); **make a stopover** hacer escala 7

**store** tienda (f) 2

**story** cuento (m) 8; historia (f)

**stove** estufa (f) 4

**straighten out / up** arreglar 4

**straightened up** ordenado/a 4

**strange** extraño/a

**stranger** desconocido/a (m/f)

**strategy** estrategia (f)

**strawberries** fresas 9; frutillas (fpl)

**street** calle (f) 4

**street map** plano de la ciudad (m) 7

**strength** fuerza (f) 10

**stress** estrés (m) 10

**stressful** estresante

**strict** estricto/a 3

**strike** golpear 8

**stroke (swimming)** brazada (f)

**stroll** pasear

**strong** fuerte 8

**structure** estructura (f)

**stubborn** terco/a 3

**stuck-up** presumido/a 3

**student** alumno/a (m/f) 8; estudiante (m/f)

**student desk** pupitre (m) 1

**studies** estudios (mpl)

**study** estudiar 2; **I'm studying . . .** Estudio . . . 1; **study abroad** estudiar en el extranjero; **What are you studying?** ¿Qué estudias? 1

**study** estudio (m)

**stuffed** relleno/a

**stuffed pepper** chile relleno (m) 9

**stupendous** estupendo/a

**stupid** tonto/a 1

**style** estilo (m)

**subject** asunto (m)

**subjunctive** subjuntivo (m)

**substance** sustancia (f)

**substitute** sustituir

**suburban** suburbano/a

**succesively** sucesivamente

**success** éxito (m)

**successful: be successful** tener éxito

**sudden** súbito/a

**suffer** sufrir

**sufficient** suficiente

**sugar** azúcar (m) 9

**suggest** sugerir (ie, i) 10

**suggestion** sugerencia (f)

**suit** traje (m) 5

**suitcase** maleta (f) 7

**suitor** pretendiente (m/f)

**summary** resumen (m)

**summer** verano (m) 5

**sun** sol (m)

**sunbathe** tomar el sol 2

**sunblock** bloqueador solar (m)

**Sunday** domingo 2

**sunglasses** gafas de sol (fpl)

**sunny** soleado/a; **be sunny** hacer sol; **It's sunny.** Hace sol. 5

**supermarket** supermercado (m)

**superstitious** supersticioso/a

**supervisor** supervisor/a (m/f) 11

**supplement** suplemento (m)

**support** apoyo (m)

**Supreme Court** Corte Suprema (f)

**sure** seguro/a; **be sure** estar seguro/a 10

**surgeon** cirujano/a (m/f) 10

**surgery** cirugía (f) 10

**surprise** sorpresa (f)

**surprise** sorprender 11

**surprised** sorprendido/a 2, 4, 6

**survey** encuesta (f)

**surveyor** encuestador/a (m/f)

**survive** sobrevivir

**suspect** sospechoso/a (m/f)

**suspense** suspenso (m)

**suyo/a** their

**sweater** suéter (m) 5

**sweatshirt** sudadera (f) 5

**sweets** dulces 9

**swim** nadar 2

**swimming pool** piscina (f) 2

**swimsuit** traje de baño (m) 5

**swollen** hinchado/a 10

**symbol** símbolo (m)

**symphonic orchestra** orquesta sinfónica (f)

**symptom** síntoma (m) 10

**synagogue** sinagoga (f) 2

**syndrome** síndrome (m)

**synonym** sinónimo (m)

**synonymous** sinónimo/a

**system** sistema (m) 11

**systematically** sistemáticamente

## T

**tabacco** tabaco (m)

**table** mesa (f) 1

**table (graphic)** tabla (f)

**tablet** pastilla (f) 10

**take** llevar 5; sacar; tomar 2; **take a bath** bañarse 5; **take a nap** dormir (ue) una siesta 4; **take a picture** sacar una foto 5; **take a seat** tomar asiento; **take a shower** ducharse 5; **take a trip** hacer viaje 3; **take away** llevarse 5; **take care of (yourself)** cuidar(se) 10; **take off** despegar 7; **take photographs** cargar fotos, sacar fotos

**tale** cuento (m) 8

**talent** talento (m)

**talk** hablar 2

**talkative** hablador/a 4

**tall** alto/a 3

**tariff** tarifa (f)

**task** quehacer (m)

**taste** gusto (m)

**tattoo** tatuaje (m)

**taxes** impuestos (mpl) 11

**taxi** taxi (m) 7

**taxi driver** taxista (m/f)

**tea** té 9; **hot tea** té caliente (m) 9; **iced tea** té helado (m)

**teach** enseñar

teacher maestro/a *(m/f)* 8
team equipo *(m)* 8
technical técnico/a
technical service servicio técnico *(m)* 11
technique técnica *(f)*
technology tecnología *(f)*
telecommute teletrabajar
telecommuting teletrabajo *(m)*
telephone teléfono *(m)* 2; **on the telephone**
    por teléfono 11; **public telephone**
    teléfono público *(m)* 7; **telephone**
    **number** número de teléfono *(m)*
telephonic telefónico/a
telephony telefonía
television (TV) televisión (tele) *(f)*;
    televisor *(m)*
television set televisor *(m)* 1, 4
television viewer televidente *(m/f)*
tell contar (ue) 4; decir (i) 4
teller cajero/a *(m/f)* 11
temperature temperatura *(f)* 10
temporary temporal
tendency tendencia *(f)*
tennis tenis *(m)*
tennis court cancha de tenis *(f)*
tennis player tenista *(m/f)*
tennis shoes tenis *(mpl)*; zapatillas de
    tenis *(mpl)*
tenth décimo/a
term término *(m)*
terrace terraza *(f)*
terrain terreno
territory territorio *(m)*
terrorism terrorismo *(m)*
terrorist terrorista *(m/f)* 12
testimony testimonio *(m)*
text texto *(m)*
textbook libro de texto *(m)* 3
than que
thank you gracias 1
thanks to gracias a
that que 1; **that (those)** ese / esa (esos /
    esas) 3; **that (those) (over there)**
    aquel / aquella (aquellos / as) 5; **that**
    **which** lo que 8; **that's right** así es 9;
    **that's why** por eso 8
the el, la, los, las
theater teatro *(m)* 2
their su(s) 3
theirs suyo/a 9
them ellos / ellas 2; les, se; los, las 6
thematic temático/a
theme tema *(f)*; tema *(m)*
themselves se 6
then entonces 2; luego 8
theory teoría *(f)*
therapist terapeuta *(m/f)* 10
therapy terapia *(f)* 10
there allí, allá

there is, there are hay 1
therefore por eso 8
they ellos/as 1
thin delgado/a 3
thing cosa *(f)* 1
think opinar; **think (about)** pensar (ie)
    (en) 4
third tercero/a
thirsty: be thirsty tener sed 3; **make**
    **thirsty** dar sed 9
this (these) este / esta (estos / as) 5
thought pensamiento
thousand mil *(m)*
thrilling emocionante
throat garganta *(f)* 10
through here por acá
throw up vomitar 10
Thursday jueves 2
thus así
ticket billete *(m)* 7; boleto *(m)* 7;
    pasaje *(m)* 7
till menos; hasta 2
time hora *(f)* 2; tiempo *(m)*
times: at times a veces
timid tímido/a 1
tired cansado/a 1, 4
title título *(m)*
to para
to where adónde
today hoy 1, 2
together juntos/as 2; **get together**
    encontrarse (ue) 5
Tokyo Tokio
tolerance tolerancia *(f)*
tomato tomate *(m)* 9
tomorrow mañana
tone tono *(m)* 11
tonight esta noche
too demasiado 2, 5; también 1
too much demasiado 2, 5
tool herramienta *(f)*
tool bar barra de herramientas *(f)*
tooth diente *(m)*
totalitarian totalitario/a
totally totalmente
tourism turismo *(m)*
tourist turista *(m/f)*
tourist guide guía (turístico/a) *(m/f)* 7
tourist guidebook guía (turística) *(f)* 7
tradition tradición *(f)*
traditional tradicional
traditionalism tradicionalismo *(m)*
traffic tráfico *(m)* 4
tragedy tragedia *(f)*
train tren *(m)*
train entrenar 11
tranquility tranquilidad *(f)*
transaction trámite *(m)* 11
transform transformar

transformation transformación *(f)*
transition transición *(f)*
translate traducir
translation traducción *(f)*
transmission transmisión *(f)*
transmit transmitir
transparent transparente
transportation transporte *(m)*
trash basura *(f)* 4
travel viajar 7
travel agency agencia de viajes *(f)* 7
traveler viajero/a *(m/f)*
traveler's check cheque de viaje *(m)*
traveling itinerante
treat tratar (de) 8
treatment tratamiento *(m)* 10
tree árbol *(m)* 4
triangle triángulo *(m)*
trimester trimestre *(m)*
trip viaje *(m)* 3; **take a trip** hacer viaje 3
true cierto/a; verdad; verdadero/a
trumpet trompeta *(f)*
trust confiar
try probar (ue) 7; tratar (de) 8; **try on**
    probarse (ue) 5
T-shirt camiseta *(f)* 5
Tuesday martes 2
tuna atún *(m)*
turbulence turbulencia *(f)*
turn (an age) cumplir 8
turn off apagar 11
turn on encender (ie) 11; poner 3; prender
type tipo *(m)*
typical típico/a
typically típicamente


## U

ugly feo/a 1
ultimately últimamente
uncle tío *(m)* 3
under debajo de 2
underline subrayer
understand comprender 3; entender (ie) 4;
    **I don't understand.** No comprendo. 1
understanding comprensivo/a 3
undocumented indocumentado/a
unemployed desempleado/a
unemployment desempleo *(m)*
unfaithful person infiel *(m/f)*
unfortunately desafortunadamente 4
uniform uniforme *(m)*
union unión *(f)*
united unido/a
United Nations Naciones Unidas *(mpl)* 12
United States Estados Unidos *(mpl)*
university universidad *(f)*
university (adj.) universitario/a

university band tuna
university band member tuno
university course curso universitario (m)
unknown desconocido/a 2
unnecessary innecesario/a
unpleasant antipático/a 1
until hasta 2; hasta que 11
unusual inusual
up arriba
upon: a; upon . . . ing al + infinitive 7; upon request a petición 11
upset molesto/a 2, 4
urban urbano/a
urgent urgente 10
us nos 6; nosotros/as 2
use usar 2; utilizar
use utilización (f)
useful útil 1
user usario/a (m/f)
utility utilidad (f)
utilization utilización (f)

V

vacation: on vacation de vacaciones 7
valuation valoración (f)
value valor (m); valorar
varied variado/a
variety variedad (f)
vegetables verduras (fpl) 9
vegetarian vegetariano/a
vehicle vehículo (m)
velocity velocidad (f)
verb verbo (m)
verb tense tiempo verbal (m)
verify verificar
versatile versátil
version versión (f)
very muy; very well muy bien 1
vestige vestigio (m)
via por; vía
vice versa viceversa
victim víctima (f)
victory victoria (f)
videogame videojuego (m)
view vista (f)
view of . . . vistas a . . . 7
vigilant: be vigilant vigilar
vinegar vinagre (m)
violence violencia (f)
virtuouso virtuoso/a (m/f)
visit visita (f); visitar 7
visitor visitante (m/f)
vitality vitalidad (f)
vitamins vitaminas 9
vocabulary vocabulario (m)
voice voz (f)
voice mailbox buzón de voz (m) 11

voluntarily voluntariamente
voluntary voluntario/a
volunteer voluntario/a (m/f)
vomit vomitar 10
vote votar
voter votante (m/f)
vowel vocal (f)

W

wage sueldo (m) 11
wait esperar 7; wait on atender (ie) 11
waiter camarero/a (m/f); mesero/a (m/f)
waiting room sala de espera (f)
wake up despertarse (ie) 5
walk caminar 10; pasear
wall pared (f) 4
want desear; querer 2; querer (ie) 4, 10
war guerra (f)
wardrobe armario (m) 4
warm cálido/a; caluroso/a
warm up calentar; calentarse (ie)
warn advertir
warning advertencia (f)
wash lavar 4; wash one's hair / one's face lavarse el pelo / la cara 5
washbasin lavabo
washing machine lavadora
waste basket papelera (f)
watch reloj (m) 1
watch mirar, ver 2; vigilar
watch out ojo
water agua (f, el) 4
waterfall catarata (f)
waterski hacer esquí acuático 2
way manera (f)
we nosotros/as
weak débil
wear llevar 5
weather tiempo (m) 5; The weather's good / bad. Hace buen / mal tiempo. 5; What's the weather like? ¿Qué tiempo hace? 5
weather report pronóstico del tiempo (m) 12
web red (f) 6
web page página web (f)
web page design diseño de páginas web (m) 11
web site sitio web (m)
wedding boda (f) 8
Wednesday miércoles 2
week semana (f) 2; last week semana pasada (f) 7
weekend fin de semana (m) 2
weekly semanal
weird raro/a 3
welcome bienvenido/a 7

welcome dar la bienvenida
well bien 1, 4; pues; I'm doing very well, thank you. Estoy muy bien, gracias.
well-being bienestar (m)
west oeste (m); west of al oeste de 2
What? ¿Cuál(es)? 2; ¿Qué? 2; What are you studying? ¿Qué estudias? 1; What classes do you have? ¿Qué clases tienes? 1; What color is it? ¿De qué color es?; What does . . . mean in English? ¿Qué significa . . . en inglés?; What is the date? ¿Qué fecha es? 5; What is your name? (fam.) ¿Cómo te llamas? 1; What is your name? (form.); ¿Cómo se llama usted? 1; What's . . . like? ¿Cómo es . . . ? 1; What's the weather like? ¿Qué tiempo hace? 5; What's wrong with you? ¿Qué te pasa? 10
wheat trigo (m)
wheel rueda (f)
When? ¿Cuándo? 2
Where? ¿Dónde? 2; Where are you from? (fam.) ¿De dónde eres? 1; Where are you from? (form.) ¿De dónde es usted? 1
Which? ¿Cuál(es)? 2
while mientras 8, 11
while rato (m)
white blanco/a 4
white-haired canoso/a 3
Who? ¿Quién(es)? 2
whole entero/a 9
whole-grain integral 9
Whom? ¿Quién(es)? 2
Why? ¿Por qué?
win ganar 8; win the heart of enamorar
wind viento (m)
window ventana (f) 1, 4; counter window ventanilla (f) 11; window (of a vehicle or box office) ventanilla (f) 7
windy: It's windy. Hace viento. 5
wine vino (m) 3; red / white wine vino tinto / blanco (m) 9
wine glass copa (f) 9
wine shop bodega (f)
winter invierno (m) 5
wish desear 2, 10
with con 1, 2; with an accent con acento 1; with attention con atención 8; with me conmigo 2; with respect to respecto a; with you contigo 3
withdraw retirar 11
withdrawal retiro (m) 11
within dentro de
without sin; without an accent sin acento 1
witness testigo/a (m/f)

**woman** mujer *(f)*; **businesswoman** mujer de negocios *(m)* 8; **policewoman** mujer policía *(m)* 8

**woods** bosque *(m)* 7

**word** palabra *(f)* 1

**word processor** procesador de texto *(m)* 6, 11

**work** obra *(f)*; trabajo *(m)* 2

**work** funcionar 4; trabajar

**work days** días laborales

**workbook** cuaderno de ejercicios *(m)* 1

**worker: construction worker** obrero/a de la construcción *(m/f)* 8; **factory worker** obrero/a de fábrica *(m/f)* 8; **social worker** trabajador/a social *(m/f)* 8

**world** mundo *(m)*

**worldwide** mundial 6

**worried** inquieto/a; preocupado/a 8

**worry** preocupar(se) 10

**worse** peor 4

**write** anotar; escribir 3; redactar; **How is that written?** ¿Cómo se escribe? 1

**writer** escritor/a *(m/f)*

**writing** redacción *(f)*

**wrong** equivocado/a 11

**X-ray** radiografía *(f)* 10

**yard** jardín *(m)* 4

**year** año *(m)*; **be . . . years old** tener . . . años 3; **per year** al año 2

**yell** gritar

**yellow** amarillo/a 4

**yesterday** ayer 7

**yield** rendir

**yogurt** yogur *(m)*

**you** *(pl.)* ustedes

**you** *(pl. / fam.)* vosotros/as

**you** *(sing. / fam.)* (to/for) **you** ti 2

**you** *(sing. / fam.)* tú; **How are you?** *(fam.)* ¿Cómo estás? 1; **You like . . .** Te gusta(n) . . . 2; **You look . . . to me.** Te veo . . . 10

**you** *(sing. / form.)* usted; **How are you?** *(form.)* ¿Cómo está usted? 1

**young** joven 3

**younger** menor 3

**youngest** menor 3

**your** *(pl. / fam.)* vuestro/a(s) 3

**your** *(sing. / fam.)* tu(s) 1, 3

**your** *(sing. / form./; pl.)* su(s) 3

**yours** *(pl.)*, **yours** *(sing. / form.)* suyo/a 9

**yours** *(pl./fam.)* vuestro/a 9

**yours** *(sing./fam.)* tuyo/a 9

**youth** joven *(m/f)*

**zone** zona *(f)*

# Credits

## Photo Credits

**VOLUME I COVER:** Murat Taner / Getty Images, Inc. - Photographer's Choice; Tom Merton / Getty Images Inc. RF; Peter Adams / Getty Images/ Digital Vision; Nick White / Getty Images/ Digital Vision; Masterfile Royalty Free Division; MalibuBooks/Shutterstock; Stephen Coburn / Shutterstock; Jose Luis Pelaez Inc. / Getty Images, Inc. - Blend Images.

**VOLUME 1:** p. 2 © GoGo Images / Jupiter Images Royalty Free; p. 4 (top) © Peter Menzel / Peter Menzel Photography; (middle) © Photos.com (bottom) © Michael Jung / Shutterstock; p. 6 (left) © Juan Silva / Getty Images Inc.-Image Bank (right) © Terry Vine / Getty Images Inc.-Stone Allstock; p. 21 © Rudi Von Briel / PhotoEdit Inc.; p. 28 (top) © Photolibrary.com; (left) © Providence College; (right) © Providence College; p. 30 (top) © GoldPitt LLC; (middle) © GoldPitt LLC; (bottom) © GoldPitt LLC; p. 34 © Juice Images/Fotolia, LLC-Royalty Free; p. 41 © Robert Fried / Robert Fried Photography; p. 62 (top) © GoldPitt LLC; (middle) © Jupiter Unlimited; (bottom) © GoldPitt LLC; p. 66 © Monkey Business Images / Shutterstock; p. 75 © PureStockX; p. 81 © Losevsky Pavel / Shutterstock; p. 84 © Jupiter Unlimited; © Rob Lewine / Rob Lewine Photography; p. 92 (top left) © Hoby Finn / Getty Images, Inc.-Photodisc / Royalty Free; (top right, left) © ColorBlind Images / Jupiter Images; (top right, right) © EyeWire Collection / Gettty Images, Inc.-Photodisc-Royalty Free; (bottom) © Jose Carrillo / PhotoEdit Inc.; p. 94 (top) © GoldPitt LLC; (middle) GoldPitt LLC; (bottom) GoldPitt LLC; p. 98 © Jupiter Unlimited; p. 101 © Spike / Getty Images, Inc.-Photodisc/ Royalty Free; p. 111 © faberfoto / Shutterstock; p. 116 © Image Source / Jupiter Images Royalty Free; p. 117 © Getty Images, Inc.-Stockbyte, Royalty Free; p. 122 © Jupiter Unlimited; p. 124 © Lucas Jackson / CORBIS-NY; p. 126 (top) © GoldPitt LLC; (bottom) © GoldPitt LLC; p. 130 © Photos.com; p. 139 © Jupiter Unlimited; p. 143 © Jupiter Unlimited; p. 145 © Alvaro de Leiva / AGE Fotostock America, Inc.; p. 148 (left) © Jupiter Unlimited; (right) © Jeff Greenberg / Omni-Photo Communications, Inc.; p. 151 © Ken Welsh / AGE Fotostock America, Inc.; p. 158 (top) ©

GoldPitt LLC; (middle) © GoldPitt LLC; (bottom) © GoldPitt LLC; p. 162 © Jupiter Unlimited; p. 164 © Microsoft Corporation; p. 165 © Terry Vine / Getty Images, Inc.-Blend Images; p. 168 © Jose Luis Pelaez, Inc. / Getty Images, Inc.-Blend Images; p. 169 © Peter Byron / PhotoEdit Inc.; p. 170 (top) © Photos.com; (bottom) Pearson Education / PH College; p. 171 © Jupiter Unlimited; p. 174 © Turba / Corbis RF; p. 175 © Jupiter Unlimited; p. 176 (top right) © El Pais New Service; p. 178 © Colin Anderson / Jupiter Images-PictureArts Corporation / Brand X Pictures Royalty Free; p. 179 (left) © Jupiter Unlimited; (right) © Jupiter Unlimited; p. 180 (left) © Jupiter Unlimited; (right) © Jupiter Unlimited; p. 181 © Jupiter Unlimited; p. 182 © Jupiter Unlimited; p. 183 © Keith Bendis / Getty Images / Stock Illustration Source-Royalty Free; p. 184 © Imagezoo/Images.com / Getty Images / Stock Illustration Source-Royalty Free; p. 186 © Jupiter Unlimited.

**VOLUME II COVER:** Murat Taner / Getty Images, Inc. - Photographer's Choice; Tom Merton / Getty Images Inc. RF; Peter Adams / Getty Images/ Digital Vision; Nick White / Getty Images/Digital Vision; Masterfile Royalty Free Division; MalibuBooks / Shutterstock; Stephen Coburn / Shutterstock; Jose Luis Pelaez Inc. / Getty Images, Inc. - Blend Images.

**VOLUME II:** p. 188 © Jose Fusta Raga / AGE Fotostock America, Inc.; p. 190 (top) © Cosmo Condina / Creative Eye / MIRA.com; (middle) © Demetrio Carrasco / Dorling Kindersley Media Library; (bottom) © Peter Bowater / Photo Researchers, Inc.; p. 191 (top) © Adalberto Rios / Getty Images, Inc.-Photodisc / Royalty Free; (bottom) © Jupiter Unlimited; p. 193 (left) © Frank Herholdt / Getty Images, Inc.-Stone Allstock; (right) © Hans Weisenhoffer / Getty Images, Inc.-Photodisc / Royalty Free; p. 194 © newstream rf/Alamy; p. 199 (bottom) © Kymata/Alamy; p. 207 © Nuria Alonso García; p. 209 (top) © Suzanne Murphy Larronde; (bottom) © Patricia Rush; p. 214 © Alexander/Fotolia; p. 215 (bottom left) © Photos.com; (bottom middle) © Michael G Smith / Shutterstock; (bottom right, top)

# Index

Mar Cantábrico

Golfo de Vizcaya

FRANCIA

OCÉANO ATLÁNTICO

La Coruña
Lugo
GALICIA
Pontevedra
Vigo
Orense
Braga
Oporto
Coímbra
Lisboa
Setúbal

PORTUGAL

Avilés
Gijón
Oviedo
ASTURIAS
CORDILLERA CANTÁBRICA
León
CASTILLA Y LEÓN
Zamora
Valladolid
Salamanca
Ávila
SIERRA DE GUADARRAMA
EXTREMADURA
Cáceres
Mérida
Río Guadiana
Badajoz
Almadén
SIERRA MORENA
Río Guadalquivir
Córdoba
Huelva
Sevilla
SIERRA NEVADA
Málaga
Costa del Sol
Jerez de la Frontera
Cádiz
Algeciras
Estrecho de Gibraltar
Tánger

Santander
CANTABRIA
Bilbao
San Sebastián
PAÍS VASCO
Pamplona
NAVARRA
Logroño
Burgos
Palencia
LA RIOJA
Río Ebro
Segovia
Madrid
COMUNIDAD DE MADRID
Río Tajo
Toledo
ESPAÑA
Río Júcar
Ciudad Real
CASTILLA LA MANCHA
Albacete
VALENCIA
Linares
Jaén
ANDALUCÍA
Granada
Almería
Murcia
MURCIA
Cartagena
Alicante
Valencia
Castellón
ANDORRA
Andorra la Vella
PIRINEOS
CATALUÑA
Lérida
Costa Brava
Zaragoza
ARAGÓN
Tarragona
Barcelona

Menorca
Palma de Mallorca
Mallorca
Ibiza
Formentera
ISLAS BALEARES

Mar Mediterráneo

Ceuta (Esp.)
Melilla (Esp.)

ÁFRICA

ÁFRICA

Santa Cruz de la Palma
La Palma
Gomera
Hierro
Santa Cruz
Tenerife
Gran Canaria
Lanzarote
Arrecife
Puerto del Rosario
Fuerteventura
Las Palmas

ISLAS CANARIAS (ESPAÑA)

OCÉANO ATLANTICO

ÁFRICA

Malabo
CAMERÚN
GUINEA ECUATORIAL
OCÉANO ATLÁNTICO
GABÓN

**España y África**

# América del Sur

ESTADOS
UNIDOS

Mexicali
Tijuana
Nogales
Ciudad
Juárez

*Río Bravo del Norte*
*Río Grande*

Nuevo Laredo

*Golfo de
México*

Monterrey

SIERRA MADRE OCCIDENTAL
SIERRA MADRE ORIENTAL

*Baja California*
*Golfo de California*

MÉXICO

Guadalajara

Comala

México, D.F.

Veracruz

Taxco

• Mérida

*Península
de
Yucatán*

Acapulco

Oaxaca

Palenque

Belice

Tikal ✪Belmopan
BELICE

GUATEMALA

Quetzaltenango

• Copán

Guatemala ✪

*Volcán Izalco* ▲ San
Salvador ✪

EL
SALVADOR

OCÉANO

PACÍFICO

*Islas
Galápagos
(Ec.)*

**México, América Central y el Caribe**